THE MARVEL STUDIOS PHENOMENON

THE MARVEL STUDIOS PHENOMENON

INSIDE A TRANSMEDIA UNIVERSE

Martin Flanagan, Mike McKenny and Andy Livingstone

Bloomsbury Academic
An imprint of Bloomsbury Publishing Inc

B L O O M S B U R Y
NEW YORK · LONDON · OXFORD · NEW DELHI · SYDNEY

Bloomsbury Academic

An imprint of Bloomsbury Publishing Inc

1385 Broadway	50 Bedford Square
New York	London
NY 10018	WC1B 3DP
USA	UK

www.bloomsbury.com

BLOOMSBURY and the Diana logo are trademarks of Bloomsbury Publishing Plc

First published 2016

Library of Congress Cataloging-in-Publication Data
Names: Flanagan, Martin, author. | Livingstone, Andrew, 1987– author. | McKenny, Mike, author. Title: The Marvel Studios phenomenon: inside a transmedia universe/ Martin Flanagan, Andrew Livingstone, Mike McKenny. Description: New York: Bloomsbury Academic, 2016. | Includes bibliographical references and index. Identifiers: LCCN 2015041803 (print) | LCCN 2015045820 (ebook) | ISBN 9781501311895 (hardback) | ISBN 9781501311857 (epdf) | ISBN 9781501311864 (epub) Subjects: LCSH: Marvel Studios–History. | Motion picture industry–United States–History. | BISAC: BUSINESS & ECONOMICS/Industries/ Media & Communications Industries. | PERFORMING ARTS/Film & Video/Direction & Production. | COMICS & GRAPHIC NOVELS/Media Tie-In. Classification: LCC PN1999.M25 F68 2016 (print) | LCC PN1999.M25 (ebook) | DDC 384/.806579493–dc23 LC record available at http://lccn.loc.gov/2015041803

ISBN: HB: 978-1-5013-1189-5
ePub: 978-1-5013-1186-4
ePDF: 978-1-5013-1185-7

Typeset by Deanta Global Publishing Services, Chennai, India
Printed and bound in the United States of America

In Memory of Chris 'Channy' Chan: Superhero of the Bass

CONTENTS

Contents

ACKNOWLEDGEMENTS

Martin Flanagan

Ruth Hannan's support, as ever, was unconditional, unwavering and inspiring. My parents Bridget and Gerald Flanagan also deserve my thanks, and have seen far too little of me during 2015, which I intend to rectify. I am grateful to Kieron Flanagan for helping to locate resources, and to Elvira Uyarra for a loan that got me through technical difficulties. The staff of the University of Salford, particularly in the library and the School of Arts and Media, have made me very welcome since 2014, helping me to be in a settled place, which helped with this work. Katie Gallof, Mary Al-Sayed and all at Bloomsbury have been a pleasure to work with.

When I was small, a school friend gave me some Marvel comics that later on I came to regard as my 'starter pack' into a life of following its amazing universe. Though I'm more critical these days, I still regard this as an important, fortunate moment, so I would like to thank Robert. Later on, when I started thinking about a book on Marvel, I quickly realized that there were two other people whom I wanted to be part of the fun. Mike and Andy have been fantastic collaborators, not just in the energy and excellence of their ideas, but their grasp of the organizational needs of a project with three authors, and their willingness to give everything to it. So I thank my co-authors most profusely. I feel that we have produced a book that reflects many enjoyable conversations. Mike, in particular, has assisted with editing to a greater extent than he had originally signed up for, and I am grateful for that support.

We all would like to thank the anonymous (and known) readers for their helpful comments. Sincere and special thanks to Martin Hall for his advice on chapters. Additionally, I am grateful to the people with whom I corresponded about Marvel for keeping me in the zone, particularly the members of the 'Back Issue' forum.

Portions of Chapter 4 previously appeared in *Scope: An Online Journal of Film and Television Studies*, issue 26 (February 2014). I'd like to thank the issue editors, and the journal editors Mark Gallagher and Julian Stringer. Elements of the discussion of Pixar in Chapter 7 are reworked from Chapter 5 of Martin Flanagan, *Bakhtin and the Movies: New Ways of Understanding Hollywood Film* (55–80), and are republished with kind permission of Palgrave Macmillan.

Mike Mckenny

First and foremost, I would like to thank my wonderful family. My wife Tasha especially, but my eight-year-old son Corey and my two-year-old daughter Mischa as well, have all, in their own unique ways, given me an immeasurable amount of love, support and above all, patience, through what has been a gruelling period of work. They are my infinite source of inspiration and drive in life. I also couldn't have ever been in the position I'm in today if I wasn't supported by my parents John and Lynda McKenny, and Kelly McKenny is the most dependable sister you could ask for, helping in many ways throughout the writing of this book. Thanks to Josh Tucker for his technical wizardry and Ross Holroyd for selflessly giving so much of his own time, helping me talk through ideas and offering an external perspective.

A special thank you must go to my employer Access Solutions Northern Ltd, who despite being a small business with very real and pressing financial considerations, afforded me a great deal of flexibility in my working arrangements, without which I would have seriously struggled to complete this work. I'd also like to acknowledge the external users programme at the University of Bradford's library, which ensured I had both an incredible access to knowledge, as well as the right working space to get my mind in gear.

I'd like to save a special acknowledgement for any and all creative individuals that have inspired us throughout this project; not just academics, filmmakers and comic book creators, but the inspirational people in all fields, putting passion and energy into the objects they create or acts they perform, so that the world can be a richer place.

Finally, a deep thank you to my co-authors for making all of this, not only possible, but also a thoroughly enjoyable experience. I have a great admiration for both and words can't describe how much of a pleasure this exciting – albeit at times very intense – journey has been. Thanks in particular to Martin, for the honour of coming to me with the idea in the first place, and introducing me to Andy.

Andy Livingstone

With much admiration, I'd like to thank my two co-authors for pulling this off with such patience and dedication. This book was written during the most difficult period of my life, and if there were ever two people I could depend upon to make sure we endured, it was Mike and Martin. They are both heroes to me, and will remain lasting friends.

Although Martin has already been mentioned, I'd like to thank my other former lecturer Martin Hall for his steady supply of support/insight/beer, and for introducing me to The Cornerhouse, who would become my employer and nurture my love of cinema.

To my parents, Val and Phil Livingstone, who introduced a noisy toddler to the world of superheroes with a Spider-Man costume; words cannot express my love and thanks. Some things never change, and there is always a costume hanging in my wardrobe, just in case. To my brother Matt, who has always supported and looked out

Acknowledgements

for me, I hope one day to be as good a brother to you as you've always been to me. To Claire Dorsett, who would always cheerfully admonish me for doing anything other than research; it paid off.

Finally, I'd like to thank Janine Farran for allowing me to 'waffle on' about all things Marvel for hours on end, and for accompanying me to see the many Marvel Cinematic Universe (MCU) releases. I always knew you secretly hated comic book movies, so your perseverance will never be forgotten.

MF, MM and AL – October 2015.

ABBREVIATIONS

MCU texts

A:AOU = Avengers: Age of Ultron (Film)

AoS = Agents of S.H.I.E.L.D. (Television)

CA:CW = Captain America: Civil War (Film)

CA:SS = Captain America: Super Soldier (Videogame)

CA:TFA = Captain America: The First Avenger (Film)

CA:TWS = Captain America: The Winter Soldier (Film)

GOTG = Guardians of the Galaxy (Film)

IM2 = Iron Man 2 (Film)

IM3 = Iron Man 3 (Film)

Marvel specific references

MCU = Marvel Cinematic Universe

MU = Marvel Universe

MS = Marvel Studios

MCC = Marvel Creative Committee

UU = Ultimate Universe

FF = Fantastic Four

SSR = Strategic Scientific Reserve

WSC = World Security Council

EIC = Editor-in-Chief

INTRODUCTION: THE ROAD TO MARVEL STUDIOS

Introducing the universe: A master plan?

> For the more we learn about the seemingly endless universe … the more we realize that it all seems to be part of some awesome, intricate *master plan*!
>
> (Reed Richards, *Fantastic Four* Annual #6, 1968)

The intellectual property (IP) associated with Marvel Comics has attracted a string of corporate takeovers and mergers, an ultimate purchase by Disney, and millions of devoted readers/fans, in the decades following its inception in 1961. The compelling content resides in the characters, locations and story events making up the 'Marvel Universe' (MU). Spider-Man, Iron Man, Thor, the X-Men, the Avengers and their accompanying villains have spent five decades waging war on one another across locales like New York City, the extra-dimensional 'Negative Zone', technologically ascendant African land Wakanda, and exotic worlds such as Hala and Sakaar. The legends of these battles are told in story arcs and multi-issue/multi-title 'events' like 'The Galactus Trilogy' (1966),[1] 'Planet Hulk' (2006–7), 'Extremis' (2005), 'Winter Soldier' (2005–11), 'The Kree-Skrull War' (1971–2),[2] 'Secret Wars' (1984–5), 'Acts of Vengeance' (1989–90), 'Civil War' (2006–7) and many more. Certain of these arcs are sufficiently character-defining that they have informed texts of the MCU[3] such as *Captain America: The Winter Soldier* (*CA:TWS*) and *Captain America: Civil War*, *Iron Man 3* (*IM3*) and several episodes of ABC Television's *Agents of S.H.I.E.L.D* (*AoS*) (the last two both inspired by 'Extremis'). In addition, key arcs have given rise to a Marvel Studios Animation ('Planet Hulk'), and film adaptations from outside of the MCU (*Fantastic Four: Rise of the Silver Surfer*, (Tim Story, 2007), draws heavily on 'The Galactus Trilogy'; *Spider-Man 3* (Sam Raimi, 2007) is informed by the events of 'Secret Wars'). Such activity testifies to the enduring power of the characters and situations appearing under the Marvel banner since the early 1960s. Even where comic arcs have featured characters originally established in other corners of fiction, the saga as a whole makes up a distinctive and fully realized fictional universe; one of the most extensive in recent Western popular culture, fit to be called 'the great mythology of the modern world' (Howe, 2013: 6).

Our argument is that the transference of this 'fully realized universe' concept, from the pages of comics to the big screen in the form of the MCU, must be regarded as a key moment of recent film history. Each of our eight distinct chapters, arranged thematically rather than chronologically, will add a new dimension to what we hope shall be a varied and convincing view of this 'phenomenon' of Marvel Studios (MS). We hope to reveal its unique nature within the contemporary media landscape (however, relating it to the 'norms' of that landscape) and show that it is worthy of study as an addition to Film Studies' repertoires around genre, narrative form, industry and more. We particularly argue that new conceptions of studio identity, floated by writers concerned with tracking the continuing relevance of older Hollywood practices and philosophies *within* the new, can be extended with reference to Marvel.

Brief summaries of each chapter can be found at the end of this introduction (Section IV), but the focus presently will be to lay the foundation of a broad understanding of Marvel, what it is and where it has come from. Our intention has been to assemble an introduction that will orientate a reader in possession of only a surface knowledge of Marvel's history and characters, while providing many useful highlights for the initiated. As such, illustrative examples – spread across three sections loosely separated both chronologically and thematically – will help convey the following essential elements: the heritage of an aesthetic and thematic 'house style' in Marvel Comics (Section I); Marvel's fluid organizational identity (Section II), and Section III will cover how commercial and creative needs have been traversed by an evolving (sometimes haphazardly) attitude to the utilization of characters (IP). This overview will lay the foundation for a well-rounded understanding of Marvel, indicating the kinds of events that we see as significant and which define our primary focus, so that the reader can then approach the more nuanced chapters thereafter in an order that suits their needs (though, we recommend going through them sequentially).

I. A silver age 'Big Bang' from the House of Ideas

In the early 1960s, Marvel's characters were not the only superheroes on the block. The company had competition, and its characters took their place in a hero-filled postwar world only after a decade where horror, crime and romance comics represented the mainstream.[4] Most notably, of course, competition came from industry leader DC (once 'National') Comics (Wright, 2003: 182). DC was the home of Superman, Batman and the Justice League of America, but other superhero publishers (such as Charlton, active 1946–85 and Gold Key Comics, active 1962–84) also found success. As Wright points out (2003: 183; 203), as a shift in editorial direction, Marvel's early 1960s return to superheroes actually followed the lead of DC; by summer 1961, DC had already explored the existence of a more convoluted superhero ontology in landmark issues such as 'The Flash of Two Worlds' by Gardner Fox (*The Flash* Vol.1, #123).[5] However, Marvel would quickly show a strong commitment to the 'shared universe' concept, and this would lend the company a priceless identity. Hitting its stride under the stewardship of writer-editor Stanley 'Stan Lee' Lieber, in conjunction with the prolifically imaginative and talented writer-artists Jack Kirby and Steve Ditko,[6] among several others, Marvel became the first publisher of superhero fiction to have its characters coalesce into a *coordinated* 'universe' (Wright, 2003: 218).

The approach set in quickly: new Lee/Kirby or Lee/Ditko creations like the Hulk, Spider-Man and Doctor Strange followed the Fantastic Four (FF) onto the same, crowded New York City streets within less than twenty-four months of the November, 1961 publication of *Fantastic Four* #1. Indeed, when Spider-Man earned his own title (dated March[7] 1963), the FF appeared on the cover, suggesting a universe that was already in play, a bigger narrative which newer heroes simply joined. Interactions that in the earliest issues might have seemed opportunistic (designed chiefly to raise the profile of new or lesser heroes) gradually developed a sense of an overall *plan*: such that an issue of one team's adventures (*Fantastic Four* Vol.1, #73, 1968) could feature another character, Thor, crossing the same Manhattan landscape, while in the midst of his own adventure (in the events of *Thor* Vol.1, #150–1, referenced in the other issue). Of course, such a device was also a manifestation of an entrepreneurial editor who understood the power not only of 'To be continued...', but also of the (often insoluble) conundrum of 'could Thor defeat [strongman of the Fantastic Four] The Thing?', or its equivalent.

As time passed and the Marvel Universe (MU) developed a galactic, pan-dimensional reach, and characters from alternate realities and timelines began to appear, there was an increasingly evident suggestion that the unfolding of this universe would know no bounds (Howe, 2013: 72). Miss an issue, and a reader could miss the start of something big; importantly for the future value of the library and brand, the events of the MU made up 'one grand narrative ... everything that happened in one title could have an impact on all of the others' (156). This would one day serve Marvel, along with the other major comic publishers, well, when publication format changes introduced hard and soft cover collections of previously printed issues that could keep defunct titles and 'resting' characters in lucrative circulation. Thus, longevity came to a medium that had once been thought of as disposable and only appropriate for young children (Miller, 2011). Indeed, for decades, posterity had been far from the minds of the creative teams planning the production of superhero comics.

This situation changed as Marvel upped the stakes of the shared universe concept in superhero fiction and, for different reasons, both the fan community and potential licensees started to demand stable, canonical versions of characters. This encouraged an increasingly organized and codified approach to the burgeoning MU. The direction that Lee initiated in 1961 has defined Marvel in popular thought, but it is pertinent to remember that the company's portfolio does not consist solely of superheroes. Just as horror themes, popular before the 1954 introduction of the Comics Code, returned to inflect the 1970s MU, other genres have epitomized the company's offering at certain points. The 'Timely Comics' phase saw romance comics as one staple of the product line, and once the MU was up and running, efforts to integrate characters dating from the 'vaults' of the company were made.[8] What eventually became labelled a Marvel 'multiverse' found a way for characters of all kinds to participate in mainstream continuity.[9] Limited diversification into non-superhero storytelling has been further enabled in various imprints and sidelines,[10] but above anything else, the MU is known to global audiences as a domain of superheroes. While acknowledging the various genre 'tweaks' on this formula apparent in its productions,[11] this is the capacity in which the MU provides a model for the MCU.

Understanding the universe

The shared universe element is, according to our argument, an essential differentiator both in Marvel's comic book universe, and later in the production philosophy of MS – it is from this that Marvel draws the 'competitive advantage' (further defined in Chapter 6) that allows the MCU to flourish. Before we proceed too much further, a working definition of a fictional universe may be beneficial.[12] A fictional universe may be defined as a textual environment in print, film, online or other medium (often multiple media) with defined discursive borders. These borders mark it off from leaking into other, competing universes (the Oz of L. Frank Baum's books from Tolkien's Middle Earth, say), but also serve to (selectively) demarcate it from the 'real world' and real history ('A long time ago in a galaxy far, far away ...'). It may encompass a number of significant, related works within one artistic oeuvre (Krzysztof Kieslowski's *Three Colours* trilogy (1993–4) or Kevin Smith's 'Askewniverse'), or a stable world populated by characters established in once unrelated, discrete narratives that – for reasons that may be commercial as well as, or instead of, creative – are gradually drawn together under a brand association with the rights holder's series of IP assets (the Disney or Warner Bros. cartoon universes). A fictional universe, then, may emerge from rigid planning, or it may evolve gently.[13]

In our working definition, a fictional universe is (obviously) not real, but its ontological properties and premise may evoke real states, and it shall display consistent psychological and – of course – narrative continuities (Eder et al., 2010: 7). Principles of space and time within the diegesis need not resemble those of the real world, but their logic will be adhered to consistently throughout any text set within the universe. It is important that a universe sets its own 'rules' for a reader, and maintains them; in summarizing, Thomas Pavel, Marie-Laure Ryan (2013) explains that the literary text 'establishes for the reader a new actual world which imposes its own laws on the surrounding system, thereby defining its own horizon of possibilities. In order to become immersed in this world, the reader must adopt a new ontological perspective, thereby entailing a new model of what exists and what does not'.[14]

A distinction may be drawn between serial texts which depend upon a fairly stable character or sets of characters, and texts that are but one part of an interlocking, mutually impacting design. In serial texts which transpire in 'one-off' environments, there is a sense of impermanence because, apart from fundamentals, the next text in the series essentially wipes the slate clean (this, with few exceptions, is the case with the rolling diegetic present of the first twenty films in the James Bond series – see Flanagan, 2009: 65–6). By contrast, in mature, continuous fictional worlds, characters display *history*. We can say, then, that a fictional universe allows events to accrue history; that this history affects characters, and is something of which they are aware.[15] A fictional universe thus emphasizes the operations of time more than does a serial text; but this is not to say that the time transpiring in the MU closely tracks the time of its readers' world.[16] This fact has inevitably presented a problem in how the developed MU is interpreted, since the MU may choose to anchor certain events in relation to historical markers (like the Second World War or the Cold War) while virtually ignoring the passage of time in the ages of characters. Exemplifying this is the problem of maturation in certain characters; Franklin, the child of Reed and Sue Richards of the FF, has yet to advance past the pubertal stage despite having appeared as a toddler in 1980s comics.[17]

What we have termed the 'maturity' of a fictional universe could be alternatively expressed as the internal consistency that is maintained as it expands. The detail that goes into its construction will be initially mapped by creators but may be monitored and, occasionally, codified and even corrected by users/fans in documents like Mark Gruenwald's 1977–9 fanzine *Omniverse* (which led to the Gruenwald-edited manual *Official Handbook of the Marvel Universe*),[18] or the concept of the 'Buffyverse' (a term derived from the fandom of TV show *Buffy the Vampire Slayer*, 1997–2003). The more history and story event accrued by a textual universe, the more complex the guidance needed to orient new fans. Accordingly, the world of media fandoms (in which comics and their adaptations are a major strand) has seen the wide circulation of terminology that describes various strategies for how continuity is managed (as noted above, complex continuity may not have played a major role in superhero culture before the 1960s, but the form seems particularly well-suited to reflections on how textual worlds are constituted).[19] The phenomenon of creators/producers changing the explanation for a past event to suit new purposes, or annulling the event (erasing it from canon), is known as 'retconning' (for retroactive continuity). A 'reboot', which can be full or partial, is when a continuity that has grown complex (or unpopular) is simplified and/or restarted (essentially, allowing the resetting of any aspect beyond fundamentals like character names). For instance, *Casino Royale* (Martin Campbell, 2006) relaunched the James Bond cycle with a new star and status quo for the character, and the 'New 52' event reset the mainstream DC Universe in 2011. William Proctor (2014) asserts that where makers of fictional universes desire to introduce 'fissures, cracks and counter-factual narratives', a 'multiverse' concept may be employed. He contends that Marvel uses a branching 'multiversal' structure of many levels, featuring interlocking universes, alternate timelines and 'what if' divergent realities, to 'rationalise divergent continuities by situating them within a nexus of parallel worlds'. Thus, extra stories are allowed to take place and 'count' for something, without interfering with 'official' events. The centre of Marvel's multiverse, and home to the most stable, definitive versions of the major characters, has become known by the designation 'Earth-616'.[20]

For clarity, then, it is worth underlining that in the present work, 'MU' shall be used to refer to the Marvel *Comics* Universe (more properly, the multiverse), which officially started with *Fantastic Four* #1 in 1961,[21] and is still going strong today.[22] The 'MCU' refers to the particular iteration of familiar Marvel characters that has unfolded, in an organized and ostensibly seamless continuity on screen since the release of *Iron Man* in 2008. As a designation, MCU encompasses all of the major 'shared universe' MS texts discussed herein.[23] Where the two differ in salient ways, care will be taken to orient the reader to their relationship.

House style: The Marvel worldview

Although very much a product of pop culture, the MU exhibits a complexity, breadth and internal diversity that have raised comparisons with the mythologies of various literatures, periods and cultures (Lang and Trimble, 1988). Despite the fullness and range of the material, certain thematic tropes feature with enough regularity to be regarded as key concerns. One is the development of teenaged and youthful characters that would fulfil a need for identificatory figures for young readers; from the 1940s onwards, teen characters would frequently be paired with older mentor figures (as in Captain America and Bucky, themselves following the Batman/Robin template). Indeed, in a post-Comics Code era, when adolescent readers were deserting the sanitized comic book for other attractions in a crowded entertainment field, Marvel stepped up its emphasis on youthful characters and their problems (Wright, 2003: 181–2), culminating in the September 1963 debut of its most exciting young team, the X-Men.

Another consistent characteristic concerns the motivations behind why Marvel characters don masked personas (or, in the case of the transforming Hulk, express their internal rage). Almost invariably, these stem from traumatic personal histories, with the deaths of loved ones – particularly but not exclusively parents, or parental surrogates – figuring heavily (Daredevil; Havoc and Cyclops of the X-Men). Some, like Spider-Man/Peter Parker, would be forever defined by the truncation or disturbance of their Oedipal narratives. Even copyright-free Norse god Thor, written by Lee and Kirby from 1962, regularly tussled with father Odin. With these Marvel heroes, concerns with the figure of the outsider and their place within the social fabric gather around an Oedipal narrative that, over time, solidifies into an ubiquitous structuring presence. Foreshadowing the countercultural direction that superhero comics took later in the 1960s (Wright, 2003: 230), the Oedipal trope also carried a certain allegorical burden, in that it mirrored the struggle to receive the understanding of a deeply suspicious, patriarchal establishment that marked comics' response to the Wertham campaign of the 1950s.[24]

As opposed to the more straightforwardly upstanding heroics of DC Comics (Scott, 2012: 121), the Marvel house style would pivot around a brand of tormented heroism that was woven through key 1960s outcasts like the Hulk and the X-Men. These heroes displayed self-doubt and anxiety, awareness of their own 'dark side' or a profound sense of irony regarding their own powers. A regular trope was the perception of heroic powers not as gifts, but as a curse or unbearable responsibility (Spider-Man, the Hulk, the Thing); by the time Marvel had really hit its stride, a succession of horror-inflected characters like Werewolf-by-Night and Ghost Rider appeared, some of whom were literally cursed. These heroes were neither content with their powers, nor always sure of how best to use them; so, in their own way, characters as far from each other on the heroism-to-antiheroism spectrum as Captain America and the Punisher equally measured out the gap between American idealism and American reality (Pustz, 2012: 140; Scott, 2012: 122). This was fitting for an American decade, the 1970s, defined by 'paralysis ... stagnation and drift' (Pustz, 2012).

The tendency towards brooding (anti)heroes, who examined the rules of society as well as working at upholding them, undoubtedly owed something to Bob Kane/Bill Finger's Batman; all the same, Marvel – in the previous form of 'Timely Comics' – could date the even more ambiguous villain-turned-hero trope to the debut of the Sub-Mariner, within only a few months of Batman's initial 1939 appearance.[25] At Marvel, it seemed as if the era of 'Monster as Hero' (Thomas and Sanderson, 2007: 112) never really ended, surviving as a major aspect of Marvel's successful characters into the 1980s and beyond (Wolverine, Punisher and former Spider-Man enemy Venom enjoyed their greatest popularity in the 1990s). The MU could be downbeat, and in times of national strife, bristle with social relevance, but even in a malaise-stricken 1970s, there was still fun to be had and action to be savoured. If struggles with the responsibility of being powered became something of a Marvel trademark, another part of the company's evolving 'house style' was to do with the backdrops to adventure; these generally transpired against more 'realistic' surroundings when compared to the generic, composite cities of DC's costumed adventurers (Hell's Kitchen, Greenwich Village and Queens rather than Metropolis or Coast City). This suited the Marvel specialty of interlacing adventure with the hero's domestic and emotional struggles (romantic, financial or familial). It has already been pointed out that the involuntary loss of parents sets many Marvel crime fighting careers in motion, yet problems resulting from the structure of families are not limited to those around absence. Teams like the FF and the X-Men featured squabbling siblings, and the insecure bickering among 1970s Avengers teams became legendary (see Chapter 5).

Although present-day Manhattan settled into the role as fulcrum of Marvel's universe (locating the Sanctum Santorum of Doctor Strange on Bleecker Street, the Baxter Building – home to the FF – on Madison Avenue, among many other correspondences with the real city map), it was not long before creative teams wanted to spread their wings into other places, periods and even times. Dimension-crossing characters like Lee/Ditko's Doctor Strange were added to institute a 'magic' side to Marvel that plays a key role in the universe to this day,[26] while Reed Richards kept the portal to the outlandish 'Negative Zone' within the headquarters of the FF. As Sean Howe explains, a key moment was the introduction of gods from the Norse pantheon, in tales binding their legendary realm of Asgard to the Midgard/ Earth of the other heroes; this represented a kind of statement about how Lee and Kirby saw their new characters. Playfully disparaged by Lee, not long before, as 'long-underwear characters',[27] these heroes were now being presented in terms of a tradition as long, dignified and universal as those drawn from mythic literature. 'It wasn't just the awe-striking powers that made these stories operatic. There was also the classicism of the narratives – quests for mystical objects, preparations for battle – and themes of duty, heritage and mortality, that seemed wholly unrelated to the alien-punching stories from the newsstand competition' (Howe, 2013: 71). The presence of archetypes recognizable to many cultures helped to fuel Marvel's expansion, making the MU a place where readers should not be surprised to find a revision of Cain and Abel in a social system that resembled Imperial Rome,[28] various Promethean explorations of the responsibility of scientific creation,[29] or tales – such as the Incredible Hulk's – that took fables like 'Beauty and the Beast' and updated them with atomic age cautions. A quality of 'Shakespearean' gravitas and consequence obtained (Howe, 2013: 71), kept in balance by the playfulness and earthbound reflexivity of Lee's ringmaster-style persona and narrational techniques. The contrapuntal formula worked. 1965 would see the Norse legends followed into MU continuity by the gods of Mount Olympus; apparently, the expansive MU could accommodate both systems.[30]

An enormous superhero terrain was gradually being mapped. In this, Lee, as Editor-in-Chief (EIC), may have been carrying out the orders of publisher Martin Goodman, the head of Magazine Management Company, parent to Marvel (Genter, 2007: 953), but it was Lee's personality that was coming, unstoppably, to the fore. Full credit was not always forthcoming, but Lee's artistic collaborators were incredibly important in establishing and developing many of these concepts.[31] Bill Everett returned to the fold having created The Sub-Mariner (Prince Namor) in 1939; like Joe Simon and Kirby's Captain America, the character was revived by Lee.[32] Ditko, Don Heck, Dick Ayers and others were major collaborators. None was more important than Kirby who, quite apart from his other contributions, accompanied Lee (providing plotting as well as art) on an uninterrupted 102-issue run of the main *Fantastic Four* title. This series would seed many of the characters that would define and sustain Marvel for decades.

Within a few years, the evolution of Marvel's style was evident to readers from playgrounds to barracks and college campuses (and, increasingly, to other parts of the entertainment business as well as corporate observers). Crucial to mention with regards to the development of this strong personality and point of view was the editorial voice cultivated by Lee in the 1960s. No doubt originating as a selling tactic, in time this became an essential component of the company's DNA. This mode of address would explicitly aim to draw readers into a relationship not only with the company's heroes and titles, but also with other 'true believers' or 'zombies'. The fans were painted as zealous loyalists, nonconformist to a man yet paradoxically happy to 'march' along with Lee and Marvel (Duncan and Smith, 2009: 180). Letters pages and the 'Bullpen Bulletins' page (including 'Stan's Soapbox' columns from 1967) were 'written in a style which might be characterized as High Hipster', according to the novelist Jonathan Lethem (2003), and framed as missives from the heart of a carnivalesque 'Bullpen' staff culture that may have been far from the truth. Readers were made familiar with the various staffers, who were known by jovial nicknames like 'King' Kirby and 'Fabulous Flo' Steinberg. Playful though it was, this address to readers was ingenious in its directness, stamping Marvel with a sense of identity and distinct worldview unknown elsewhere in American comic publishing; when DC tried to imitate Marvel's hip and offbeat style, the results fell flat (Wright, 2003: 224–5).

Lee's promotion tipped readers off about the development of the MU and sent up both itself and the 'Distinguished Competition', adding a friendly face to Marvel (and building the fame that has seen Lee make a cameo appearance in every MCU film to date). As early as *Fantastic Four* Vol.1, #3 (March, 1962) readers were being complimented on being 'a cut above average', and for writing 'intelligently' in to the magazine, but for all that the image of a smart conversation between equals was splashed across columns and bulletin pages, the same tone was infiltrating the comics' narration.[33] Rather than breaking the spell for the reader, Marvel's editorial voice and the diegetic world seemed of a piece.[34] This technique crystallized, famously, in *Fantastic Four* Annual #3 (1965), the final panel of which saw party crashers 'Stan Lee' and 'Jack Kirby' excluded from the much-hyped wedding of Reed Richards and Sue Storm – for the lack of an invitation.[35]

The editorial voice had become another component that was quintessentially Marvel. And while it may not quite have been the voice of a generation – Lee turned forty a couple of months after the late 1962 first appearance of Spider-Man[36] – Lee's patter and Kirby's talent for designing freakishly 'other' science-fiction landscapes and characters helped Marvel to speak with the nonconformist voice of the 'hipster'. The glory reflected across the entire universe: already well known for taking outcast characters and making them into stars, Marvel began to seem rebellious at heart, more likely to challenge establishment values and explore the fairness of the system, than was the work emerging from DC Comics. DC's universe, even into the late 1960s, was known as a wilful realm of 'black and white' moral certainty (Wright, 2003: 224). Although DC would eventually adapt to the new style, Marvel's mission became more evident as the 1970s wore on, against the setting of a comics industry courting attention and critical acclaim in the pursuit of 'relevance' (Wright, 2003: 233–4). The values espoused in some of Lee's editorials gave readers (many of whom were university students) something to align with, as did the risk-taking approach adopted by the publisher in groundbreaking controversies like Spider-Man's 1971 drugs issues.[37] *Amazing Spider-Man* Vol.1, #96–8 (1971) were written by Lee at the behest of the Department of Health, Education and Welfare but rejected by the Comics Code Authority; Marvel published them anyway.

Despite Marvel's reliance upon sci-fi, cosmic, horror and even occult characters and plots, one of the effects of this period was to construct a lasting association between Marvel's products and the real world. This coexistence of space opera and street level social critique in the same universe was as much a matter of style as content. Howe reports that the 'real world' direction was noted at the time by iconic alternative newspaper the *Village Voice* (2013: 60). Although one of the most gripping and admired runs of 'relevant' comics was DC's *Green Lantern/Green Arrow* (1970–2) by Denny O'Neill and Neal Adams (the latter brought a realistic art style to epic Marvel storylines like 'The Kree-Skrull War'),[38] Marvel always seemed to have the edge on unforced 'relevance'. As correspondents used letter pages to hold a debate over whether superheroes belonged in the Vietnam War (Wright, 2003: 240–4), Marvel seemed to have established a credible platform where ideas of moral equivalence and compromised societies could be handled; in this universe, paragons brandishing eternal values were in short supply. This enabled riskier stories dealing with essentially unpunished crimes like the death of Spider-Man's girlfriend Gwen Stacy, or Captain America's feelings of betrayal by his own nation (Pustz, 2012: 139–40). By naturalizing such serious, 'relevant' themes and complex moralities into stories and characters from such an early stage, Marvel enhanced the signature style of its comics; importantly, it also prepared MCU fans of later decades – some of whom had little more than a passing familiarity with comics – for new iterations of characters (or rather, for characters whose moral perspectives did not have to be fixed in the fading relevance of an early 1960s 'structure of feeling').[39] Some of these iterations will be discussed in later stages of this book; here, we note that MS's projects have largely been able to follow riskier themes without seeming to jar with 'innocent' earlier versions, a move that would risk drawing the ire of long-time comic readers.[40]

This section has aimed not to provide a chronological overview, but instead to highlight some narrative and thematic Marvel 'hallmarks' that should give readers a handle on the company's artistic essence and origin. That parts of this essence carry over into the MS releases (negotiating and transcending shifts in format) is a contention to be explored over the course of this book. The various aspects of theme, style, voice and worldview described in this section add up to Marvel's identity, an identity with considerable public recognition and significance. Predominantly, the creation of this identity has been conducted on a diegetic plane. However, the reputation of Marvel Comics (and the associated subsidiaries and partners connected with the immensely valuable IP contained in the MU) also obtains as the public image of a business; one which has required constant management and control, sometimes through times of considerable corporate instability. We shift focus to such matters in our next section.

II. 'Suits' and 'Creatives': Organizational identity and surmounting internal conflict

As the MU continued to expand, the piling up of parallel character histories and sub-universes was inevitable, resulting in some obfuscation of character identities and requiring some creative solutions from the comics division; a fresh and significant idea emerged in conjunction with Marvel characters becoming big news at the international box office, and we shall look at this 'Ultimate Universe' (UU) approach shortly. Another identity problem that was less than secret had been playing out around Marvel itself. As a business, Marvel had been changing hands regularly since the late 1960s, when it was first the subject of acquisition.[41] Marvel's identity demanded vigilance and careful management, as did the MU itself, the difference being that the former was a struggle in which editorial could have little influence. In an ever-present tension between art and commerce, Marvel is no different to any organization operating in the creative industries. In order to excel in its competitive environment, such an organization must offer more than the competition; for a creative entity, this translates as innovation. Yet, as is the case with Marvel, it also has to operate within the constraints of financial pressures, with management edicts sometimes handed down from executives far removed from hard-won, specialized business wisdom (Wright, 2003: 256). To put this in essence, and no doubt reductively, this leads to a state where 'the creatives' are distant from 'the suits'. Those that control financial sources, and benefit only from their short-term return, can significantly affect how the organization acts, and thus, its standing with its many stakeholders. However, Marvel could never quite separate the creatives from the suits, and instead, as we'll see, pursued a reconciliation of the two – with uneven results.

The purpose of the following section is to track certain key business actions undertaken by Marvel, examining how these actions have influenced organizational identity, as well as assessing where identity may have had a causal effect on certain courses of action. The resulting identity then reverberates in the public image adopted by Marvel, not only through its own communications, but also in favourable media coverage. Realizing that these strands are never completely discrete, we will piece together the story of how Marvel products entered the cinematic consciousness.

Although Marvel is synonymous with certain extremely creative, influential and some considerably famous individuals, this discussion adopts a position of treating the organization as an entity (an 'it' rather than a 'they'). This is because the personalities within the organization are only part of the cumulative image, or identity, of the organization as a whole. The many varied stakeholders interested in, and/or affected by, its activities – customers, competitors, industry analysts, investors, suppliers, employees and many others – develop a specific, and indeed, emotional view of an organization; it is, to them, a sentient being. Organizational identity is a fluid and multifaceted notion that Mary Jo Hatch and Majken Schultz define it as 'a dynamic concept of identity that is both rooted in the organisation's history and heritage *and* in its relationships to other identities and images that swirl around and interpenetrate it at any given moment' (2004: 5). This 'rootedness' in organizational history means that such an identity can have profound and lasting effects on strategic decisions and operational interactions with the aforementioned stakeholders. Yet, its dynamic nature implies that this identity is constantly in flux, changing over time as a result of those very interactions and decisions. In effect, a symbiotic relationship – where identity and actions shape one another – ensues. Seen in this way, the organization itself makes decisions, holds opinions, even espouses a 'worldview'; in the case of Marvel, the semantic richness of its literary holdings – their many meanings – makes the application of such an approach necessary. By treating Marvel as an entity, we intend to bring out the elements that transcend individual creative talents, passing corporate owners, and changing editorial departments.

In the twenty-first century, Marvel is known for supplying characters experienced by audiences in diverse media; it maintains the desired fun and approachable image, updating for a lucrative family market what was once the more chaotic, hip and 'freewheeling' (Howe, 2013: 93) image. At the same time, its enduring success and market dominance – despite some well-documented events towards the end of last century that will be examined presently – lend an air of legitimacy essential to capture the trust of financial markets, for whom Marvel needs to be a viable investment or partner. This balancing of multiple identifying features – faces that turn towards consumers and towards business – is fundamental to Marvel's position at key stages in its history, reminding us of a trait of organizational identity highlighted by Stuart Albert and David Whetten: 'There is no one best statement of identity, but rather, multiple equally valid statements relative to different audiences for different purposes' (2004: 93). Albert and Whetten go on to specify what they term the 'ideographic form' of organizational identity, where there is 'a struggle, not simply over alternative budget proposals, but over the very soul of the institution' (97). Marvel's understanding of this, and ability to project its identity in different ways to the desired audience at the right time while maintaining its creative 'soul', is key to successful periods in its history. To achieve this balance is not a simple task, and although this feature will be covered in much more depth in Chapter 2, a brief overview of the company after the 'freewheeling' 1960s were left behind will illustrate how the failure to maintain this balance can result in a fractured organization (and, in Marvel's case, nearly led to financial and artistic ruin).

Not-so-secret wars

In the decades following its meteoric 1960s rise, Marvel struggled to expand in order to deal with the escalation that it had itself triggered in the comic book market. Although as a subsidiary of Magazine Management it was operating within a wider industrial structure, the running of Marvel Comics was ostensibly left to comic book writers. Howe explains that through savvy business manoeuvres from Martin

Goodman, in 1971 Marvel overtook the market share of its largest competitor DC, so that 'for the first time in its history, Marvel comics was the number one comic book company in the world' (2013: 116). In terms of its organizational identity, the steps needed to accomplish this industrial feat, such as an escalation in number of titles, could arguably compromise attempts to maintain reputation; Howe adds that 'Marvel had lost … its underdog status now' (117). This came after creative control issues had already led to fragmentation, with many of the personalities synonymous with the 1960s era departing: by 1970, Ditko and Kirby had left Marvel, and Stan Lee had stepped aside as EIC to spend time trying to steer the company's characters and general IP into other media – specifically, Hollywood – waters.

A disorganized, yet earnest attempt to maintain Marvel's essence and reputation followed, as Roy Thomas, with the company since the mid-1960s, stepped up as EIC. A product of comic fandom himself, Thomas attempted to harness the creative energy that was gathering through fanzines and the emergent convention circuit, embodied in talent that had been reared on 1960s Marvel publications. In the period after Thomas's promotion, notes Howe, 'Marvel's line expanded … pages were filled with the work of more than a dozen new artists that synthesized their forerunners' visual trademarks into ever more intricate styles' (2013: 125). Writers such as Steve Englehart and Steve Gerber, among others, pushed the boundaries of what had been seen in comic books. This period of 'hands off' editorship from Thomas spurred creativity and 'ushered in Marvel's most unpredictable – and often downright subversive – era' (Howe, 2013: 135), as inspired but sometimes disruptive young creators managed to 'refract the superhero world through a prism of boomer values' (135). Although not in the majority at first, these subversive creators operated in the margins on an ever-increasing roster of lesser-known characters where they earned swelling readerships, helping them to work their way towards the headline titles, such as *Captain America* and *The Avengers*.

The innovation and risk-taking that such as Gerber brought to Marvel in the 1970s was helping to incubate a dedicated cult readership. This had the potential to ensure long-term financial success, if management could only recognize 'the wisdom of selling comic book fantasies directly to those who dreamed about them the most' (Wright, 2003: 253), by which Wright means the fans, who were in it for the long haul. Thomas attempted to maintain a high level of creativity amid the pressure of satisfying the short-sighted commands of owners Cadence Industries, but ethical concerns about the treatment of freelancers forced him to leave. A flurry of changes in the EIC position followed, with many more promoted writers struggling with similar problems: Marv Wolfman fought Cadence over cost-cutting, while his successor Gerry Conway painted a picture of a 'toxic' environment; 'a cesspool of politics and personality issues' (cited in Howe, 2013: 185). Respected writers left Marvel following disputes over freelancing terms, or were handed the poisoned chalice that was the position of EIC.

In late 1977, the EIC role finally settled with Jim Shooter, the man primed to define Marvel's next era. In contrast to Thomas's fan's-eye trust in, and backing of, creators, the Shooter period unravelled Marvel's reputation for harbouring creativity. A new 'hands on' approach reigned in experimentation and creativity, at one point instituting 'a rule against stories that stretched for more than two issues' (Howe, 2013: 237) through fear of alienating new readers. Shooter aimed to homogenize art styles; the design he wanted to impose summed up by 'a grid of six or nine uniformly sized panels of eye level, medium-sized shots that sacrificed dynamism for absolute clarity' (238). This era reached its apex with 'Secret Wars' (*Marvel Super Heroes Secret Wars* Vol.1, #1–12, 1984–5). A charitable way of explaining the new direction indicated by the miniseries is offered by comic store owner Diana Shutz: where the 1970s era had offered autonomy to creators, by the 'advent of *Secret Wars*, it seems to me, Marvel was trying to redress that balance and pull things back in favour of the characters, not the creators' (Shutz, cited in Howe 2013: 264–5). The series came about at the behest of toy company Mattel, whose research had identified the words 'Secret' and 'Wars' as 'words that made kids go wild' (Howe, 2013: 263). The comics took on the value of advertising brochures to stoke children's interest in Mattel's superhero toys.

The broad 'event' structure, where more characters could join in and play passing roles, certainly helped 'Secret Wars' to exploit the MU. Less driven by creators than by Mattel's priorities around characters, it approached story in such a way that second-stringers like Falcon and villains like Kang could enter the spotlight alongside the high-profile likes of Spider-Man, who would already be expected to register high sales in toy form. Long-term readers may have preferred to think that the *Secret Wars* style was more of a single issue, 'impossible story' or reversible dream narrative, but the fact was that this approach to comic book creation was meant to stay. This was confirmed when the inevitable sequel was announced (Howe, 2013: 279). *Secret Wars* was successful, but by combining the exploitation of diversity within the MU with a move to homogenize storytelling style, it seemed a corruption or, at best, unintended consequence of the open-ended universe building that had gone on during Kirby, Lee and Ditko's most fertile period. This renewal of Marvel's identity was a controversial one that tipped the balance away from creativity and towards commerce. Despite high sales for comics like *Secret Wars*, the emphasis on short-term returns did not prove to be sustainable, and carrying on in this image, the 1990s led to further strife.

Every character needs an origin

As a storytelling organization, Marvel understands the significant comic book convention of the 'origin story', in which lies the core identity of a hero (or villain). If focus is lost, the origin story serves as baseline reference for a true interpretation, but superheroes that have become dated, or overlooked by time, are sometimes given a story arc that reinterprets, or simply retells their origin story to better resonate with contemporary readers (a good example would be the shift from the specifically Vietnam-era 1963 origin of Iron Man to the Middle Eastern 'terrorist plot' of the

2008 MCU iteration). Following the business tumult and artistic criticisms of the 1980s, Marvel began a reconstruction, or recalibration, of its organizational identity, seeking to reconnect with the image of its 1960s origins. As we have seen, public understanding of this original identity resounds with fond memories of the times when Lee, Kirby et al., embarked on a game-changing reinvigoration of a floundering superhero genre. When it most needed it, in the late 1990s, the company went so far as to base an advertising campaign upon assuring fans that its comics were returning to their roots (Wright, 2003: 283), a clear illustration of Hatch and Schultz's view that a viable identity is 'rooted in the organisation's history and heritage' (2004: 5). Plainly, then, a specific characterization was consciously sculpted at times, and leaving aside the validity of Marvel's self-narrating claims with respect to the part that other companies played in resurrecting the superhero, Marvel's successful placement of comic storytelling on an industrial footing has ensured that this is the narrative on which comic book lore has come to depend. Two main features – faith in creators, and the narrativization of industrial events – become apparent as common themes linking Marvel's success in the 1960s with the achievements, four decades later, of MS. The crafting of a public narrative emphasizing these crucial aspects – creativity and financial viability, maintained in a scrupulous balance – supported the company's entry into independent film production. Marvel's preferred way of seeing, and discursively constructing, itself often summons up this narrative.

By 1990, Marvel had adjusted to comics' new reality, where traditional news-stand sales were all but irrelevant and direct sales to the niche fan audience through comic book stores were all important (Wright, 2003: 280).[42] The company entered the new century having tentatively navigated Cadence/Shooter's roll-back of creative freedoms, as well as business and market changes that saw its comic book portfolio shrink to a lesser role in the overall generation of revenue, and the high comic sales of the early 1990s plunge in the second half of the decade (2003: 283). This new, post-2000 era was characterized by a renewed emphasis on star creators, as Marvel attempted to distance itself from the creativity stifling image it had acquired in the 1980s (typified by the 'Secret Wars' event). Unlike a previous generation under well-meaning but essentially powerless EICs stretching from Thomas's commencement to the appointment of Shooter, this new stable of creators arrived, at the right time, and apparently lacking a bitter sense of entitlement, into the stewardship of Joe Quesada (who became EIC in 2000). Representing hopes that the Marvel 'feel' would be restored, Quesada instructed creators to express themselves.

What we have framed, up to now, as a reversion to first principles or self-proclaimed return to roots, served Marvel well in the new century. A little comment, germane to the cinematic subject of this book, may be added on the matter of this resurgence of fortunes, which rose simultaneously with the move to bring creators into the fold, endowing them with increased power and credit. Given that the business practices of the 'Big Two' publishers had alienated key creators like Frank Miller and Alan Moore (not to mention the shabbily treated likes of Kirby, and – going back to the dawn of the Golden Age – DC's Siegel and Shuster, creators of Superman), the ease with which new superstar artist-creators such as Brian Michael Bendis were prepared to publicly identify with one of those same publishers was striking. This spoke to the peaking of a new morale that had been building for writers and artists under reformed agreements that improved upon the poor remuneration and rights afforded to employees of Kirby's vintage (Wright, 2003: 256–8; 262); in addition, it identified a new and well-timed philosophy of production. This philosophy involved linking star names (and – just as significantly – those names blessed with fan credibility) to major titles in a fashion owing more than a little to Hollywood practice. A comparison of the figure of the filmic author, in the early 2000s enjoying their own period of 'mainstreaming',[43] with the Big Two's hiring policy on name creators should not be made superficially; indeed, in discussing the general principle of comparing film and comic *auteurs*, Gregory Steirer (2011: 272–4) notes the need for further reflection and interrogation to strengthen the approach. Yet, given the increasing mirroring between comic storytelling and commercial strategy[44] and film practice during the 1990s and early 2000s, it does not seem outrageous to link the manner of Marvel's resurgence with an auteurist model which – in a careful and calculated way[45] – was re-embraced by Hollywood studios during the same period.

Marvel was making a public show, and bold identifying statement, of once again holding the creator in high esteem. This seemed to release credibility and excitement through the organization as a whole. Many of the new appointments had made their names in independent comic publishing, and brought with them the cultural prestige of non-superhero work, or sophisticated, cerebral 'twists' on the genre. Alongside Bendis (*Ultimate Spider-Man* 2000–present[46]; *New Avengers* 2005–10; *Alias* 2001–4) worked writers such as Mark Millar (*Ultimate X-Men* 2000–3; *The Ultimates* 2002–7; *Civil War* 2006–7), Warren Ellis (*Doom 2099* 1994–6; *Ultimate Galactus Trilogy* 2005–6; *Moon Knight*, 2014), and Ed Brubaker (*Captain America* 2005–12). These writers were responsible for a considerable amount of rebranding and re-energizing of Marvel's characters, the updating of identities and environments having an impact on Marvel's organizational identity as a whole, particularly in the sense of repurposing many aspects of the MU to better suit the drift towards Hollywood. Bendis and Millar, in particular, fed off the energy that seemed to conduct between Hollywood and comics, working cinema motifs and personalities into both major story arcs ('Hollywood' in Bendis's *Ultimate Spider-Man* Vol.1, #54–9, 2004) and the fabric of their issues. Before long, Marvel was drawing its authorial *cachet* direct from the source, enlisting hip, comic-friendly directors, often drawn from indie or niche filmmaking scenes (Kevin Smith, Reginald Hudlin and – auspiciously for MS – Joss Whedon) to script major characters. Starting in 2005, with artist Steve Epting, Brubaker produced a hugely acclaimed Captain America arc ('Winter Soldier') that, within a decade, would explicitly provide the second phase of the MCU with its signature film.

Going ultimate

Perhaps the purest innovation of this period – although typically, such innovation paid due respect to the original 1960s breaking of universal ground – was the formation of the 'Ultimate Universe'. An extended example of Marvel's use of alternate timelines and counter-factuality within the wider multiverse, the UU allowed Marvel to experiment with ideas and create situations that could not be executed in – and would not affect – the established Earth-616 MU, with its rich history and restrictions on permanent change. The UU was the epitome of major comic company reinterpretation and reappropriation, as its headline characters had their origins re-situated in the contemporary world, attempting to tap into core values but simultaneously wiping away decades of narrative baggage that had been identified as off-putting to new readers. Importantly, these were the readers – and potential readers – who were discovering Marvel characters at the cinema (the X-Men came to theatres in 2000).[47] These reinterpretations were friendly to new international cinematic incarnations; for example, Sony's 2002 launch of what became a Spider-Man trilogy. It was not coincidental that the founding characters of the UU were Spidey and the X-Men.

Bendis, possibly more than other top-level Marvel creators, personifies a public commitment to allowing artists the scope they need to define themselves, the characters they are working on (albeit neatly fitting in with established Marvel aesthetics/conventions), and by extension, the unfolding Marvel 'drama' itself. More than a decade on from the October 2000 first issue of *Ultimate Spider-Man*, Bendis was still working on the title and imbuing the character with fresh notes and changes that attempted to update the wall-crawler. Just as Bendis's interpretation of Spider-Man sat comfortably alongside Sony's, his current run on comic title *Guardians of the Galaxy* (*GOTG*) (Vol. 3; 2013 – present) helped to prepare audiences for the release of MS's first strike into basing a major feature on characters with almost no public profile (which is the subject of Chapter 6). Of course, unlike with the Sony arrangement, Marvel themselves produced James Gunn's *GOTG* film, meaning that the cohesion between the two could be planned to a far greater degree. Opportunities for synergy – particularly relaunches or the renumbering of comic series – would therefore not be passed up, as they were in the early days of Marvel's filmic presence (see Howe, 2013: 405).

Designed to attract new readers by letting creators' imaginations loose in a world lacking the strictures of Earth-616 continuity, 'Ultimate' comics filled the role of testing the ground for new ideas on how characters could fit into contemporary society. New series like *The Ultimates* – Millar's reimagining of Marvel's premier superhero team the Avengers for a more cynical, 'realistic' universe and time – extended inspiration for cinematic ventures that, in several cases, would actually be realized (showing proof, in other words, to decision makers and financial backers that characters had contemporary relevance but also, in the hands of artists like Bryan Hitch, spectacular visual possibilities). Far from the conditions experienced by writers and artists under

Jim Shooter and, indeed, Lee (this, arguably, prompted by paymasters like Cadence Industries), Bendis cites the creative freedom that he has been given under Quesada as a defining feature explaining his allegiance to Marvel. He describes the company as 'forward thinking', and summarizes management's attitude as more concerned with long-term creativity than short-term profit potential: 'We don't care if it sells – why should we do this?' (Bendis, cited in George 2009). Defining his position on this approach, Bendis uses an example from an early issue of *Ultimate Spider-Man*. The writer decided to spend the whole issue's span in Peter Parker's bedroom, as Parker discloses his secret identity to his would-be girlfriend Mary Jane Watson. Bendis's point is that, bold move for an action-oriented character though this is, it still recognizes a valid tradition of soap opera in the character dating back to Lee and Ditko, and rendered just as significantly in the Raimi films. 'I don't have to work there', says Bendis in highlighting the main reasons he gives his loyalty and creativity to the company, 'but I love to work there. And they brought that out in me' (cited in George, 2009). Materially for our discussion, Derek Johnson recognizes the same mentality (that of allowing creators to express themselves) in relation to the MS message: 'With actors and licensees signing deals with Marvel instead of Hollywood studios, executives presented the fan-managerial Marvel brand as a cultural space in which contracted labor could feel affection, affinity, and belonging' (Johnson, 2012: 20).

Not long after Millar had redefined the Avengers under the aegis of the 'Ultimate' project, his creativity was directed towards classic Marvel characters in the established Earth-616 MU. Drawn to complex themes and stories that could set beloved characters among contemporary political events, in 2006–7, Millar, alongside artist Steve McNiven, produced *Civil War*, a miniseries that has been crucial for modern Marvel. Both series have since had elements from their pages realized onscreen in MCU titles.[48]

Wishing to effect coordinated production throughout its cinematic universe, Marvel established the Marvel Creative Committee (MCC), bringing together comic book creators like Bendis and film industry personnel.[49] Johnson states that 'with film and television producers, comic book talent, and marketers all pooling their expertise, this committee sought to impose creative coordination across film productions' (2012: 13).[50] Not only have the themes and storylines originating within the comic books found expression in cinematic form, then; so too, has the collaborative culture infusing the planned mode of production of the comics. Effectively, the MS experiment incorporates an attempt to replicate the conditions of the creative committees that guide the development of the comics' multiverse. The oft-publicized strategy of attracting creative individuals that have built their reputations in acclaimed, independent endeavours already in receipt of some cultural legitimation can be seen in MCU films such as Shane Black's signature *noir* inflections in *IM3* (drawing on Black's reputation built upon the stylish, career-reigniting thriller *Kiss Kiss, Bang Bang* (2005)). The most telling examples of a circuit of value travelling from comics to film and back, surround Joss Whedon, creator of *Buffy the Vampire Slayer* (1997–2003), and *Firefly* (2002–3).

Renowned for his relationship with, and address to, fans, Whedon – a former Marvel writer steeped in the history of the comic book universe (Whedon, 2002), who had previously been tasked, alongside artist John Cassaday, with a reinvention of the X-Men (*Astonishing X-Men* Vol.3, #1–24, 2004–8) – was brought on to direct and cowrite *The Avengers*. The film proved pivotal, capping a run of almost unequivocally successful releases by drawing together strands, both classic and fresh, of the burgeoning MCU. The publicity and fan approval that Whedon's involvement received in the popular film press and across social media confirmed that Marvel's intended message about its policy of trust in authors was hitting home. On the verge of *The Avengers'* release – the biggest gamble to date in proving the efficacy of a shared universe-fans familiar with Whedon's work could see the long-term intent of appointing someone like this to a position bearing greater responsibility than previous writer/directors had carried in the MCU, yet, to Hollywood, Whedon, who had achieved relatively few 'hits' with his more *auteur*-branded work, could still represent a risk. As a responsible creator, he would ensure 'a particular tone for the MCU, a consistency that would emphasize attention, careful thought and intent behind each extension as it was added' (Hadas, 2014: 14). Highlighting how Marvel attempted to guide how this news was received, speaking at the press junket for *The Avengers*, studio figurehead Kevin Feige drew attention to Whedon's respect for character roots, as well as to his varied but linked body of work (Richardson, 2012). This may not have possessed the effortless ebullience of the 1960s editorial style, but fan-pleasing it certainly was. Whedon's involvement represented a marker of confident creativity, instilling faith in the reality of Marvel's upward trajectory. Followers were assured that the present incarnation of the company's media strategy would not be another fly-by-night, inauthentic one, Whedon's appointment offering 'proof that Marvel are not opportunistic media land-grabbers, but inspired architects' (Hadas, 2014: 14). Confirming the findings of Johnson, and as we shall explore to a greater extent in the course of this work, the way that Marvel has more widely orchestrated a narrative surrounding its cinematic endeavours pursues a similar effect.[51]

Taking control

The process will be analysed to a far greater extent in the body of this book, but viewed in the context of organizational identity, Marvel's decision to independently produce films using its own characters needs to be understood as an exercise in *control*. When considering how its characters might proffer clues to any 'worldview' that the modern Marvel might possess, a key point to consider is the influence that an independent status grants to Marvel in terms of managing its most highly exposed characters in blockbuster films and the impact exerted, through this, on its own public identity. Marvel's independence retakes from third party producers the authority for crafting lasting, public interpretations of these characters. It has been pointed out that Marvel, in any case, has more to lose by way of reputation when the quality of the output is low (Stork, 2014: 88); any negative reaction to the Spider-Man films produced by Sony, or the X-Men and Fantastic Four films (FF) films produced by Fox would have a deeper impact on Marvel than it would on the production companies. Further, outside the creative perspective, the lack of control could have a negative impact upon the organization's financial fortunes, as highlighted by Devin Leonard (2014a), who states that Marvel's 'shares rose as movies opened and fell when there was nothing in the theatres. But the company couldn't order Sony to put out the next *Spider-Man* film'.

Marvel has positioned itself to address this potential lack of control, and shield its public identity from such business weaknesses. Control is thus an essential theme that runs through this book. A brand that is distinctly tied to the cultivation of characters, stories, myths and universes, Marvel uses an ingrained public association with expert character-building to prop up its own identity, just as it would craft the identity of Steve Rogers (Captain America) or Tony Stark (Iron Man). Industrial events and histories thus become narrativized, as Derek Johnson articulates in describing MS's brief period of true independent production – following the securing of $525 million in 2005 to invest in the MCU's opening films *Iron Man* and *The Incredible Hulk*, leading up to the Disney acquisition of December 2009:

> While Marvel's narrative strategies were compatible with Hollywood's story-telling traditions, its institutional strategies in pursuit of industrial convergence proved less so, requiring another set of narratives – stories about Marvel itself – to manage the contradiction and give commonsense meaning to Marvel's objectives.

> (2012: 15)

During this time, Johnson explains, Marvel manipulated trade press coverage and used evocative language in its public discourse because it wanted to drive home one crucial idea: that its entry into film production was a form of 'destiny' fulfilled. 'Drawing on narrative tropes central to Marvel's core brand identities' (2012: 22), this formed the implication that the venture 'was inevitably predisposed to success' (21–2). Such 'trade narratives' – as termed by Johnson – became 'primary cultural gateways through which investors, potential partners and consumers alike would have begun to articulate, reproduce, and negotiate meanings about Marvel' (15). Thus, all public acknowledgement of business actions had to support the (ultimately successful) attempt at 'rebranding, self-presentation, and self-reflexive legitimization' (4) that would announce Marvel's arrival as a film producer. Noting the impact that these stories had upon Marvel's identity, Johnson postulates that, as an upstart, inexperienced production entity, Marvel at the time was seeking to disrupt the industrial order; however, judicious use of the trade press dampened any impression of 'rocking the boat' of an industry it planned to work within.

As a discursive manifestation of the control that we identify as a theme in Marvel's public affairs, Johnson is quite correct about the narrative that has been constructed.

It is a message that relies on a specific self-characterization. Marvel has cast itself once again as the 'underdog', reclaiming valuable parts of that original 1960s identity, but retooling them in a way that befits corporate Hollywood traditions and culture. The process of self-promotion accentuates Marvel as an entertainment producer in proud possession of an unsurpassed understanding of fans and creativity. Colourful comic book overtones accompany this, lending a Manichaean aspect to what would otherwise be a straightforwardly dull corporate story: 'Casting Hollywood as the villain and Marvel as the hero ... these trade stories reinforced Marvel's core comics expertise as a rationale for its growing "superpower" in a converged film industry' (Johnson 2012: 22).

Today, MS is part of Disney, of course, but careful public relations keep the message strong and consistent. A recent example of this strategy in process can be seen in the release of *Captain America: The Winter Soldier*. *Bloomberg Businessweek*'s industry-slanted coverage highlighted phrases that identified Marvel/Disney's 'historic brand building' and a post-*Avengers* 'trickle-down effect where every movie that comes out after is benefiting' (Phil Contrino, cited in Livesey, 2014). A comprehensive feature article by Leonard (2014a), timed to coincide with the release of *The Winter Soldier*, failed to disprove any of the major points of Johnson's analysis of Marvel's trade message. It incorporated an interview with Feige, who has been called the 'one man' holding Marvel's 'film fibres' together (Kit, cited in Johnson, 2012: 17). The image even invokes the sense of a complicated, growing universe controlled by a committed, perhaps super-strong individual. Leonard attributes to Feige 'a special understanding of comics, fans, superheroes, and narrative', further noting that 'the fans' in attendance at a Marvel premiere in Los Angeles recognize Feige in public (and chant in support). Confirming Johnson's analysis, such trade press surrounding *The Winter Solider* accomplishes two desired outcomes on behalf of Marvel: making it appear creatively dominant and financially sound (as per Leonard's assertion: 'Marvel has made consistent hits, which is supposedly impossible in a creative business'); and concentrating the most positive aspects of the Marvel story into an authorship figure, Feige, who, in this instance, becomes a sort of Stan Lee for this phase in the history of Marvel. Soon after Leonard's article appeared, *The Winter Soldier* was virtually doubling the worldwide box office of its 2011 predecessor. Marvel, and Feige, did not arrive on the cusp of such success by accident, as we hope our discussion demonstrates. For this introduction's final section, we will retrace the final steps of the transition that led to Marvel's virtually unprecedented gamble on becoming a film industry 'superpower'.

III. Movie hopes and false starts

The commercial pinnacle of summer 2014 probably seemed like a pipedream at the end of the 1970s, yet Marvel continued to make the effort to unlock the potential of its character catalogue in other media. Some early success in animated adaptations had not been followed through in live-action, so Marvel's intent was clear when conducting negotiations with an American television network for the production of the shows that became *The Amazing Spider-Man* (1977–9) and *The Incredible Hulk* (1978–82).

> CBS agreed to finance two-hour pilots for eight [shows based on Marvel characters]. … For the first time in a decade, Marvel would be transmitted into American living rooms. Hopefully, the children in those living rooms would go out and buy some comic books.
>
> (Howe, 2013: 196)

At this point, Howe asserts, Marvel followed a logic that television production – limited in its profitability by the nature of licensing – could be a way of driving important comic sales, rather than representing any ultimate media incarnation for these characters. For a while, the primary strategy for maximizing Marvel's assets cinematically or on television had been to add to such licensed deals. Why did the efforts of Stan Lee, who moved to Los Angeles in 1979 to spearhead Marvel's film and television fortunes, concentrate on this tactic? Among the advantages yielded by licensing, the ability to efficiently circulate characters while subtly circumventing notions of the transference of proprietary rights (meaning characters are *loaned* to, not *owned* by, other interests) was undoubtedly pertinent. As much is disclosed by the text of the *Variety* advertisements taken out by the company in the 1970s, which make clear that licensed characters remain 'Marvel Characters':

> All Marvel Characters have their own identity – their own *personal* story – and the potential for outrageous stardom. … Daredevil is but one of over 100 exciting Marvel Characters ready to star in your next motion picture or television production.
>
> (Unknown, cited in Howe, 2013: 216; emphasis in original)

In fact, at the point when the *Variety* advertisements were canvassing support for the idea that 'Marvel Characters' could hold up in a brand new media spotlight, the value of characters as brand representatives to be harnessed in potent commercial partnerships was outstripping the revenue coming in from a shrinking comic book market (Wright, 2003: 259). The convincing new plan that eventually led to MS would only materialize once Marvel had re-appraised certain assumptions on which its media hopes were built. A more immediate change requiring attention was the emergence of comic stores and the implications of this for the American comic book market; disappearing mass (news-stand) sales prompting a transition to a fan-servicing address (Wright, 2003: 253). Within a decade, there would be bonuses to be had in this changed market, in the form of massive (but transient) sales, with collectability and speculation the new watchwords. But another bout of company soul-searching ensued first.

Far from the romanticized 'Golden Age' of the Second World War era and after, the 1990s attracted lamentation as 'The Dark Age of Comics' (Voger, 2006). The designation is sometimes narrowly applied in connection to the industry-wide financial crisis brought on by the collapse of the speculator market. However, the term more widely addressed the comparatively gritty, introspective and melancholic tone, and brooding anti-heroes (a step beyond even those of the 1970s), which populated the newly frank pages of comic books. Independent publishers had risen to prominence and strong sales bearing such aesthetic recipes as manifestoes, and executing them using expertise gained at the 'Big Two' companies. Among these upstarts, famously, was Image Comics (formed by, among others, ex-Marvel alumni Todd McFarlane (*Spider-Man*) and Jim Lee (*X-Men*)).

With Marvel, somewhat reluctantly, participating in a market-wide tonal shift, the company was partway through an incomplete metamorphosis, its identity seemingly more fluid than ever during the 1990s. By mid-decade its independent standing was in trouble and stock price in free fall (Howe, 2013: 356). The bottom had promptly fallen out of a speculator market that had prompted stellar sales for *Spider-Man* Vol.1, #1 (1990) and *X-Men* Vol.2, #1 (1991).[52] Almost totally committed to the direct market, the major companies arguably underestimated the collective intelligence of the most loyal elements of readership; those who invested in story, and the consistency and integrity of their preferred fictional universe. Revenue streams declined at crippling speed, and Marvel filed for bankruptcy in 1996.

Considering the self-image that Marvel had projected for years – that of a 'House of Ideas' issuing from a Bullpen-grown creative source under mavericks such as Stan Lee or caring fan-surrogates such as Roy Thomas – it may seem surprising that the saviour of the business came not from behind a Marvel desk, but from the world of licensed exploitation of Marvel's IP. Merchandizing company Toy Biz was prescient in realizing that a solvent Marvel was necessary to the maintenance of prosperity in its own licensed operations. Capitalizing upon Fox's syndicated *X-Men* (1992–7) and *Spider-Man* (1994–8) cartoons, Toy Biz was a thriving action figure business, dominant in its field through monopolizing Marvel's incredibly lucrative toy merchandise rights. With its market relevance entirely dependent on the circulation of Marvel characters, the company, under the direction of Avi Arad and Isaac 'Ike' Perlmutter, made the crucial decision to merge directly with the crisis-hit Marvel Entertainment Group in 1998, rescuing it from bankruptcy (Raviv, 2004: 242). Not only did this narrow the interests of Toy Biz to exclusively Marvel-related products (the business renaming itself 'Marvel Toys'), it was a decision that would take Toy Biz entirely out of the manufacturing sector.

Showing little trepidation towards the venerated status of characters within a 'Bullpen' culture (not to mention the issue-by-issue consistency significant for the niche fan audience), and seizing instead upon their value to mass consumers, Arad and Perlmutter began a programme of property licensing with the goal of re-balancing the Marvel ledgers. Arad and Perlmutter were emboldened by their detailed knowledge of how rapidly and to what scale these properties were able to shift products, although Lee had recognized much earlier that Marvel's stable of characters was resilient enough to underwrite huge revenues for commercial partners. Freed into commercial exposure, the much-loved and hugely recognizable characters might just function as ouroboric, self-perpetuating advertisements for themselves. As with the earlier CBS deal, Spider-Man and the Hulk were floated to outside interests in deals crafted to court the eye of potential licensees. In an echo of the keynote found in the 1979 *Variety* advertisements, Toy Biz simply recognized – albeit from a different standpoint and, perhaps, a more intensely commercial motive – that the character-led strategy worked, and that executing this tradition more ruthlessly (more favourably to Marvel) would aid the construction of an entertainment player of serious scale and complexity. Of course, the development of a product that marries popular characters and franchising is not unique to a discussion of Marvel, comic-book characters or even cinema. Franchise entertainment, with cinema occupying a privileged space atop the synergistic pyramid, was well-established by the 1990s. The specific aptness of superhero stories for multi-media adaptation had even been demonstrated in 1989 by Tim Burton's version of DC Comics' *Batman*, to the tune of almost half a billion dollars of worldwide box office takings and countless further millions in merchandizing deals.[53] If this was the new reality, Marvel, having signed off cheap versions of *Captain America* (Albert Pyun, 1990) and others, was very much lagging behind.

The character strategy

As a comic publisher centred – in reality, symbolically, or both – upon a romanticized 'Bullpen' notion (and earlier, in more formal terms, the 'Marvel Method'), Marvel had long understood its own mission as the 'creation and marketing of characters' (Raviv, 2004: 12). Where ambitions exceeded the boundaries of comics and flirted with other entertainment channels, the prevalent view took characters as a one-way referential valve for consumers. This would treat potential multi-media properties as, first and foremost, advertising for their parent publications, rather than a source of revenue in themselves. The consolidation of brand identity was important, but the link between the commercial potency of characters and the health and expansion of the MU itself seemed to go unrecognized. Both Johnson and Howe attribute to Stan Lee a vision of what was needed and a desire to change things, but access to a way of effecting the change eluded Lee, the company, and its various corporate controllers in the 1970s and 1980s. In particular, Johnson describes how Marvel lacked both 'the institutional power to move its property out of the comics market ... [and] the right type of content to forge a strategic partnership with film and television institutions' (2013: 85). The solution was surely in-house production, supported by investment from outside agencies; but Marvel was not in a credible enough shape to persuade anyone of the soundness of this premise, at least to the tune of the serious capital backing that would be needed to compete properly in modern blockbuster cinema.

Meanwhile, Marvel characters continued to receive exposure in the mass media. Arad and Perlmutter took the catalogue, and applied acumen gained when the Reagan incumbency relaxed laws pertaining to television advertisement of products for children. Even prior to the merger, the production of *X-Men: The Animated Series* was no doubt driven by Toy Biz's awareness of the success of *GI: Joe, A Real American Hero* (1983–4).[54] Before Arad and Perlmutter's arrival, Marvel had attempted to bring the X-Men to the lucrative Saturday morning cartoon market once already, only to have its attempts rejected by CBS in 1984 (McNeill, 1984: 22). Even with Toy Biz expertise on board, a joined-up strategy of distributing the characters into the media slots where they could have the most impact was still elusive; old, one-off strategies were hurting Marvel. Previous regimes had signed off on agreements that were short-termist in profit but long in duration; the binding, time-contingent strictures of some of these agreements became famous (Marvel's travails in this area even became the target of satire and parody).[55] Until this situation was resolved, Marvel would not be able to reap the full benefits of its characters, and many windows for improved revenue would continue to be missed; as Leonard (2014a) states, because there were so many variables under such arrangements, 'movie release dates would get postponed, and investors would dump Marvel's stock'. Where properties rested in the hands of third parties, Marvel did not possess the right to exert control over aspects such as a coherently organized and commercially maximized release schedule (with opportunities for synergy across the comic line).

Although Marvel had recently reclaimed some properties, when insolvency was faced in 1996–7, there was little option but for one of the pillars of comics' 'Big Two' to consider shopping yet more assets. Yet, whatever negative consequences were to follow for Marvel, it is important to bear in mind at this juncture that the revenues yielded by such licences were imperative to Marvel's survival, however inherently disadvantageous the loss of characters into various deals might appear.[56] It is only through the financial hardship faced by Marvel and its reaction of expanded licensing that a (non-coordinated) representation of the MU began to appear on cinema screens with the isolated productions of the late 1990s (see Appendix: Timeline). What would, in turn, ignite the spark of hope for cinematic control of its premium properties – what became the MCU – was the remuneration flowing back through royalty payments received from these franchises. The internationally popular X-Men and Blade franchises also stood as a serious 'calling card' to future investors. Thus, the desperately needed recovery strategy which would take Marvel into Hollywood was set in motion, but far more work would have to be put in to sustain both this plan, and the company (Johnson, 2007: 71).

Collaborative but contested

Today, MS is free to deploy any of the characters first rendered into the MU as long as the rights to such characters have not been previously sold to an outside production interest (in which case MS must either negotiate for the use of the property or wait for the rights to expire). There is an awareness even in casual movie fandom that, due to these deals, MS is not free to place on screen any arc, relationship or character of its choosing. This demonstrates the almost unique position MS occupies in illustrating for audiences that a modern transmedia company springing from another form can symbolize both the splintering of classic paradigms of production and, simultaneously, the need to uphold the value of a cinematic presence.

Expounding upon the business model of Disney, in terms of the branding and licensing of properties, Janet Wasko – by way of a 1998 *Economist* article – posits a model which privileges the centrality of specific characters operating within a larger, nebulous universe. Rather than a case of vertical or horizontal integration, the image to which Wasko refers involves 'a wheel, with the brand at the hub and each of the spokes a means of exploiting it' (Anon. cited in Wasko, 2005: 170). This highlights a relationship between the circulation and licensing of characters within multiple markets, as each spoke pertains to a specific arm of production or utilization that represents the influence of a character extending into different media, with the success of the 'spokes' reaffirming and strengthening the centre in a kind of feedback process.

In forming its model, Marvel has found itself not only harnessing the synergistic potential of a process like the one described by Wasko, but also adapting it to accommodate multiple, synchronous productions (the unfolding cinematic Avengers Franchise (AF)). The feedback potential of the wheel/hub/spoke arrangement, being involved as it is with ownership rights and balance sheets, is often managed at an executive level, which makes possible the coordination of brand synergy. Proliferating remakes, re-imaginings, 'ret-cons' (retroactive continuity) and re-mediations all burden the individual spokes of a character wheel, adding tension and serving to muddy the waters of hard-won character identity. The capacity is there to produce confusion and contradiction within a character's collectively accepted persona/brand; to 'taint' or distort the character, essentially. The decisions by MS to re-invent already 'cinematically primed' characters (such as the Hulk, who starred in his own moderately successful cinema release *Hulk* (Ang Lee) for Universal in 2003, and more recently, the resurrection of Daredevil – also subject of an unrelated 2003 film: *Daredevil* (Mark Steven Johnson) – in a 2015 Netflix series) is therefore a calculated risk worthy of study. In salvaging licensed properties deemed franchise failures, MS exposes itself to more brand peril than would ideally be the case, but it has worked to protect itself from this in various ways, as we shall see.

Johnson (2007) leads the way in articulating these kinds of complexities in his work on the character Wolverine. Although not a primary focus of the present book – due to the kinds of rights provisions we have just highlighted – Wolverine, alongside Spider-Man, is the most popular Marvel character operating on film outside the MCU. He is also the most prolific, appearing in all seven of Fox's X-Men films between 2000 and 2014. Johnson's dedicated study provides an insight into the aberrant readings of a popular character, assessing how characters adapt under the effect of re-mediation, and asking in his title: 'Will the real Wolverine please stand up?'[57] As work like this reminds us, full understanding of how MS is able to make its production strategy fit for transmedia exploitation requires reflection upon exactly *what* is being 'transmediated'; hence our dwelling, in this section, on what it was that made MU characters attractive in the first place. Rendering tangible some kind of ultimate/primary meaning of what a character *is* may be difficult, but defining what it is about the source comics that makes MS's transmedia ventures unique is a realistic ambition. Narrowing this down, we continue to return to the shared universe concept.

Elsewhere, Johnson (2013) has elaborated on the relationships formed from franchisement, alongside critical responses to it. Analysing the tensions between separate elements operating within the same brand umbrella, he locates consolidation in a process which he characterizes as 'collaborative but contested' (7). As the study of Wolverine bears out, the maintenance of a stable core and feel to a character, much less keeping it consistent with wider Marvel traditions, is much more challenging as more licensees become involved in its media exploitation. A set of problems elucidated in John Caldwell's book *Production Culture* (2008) is particularly relevant, hence Johnson's employment of a delineation made by Caldwell regarding the 'tensions between the singular, homogenous brand images of media franchises and the heterogeneous production companies working to produce them' (Johnson, 2013: 15). Although making money, MS needed to negotiate a route out of the forced 'heterogeneity' – and jeopardy to its own identity – that resulted from handing its properties over to multiple production entities. Yet, by the turn of the millennium, the financial footing to support in-house production still eluded Marvel, leaving it unable to turn down the financial boons offered by licensing.

As we have seen, Marvel had long – but ineffectively – pursued a rudimentary transmedia agenda. Recognizing the potential held within its connected universe of characters was one thing, but forming 'spokes' to transmit that value was another. In fact, the licensing revenue gains had to be re-conceptualized as strengthening the brand and the recovery process, with a typical assumption – that ceding control of properties made its in-house realization more distant – de-emphasized, and a longer term view of how to win control instigated. Marvel's representatives had suffered from two impediments in negotiating those early television deals. First, hands were tied by corporate management that may have held the same fiscal motives but looked to different methods. Second, the comic book company lacked shrewdness in how it confronted the 'gatekeepers' (Johnson, 2013: 85) of the filmed entertainment world. Arguably, that world needed to change to accommodate Marvel, and change it did.

Transmedia Marvel: 'It's all connected'

When Toy Biz merged with Marvel, Avi Arad took an immediate interest in purifying Marvel's confused filmmaking plans, and increasing the likelihood of steering its own properties into Hollywood. The initial reinvigoration of superhero fictions unfurled in a new, late 1990s media reality of total franchisement, with MS limited during this period, to pre-production. Its poor corporate shape in the mid-1990s hampered Marvel; its media ambitions were defined by licences that, although profit-making, were essentially sacrificed to further the interest of other media producers. Yet, with Arad driving policy, some success attended this first stage, with the first significant licensed release being *Blade* (Stephen Norrington), in 1998. Marvel became far more actively involved in the process of jump-starting productions (commissioning scripts and talking to directors, for instance). MS was not yet a true producer, but Marvel's properties drove the filmic revival of the 'superhero' genre anyway.

Emboldened by experiences with characters such as Blade – perhaps the least renowned character to hit screens, yet an immediate success, proving the strength of the MU as a whole, as well as its capacity to be flexible when it comes to genre[58] – as well as the more obviously bankable X-Men and Spider-Man, Marvel began trialling smaller partnerships (for instance, in the production of DVD animated features in a deal signed with 'mini-major' Lionsgate in 2004). As a result of these developments, what we now understand to be 'Marvel Studios' moved closer into being. The story will be more fully recounted later, but deals made between 2004 and 2008 saw the movie rights to a series of MU characters (of varying public resonance) themselves being used as collateral in raising a substantial ($525 million) line of credit (Johnson, 2012: 11). Over the same period, rights that had rested with other studios were systematically bought back (for instance, those controlling Iron Man and the Hulk). This enabled a series of medium-to-high budget films to be planned; crucially, they were conceived in a coordinated roll-out. With financing and distribution secure, a pre-meditated interlocking quality could be imparted, its target being a replication of the way the MU had worked on the page since the early 1960s. Groupings of intended films became known as 'phases': Phase I, Phase II and so on, a use of term that interestingly implies development, but also holds a connotation of scientific experimentation.

MS had barely achieved its independence when Arad quit in 2006 (McAllister et al., 2006: 111). David Maisel was appointed Chairman, and Kevin Feige was installed as President of Production, casting a new 'face' upon the new enterprise (Hadas, 2014: 11). Shortly, production commenced on *Iron Man*, a film that would open to almost $100 million at the US box office in May 2008,[59] impressing Hollywood and proving to Wall Street backers Merrill Lynch (as well as future investors) that MS was a fast learner. It was quickly gathering the experience – and forming the necessary artistic relationships (Johnson, 2012: 20–1) – to produce hit movies with significant opportunities for true transmedia storytelling.[60]

A transmedia franchise can be construed as a single commercial entity deployed across multiple mediums, with content built by aggregate across disparate formats, which converge together in a fluid unity. Within a coordinated narrative context like that of the MCU, the different appearances strengthen not only brand identity (which could be said of any entertainment producer with a variety of outlets in which to expose and monetize characters), but also the story repository or 'canon'. MS utilizes franchising as part of its wider transmedia exploitation plan; as Hadas (2014: 13–14) points out, the interests controlled by MS/Disney include non-MCU, but still vaguely coordinated material (like the animated shows *Hulk and the Agents of S.M.A.S.H, Avengers Assemble* (both 2013–) and *Ultimate Spider-Man* (2012–), shows which form their own shared universe and exploit images and versions of characters established in the MCU, but are not part of that shared story world; they can deploy a full spectrum of MU characters to join in – such as Spider-Man or Wolverine – since rights pertaining to live-action treatments do not apply).

One of the public relations tactics necessary to a successful launch, as we've seen, had been that of convincing the audience (and the film business) that this strategy – the establishment of a production line extending Marvel comics into varying screens – was so natural as to constitute a 'destiny' (see Johnson, 2012). In the event, the window of genuine independence was short; not much over one year, if counting from the release of the first film. The current state of direct ownership by parent company Marvel Entertainment (itself a wholly owned subsidiary of The Walt Disney Company) permits the – somewhat problematic – 'official' accreditation of MS movies as the movies of the MU. In fact, by displaying a shared corporate parentage with Marvel films from other studios (via the prominent production company logo in movie titles) and stipulating that only certain distinctions (such as cameo appearances from Stan Lee himself) be allowed in the wider Marvel Entertainment cinematic family, what could have been a threat to a unified identity appears to have been negotiated. A system of endorsement has effectively been created, signalling a superiority over non-MCU franchises like X-Men or Ghost Rider (previously held by Sony Columbia, 2007–12), but nevertheless taking into account compliance with the overall health and credibility of the overarching brand.[61] And, as the page-turning imagery in Marvel's iconic logo announces with each film text, a notion of stories, rooted in print origins, remains the symbol of the company's artistic compact with audiences. The logo signifies both a source point for stories/characters, and a hallmark of quality control; noticeably, it is not preceded by any markings relating to Disney (Stewart, 2013).[62]

Behind the shield

In exploring the translation of Marvel's famous character catalogue into moving image, it is important to understand how seizing the transmedia opportunities offered by emergent technologies and varied platforms has served Marvel. With

The Avengers marking the peak of 'Phase I' in summer 2012, and 'Phase II' well underway thereafter, Marvel took further steps to consolidate its assets under unified *control*. The most recent major decisions to be unveiled specifically relate to its newly minted television (network and online subscription) franchises. These are new spokes meant to expand the transmedia story, link characters to further potential revenue opportunities, and thus indicate where the company most desires to next make its mark. Marvel's *Agents of S.H.I.E.L.D.* (ABC-TV, 2013–)[63] (hereafter *AoS*) – itself the most successful extension of a Marvel property onto live-action weekly television since the 1970s shows mentioned earlier – has been followed onto network television by *Agent Carter* (ABC-TV, 2015–), while *Daredevil* (2015–) and *Jessica Jones* (2015-) join the TV fray via the alternative route of streaming service Netflix, with related series' promised to follow. In discussing the concept of fan 'loyals' (a type of consumer behaviour defined by a characteristic obsession with participating in properties in their totality), Henry Jenkins (2008: 74–9) provides a perspective that helps to contextualize Marvel's confidence in these more bespoke methods of releasing television material to fans, as well as the audience tail-off experienced by *AoS* in its maiden season (see Kendrick, 2013). While this instance relates exclusively to television audiences, the specific behaviour recalls patterns in the historic consumer base of Marvel itself, forcing us to reinterpret and temper the notion of a bleed of less committed viewers. Jenkins' designation describes a broad mode of fandom that is undaunted by the prospect of so-called appointment television, and from this we are able to postulate that instead of the *AoS* audience loss representing a kind of decay, it is perhaps more apt to interpret the figures in terms of a process of the show *acquiring* its 'loyals'; that is, the correct, inevitable audience.[64] Perhaps it goes too far to claim this loss of audience as a deliberate tactical move by Marvel, yet it is possible that the eventuality was anticipated and accommodated for (Kendrick, 2013). However, the issue of why Marvel texts do not (yet) adapt to the network television audience in a way comparable to its conquering of the mass theatrical audience remains cloudy.[65] The decision to move the new shows to an on-demand service makes sense, given the benefits in comparison to network television: the theme of *control* returns, with a network tending to orient its commissioning decisions around advertising revenue and audience timeslot profiling. As our later discussion of *AoS* will suggest, the popularity of an on-demand service, coupled with typical modes of consumption of Marvel media output, provides an opportunity for the development of unified content to be continued and indeed, furthered, across simultaneous properties, all held within the Netflix platform.

In fact, *AoS* brings together many of the most pertinent issues relating to MS's execution of transmedia planning, and requires scrutiny on elements beyond its reception. The show – advertised by an appropriate Twitter hashtag, '#ItsAllConnected' – harbours perhaps the best symbol of how cross-media storytelling is incorporated into the overall transmedia storytelling strategy. On one level, the show acts as a vehicle for Agent/Director Phil Coulson (Clark

Gregg), a leader of world security organization S.H.I.E.L.D. who has existed as a bridging 'touchstone' character spanning the whole MCU since *Iron Man*. The non-powered Coulson was given a special role in Whedon's *The Avengers*; the all-too-human rallying point for a disparate and brittle group of heroes. This aspect has carried much of the show's narrative potency, but other functions of the series bear sustained discussion. Appropriate ways of approaching the show concern its 'world-building' capacity, and the examination of its mandate for tie-in media events that reflect and sustain interest in the MCU as a whole. In scope here are features such as the show's extension of the narrative of *Thor: The Dark World*, and its simultaneous participation in events presented within (*CA:TWS*) in an innovative recasting of the relationship between theatrical cinema and network television. *AoS* focuses one further idea which is important to our overall discussion of MS and the universe which it elaborates. This concerns the show's deployment of 'tactical overlap', by which is meant its ability to produce characters and events of significance that can serve the narratives of other properties and vice versa. While the show's first season sought to add flesh to events first glimpsed in MCU movies – such as dealing with the fall of S.H.I.E.L.D. following *CA:TWS* – it wasn't until the second season that it began to reciprocate. This development ran parallel to the steady introduction of more powered, mysterious individuals known as 'Inhumans' (see Chapter 5). Had the evolving Inhumans storyline not seemed to carry such weight, and arisen within the show, *AoS* could have been relegated to a position that Marvel's videogame division finds itself occupying: a vulnerable and problematic space with regard to the accepted, credible and canonical structures of the MCU, potentially invoking the failed status of a franchise 'parasite', feeding off the 'host' body of the film series without contributing original material. This would be an application of the tainted view of media franchising as creatively bankrupt and 'mechanistically' self-perpetuating beyond any innate creative logic (Johnson, 2013: 2). Thus, some recent expansionist moves introduce important reservations to deeming the overall roll-out of the MS business plan an outright success (as discussed in Chapter 8).

No doubt, things were a little simpler when Lee, and the other agents charged with negotiating on behalf of Marvel, sought to make inroads into television production back at the time of the CBS deals. The hope that Howe articulates ('the children in those living rooms would go out and buy some comics') would appear less relevant as each decade passed, and the comic market turned in on itself. A 'joined-up' media strategy required far greater structural change, and tethering to a different vision, than it seemed in the late 1970s, not to mention when initial animation deals were signed in the 1960s, or when Lee and Kirby put *Fantastic Four* #1 together in 1961. But when Lee studied what the company's reputation and value actually rested on, the correct conclusion was nevertheless drawn, and the way forward started to take shape. The huge value of the character catalogue needed to be given due recognition as the place where consumer response coalesced, and, therefore, the place where the formula to success lay. To some extent, it even seemed necessary to divorce comic sales from the primary business equation. Nobody ever claimed that Marvel's origin story was simple, or one-dimensional.

The manner in which Captain America, Iron Man, Thor, Hulk and all their comrades (rights allowing) have been subsequently distributed and exploited is the story of how the MCU was built. Although now commanded by Disney, suggesting that the operational creative chain may have lengthened or become more complicated (Lussier, 2014), control – within the parameters mapped out by such as Feige and attendant MCC – appears to remain with MS. Even before Disney, it consciously reduced its involvement in the process of licensing character rights to experienced film producers, despite access to decades' worth of contacts and the tactic's proven status as a source of cash flow. Through this decision, Marvel sought to regain control over its characters, over people's perception of the same, and, by extension, ultimate control over its own public 'face' and identity. There have been losses in reputation; the battle scars of corporate drama experienced by Marvel as a business over five decades may have been accepted and absorbed, but they no doubt took a toll on the pure image of a freewheeling 'House of Ideas' at various times. There are many dimensions, reboots and revisions in the distinctly Marvel narrative of organization, management, and story-making. Many of these challenges may have originated in the life cycle of a small, overlooked comic book division of a magazine publishing firm, but their impact is felt years later on the road to Marvel Studios.

IV. Eight distinct spotlights

Having outlined key developments in Marvel's history, and signalled our approach to understanding them, the chapters that follow will be more specialized, allowing us to uncover much more depth. There are many instances where they may thematically overlap; wherever this is the case, care has been taken to signpost and guide to a related discussion elsewhere in the book, in such a way that will not disrupt the flow of the particular chapter, but will quickly give the reader the option to access the information.

The first two chapters are particularly industrially focused, with Chapter 1 – **'Films Lead Policy': Marvel's Industrial (R)evolution and the Birth of a Studio** – pondering the steps of Marvel's transition from a troubled publishing company into a successful player in a broad entertainment arena. Existing models of Hollywood production cultures will aid in evaluating Marvel's proposed period of independence, its position within The Walt Disney Company, and its general position and status within global film entertainment. This is followed by Chapter 2 – **An Organization of Storytellers: The Marvel Story, According to Marvel** – which proposes that having a stable and consistent organizational identity is key to success in the creative industries. It will identify the core of Marvel's identity as balancing sustainable business logic with the creativity of storytellers. The adherence to these core principles will be identified as key to its successful 'origin story' and a resurgence – following a tumultuous period of bankruptcy as it strayed from this identity – that has been self-reflexively narrativized on an industrial level thanks to its own expertise as a storytelling organization.

The next three chapters favour a more thematic approach and engage with key filmic texts. In Chapter 3 – **'Doth Mother Know You Weareth Her Drapes?': The Genre Tactics of Marvel Studios** – we discuss the problems with reckoning 'superhero film' as a genre of its own. MCU films sit within a genre designation ('action-adventure') that is known for a fluid approach to iconography, seeing it as prone to merge with the likes of sci-fi, fantasy, and others. This chapter examines MS's forthright approach to such territorial issues, juggling the maintenance of fidelity to genre norms while also extending the definition of the superhero field. Chapter 4 – **Captains America** – takes as its focus a single character, asserting that Captain America is the heart and epicentre of the MCU. By analysing points throughout the universe, including his solo features, his centrality within the Avengers films and his impact upon many other texts in the MCU, Cap's continuing, fluid relevance through different eras, incarnations and surrogates shall be evaluated. In contrast to the single character focus, Chapter 5 – **Teams/Screens** – zooms out, emphasizing that Marvel's modern dynasty of powered heroes was founded on the concept of the 'team book', and therefore the populating of narratives with many heroes (not always facilitating a smooth harmony) is a Marvel specialty. Thus, the chapter asks how this superhero team heritage – from Coulson's S.H.I.E.L.D. squad to the Guardians of the Galaxy – has informed the wider MCU.

Chapters 6 and 7 refocus on industrial matters, albeit with slightly different agendas, bringing the significance of such industrial developments out through sustained textual analysis. Chapter 6 – **Star-Lord, Who?:** *Guardians of the Galaxy* – **Raiding the 'B-List' for New Legends** – postulates that having scored major hits with some of its most recognizable, so-called A-list characters, MS faces the risk of market saturation. This chapter highlights James Gunn's film as spearheading a response to such a risk, as Marvel draws deeply on its rich catalogue to show that its character base goes much further than the AF. The exploitation of these within subtly expanded genre environments will be foregrounded. Chapter 7 – **'A Little Old-Fashioned...': Marvel Studios and Pixar** – then situates MS within its contemporary landscape, asserting that it begs comparison to another organization that trades on similar values. Marvel's Disney stablemate, Pixar Animation Studios, situates itself as innovative, at the cutting edge of technology and character creation, yet at the same time, recuperable in terms of entrenched Hollywood production traditions. This chapter ponders the similarities between the two, studies their reception, and analyses what the public images of these custom studios contribute to their corporate parent (asking whether the influence regarding Disney runs in only one direction).

Chapter 8 – **Tie-ins, Tie-ups and Let-downs: Marvel's Transmedia Empire** – has an apt catch-all theme as it assesses MS's connected feature films, 'One-Shot' short films, videogames, in-continuity tie-in comics, network television shows and on-demand subscription television, as an instance of transmedia storytelling, and compares the use of such a portfolio to the norms of media franchise licensing. We then finally tie these chapters together in the **Conclusion**, tracking the pervasive themes that arise throughout, taking stock of the Marvel Studios Phenomenon, as it appears today, and asking what might lie ahead in the studio's future.

CHAPTER 1

'FILMS LEAD POLICY': MARVEL'S INDUSTRIAL (R)EVOLUTION AND THE BIRTH OF A STUDIO

Introduction

In June 2015, sweeping changes were coming to the comics of the MU, designed to hit over the summer. To prepare fans, Marvel released a free preview detailing several of the 'All-New, All-Different' titles that would establish the characters' new status quo. EIC Axel Alonso welcomed readers to this new phase with a message:

> What was your first encounter with the Marvel Universe? Did you pull a comic book off a spinner rack at the five and dime like I did, or did you float out of a movie theater, your mind blown by what you saw on the Silver Screen [?] … If you liked that feeling, you're going to love what's in store for you in All-New, All-Different Marvel.
>
> (Alonso, 2015a: 4)

Statements from the management of MS intimate that the masterplan controlling all of Marvel's joined-up entertainment activity radiates from its filmic output (according to former executive Justin Lambros, speaking about the relationship between the videogames outlying Marvel's convergence circle, and the film releases at its heart, associated products were meant to 'take the lead from the films', and even material sourced in comics would be 'filtered' through this matrix – Lambros, cited in Johnson, 2013: 97–8). If the direction of the MCU is creatively led by films, Alonso's statement seemed to do more than offer helpful contextualization; it seemed to admit something new. This was the fact that from this point, new Marvel comics would similarly take a lead from the needs of, and the character iterations appearing in, the MCU. Implicitly accepted in the statement was the idea that quarters of comic-reading fandom – the spinner rack-lurkers who may see themselves as having stood by Marvel Comics through long, frequently lean times – might not be happy, but Alonso attempted to remind them of the bond they shared with recent converts (What difference where a 'true believer' discovers their interest?).

This indivisibility of publishing and filmic aims would now, it seemed, dictate events within the pages of comics that, prior to this 'subordination' (Johnson, 2013: 98), had seemed to represent the purest level of Marvel characters' authenticity and existence. After all, Alonso had presided over a year in comics where Phil Coulson, an MCU invention, had materialized leading a S.H.I.E.L.D. team and linking with the already resident Quake/Daisy Johnson/Skye (familiar to television viewers from *Marvel's Agents of S.H.I.E.L.D.* – see Chapters 5 and 8); a half-century before (calibrated to the passing of time in mainstream Marvel continuity), Agent Peggy Carter, another TV star, had been shown to have adventured alongside the father of Tony Stark/Iron Man in the 1950s.[1] Characters were converging and completing a 'feedback loop' – from comics to films, back to comics. The versions played by Hayley Atwell (Carter) and Chloe Bennet (Daisy/Skye), with which millions of cinema and TV viewers were familiar, were the new yardstick for how those characters should appear in the MU. The implication was that things happening in Marvel comics should not *contradict* what is going on in the MCU, and the shape that the new status quo was taking would precisely accommodate this.

Around eight months before Alonso's introduction to 'All-New' Marvel Comics, Kevin Feige announced the 'Phase Three' MCU titles at a pumped-up press event in a Hollywood theatre. This event laid out two decades' worth of connected production: the MS slate stretching on towards 2028, comprising a total run of twenty-one features. The day confirmed the completion of a remarkable turnaround of Marvel, the business.[2] A troubled comic publishing company had not only 'planted [its] flags', as Feige put it, into the new billion-dollar territory of filmed entertainment – it had shown, via the currency of success, that it belonged there. It is the right time to reconsider the meaning of certain steps of this transition in detail. As this work proceeds, the motives and mechanics of Marvel's history of attempts to become a film and television industry player, and the recipe for its recent success and stability, will be given their due. In the present chapter, we view the pattern as a whole. Our assessment will be framed via a few key questions:

- *What is a studio? How does one operate? Can periods in the history of American cinema be differentiated by distinct ways of operating?*
- *Can the models of past Hollywood production cultures put forward by Film Studies tell us anything about Marvel's status and position in global film entertainment today?*
- *When it acquired its capital and struck out into production, was Marvel Studios 'independent'? What do we mean by saying that it was?*
- *What is the place held by Marvel Studios and its plans within the Disney empire?*

Before we do this, it would help to highlight the roles and identities of key personnel that currently give, or in the past have given MS its shape and structure. We will discuss the concept of 'studio authorship' later on, but clearly, individuals and management structures above and around creative personnel, casts and crews, constitute a large part of the studio's business, and help to foster its values and identity.

MS grew out of Marvel Films in 1996, but owes its current status and shape to significant changes in the mid-2000s. Prior to this, headed by Avi Arad, the company was a pre-production hub, exposing Marvel characters through licensing deals with studios such as Fox, Sony and Lionsgate. One such deal brought Feige into the fold (working with Arad as executive producer on Fox's *X-Men*); he officially took the position of Arad's second-in-command in 2000 (Anon., 2009a). As will be detailed in Chapter 2, both Feige and Arad took a creative producing approach, but the appointment – that of David Maisel – that changed the MS trajectory was, tellingly, more commercial in nature (closer to the heart of Arad's business partner – and Marvel purse-string holder – Ike Perlmutter, who has presided over the organization since it emerged from bankruptcy). Maisel joined as MS President and Chief Operating Officer in 2004 (Anon., 2004a) and is credited with pushing the organization into the arena of (then) independent production for which it is now recognized (Maisel it was, who secured the $525 million required to sponsor this production). As a result, in 2005, Maisel was promoted to MS Vice Chairman, and Executive Vice President – Corporate Development in the wider Marvel Entertainment. Installed in this role, with film production on a continuous footing, he is credited with brokering the 2009 deal between Marvel and Disney, following which he left the company (Anon., 2009b). Amid Maisel's rise within the company, Arad departed in 2006, reportedly over creative differences between the two (Leonard, 2007), an account later disputed by Arad (Busch, 2014).

Since Maisel's exit, still under the oversight of the (by reputation) austere Perlmutter, studio business revolves around three individuals, each with some creative urgency and identity: President of Production, Kevin Feige; Co-President (since 2009), Louis D'Esposito, who was formerly President of Physical Effects; and Executive VP of Visual Effects and Post-Production, Victoria Alonso (DeMott, 2009). The three executives, around whom a core team is often maintained from production to production (Masters, 2014), imbue the governance of MS with a front that stresses a creative interest and leadership kept in balance with executive responsibility (see Chapter 2). Alonso, for instance, expounds a collaboratively creative approach encapsulated in the 'Marvel Process' – the subject of a keynote she delivered at 2014's Visual Effects Society Production Summit (Giardina, 2014) – but maintains the fiscal discipline instilled in the company by Perlmutter by ensuring that production is undertaken efficiently (Cohen, 2015). Placing a constant and stable team, with a shared background in various elements of creative producing,[3] at the heart of how productions are assembled on the studio side mirrors, but also enables, the more directly influential combinations of directors, writers and crew (although here we should take care to not always take the filmmakers' and studio's word at face value, as is explored later). Significant to the expansion of Marvel's game-changing MCU, Marvel Television was established in 2010, following the Disney sale, after which its operation was moved to the Disney-owned ABC studios (Andreeva, 2012). Here, Jeph Loeb takes a Feige-like position in overseeing television content, which increasingly features in the world-building transmedia enterprise of the MCU (see Chapter 8). The direction of both divisions, still under the auspices of Marvel Entertainment and the control of Perlmutter, is monitored by the MCC.[4] Up to late 2015, the MCC's remit appeared to have straddled both film and television operations, but Tilly (2015) as well as Masters and Belloni (2015) provide accounts that suggest more fluidity to this situation.

What do we talk about when we talk about Marvel Studios?

The period when the 'Studio System' – a specific organizational way of structuring business that drew together the largest, most successful and recognizable entities of Hollywood cinema – held sway varies according to the observer.[5] Most accounts will extend as early as the late 1920s and as late as 1960. The Studio System is a device for describing how economic arrangements were laid out; the *product* that resulted, and its particular aesthetics, is better described with reference to notions of 'classical cinema'. Taken together, they capture the idea of a factory-like system geared up to make a standardized, effective product to the pleasure of audiences. Aspects including script, *mise-en-scène* (the meaningful contents of the film frame), casting and so on had principles of formula applied to them (the genre system; the star system) so that what worked could be repeated. The parts of the company selling the film knew how to sell: stars and genre (and even, more rarely, the director or producer) would be used so that audiences could relate new films to previous successes, often coalescing around a notion that identified the releasing studio with preferred genres or the striving for a particular atmosphere (glamour, realism, classiness, etc.). Control over the most crucial parts of the process – producing the film, distributing into theatres, and making sure the end result had the best chance to sell tickets – was kept within the company in the case of the largest studios like Paramount, Fox and Warner Bros., which owned theatre chains; the coordination of these three stages was known as 'vertical integration'. The model was one of mass production, informed by principles of 'Fordism', and it addressed audiences as an 'undifferentiated mass market' which was 'served … [with] a limited array of standardized mass-produced commodities' (Smith, 1998: 6).[6]

Film Studies looks beyond the pure economic description to approach the 'Studio System' era in terms of a particular relation between system and creativity (the classical cinema). The era's values and how the studios functioned is delineated in fascinating detail in studies such as those of Bordwell, Staiger and Thompson (1991), and Schatz (1998), and every subsequent study of Hollywood – even ones taking up the story decades after the apparent end of this phase – build on such works. What does Film Studies identify as the typical features of a company that extends, in relevance, from the classical into the contemporary ('post-classical') era?[7] Looking a little more deeply, how has the notion of the studio been broken down?

We might take the case of Disney, Marvel's current corporate parent, as elucidated by Janet Wasko (2001). Over a brief few pages, Wasko underscores various points of importance in the process by which Disney eventually became the most emulatable of all those media brands still retaining a core interest in theatrical film (Grainge, 2008: 49). Wasko follows the studio from its unlikely start in 1923, beginning as a privately owned production outfit releasing through a de facto 'Big Five' studio in RKO[8] (until RKO's financial instability in the early 1950s persuaded Disney to form its own subsidiary for distribution), and into the modern era of conglomeration. Wasko notes the features and policies that made it so fit for this era, among which are its capacity to ride waves of 'technological change'; its adaptation to the potential of merchandising at home and outside the US; and, its commitment to 'synergistic ... global expansion', including the hugely important ownership of a television network (2001: 17). Alongside such features of business strategy designed to return profit to investors in the publicly traded (since 1957) company, Wasko isolates aspects of what we might crudely call 'content': IP; the 'proliferation of Disney images and characters', some of which were eventually 'modernized' as the company adapted to new times (2001: 17–8).[9] Wasko's profile sets out the deployment of this IP within the various strategies planned and driven by individuals whose management influence centred on successfully building the company first of all into a rival for its former distribution partners Columbia, UA and RKO (under Walt and Roy Disney), and later – under CEO Michael Eisner – rebuilding it in the corporate image of connected entertainment behemoth that would fix it as the envy of 1990s Hollywood; and more widely, allow it to epitomize the dream of situating that IP production, protection and exploitation far beyond theatrical film within international 'leisure markets, ... television, tourism, theme parks and consumer merchandise' (Grainge, 2008: 44).

Elsewhere, Wasko categorizes this overview as within the remit of the political economy tradition, which she points out has been fruitfully applied in communications research since the late 1950s (2001: 28–9). The study of ownership and control is the crucial element informing the approach; although not obviously textual in the way of other preoccupations of media research, this focus keeps together political and economic dimensions, thereby rendering a type of analysis that can serve as the ground for ideological analysis. However, Grainge raises a key limitation of political economy approaches to those global media brands that trade in populist image production, this being the 'generalizing impulse' that assumes 'impoverishment' of cultural life as an automatic by-product of the imposition of brand marketing (2008: 7). This book does not embrace political economic methods to an extent which could concern Grainge, but it is apt at times to point out that the dominant influence of brand-aware strategies in the Disney-owned Marvel of the last seven years may be an intensified (more successful) version of pressures that the smaller, more 'innocent' Marvel Comics of the fan-favourite 1970s period had already experienced.[10] Where a genuine connection between fans' interests and emotions seems to be met inside MS, it is right to acknowledge it (and as Alonso's statement above shows, the company is willing to base its own marketing on the premise that this does occur). This is hardly to say that every step the studio takes is calibrated to fans' desires, or even avoids fans' displeasure (even if we could arrive at a single definition of the 'fan') – if it were, the readers who first experienced Marvel at 'the five and dime' would need no reassurance.[11]

Modern Film Studies acknowledged that, with the waning of the once-dominant classical studio model, film company structures expanded to take in a differently constituted type of business, reflective of major changes both in the structure of capitalism, and of how production and revenue were interlinked in a more modern cinematic era. We will find that there is some ambivalence in the views of how major such changes really were; but the Hollywood studio mode of production certainly altered to adapt to, and ride out, new trends in genre, exhibition, home entertainment, international sales and technical capabilities. Across these aspects, a new dialogue was arguably initiated between 'independent' and established interests; new ways of working were found; the blueprint of classicism was revised. For some critics, the old studio-brands craved the structures of old (and beyond economics, there are other levels on which mainstream style might wish not just to understand how 'independents' could succeed, but to neutralize some of their spikier edges). Finding this impossible, in compensation, they took an interest in their own histories, and even started to represent these in screen 'metanarratives', carving allegorical studio stories into their fictions (Connor, 2015: 13 and *passim*).[12] Marvel – a publisher that used to regularly drop 'Easter Eggs' featuring its EIC, artists and production staff (the whole 'Bullpen' on certain occasions) into the comic diegesis – would surely fit in.[13] In other words, independent companies (Marvel itself was one, of a kind, albeit unusually well-funded, in the pre-2009 era), and the concept of independence itself, increasingly demanded attention.

'All-New, All-Different'?

As Derek Johnson (2012: 1) rightly points out, a unique factor in MS's rise is that from the beginning it has relied on expertise from a different media industry, even staking its public name on this distinction (defining its mission as producing narratives and characters in ways which maintain fidelity to creative principles set in the 1960s). The amalgam of business knowledge which saved Marvel as a vibrant publishing concern (via the business acumen brought in via Toy Biz executives Avi Arad and Ike Perlmutter) seems to reverberate here. The concept of *convergence* is currently the fashion for understanding production modes. If convergence must be understood as the circulation of content via a combination of 'old' and 'new' paradigms,[14] MS as a transmedia producer surely qualifies for analysis in this way. Its appeal and address is in fact more layered than most, since it often explains its film production with reference to storytelling values enshrined in comics five decades ago. One way this can be seen is Marvel obliterating (through a corporate/financial 'reboot' – discussed in Chapter 2) its previous history of media adaptation failures.[15] What re-emerged in 2006–9 as a standalone blockbuster producer named 'Marvel Studios' was turned towards a new era. This was an era which, despite later branching into network television, 'on-demand' subscription television, videogames and tie-in comics – all consciously masterminded via a shared universe approach – was announced in April 2008, tellingly, with that most classic of forms: the theatrical feature film (*Iron Man*).

To an extent, the twist on convergence represented by MS's application of its serial stories to convergent media practice is identified by William Proctor's observation that 'a film series as connective tissue with other mediums linking in from the outside is a rather new approach' (Proctor, 2014). In another sense, though, what MS practices is not that new: its agenda underscores 'the continued centrality of film in converged media economies' (Johnson, 2012: 2), actually preserving theatrical cinema in its familiar privileged place, where it exudes a symbolic power that other stages in media transmission cannot match (Connor, 2012: 523).[16] This can be plainly observed in the subservience of television episodes to theatrical films when it comes to releasing narrative material (see Chapters 5 and 8).

In all this, Johnson detects a paradox: 'For all its success in reframing blockbuster film as a market for comic book properties, MS remained a contradiction – a reminder of the continued significance of cinema even as convergence meant redefining the film industry around external content, companies, and creators' (2012: 2). On this logic, one implication we might draw holds comics up as the pure form of Marvel's IP, but the theatrical movie is affirmed as that which can best advertise them to new consumers. After this, their diffusion into progressively less prestigious media forms like continuing television (or, indeed, back into comics)[17] is more efficiently achieved (with a risk that older consumers and comics-only brand loyalists must be persuaded to buy in, as per Alonso's statement). So, one major challenge for MS has been the management and reconciliation of the apparent newness of its exciting cinematic project with the solid history and prefigured 'destiny' (Johnson, 2012) often professed as inhering within the history of Marvel, comics publisher. The history runs deep, or needs to appear so – just as Nick Fury's 'Avengers Initiative' appeared radical to Tony Stark (and extra-diegetically, to audiences) in the closing moments of *Iron Man*, but later is revealed to be the newest incarnation of a post-Second World War search for world security that has taken many forms.

It is important to attend to how Marvel has plotted and realized a transmedia storytelling strategy that maximizes industrial systems geared to convergence, while (initially) shaping an image of itself as the most potently, independently creative new/old 'kid on the block' of popular Hollywood production. In this vein, its post-2009/Disney purchase story asks to be understood as consolidating an image of a radical yet proven (and thus, fiscally responsible) content producer; and, further, one that can strategically harmonize with the image and aims of its parent, The Walt Disney Company (in terms of 'old/new' media values, a Hollywood stalwart).

The December 2009 transaction, folding Marvel into Disney, saw an exchange of reassurances from one 'side' to the other, so that the safety of the move could be transmitted to shareholders and public. Along with those of Pixar (see Chapter 7), Marvel properties were represented as 'the centerpiece of [Disney's] strategy of integrating intellectual property throughout … business units'. Disney CEO Robert Iger spoke of charming Marvel's then-owner Perlmutter with the promise of being a good 'steward' to his brand (Miller, 2015). Along the way, the concept of convergence will help us in elucidating this narrative. But it is also of benefit to set out some earlier ways of understanding large-scale film production, indicating that MS's industrial presence can actually be read in terms of historical modes and patterns, despite the press concentration on innovation. In fact, a blend of 'old' and 'new' obtains: perhaps, the Captain America-style 'super-serum' of convergence grafted onto the durable host of Hollywood studio planning and identity. Marvel itself accommodates a discourse foregrounding notions of responsible legacy-guarding and adherence to consumer-pleasing, historically minded creative formulae, at the same time as shaking up a staid Hollywood via reimagined modes of production (Johnson, 2012: 2). In investigating this, we will, of course, in time arrive at the texts and the thematic, generic and stylistic features exhibited by them, which rearrange Hollywood's popular genre codes; testifying, as Stork puts it, to how 'Marvel essentially set out to rewrite film history to recast the superhero genre's contemporary status' (2014: 90).

Studio stories

At one time, creative control was defined in a way that was highly mediated by the mass production model outlined earlier. The need to keep distribution 'pipelines' fed dictated large parts of Hollywood's production system, which was managed in a way that tightly proscribed (or at least, de-emphasized) individual creativity or 'art'. At its smoothest, this supported the system and its products towards maintaining consistency and stability. However, in time, and with the changing status of cinema within the arts landscape as a whole, this tight regulation encouraged the romantic notion of the outsider-*auteur* to flourish (the idea of promoting directorial control had always been tolerated by Hollywood in terms of some of its most reliable moneymakers and winners of prestige, but it was one thing to pump up reputations and another to allow individuals to alter the system). The earliest American popularization of auteurist notions in relation to large-scale film production, by Andrew Sarris, defined individual expression in an inverted relation with the idea of the producer. This role became negatively identified with studio (management, financial) interests (1968: 31). At many points in this book we shall have cause to view Marvel's Kevin Feige as epitomizing a contemporary remodelling of bits of both roles – but, tellingly, for how all of the industry, the public and criticism continue to understand the flow of creative credit as well as the flow of money; Feige is a producer rather than a director.[18]

Hollywood's first move into blockbuster production – fixed within general film history as the 1950s, when practices set up with the transition to sound underwent their first serious modification for changed times – was a 'rational adaptation' by risk-averse companies (Garvin, cited in Buckland, 2003: 88). Changing conditions of that decade saw audiences drain away, and production slow down as Hollywood dealt with the effects of the Paramount ruling[19] rippling through its system; a '"make 'em big"' (and fewer) philosophy ensued. 'With supply reduced, the companies ... knew demand from exhibitors increased' (Casper, 2007: 43–4). Today, studios are mostly distributors, letting others produce; a post-Fordist, postindustrial sector resorts to different methods to manage film production. In the days of the 'backlot', supervision was central and immediate (albeit with executives mostly involved in finance/sales separated from 'front office' production work by a bi-coastal arrangement); today, films may be commissioned from any part of the world where conglomerate-owned American studios have spread themselves and, equally, production may be carried out anywhere (Thompson, 2007: 330).[20]

Hollywood companies have always sustained themselves by routinized genre production at a medium level of investment, but in the modern era, films take more effort to put together and thus, bets on profits are no longer spread across a wide range of films. Despite their usual high cost, the value of the blockbuster film/franchise was amplified by the changes we have described. Their production, fairly obviously, was much less predictable and controllable than at the height of the studio system; but the rewards were large (Miskell, 2014: 3). Happily for the studios (and shareholders), risks on blockbuster production could be defrayed with the splitting of distribution rights across territories, a method that can be complex but is capable of raising a huge proportion of the funds needed to support a high budget project (Grainge, 2008: 135).[21] This is not to say that some of the sums involved do not represent a significant risk, nor that turning to formula and striving to repeat or re-implement successful aesthetic strategies guarantees an improved result.[22]

In this landscape, critics have mused on whether the identity of the single film, or, more pertinently, the franchise carries more value than does that of the studio. Kristin Thompson argues that 'audiences do not attend a film because it was made by Paramount or Warner Bros'; these days, 'the franchise is often the star' (2007: 5, 6). A rare, exceptional case may be Pixar (see Chapter 7), a producer whose image quickly coalesced into a meaningful brand which transcended individual films and genres (within the production area – less hermetic today than in the early days of *Toy Story* – of CGI animation).[23] Again slightly out of step with Thompson's broad diagnosis of current practice, Marvel's brand ambition seems to have been set on establishing a studio style and unified serial approach to releases from the beginning: note the strict use of title graphics to delineate a 'Marvel Studios' release from the now devalued, plain 'Marvel' appearing on licensed productions like Fox's *X-Men* films.[24] Once simply there to denote proprietorship, studio logos and idents have increasingly grown connotative; a number of critics have worked on how meanings transfer from the logo shots that begin texts into the narrative proper (Grainge, 2008: 69–87; Connor, 2015: 19–30).[25] The animated logo sequence announcing a MS release famously contains story – precisely, a representation of a comic story being consumed and presumably enjoyed – within it. The studio identity makes an attempt to re-envelop the film text, despite critical arguments to the contrary. It is as if there is no point in seeking a cohesive 'studio-brand' without accepting one important precept: that contemporary Hollywood is a space in which the business deal that supported the film's making inseparably builds a 'path' that leads into the very film narrative (Connor, 2015: 1; Christensen, 2012: 321). This suggests that attention needs to be paid to the way in which studios form and reform themselves, and how that story is told, and retold.

The value of creative

As if in response to the assumption captured in Thompson's comment (that the identity of a single film/franchise is more powerful than that of its hosting studio), the nascent studio-brand of MS would stake everything upon the 'shared universe' concept that has become abbreviated as 'MCU'. The MCU is deployed to engage audiences in a rolling programme of linked works, while repeatedly citing the value of its earlier blueprint in comics, the MU. As Stork attests, the release of *The Avengers* was a crucial symbolic stage of this project; its relevance to the 'creation myth' of MS's mode of storytelling – what Stork describes as the film's status as 'a battle cry ... [and] public reference point for [Marvel Studios'] emerging business model' (2014: 78) – shall be addressed in the next chapter, and in Chapter 5.

The shared universe approach is often identified as the source of MS's distinction within the Hollywood environment (Hadas, 2014: 7; Ayodeji, 2013). Yet, the more the overall picture is studied, it becomes clear that in other respects, MS owes its success to bold decisions about embracing more traditional realities. Johnson's argument (2012) is that narratives about Marvel are used to justify its uniqueness and to underline the validity of its mission to film its own characters, but in a way that limits undue anxiety and alienation in its new studio neighbours and partners. Yvonne Tasker notes how the superhero genre in general comfortably fits the commercial production logics developed by Hollywood for spectacular action since the 1970s, which, elsewhere in the same work, she affirms are themselves a development of those older American cinematic forms privileging action (Tasker, 2015: 181 and *passim*). Chief convergence scholar Henry Jenkins maintains that even 'the dominant classical system' can accept 'alien aesthetic norms' as long as a sufficient period of accommodation has been observed (1995: 114). We would argue that, for all MS's need to appeal to Hollywood stalwarts, its 'norms' are not that alien or new (although its ways of *exploiting* those norms through new channels deserves to be called innovative) and so, this section asks: Which older production methods, norms and rationales has MS selectively incorporated? As a Hollywood studio – involved in production as much as any stage – what is its lineage? And where does creativity sit within this?

*****

As the period after the Studio System got underway, in various ways documented by Crofts (1998), Cook (1998) and many others throughout the literature surrounding post-1970s Hollywood, the importance of creative control registered once more in industrial discourse. After the mergers and buyouts of studios like MGM and Warner Bros. in the late 1960s, the business progressively honed public relations operations through the next few decades. Ideas around creativity were re-embraced, if selectively. This was also, however, the era when new 'model[s] of [studio] authority' (Christensen, 2012: 324) grew to match the modes of creativity that accompanied artistic high points such as the 'New Hollywood' or 'Renaissance' period (late 1960s–mid-1970s) and the post-*Sex, Lies and Videotape*/Miramax era, where independent successes encouraged the major studios to investigate quasi-independent ways of doing things (see Wyatt, 1998).[26] Both critically acclaimed periods provoked responses from studios, which sought to accommodate personal filmmaking approaches that would have been easier to quash or regulate in studio system days.

The rise of an independent/'artistic' sector of cinema, incorporating the strengthened personal point of view that helped to revive 1970s commercial filmmaking, thus installed certain filmmaking styles and practices as central. Clearly, the definition of the filmic author shifts just as does that of the studio[27]; but filmmakers who could reintegrate the stages of production and distribution via compelling franchisable products continue to prove magnetic to studios (Flanagan, 2004a, *passim*). Steven Spielberg represents one strain of this type, MS's Joss Whedon a later form (given Marvel's expansion, it is interesting to note how many of this type brought significant experience from television). Spielberg's career path moved in the direction of increased control (Grainge, 2008: 47) – little wonder, considering the easily explicable way in which facets of authorship and 'the business' combine in him. Spielberg's name and power was lent to the 'creation' of a new studio in Dream Works in the late 1990s, while New Zealander Peter Jackson, coming from a culturally external position to Hollywood but exhibiting thorough familiarity with its genre 'language', owns parts of at least six connected companies (from studio spaces to postproduction facilities to digital and practical workshops), into which flowed the $330 million budget[28] provided by New Line Cinema and its international partners on the archetypal early twenty-first-century franchise, *The Lord of the Rings* (Thompson, 2007: 291). The fact that New Line, a former independent company with a 'renegade' industry reputation (Grainge, 2008: 135), was able to launch the ambitious, expensive and rather studio-like *Rings* saga staked out the kind of territory MS had in mind (Johnson, 2012: 3), even when the fact that New Line was operating within the aegis of Time Warner, albeit with autonomy, was accounted for. *Lord of the Rings* was a project on which even Disney, through its subsidiary Miramax, had once passed. Tellingly, and reflective of broad changes in the routes smaller companies were taking to Hollywood power, New Line grew out of independent and specialty film distribution. It was 'known for a tradition of giving more room to the filmmaker' (Porras, cited in Thompson, 2007: 81).

Control I: Authorship

This early 2000s Hollywood was a domain where parts of popular auteurism were steadily being reintegrated into studio operations (Flanagan, 2004a: 20–2), and it saw superhero movies and comic book adaptations being invested in as never before. The kind of manoeuvring for industry-player status that MS undertook just a few years into the decade saw creativity and authorship play out on different levels. There was inevitably a connection to traditions established in print. In the Introduction, we saw how the insider-ish editorial 'voice' commanded by Stan Lee combined properties of unifying narrational sensibility and promotional tool. This bound together the market potential of different titles, forming an interlocking 'Marvel space' in which, say, Spider-Man and Daredevil's patches were 'just around the corner' from each other. This continued for decades after under various EIC surrogates starting with Roy Thomas. This voice, and the increasingly recognizable image of Lee, unified a feel and an approach which simply said 'Marvel' (the powerful volume of this voice was also used, arguably, to institute a picture of the industrial process in comic production at Marvel that was detrimental to vital artistic contributors).[29]

Respecting the different medium and applicable production logics, the situation regarding the wielding of authorship at MS needs to be understood: various cases may and have been made. Matthias Stork contends that Marvel's 'notion of authorship and control is evidently imagined in a corporate-industrial dimension ... [differing] significantly from the predominant discourse centred on directorial influence and auteurism in franchise filmmaking' (2014: 82). This may actually be comparable to how Lee ran things, and less so to privileged forms of cinema authorship: a crude reading of this seems to suggest a model that diverts power back to management and the process (except where figures like Jackson and Spielberg can play the game well enough, for long enough, to build their own empires). Might there be other ways to understand this? Marvel channels authorial power into the form that best serves its continuing serial plan: the shared universe. Each successful release, while undoubtedly burnishing the reputations of individual directors like Jon Favreau, Kenneth Branagh or Whedon (and, importantly, requiring the input of their personalities), counts in weight added to the credibility of the studio-brand. Although not denying the presence of name directors (highly rated figures like Branagh or *auteurs*-in-waiting recruited from more modest fields of cinema), a formula was struck in official posters from a relatively early stage, with a legend – 'From the studio that brought you *Iron Man*'; 'From the studio that brought you *The Avengers*'[30] – that insisted upon a coherent studio identity. The promotion of a studio identity over an individual one is Marvel's right, of course, and not unique; but for our analysis, the tendency (along with the publicity afforded to *auteur*-producer figure Feige) notably conjures a certain Old Hollywood, Fordist flavour: reintegrating the old in terms of the new.

Some of the ambiguities of such views of power, which in refusing to divide neatly, brings its own tensions to MS's public presence, are unpacked in later chapters; but Marvel's attitude to control as it relates to authorial figures/values may not be so clear-cut. As much as studios retrieved power in the second half of the 1970s, the 'high concept' product styling that emerged as the dominant trend in the next decade stamped the idea of homogeneity upon perceptions of studio film production. Criticism suggested that the fluidity, contingency and organizational mode that was the new norm in studio practice seemed to swallow individuality, enervate narrative, and result in films cut to the creative measure of marketing agendas and sequel prospects.[31] This pattern, borne of various influences, had perhaps been observable since the aforementioned 'New Hollywood' (see Elsaesser, 1998: 192) but was rigidly formularized in the popular works of certain producers like Don Simpson and Jerry Bruckheimer. Here, the double valence of the slippery term 'New Hollywood' presents itself: it has been used to encompass the tradition of risky, personal American art-filmmaking that occupied the mainstream for a few years around 1967–75, but at the same time – this, the sense used in Tom Schatz' famous essay – to signify the shift to (or resumption of) a 'blockbuster syndrome' immediately after this period, demonstrating the 'staying power of [both] the major studios ... and of the movie itself' (Schatz, 1993: 8–9).[32] What can be taken from this, whichever sense is invoked, is that a successful but incoherent (1993: 34) Hollywood phase led to an acceptance that authorial talent (mainly, but not solely, directors) could help to gel a fragmentary production process. Such authors, in participating, enhanced their own market value (Grainge, 2008: 46; Buckland, 1998: 169).

In seeking to delineate the past and present elements in Marvel's relationships to studio practices, we might say that MS, as a modern studio identity or studio-brand maintains a relationship to individual creativity that would have been unfamiliar and most probably unnecessary for the more traditional, top-down classical studio identities. The fact that this policy is provisional, though, seems to be evidenced in MS's own recent history: 'geek'-pleasing and critically praised individuals like Whedon[33] are given a degree of control to 'play in Marvel's sandbox', but ultimately may see their charges eventually handed over to the less palpably auteurist likes of the Russo brothers, as a new cycle begins.[34]

Control II: Film production logic ('Meet the New Boss....')

With these kinds of changes, studios no longer control the everyday business of production as they once did. Hollywood long ago shifted to a culture where the deal was the situation that actually produced the film, circumventing some of the centralized power and oversight of the studios as they had existed from the 1920s to the1940s. Today's studio can best maximize the reflected glory of being associated with creative successes, if it invests heavily in the idea of *guaranteeing* something: a quality family experience (Pixar), the capture of Academy Awards (Miramax). This is a lesson that MS has absorbed from a combination of old Hollywood and the successful and culturally meaningful 1990s 'major independents' (Wyatt, 1998), such as Miramax and the already discussed New Line.[35] Working with Marvel on the successful *Blade* (Stephen Norrington, 1998) – harbinger of a stream of licensed movies to come in the early 2000s – New Line's Bob Shaye applied lessons in dealing with exploitation and low-grade genre cinema that led directly to huge grosses and Best Picture success for *The Lord of the Rings*; just as Roger Corman's fast, cheap, studio-mimicking production, at one point deeply connected to the 'New Hollywood' in personnel terms, led to James Cameron's ultra-commercial *Avatar* (2009–17) saga. Both of those super-franchises are reflections of that which MS wanted to do. They share elements of high-quality 'pre-sold' event entertainments planned into a cycle (eventually, an annual pattern as with *Lord of the Rings*; then, as MS's 'Phase II' arrived, a biannual pattern). With all three franchises, the texts themselves wrap around cutting-edge Hollywood technology, used to fashion diegeses that open onto endlessly explorable epic universes.[36]

Such super-franchises have a powerful hold on the public's imagination but, conceptually, what 'Hollywood' signifies for many people, still, is an elite cadre of legendary companies. The image lingers, despite the fact that independent production has been the norm since the late 1950s, encompassing high-as well as low-budget filmmaking and touching a range of points on the spectrum of 'cultural status' (Newman, 2011: 3). As early as 1996 – the year of bankruptcy for Marvel Entertainment Group – Marvel's plans were being reported thus:

> Marvel's idea is to control pre-production, which means it will commission scripts, hire directors and negotiate with stars. After the package is assembled, it plans to turn over the shooting and distribution to a big studio partner.
>
> (Hass, 1996)

The swing towards deal culture empowered the talent agency industry, led by Creative Artists Agency (CAA), a giant which grew so powerful it could 'challenge studio authority' (Connor, 2015: 14). However, though the changes might have forced an adaptation, Hollywood royalty like Paramount and Warner Bros. were also presented with a chance to repurpose themselves. Hillier even points out that this culture of deal-making was built in the image of old styles under the studio system (in Buckland, 2003: 89).

Key films in the post-'New Hollywood' transition into the corporate 1980s and 1990s – when Paramount and others renewed themselves around popular film formulae – include that studio's *Raiders of the Lost Ark*. As will be seen more than once in this book, this film is a major reference point for *Captain America: The First Avenger*

(Joe Johnston, 2011) – Marvel's most committed attempt to round-up the complex mythology of the MU in a cinematic nutshell and, thus, a historical piece in more ways than one. *Raiders* is emblematic, a sort of umbrella text highlighting both continuity and change in Hollywood methodology (see also Buckland, 1998) which Connor views as an allegorical 'triumph of deal-making' (2012: 533). The film illustrates – depending on the perspective chosen – both the connections with earlier practices and styles, as well as breaks with tradition. Those practices highlighted in the 1996 article – commissioning scripts, forming packages of directors and stars – may have been unusual for a comic book publisher then in near disarray (and with rights returning to the company for some, but not yet the most crucial, superheroes, it is understandable that a press strategy should encourage an impression of positivity and expert planning), but for diversified, hands-off Hollywood companies, such practices were the norm. What was different was that a Marvel arranged in the right way could generate this business momentum from its own IP, once control over that IP had been established/recovered.

It is hopefully becoming clear that, even when MS has been adopting common blockbuster methodology, the normative logic of Hollywood, the way the company manages its own profile seems to wish not to draw attention to the fact. It does not simply arrive on the scene and take a pose of tearing up the rules; its aspiration as a studio-brand features a quiet respect for history. Hollywood histories often see the concentrated auteurism of the late 1960s/early 1970s 'New Hollywood' era as marking a fundamental discontinuity with the way earlier studio organization sought to arrange creativity, but certain critics question the classical/post-classical break that is postulated. Asking whether any tangible 'revolution' ever set in to Hollywood logic, Kristin Thompson (2007: 74) wonders whether a key post-Studio System film like *Raiders* is even 'pitched' towards audiences differently from a generic predecessor like *The Adventures of Robin Hood* (Michael Curtiz, 1939) – even taking into consideration familiar arguments around the juvenilization of the popular movie audience[37] (the kind of youthful audiences which are often assumed to be the natural constituency of MS's, and superhero films more generally; however, there is little disagreement that young consumers are the target of the array of goods that accompany a Marvel or DC movie to market and can be considered part of its textuality). The inheritance of the freedom that is generally attached to the 1970s 'golden age' has not notably been linked to superhero films. We have already observed that there is room to apply Buckland's notion of the 'classical *auteur*' to directors like Spielberg, Cameron, Jackson, Whedon and Christopher Nolan, who unite production and distribution by making possible epic, connected storytelling suited to transmedia exploitation by a convergent industry. However, the more traditionally vaunted status of 'romantic *auteur*' (2003: 84–5) tends to be awarded away from significant commercial Hollywood trends. This kind of activity is more commonly attributed to the independent cinema sector. Technically an independent in industrial terms in the 2006–9 period (arranging deals that would produce self-financed films without handling its own distribution), this is ostensibly not the area in which MS has traded. The bigger picture of Hollywood trends, though, is marked by a desire to infuse mainstream practice with something from 'left field', which is becoming a key component of studio self-image, particularly in terms of the pursuit of good reviews and awards (Newman, 2011: 223–7); MS has not exempted itself from this.[38] As the term 'independent film' becomes too wide to be useful (O'Hehir cited in Newman, 2011: 223), the tendency to read 'independence' in Hollywood as necessarily an expression of some radical quality can be usefully corrected according to some critics. J. D. Connor is one of those arguing for a more nuanced perspective on this, identifying the best way to decipher contemporary independence as a value in cinema as peering 'through its reflections within studio filmmaking' (2012: 524).

In the case of MS, as Johnson has already pinpointed, there is a sense of the company pragmatically describing itself as able to work within Hollywood traditions, but encasing this in the identity of an outsider to those traditions. Yet, as Jenkins pointed out above, 'alien norms' in the form of aesthetic innovations will tend to be absorbed by the system. Marvel's appeal to an outsider identity is not a taking up of 'indie' cinema defined as a set of stylistic conventions or subject matters,[39] but rests more on the way it self-advertises as setting its own terms in relation to franchise film customs which – by implication – are accused of staidness and lack of creativity. We can detect this in the aggressive laying out of values and positions occasionally emanating from MS or its representatives. It is there in Arad's authorship-asserting declaration that the films are 'our children' (cited in Johnson, 2012: 17) (the 'our' excluding distribution powers, i.e., established studios); or in Feige's juxtaposing of the 'fresh and original' *GOTG* against jaded audience expectations of summer movie fare (Graser, 2014a). Such discourses support Marvel's self-identification in a position 'advantageously outside the Hollywood fray' (Johnson, 2012: 24) – as starting trends, and not following them; perhaps, of existing as a 'reflection' but not a clone of studio filmmaking. Marvel's self-branding narrative concerns the use of incomparable comic-storytelling experience to add an 'X' factor to Hollywood formulae that Hollywood producers never realized was missing.

The right deal

A deal-making culture may not seem conducive to long-term relationships, but one lesson of the road that MS has been on would indicate that a series of deals, worked well enough, generates its own pseudo-studio environment around it: an intangible 'backlot' that can remain standing after the main event has wrapped, and build propitious conditions for a string of releases.[40] Again as instructed by the story of Peter Jackson's realization of Tolkien's saga, the crucial element that must be secured in place is rights. Once willing (and no doubt, advised) to surrender rights for a quick cash fix, the film and television aspirations of Marvel Entertainment floundered (see Introduction). As we saw in the Introduction, Marvel transformed its characters' fortunes in mass media over the decade following the Toy Biz rescue from bankruptcy. The new strategy depended on accomplishing two things over the years from 2004 to 2008: pursuing the rights to put a series of important MU characters on film; and raising finance. Those rights would themselves provide the collateral in the gaining of the $525 million initial production fund, arranged through Merrill Lynch. Illustrated by well-publicized involvement in a recent deal to use key hero Spider-Man in future MCU productions without regaining his rights (showing that MS – sometimes painted as absolutist when it comes to rights – is actually willing to negotiate),[41] the obligations to studios dating from when Marvel was a content provider to Hollywood, as Johnson points out, are not just in the past; some are still in effect (2012: 24). For instance, those to Daredevil were allowed to expire by Fox in 2012 (Taylor, 2014), the character returning to Marvel for exploitation in a Netflix series discussed below.

With popular interest growing in Marvel's release schedule, and a fan community that seems fully 'bought-in' to the serial plan, rights themselves become a key part of the story, and perceptions concerning them can exaggerate the intricacy of the situation. The press seeks to heighten this interest, even, recently, offering pieces that contest other articles' claims around what MS has, and does not have, the right to make.[42] Dozens, or more likely, hundreds of such articles appear each week, in venues such as *Forbes*, *Entertainment Weekly*, *Business Insider* and the established Hollywood trades as well as all over the semi-professional/fan reporting networks and in 'click-bait' form (Skipper, 2014 is a representative example, his article dwelling on rights as well as speculating on new slates of films). The highly visible Feige is regularly quoted and profiled. Not everything that is published can be accurate, but it is clear that MS's approach makes the public want to peer through a window onto the behind-the-scenes stories that make blockbusters happen.

The timing of the Disney swoop for Marvel in late 2009 will have been meticulously informed by genuine intelligence on the status of some of those active rights deals, and the possibilities for resolving them; it is even conceivable that the Disney purchase did not take place sooner because the bigger company may have been waiting until the characters that could take MS to the next level had returned to the fold. What is known is that, for all the complexity surrounding the rights to depict certain characters,[43] when Marvel regains control of a character that had been out of bounds, it is made into a success. When New Line surrendered its right to make an *Iron Man* movie – the studio had worked with Arad towards an announced but never made version, with a director (Nick Cassavetes) apparently onboard, in the early 2000s (Worley, 2004) – and Universal gave up the Hulk, an inexperienced Marvel was able to create its first picture slate from the two characters. Both projects came to fruition in 2008, with combined US box office exceeding $450 million. With capital and distribution arrangements with Paramount and Universal in place, the pre-Disney MS still held enough cards to plot a reinterpretation – for a new medium or, more precisely, a new connected media ecosystem – of the MU and how it had functioned in comics. Marvel continued to work to regain other rights over the period of the first releases, and under Disney – no doubt in possession of stronger advantages – continues to do this today.

*****

J. D. Connor (2015: 13) dubs much of contemporary studio practice 'classicism at one remove'. MS seems to be one of those cases where although its developments of innovatory, even 'risky' practice (see Chapter 6) are often cited in publicity or when the studio is profiled (mainly stressing the shared universe concept or Marvel as exemplifying convergent media production), a different, older pattern is also detectable. MS actually negotiates and melds old and new in its approach; there is a certain inheritance of the agendas that constituted Hollywood before 'The New Hollywood'. A varied form of classical film production technique and style remains the most practicable method (Bordwell refers to this when he itemizes contemporary stylistic norms and gathers them under the umbrella term of 'intensified continuity', invoking the continuity style of classical editing that underpinned the reign of the studios – Bordwell, 2002), but there is no point denying that centralization in a studio cartel has gone. Many of the names – Warner Bros., Paramount, Twentieth Century Fox – are the same, but the studio function and, importantly, presence is very different. Characterizations of contemporary Hollywood as form of expression and industrial sector stress fragmentation and instability. Yet, these conditions create ways of doing business. We now move on to look at some of the non-cinema business that has been created, as Marvel formed divisions (television and to a lesser extent – as Chapter 8 will uncover – videogames, for instance), from which would flow products synced-up with the same aims, and tethered to the same MCU content, as the main event films. Perhaps surprisingly, in the Disney/Marvel era, policy around the sharing of television and film material has remained on the same course, and even – despite Disney's significant holdings in television networks – taken into account that which external partners like Netflix might bring, in offering a slightly different way to position and exploit Marvel's brand.

A joined-up brand, yet part of an ecosystem

The internet ... so helpful.

(Steve Rogers in *Captain America: The Winter Soldier*)

A consolidated 'studio identity' such as we have presented does not exhaust every relevant production mode that contemporary transmedia producers might enlist into service. A company which attempts to gather such meanings into its own sphere of control does not necessarily stand in opposition to the parameters of convergence cinema. That said, so far, our reading has aligned with such as Buckland, Thompson and Connor, who hold that the Hollywood landscape around 2000, rather than being as different as many accounts posit, was 'remarkably consistent with the one that had been built over the previous decades' (Connor, 2015: 247). The past we have invoked is that of the mature phase of major studio classicism (circa 1930–60), but even, arguably, an earlier phase until the mid-1910s when a trusted film brand such as Biograph would assure quality, applies (before stars and other 'product features' began to absorb that burden – Grainge, 2008: 45). Essentially, the pattern we are assembling enables an understanding of how the mid-to-late 2000s incarnation of Marvel took advantage of the fluidity of the post-Fordist film landscape – largely free of monolithic, film-only studio interests with rigidly divided labour – while also enjoying the reputational benefits that come from commissioning and controlling all film projects in-house, developing a 'studio-brand' signature partly by exploiting its attractiveness to a modern wave of comic-inspired film authors such as Whedon and James Gunn.

Examining MS also encourages us to think about partnerships. Partnerships hold a solid attraction and rationale even for a leader of the field such as Disney, and it has been pointed out that MS strove to render an image of itself as good to work with as well as capable of leading and going it alone (see Johnson, 2012: 23). It was the earlier partnership between Disney and Pixar – where Disney the distributor played essentially the same role as did Universal and Paramount to the early releases of MS – that allowed Pixar to find its feet (and, arguably, its audience), and store away a huge amount of credibility and goodwill for the future (see Chapter 7).[44] This goodwill might not have been as easily available with the more controversial Disney, frequently cast as hegemonic in its media dominance.[45] Marvel as a vaunted 'character franchise company' (to adopt the rather dry nomenclature used by the official purchase announcement – Anon., 2009c) had a history of working with the entertainment sector that ranged from patchy to disastrous before Toy Biz (see Chapter 2). When we turn our focus onto television, in which Marvel has become increasingly active since 2013, we can identify areas that extend and support MS as a transmedia brand, but simultaneously demonstrate how the strategic desires, and business expertise, of Disney are channelled through Marvel.

At a reported cost of $4 billion (Howe, 2013: 429), Marvel Entertainment Inc. officially belonged to Disney as of 31 December 2009. Some commentators suggested that such a move may not quite have fulfilled a tangible goal of Marvel's brand-strengthening policy dating back a decade, but neither would it have been anathema to the company (Johnson, 2007: 74). The new home of the artists and executives working on both comics and films was to be a media conglomerate of enormous size and range, 'one of the most global entities in all of business' (Robbins and Polite, 2014: 11), based on a 'compelling business model' – particularly around licensing and merchandising – which was widely seen as an aspirational blueprint by Hollywood rivals (Grainge, 2008: 49). Within this new setting, suddenly plugged into precisely the kind of transmedia opportunities that Lee had attempted to garner in the 1970s and 1980s (weakened then by the fact that licensing was Marvel's only recourse), Marvel would nonetheless maintain focus on the cinematic product. According to Johnson, the company at this time projected a feel of keeping 'film and the Hollywood way of doing things' sacred and central, increasing its likeness to a studio tradition in an ostensibly changed era (2012: 18). Nevertheless, in this new corporate environ, MS was ideally placed to re-envisage how its new MCU product could render television meaningful, and receive extra meaning in return (this, during an era where American television, in general but due to its own peculiar sectoral logic, had successfully raised its aspirations to compete with cinema on aesthetic grounds. See Akass and McCabe, 2007). As such the 'Marvel Television' wing was created in 2010, under the supervision of Jeph Loeb, a star comic writer mainly associated with Batman comics and the successful *Smallville* superhero show for Warner Bros. television (2001–11). The moves to extend the MCU to television have all been realized since the Disney purchase, although going further back and as explained in Chapter 8, viewed through a wider historical lens, Marvel heroes manifested upon television screens well before they reached cinema ones.[46]

The long-standing incorporation of television as a risk-reducing strategy playing into both horizontal and vertical integration plans is a core element of Disney heritage, meaning that Marvel's new parent truly understood the medium. With antitrust prosecutions looming, the mid-1940s was a discouraging time for moves by Hollywood studios to buy into broadcasting services on a large scale, since this would go against them in the monopoly hearings (Hilmes, 1996: 467). After the effects of divorcement had worked through the system a decade later, such distinctions had lost relevance (the old arrangement inexorably breaking up), leading to studios that were free to bring independent producers for both theatrical and TV production onto their lots. Studios reinvented a considerable part of their business as taking a leading role both in television production and the handling of syndication.[47]

Disney was a pioneer company in bonding the fortunes of its film production activity to television, the latter visualized not merely as a window to monetize a rich back catalogue, but an explicit brand-positioning opportunity, a way to generally translate its quintessential 'suburban Middle-American' address into the currency of prime-time broadcasting (Sammond, 2005: 316). Shows like *Disneyland* (later *Walt Disney's Wonderful World of Colour*, *Walt Disney Presents* and other names, 1954–92) and *The Mickey Mouse Club* (1955–9) had an ostensible function of developing the theatrical audience for new releases (establishing the early 'infomercial' form with their plugging of the new Disneyland, which opened – with full launch coverage – in 1955).[48] However, they also enveloped the audience with Disney textuality beyond the one-off screen or leisure experience, synthesizing potent 'mythmaking with … "experiential marketing"' (Christensen, 2012: 328). The Disney company's early diagnosis of television's value anticipated the eventual folding of a distinguished US network, ABC (now host to *Agents of S.H.I.E.L.D.* and *Agent Carter*) into its empire in 1996; a decade on, as part of a huge expansion into the millennium (Robbins and Polite, 2014: 12), Disney's cable TV operations were fanning out worldwide into countries like the UK, Japan and India.

Connor muses on the importance of television in new American media hierarchies:

> What might be replacing the neoclassical [studio] order? One compelling reading of this new era would contend that the principal locus of corporate reflection has simply shifted to television. … The emergence of a broad, auteurist strand of show-running, and its concomitant popular and critical endorsement may amount to what we would call 'The New Television' after 'The New Hollywood' of the 1970s.
>
> (2012: 524)

Connor's point alights on the shifting balance regarding TV and film in 'neoclassical' Hollywood, with television's power delineated not just in industrial terms (its convergence role), but in amplified creative ones. Joss Whedon's role in assigning the *Agents of S.H.I.E.L.D.* showrunners Maurissa Tancharoen and Jed Whedon, experienced collaborators from his own television work, demonstrates that the governing company Marvel Entertainment is aware of the 'popular and critical endorsement' that accumulates around him benefits the television extension of the brand. The kudos that Whedon brings convinced Marvel/ABC to foreground his name in a flurry of pre-publicity (Hadas, 2014: 10), even if relations cooled after the second Avengers film (with Whedon himself even denying a close function of inputting to Marvel Television – Tilly, 2015). However, the now two seasons-old collaboration with ABC on *Agents of S.H.I.E.L.D.* – essentially, a traditional, serial episodic show running half the year – is not the most innovative of Marvel's explorations into television. More recently, Marvel announced a foray into the more specialized 'on-demand' television sector – albeit in tandem with the biggest player in the online subscription market. How the Netflix approach might dovetail with the principles already set in place for MCU releases will be explored in more detail in Chapter 8, but broadly, this is an approach identified with the different consumption patterns ('box sets' and 'binge watching') and the urge to have control over viewing choice that are associated, at least in the earliest days of the service, with a more discriminating consumer base (Tryon, 2009: 114). Netflix's audience is said to be made up of 'urbane, globalized moviegoer[s]' (Tryon, 2013: 107), and the service attracts the technologically savvy who often watch it in conjunction with other devices. Emphasizing the impressive reach it has achieved in a few years, its viewership is more likely to be parents (Thielman, 2014), yet at the same time Netflix is cited in many articles exploring digital 'cord-cutting' among young adults (see for instance Frizell, 2015).[49]

The young adult/'millennial' consumer is a desired market segment that crosses over both with the blockbuster film address but also, potentially, a monthly digital or print-comic readership which publishers would certainly like to make more renewable (rendering Alonso's rationalization for changes to the MU at the start of this chapter understandable). Netflix's effectiveness in reaching fan niches with 'prized content' (Lotz, 2014: 255) like the smart, anarchic sitcom *Arrested Development* is demonstrable.[50] Unappreciated by advertisers and mass viewership when running on the Fox network, this resurrected show is the TV equivalent of modestly selling comics like *Captain Marvel*[51] – underlining the similarities between holding a Netflix subscription and one to the Marvel digital app or on-demand service Comixology.[52] In the way often seen with new media businesses, Netflix carried the connotations of 'a democratizing force … [in an] undemocratic industry' (Chris Anderson, cited in Tryon, 2009: 113). Disney – a focal point of the critique of 'undemocratic' trends in running a media business since the 1960s counter-culture defined the company (and Walt himself) as one strand of its 'mean, square opposition' (Hebdige, 2005: 41) – can benefit here.

Still, many consumers will remain unaware of Marvel's ties to Disney, especially if they come across a show like *Daredevil* (the first in a planned sequence of five connected shows making up the Netflix branch of the MCU) which bears the authorship stamp of Marvel itself alongside the logo of Netflix. Yet, as a subsidiary of Disney, Marvel benefits from the Netflix link-up in terms of audience development, in a further sense. Disney consumers may find it easy to have relationships with the brand as parents, but once past a certain age, the entertainment channels most commonly associated with Disney may not hold an obvious attraction for them as non-parental adults. The corporation's usual vehicles may struggle to find a place for populist fare that is not intended for intergenerational viewing, especially with the constraints of network TV standards and practices (by which Marvel's ABC shows must abide). Accordingly, Marvel's more 'grown-up' *Daredevil* carried the TV-MA rating seldom used by network programming (signifying a programme 'specifically designed to be viewed by adults … [which] therefore may be unsuitable for children under 17').[53] The violence of the show, its obvious divergence from the 'tone' of the best known MCU texts (all of which had rolled out on cinema screens with PG-13 rating in the United States/12 or 12a in the United Kingdom), as well as its lack of suitability for intergenerational viewing, were dominant features of fan discourses in the release month of April, 2015.[54] With the interlinked Netflix shows due to roll out and culminate in a *Defenders* miniseries, with a focus on characters emphasizing detection, physical strength and martial arts, we seem to have something of a 'street' or 'gritty' sub-brand of the MCU to provide diversification both from the Avengers franchise and the 'cosmic' film strand (both discussed in Chapter 6).

The handling of *Daredevil* speaks in a more general sense to how identity is constructed and distributed across business divisions, and the different options for shuffling its products through sub-brands which can be advantageous to Disney. The Marvel identity has already helped Disney to push through and maximize properties which may actually suffer from a direct branding. The 'underdog' role which we discuss as applying historically to Marvel Comics (both in the Introduction and in Chapter 2) continues to lend Marvel a certain specialness, and hold at bay calls of homogeneity or cultural imperialism even as Marvel hero-branded products roll out across the world; however, we might speculate that few in Disney's audience groups can recall when that brand represented an underdog.[55] At a time when efforts to aggrandize elements of the core Disney brand mythology seem to sit awkwardly with the public (noting here the unexceptional public reception of *Tomorrowland* (Brad Bird, 2015), about which more is said in Chapter 7), Marvel appears to offer a way to almost purge some of the negative associations of Disney for certain audience segments.

Conclusion

In MS, a structure has been raised that can handle the potential of Marvel's iconic catalogue while retaining control. The company has been much admired for it: most often hailed as a media innovator (see, for instance, Stork, 2014: 79), experimenting with 'unprecedented' strategies to maintain cohesion across texts (Sweeney, 2013: 146) and draw audiences into a 'saga' (2013: 140); but we have hopefully thrown light on how its development also displays hallmarks of more proven approaches to studio establishment, affirming the 'staying power' (Schatz, 1993: 8) of the classic major studio conception. This involves aspects like studio-branding (informed by the experiences in risky, event movie production by upstart yet growing firms such as New Line), and the value of building relationships (hard-won wisdom from the licensing days). This chapter has drawn from certain notions fitting to the Fordist/ Studio System-era to explain MS moves into Hollywood territory, arguing that these facilitated up-to-date convergent production logics, while looking to the past at the same time.

As the Introduction has shown, Marvel Comics' history is populated by staff who know better than most the trick of maintaining a brand heavily dependent on creative inventory while front office corporate landlords, those recipients of the financial success dependent on propitious creative conditions, come and go within an atmosphere of 'chaos' (Howe, 2013: 205). Shrugging off its tempestuous history, with new executives on board who were determined to learn from it, Marvel entered the 2000s in stable shape and with an 'endgame' in sight: the building of a brand with the aspiration to hold the value of a Warner Bros., a Twentieth Century Fox – or a Disney. However, arriving in Hollywood as an 'upstart', as Johnson says, MS needed a vocabulary to explain itself to rivals. Melding classical and new at the same time, MS is one firm strengthening the case for a 'neoclassicism' (Smith, 1998: 11) taking hold following the 'precarious moment' of the New Hollywood (Connor, 2012: 522). It must be remembered that as figures like Lucas and Spielberg, and their later 'classical *auteur*'/quasi-producer successors such as Jackson and Cameron asserted their stature, infusing blockbuster logic with creativity, studios drew off power from the same renewal. The artistic victories of the early 1970s arguably set the course for sharply dichotomous paths for a long period.[56]

All of those earlier changes have some relevance to Marvel's position today, as what follows shall testify. The studio is an extremely interesting case, particularly during the period from the receipt of the credit facility in 2005 to being bought by Disney in 2009. This era saw Marvel, as a producer, marked by some kind of independence (defining the studio's perception of its own identity as an outlier). Perhaps this was a moment when the niche space into which the first incarnation of MS emerged was forced open. The company enjoyed a considerable amount of room to turn its options to its best advantage by picking something old and something new from the studio playbook. Yet, it could also be said that the swift buyout by Disney – once the feasibility of the MCU had been proven beyond doubt with *Iron Man,* its in-production sequel and *The Incredible Hulk* – was a reflection of another kind of driving insecurity and instability: that the biggest entities are going to co-opt the most promising newcomers to supply their pipelines, solidifying their own positions above the 'fray'. The purchaser was Disney – once an outsider to the system, indelibly associated with a genre that before 1938 was thought to have no future in feature production; a company, even, that once could only achieve distribution by the leave of a major studio. These facts only add to the fascinating intricacy of MS's relation to Hollywood corporate history.[57] Finally, by considering partnerships and the way that the overall MCU strategy has adapted to entry into the market for streaming television, we see how the Disney–Marvel identities have learned to cooperate, compartmentalize, and even compromise. In the language of brand analysis, when it comes to certain niche areas, the 'brand equity' (Robbins and Polite, 2014: 13) of Marvel is actually more powerful (more appropriate; more credible) than is Disney's. As we have seen with *Daredevil,* this enables Disney, through Marvel, to gain some control in a sector of the market that *as* Disney, may be unavailable to it.

CHAPTER 2
AN ORGANIZATION OF STORYTELLERS: THE MARVEL STORY, ACCORDING TO MARVEL

Introduction

Throughout its sequence of hits (twelve at the time of writing from *Iron Man* to *Ant-Man*),[1] Marvel has developed from its cult standing with comic book fans into a critically recognized, credible screen enterprise drawing audiences on a scale that is the envy of its new industry. The process of meeting such a variety of success indicators has improved the recognition – and therefore future profit potential – of its key characters, while the large profit haul consolidates trust in its management capacity, which then increases its bargaining position (regarding access to funding and creative autonomy) within its corporate structure. To succeed in any one of the above criteria would be a rare and celebrated thing that requires tremendous talent in specific fields, but to succeed at them all simultaneously – instantly – and then over a prolonged period of time, requires a coherent, well-run organization. It will be postulated throughout this chapter that such coherence is achieved by having a clear, consistent and settled organizational identity: an identity that acts as a strong, recognizable brand to those outside the business, as well as a set of principles or ideals to converge upon or rally behind for those within. Mary Hatch and Majken Schultz (2004), pioneers in the field, describe organizational identity as a strategic tool that can assist in creating a competitive advantage by projecting that which is unique and inimitable about the organization. They define it as 'a dynamic concept of identity that is both rooted in the organisation's history and heritage *and* in its relationships to other identities and images that swirl around and interpenetrate it at any given moment' (5; emphasis in original). This description, along with highlighting the importance of 'heritage', foregrounds the fact that organizations are part of a social ecology; they are exposed to many influences and interact with many agents. An analysis of such influences throughout Marvel's history can lead to a better understanding of how and why its identity has developed the way it has, how this development has led Marvel towards the production of its own cinematic universe (the MCU) and how Marvel, as an organization of storytellers, has guided the construction of this identity.

Multiple identities

Marvel's position within the creative industries further complicates the process of identity generation, because it must appeal to a diverse audience, appearing in different ways to different sections of that audience without losing definition or clarity in identity. Such a dichotomy of organizational identity is noted by Stuart Albert and David Whetten (2004): 'There is no one best statement of identity, but rather, multiple equally valid statements relative to different audiences for different purposes' (93). With such an understanding, this chapter defines Marvel as an *organization* of *storytellers*; to warrant such a description it must satisfy both of these criteria. It must delight audiences by accommodating storytellers that can use traditional narrative forms, as well as innovating to surpass industry rivals, achieving cultural recognition. Yet, it must also operate as an organization, utilizing these storytellers within the parameters of the competitive environment of twenty-first-century capitalism, and affixing a happy ending – or continuation – to its own business story. Within such a model, there exists a whole spectrum between making profit at all costs and creating art that makes no concessions to commercial realities, a fact that is exacerbated within the culture industry. On this topic, Bill Ryan (1992) notes that 'it seems fundamental to recognise the distinctiveness of the culture industry. This is not simply capitalist production. It is cultural production organised along capitalist lines. It *combines* the structures of capital and art' (13–4; emphasis in original). To straddle such a dichotomy between art and commerce requires a delicate balancing act. To bring this dichotomy specifically to bear on the Marvel Studios (MS) context, if its films fail to enthral, excite, upset, or provoke some kind of emotional response in their audience, as any effective story should, they would likely be found wanting by critics and popular audiences alike. Despite how efficiently the business may have operated, the studio would not be able to access as wide an audience, and therefore would fail to maximize its potential profits. Therefore, to effect this balance, Marvel must apply frugality to thoughts of investment returns, noting that any excessive overspending could impact the potential level of financial gain; yet every corner thoughtlessly cut could expose a film's artistic shortcomings, and lead to a ruined reputation that would also impact financial returns. Further, significant to Marvel's definition of its project in terms of the shared MCU, this would not only affect the current production, but could also taint that character's brand, their associated franchise, and even the universe as a whole, therefore negatively impacting the potential of future releases. It is evident that this balancing act has ramifications for the public perception of the organization's identity. It prompts questions such as: Does Marvel succeed at business in order to tell great stories? Or does it tell great stories in order to prosper in business? Yet, perhaps it doesn't necessarily have to be one or the other, but must simply appear in the correct light for the appropriate audience.

With this in mind, Marvel's inherent capacity to tell stories – and its historic precedent of harbouring decision makers that are at once businessmen *and* storytellers – has a direct effect on the way it conducts business. Working across all layers of the organization, it is able to manipulate its own story, generating multiple complementary, or even intentionally conflicting, stories, then direct them towards different audiences. In the context of identity management, such a strategy brings its own dangers, as Marvel must be aware that failure to bring these oft-considered diametrically opposed factors into a smooth coexistence throughout the organization will lead to the perils of what Albert and Whetten term the 'ideographic form' of a dual identity. This, they warn, is

> a struggle, not simply over alternative budget proposals, but over the very soul of the institution. ... As the relative power of the various ideological groups builds and diminishes, the identity of the organization as a whole will be altered in complexion, leading outsiders to complain that the organization cannot decide what it wants to be or who it wants to serve.

(2004: 97)

It is this delineation between potential ideological oppositions of profit and art that Marvel must straddle. Its history demonstrates that when this balance has been struck, Marvel has prospered; yet when it hasn't – when an ideographic form was exposed – identity was compromised, and Marvel suffered intensely as a result. When this imbalance was redressed, and a stable identity reinstated, it prospered once more, and its cinematic universe has proven to be a pivotal development in its recent stability. Before specifically investigating such eras, and analysing their impact upon the development of the organization's identity, it would be useful to understand in what way an 'organization' is to be understood in the context of this work, and set out our view of their well-rounded place within society.

Organizations: Rationalized, rather than rational

Janette Webb (2006) takes a distinctly sociological look, not only at the identity of organizations, but also the ways in which individuals view their own identity within the framework of a world where organizations are so dominant. She stresses that although she includes businesses within the term, she pulls back from inextricably tying it to the act of running a business: 'Organisations are not solely workplaces, but are also sites of social and economic policy making, consumption, education, social welfare and citizenship' (4). She elaborates that as organizations pervade most of society – from public services, to voluntary groups, to privately owned, or publicly floated commercial entities – the general principles regarding the way individuals interact and identify with them, remain the same. In each case, she claims that although they have their codes, restrictions and set practices, organizations are more interwoven within the fabric of the rest of society than conventional organizational theory would admit: 'Organisations are simultaneously the means of regulated, standardized exchange, and are embedded in particular, personal and social relationships, institutions of civil society and cultural norms' (31). She is mindful of the complexity inherent in such intricate social constructs, emphasizing that 'organisations cannot be understood either solely as structures inhabited by passive and entirely interchangeable people, or solely as the sum of their constituent actors' (6). This line of thinking has important ramifications for notions of organizational identity, unpicking as it does the idea that an identity is pre-defined, or simply presented by organizational elites and accepted without negotiation. She therefore argues that organizations must be understood as societal entities, and as such, bear identities which are comprised of many disparate, and often difficult to control, factors. Further, this leads to the belief that organizational identity is fluid and capable of change or reinterpretation. As she opines: 'Organisational trajectories are emergent rather than planned, and rationalised rather than rational' (7). Thus, identities are subject to change, and the actions that define an organization, being rationalized, are often retroactively implemented – or forged, perhaps, by storytellers, armed with flecks of truth and objectives that cleave to creative, as well as public relations goals. It is in such a light that we wish to view the potential mythologizing of Marvel's 'origin', and the process by which the organization rebuilt a broken identity in this origin's reflected glory; a relationship between past and present that is identified in an organizational context by Dennis Gioia et al. (2004), contending that 'current needs or desired future image fuels the reinvention of the past' (361). This idea of reinventing an organization's legacy in order to fuel its current needs is important to bear in mind when considering our current understanding of Marvel's 'origin' in the 1960s, and must also be a factor when considering some of the texts upon which we have drawn, such as Dan Raviv (2004) and Sean Howe (2013). Both of these texts are detailed and comprehensive accounts of historical events, but written from the vantage point of a contemporary twenty-first-century perspective. Further, both are written in a journalistic and familiar register, bolstering their enlightening investigative work through evocative language and a sculpting of character befitting of their subject matter. In this chapter, rather than such a detailed recounting, our different mandate will be the interpretation of the events they cover, within the context of how Marvel's identity was affected. It must be stressed that the intention of showcasing an 'origin' period of Marvel's historic development is not to imply that an identity was intentionally set at the time, in order to become a spiritual beacon for Marvel over the next several decades. However, just as was suggested by Webb above, such developments are 'rationalized', rather than having been 'rational'; and what this period has come to stand for, served Marvel well when it was in danger of losing its identity completely.

An organizational origin story

In 1961, Timely Comics, part of Martin Goodman's Magazine Management, renamed itself 'Marvel Comics', taken from Timely's 1939 title of that same name. By doing so it immediately identified its comic book business with its superhero heritage, as *Marvel Comics* featured Timely's earliest superheroes Prince Namor and The Human Torch.[2] This change of name was instigated in order to keep pace with rival comic book publishers DC, and their resurgent superheroes. Under the editorship of Stan Lee, surrounded by the innovative talent of artists Jack Kirby and Steve Ditko, the organization brought to life a new sector of the comic book market: relatable superheroes with common problems. From this creative boom were borne almost all of today's recognizable Marvel characters, in the course of only a few years and through the combined minds of Kirby, Ditko and Lee (earlier characters like Namor and Captain America involving the creative talents of others such as Bill Everett and Joe Simon). It was both the relatable nature of the characters, as well as the range of innovations, that secured its identity as a 'hip' alternative to market leaders DC.

A further distinctive feature of the period, and thus an identifying characteristic for Marvel, was the unique, self-referential style of Lee's editorial address to readers (who increasingly became constructed as fans, Marvelites or 'True Believers' (Duncan and Smith, 2009: 182). His fourth wall-breaking demeanour sat Marvel alongside 1960s self-referentialism (that of pop art, movies, and certain instances of pop music for example), connecting it to the cultural zeitgeist, and gaining it recognition within a coveted, increasingly affluent and commercially savvy generation. This style, and the level of relatability that it conferred onto the individuals within the organization, facilitated a connection between organization and readers, creators and fans, which was perhaps stronger than anywhere else within its contemporary media landscape. Not only did this create consumers at that time, but also established relationships that would convert these readers into loyal 'Marvel Zombies' (Sweeney, 2013: 144), who would then reinforce Marvel's identity on its behalf in a developing conventions scene waiting to take off in the 1970s (Wright, 2003: 252). Super-fans such as Roy Thomas, inspired by Marvel's creative boom, went on to become pivotal in defining the organization's early history with a mission to preserve the flavour of its origins and maintain the identifying features that Marvel had crafted itself.

A final feature of this period defining Marvel as new, innovative and different within its competitive environment was the expansion of a shared universe. Although character guest appearances or the occasional crossover had occurred in comics prior to this stage, the fully realized expansion of a complete shared universe containing a comic book publisher's entire character catalogue became synonymous with Marvel, and thus tied to its forming identity.

The creativity shown throughout this defining period is what enabled Marvel to initiate its trajectory towards market dominance. This process brings to mind marketing theorists Al Ries and Laura Ries's (2000) assertion: 'If you want to build a brand, you must focus your branding efforts on owning a word in the prospect's mind. A word that nobody owns' (39). A word, or category, can only be owned if an organization is the first to become associated with it. DC will always have been first to create Superman, and therefore may always own the popular meanings of 'superhero'. In such an eventuality, Ries and Ries clarify: 'So what do you do if you weren't the first in a category? Quite often you can create a new category by simply narrowing your focus' (42). Marvel stood out because it shifted the focus, choosing to compete on a different level, where it could own such deviated categories as 'relatable superheroes', 'fan engagement' and in particular, an expanded 'universe'. By taking actions that became characterized as creative and innovative, Marvel became distinct within its competitive environment, but decisions were made based on commercial necessities, rather than on strictly creative impulses: Goodman ordered a comic book line to mimic DC's Justice League, but mere imitation would have failed to make the level of cultural impact achieved. It took the creativity of those individuals tasked with carrying out such executive commands to establish a unique proposition. As such, this period was founded on a balancing act that placed art and creativity on the one hand, with commercial reality and the competitive environment on the other. This process, whereby disparate incentives are at play, in tandem with a diverse combination of personalities and their contributions, underlines Webb's assertion that organizations display social variety, and are more than singularly occupied with making profit. This variety spanned Marvel: from Goodman as the corporate owner, competing in magazine publishing, to Lee as the astute, but creative editor crafting a new inclusive mode of engaging with audiences, to the storytelling innovations of the artists, to the fresh and original characters created in the midst of this. Others within organization studies, such as Barry Turner, have termed such a multifaceted approach as 'organizational symbolism'. He explains:

> The conventions within which organizational affairs are discussed must recognize this: organizations, and especially commercial and business organizations are considered to be utilitarian and formal, operating in a sterile, no-nonsense atmosphere, and managers are expected to display an economic hard headedness which will have no track with more fanciful notions. The organizational symbolists challenge this view. They point out that the world of organizations is not, cannot be solely about 'muck and brass', about ends and means, about formal discussions of business strategy within the confines of Weber's 'iron cage of rationality'.
>
> (1995: 83–4)

In deference to other, traditional approaches to organization theory, Turner posits that 'looking anew at the organizational world we can see that it is a sensual and emotional realm, replete with its own ceremonies, rites and dramas' (85). He stresses the importance of 'play' and creativity, and asserts that the rise of organizational symbolism lies 'in the attention which it draws to the manner in which the creative, humanizing, innovating aspects of culture pervade in organizational behaviour' (96). It is such a picture that we see in Marvel's origin as detailed above, and which shall be revealed as even more significant as the corporate structure that builds around the company in following decades causes the imperative of such 'play' to be forgotten, with resultant damage to its organizational identity.

The short-sighted overseers

The fact that identity does not exist in a fixed state – that it is much more dynamic than traditional notions would suggest – is posited by Gioia et al., who assert that 'the apparent durability of identity is somewhat illusory' (2004: 350) and would sooner define organizational identity as a 'negotiated, interactive, reflexive concept that, at its essence, amounts to an organizational work-in-progress' (369). As such, an organization cannot presume that its identity – and therefore the competitive advantage gained from this – will not change; in fact, they add that without fluidity in its nature, 'the organization stagnates in the face of an inevitably changing environment' (351). It must therefore strategically guide this change in a way that maintains its advantage, rather than allowing its identity to drift away from it.

Marvel's origin established such a strong identity that it supported an extended period of stability. On the storytelling side, the pairing of Lee and Kirby, particularly on their run of 102 issues of *Fantastic Four*, epitomized the creatively stable rhythm achieved, even when personal relationships within the organization were fraught with tensions.[3] Further, the style that was instigated by Kirby had become so iconic, that stability was artificially created by the imposition of his style on incoming artists (Howe, 2013: 50). On a structural level, Lee's tenure as Editor-in-Chief (EIC), particularly under a relatively unchanged corporate structure, meant that Marvel could maintain its ascendency throughout the 1960s. Even through the first significant signs of instability, initiated in 1968 when Magazine Management was acquired by Perfect Film & Chemical Corporation (which became the conglomerate Cadence Corporation Industries in 1973), Marvel could maintain its established identity thanks to creators that had been attracted to its originary core principles. This included the aforementioned Thomas, as well as writers Jim Starlin and Steve Gerber, whose work would guard and perpetuate the principles of Marvel's origin: innovation (albeit in house style); fervent countercultural references (thus retaining its 'hip' status); an expanding and increasingly intricate universe, and intimate engagement between creators and fans. This, again, allowed Marvel to showcase that such creative success is followed by economic prosperity if correctly managed; for even after periods of relative instability, a strong identity and adherence to core principles allowed the organization to prosper throughout the 1970s and into the 1980s under EIC Jim Shooter. Raviv notes that when he took the helm in 1978, 'Shooter had a huge impact during his nine-year run as editor. ... The quality of the books noticeably improved, as did sales. Marvel commanded 70 percent of the marketplace, and some of the writers and artists were earning over half a million dollars per year' (2004: 33). Yet, through years of increasing instability, time laid siege to Marvel's originating identity: its increasing size began to run contrary to the image of the scrappy underdog; creative teams broke down for either professional or personal reasons; Marvel's position as a bastion of creativity and risk-taking diminished due to the ongoing debacle regarding its complicity with an industry-wide perceived mistreatment of creators with respect to credit, entitlement and ownership of characters (Raviv 2004: 33). Successful writers and artists also knew that the threat to go across town to DC was always a valid one.[4] Such factors were exacerbated by several ownership changes that shuffled industrial incentives. When Goodman was the topmost decision maker in the corporate structure, Marvel's process worked; he might have at times been a ruthless businessman,[5] but he trusted the incentives. He knew that the creative team beneath him would deliver what this company needed in order to maintain market share, and so they were left with relative autonomy to do what they wanted to do, which was to create. Cadence's methods were different: its leadership should have been happy with Marvel's market position, but it still imposed seemingly unnecessary, and therefore disruptive changes. This was mainly indicative of the corporate environment of the time, as companies began being sold on such a regular basis. The long-term approach to business that brought Marvel market prosperity was not in harmony with the priorities of corporate owners. This was noted by Shooter as EIC:

> All the owners became shortsighted. All they were interested in was getting some money in their pockets and getting the hell out. They were not thinking about the future. … It seems that every time things look like they're going to look good, then the owners of the company end up selling it. And it falls into the hands of the philistines and you've got to start all over again.
>
> (Shooter cited in Raviv, 2004: 35)

Between 1989 and 1997, the situation became personified in the regime – attained via a convoluted system of corporate ownership and mergers – of Wall Street tycoon Ronald Perelman. He and his administration (referred to by Raviv as 'The Townhouse') made decisions that were not only bad for long-term sustainability, but were not even good for Marvel's *immediate* stability, as actions were taken that outright siphoned money out of the organization. One such manoeuvre was the floating of the Marvel Entertainment Group on the New York Stock Exchange in 1991: 40 per cent of the company sold for $70 million, with $40 million going straight to subsidiary MacAndrews and Forbes (Perelman's personally owned holdings company) (Raviv, 2004: 37). Such damaging acts of financial sleight of hand set in train a systematic breaking apart of the identity that had made Marvel distinctive. Short-term decisions were restricting creativity, robbing the organization of money, and allowing for little opportunity to maintain, or ever regain, the identifying features that had led to initial success and esteem. Despite a willingness by many within Marvel to follow DC into advancing its characters into the international showcase of feature-length cinematic releases, the short-term incentives of the corporate owners made this impossible. Film productions are long, contractual and logistically difficult to wrap up or retreat from inexpensively in a short space of time, and as Raviv identifies of The Townhouse's mentality during its period of ownership, 'no one wanted too many outstanding contracts or half-completed projects should an opportunity arise to sell the company' (2004: 38). As a result, Marvel was losing ground to DC, and to further compound the situation, just as Marvel had once supplanted its main rival by entering the market with an identity as the fresh alternative, it now appeared the uncool tyrant, as new market entrants Image Comics exploded onto the scene in 1992. Image specifically cast its difference from the 'Big Two' in terms of creator relations (on the back of the desertion from Marvel of hyped figures like Todd McFarlane and Jim Lee). Challenging Marvel and DC on the controversial mistreatment of their creative talent, Image allowed creators to retain the rights to characters they originated.

Marvel's stagnation was seemingly confirmed: far from harbouring creative talent, the company had strayed towards being viewed as openly hostile to creators; far from being at the forefront of creativity, its non-comic innovation was stifled by its parent's narrow ambitions. Its reluctance to make such deals permitted limited revenue from licensing and few options to expose its characters at the cinematic level of DC's Superman or Batman. Marvel's creative decline even culminated in fan boycotts of its products (Raviv, 2004: 69), demonstrating the harmful severing of that distinctive connection between creators and fans initiated in the 1960s. Change is inevitable, and as Gioia et al. note: 'An identity with a sense of continuity … is one that shifts in its interpretation and meaning while retaining labels for "core" beliefs and values that extend over time and context' (2004: 352). Marvel stagnated because it failed to protect core principles and change with the time on its own terms. As a result, beginning in December 1996, Marvel faced financial ruin in the form of a bloody bankruptcy, from which it almost didn't return. At several points throughout a two-year period, the entity known as Marvel was moments away from being broken into unrecognizable pieces, and scattered throughout the creative industry. Such doom was narrowly avoided thanks to the corporate pairing of Avi Arad and Ike Perlmutter, whose Toy Biz firm had a vested interest in Marvel's survival. They combined to restore the originary balance between art and commerce, convincing financial backers, and frustrated creditors, of the long-term viability of Marvel's characters, if handled correctly; this permitted the stability, and injection of creativity, that they required. Through this process, and putting an end to the bankruptcy proceedings, in October 1998, Toy Biz became Marvel Enterprises, Inc. (Raviv, 2004: 252).

Post-bankruptcy: A rising phoenix

In culmination of the tumultuous period described above, the bankruptcy, instigated by short-termist owners, had drained the firm of the monetary resources with which to rebuild that lost identity. The one thing that enabled Arad and Perlmutter to engage potential investors was that the company still held its primary assets: its characters. Their superheroics would have to function on a meta-level, as Marvel looked to understand them anew in order to reclaim the former iteration of its identity. Once free from bankruptcy proceedings, phoenix-like, Marvel regained its position as market leader in 2002, became debt free by 2003 (Raviv, 2004: 280, 296) and once again attracted the reputation of a culturally prescient, innovative storyteller. Notably, this was recognized in instances such as its reaction to the 9/11 attacks on the World Trade Center,[6] and the politically charged, definitive post-9/11 superhero story *Civil War* (Millar and McNiven 2007).[7] A closer look at the era following the emergence from bankruptcy, and building towards the present, will illuminate how Marvel made decisions that reconstructed an identity that had been so fruitful for the organization in the past, and how it exploited its nature as a storytelling organization in order to publicly amplify the industrial narrative it was creating: that of a return to former glory.

As a bona fide new entity moving forward post-bankruptcy, Marvel could openly and clearly 'reboot' its identity, wiping away years of negative reflection under the auspices of starting anew. By taking such an action, not only could Marvel dissipate the negativity drawn to it through bankruptcy, but also attempt to wipe out the much longer period where it steadily drifted from its founding principles. It could remake its own image via a contemporary reimagining of those principles. This process can be understood as an organizational adaptation of a practice common in comic book publishing: the reboot. This act was in fact embodied at the time, by Marvel's decision to create a new 'Ultimate Universe' (UU).[8] The key point, perhaps, is that at the same time that the UU reboot established a new slate for content, removing, for new readers, years of intimidating canon formation, the 'corporate reboot' followed the same clarifying intention for the business community: a back-to-roots, prelapsarian blend of the ingrained and the contemporary.

The UU, which marked the arrival of writers that would gain particular acclaim with their stories at Marvel, notably Brian Michael Bendis (*Ultimate Spider-Man*) and Mark Millar (*The Ultimates, Ultimate X-Men*) – both of whom would be important to the later cinematic translation of Marvel's superheroes – sought to pinpoint the essence of what made Spider-Man, the Avengers and other characters so appealing in the 1960s, but make them relevant to a new audience. Newly appointed Head of Publishing, Bill Jemas justified the creation of the UU as a way to 'recruit new fans who would start a lifetime of involvement with Marvel' (Raviv, 2004: 266). This same concept would also be applied on a much bigger scale, as the Marvel characters finally made it to the silver screen. By authorizing and managing the return to successful principles, Jemas – as a marketing man whose route to Marvel came through one of its troublesome mergers: Fleer/SkyBox trading cards (265) – acted as a creatively sympathetic but commercially mindful businessman, the likes of which we have identified as serving Marvel well in the past, thus helping to bridge and re-balance creativity and commerce. Jemas's commercial contributions were noted by Raviv, remarking that he 'made some controversial cost-saving decisions that angered many distributors and comic book stores, but he proved effective for Marvel's cause. His decision to restart the stories of the biggest heroes ... proved successful in spurring sales' (279). As well as aiding in the industrial narrative that accompanied such an increase in sales figures, the ripples were felt more widely, with Raviv also highlighting Jemas's impact upon creativity, going on to note Marvel recapturing the positive attention of an industry which endorsed that 'the quality of both writing and illustration improved' (279). Jemas was put in post by the astute Perlmutter at the expense of Eric Ellenbogen, who, as an outspoken critic of financial constraints introduced by Perlmutter, considering them to be shackling the creativity of the company (255), did not represent the same balance between creativity and commercial reality. The market reaction validated what Jemas was setting in place: not unfettered creativity, but a sustainable system welcoming to creativity – albeit, managed creativity.

This balance between creativity and commercially sustainable choices recreated elements of the period Goodman presided over when Timely became Marvel, and Lee's talent for promotional gusto allowed allied creative forces to flourish. The individuals that, following the bankruptcy, most encapsulated this balance were the heroes of Marvel's rescue: Perlmutter and Arad. The pair are eloquently rendered by Raviv in his extensive account, with Perlmutter playing the part of the cold, astute businessman, but the quiet, austere type, in contrast to the ego-maniacal Perelman and Carl Icahn, who were then the Wall Street tycoons also vying, ultimately unsuccessfully, for control of Marvel. Arad is cast as the creative force balancing Perlmutter's seriousness, frequently described by Raviv in ways that underline a knowing affront to business conformity. Under this image lay a mercurial mind for creative opportunity: 'Avi Arad (in black leather, picking at his sandwich) listened for any sign that his love for the Marvel characters, for toy-designing, and for movie-making could be required' (2004: 129). In another instance, Raviv describes 'Avi's sartorial splendor' (221) when, at a private club with a distinct ties and jacket dress code, Arad 'wore his most magnificent black leather jacket with a colourful Spider-Man on the back' (221). Raviv explains that 'staid lawyers and businessmen ... marvelled at Arad, "Where did you get that jacket?" "I love that Jacket!"' (221). Thus, emphasizing Arad's ability to engage with investors by rendering Marvel's creativity in simple iconic form.

Once under repair, the Marvel ship was run on as austere lines as Perlmutter could achieve, yet just as with Goodman, it is widely seen that he accepted that creativity was vital in a creative company. Hence, setting him apart from Marvel's self-interested, short-termist owners, at a time when Marvel was being driven into the ground by Perelman, Perlmutter – then affiliated with Marvel via its exclusivity deal with his company Toy Biz – understood that creation was the path to avoid bankruptcy: 'Ronald, you have to start doing things – doing things to take advantage of the Marvel characters! You have to make movies and do all kinds of things so people are going to *talk* about Marvel' (Perlmutter cited in Raviv, 2004: 6; emphasis in original). Perlmutter actively concentrated on a long-term view of business, as evidenced during an anxious 2001 lull in Marvel's recovery, when quietly, away from the public light, he managed to exploit market fears in order to buy back a host of bonds – for which Marvel would have had to eventually pay out – at far below market rate (Raviv, 2004: 281).[9] While Perlmutter appreciated the protracted surgery needed to restore company health, Arad had the different gift to look at this and translate it into an exciting articulation of creative possibilities. With impassioned pleas, he communicated the same, not only to already converted fans, but also in many instances to executives and potential investors, urging them to see the value of this body of intellectual property (IP) brimming with potential. Raviv asserts that Arad, when addressing a room full of bankers and lawyers assembled during bankruptcy proceedings to decide the fate of Marvel, 'had become Marvel's strongest "true believer", Stan Lee's dream disciple, and his enthusiasm held the complete attention of his audience. So did any mention of numbers' (177).

Trade narratives and the introduction of the MCU

Once the more patient business presence of Perlmutter was installed at the top, replacing the self-interested immediacy typified by the likes of Perelman, Marvel regained a sense of stability. The first fruit to bear from such stability was the achievement, at long last, of bringing some of its most prominent characters to the big screen, and thus being exposed to a far wider audience than ever before.[10] Yet, due to the nature of the licensing deals that saw the release of films such as *Blade* (Stephen Norrington, 1998), *X-Men* (Bryan Singer, 2000) and *Spider-Man* (Sam Raimi, 2002) (all of which were followed by several sequels), whereby other studios had acquired the rights to produce films based on specific Marvel characters, Marvel could not competently control the effects that these releases had upon its identity. Due to the very nature of temporary licensing agreements, the studio behind a film's production could not be discouraged from focusing on the short-term profit potential as opposed to the long-term sustainability and wider exploitation of the characters featured therein. This led to a situation where, following the initial fanfare that came with the above-mentioned titles, poorly received sequels and other unsuccessful releases featuring Marvel's characters highlighted the potential damage that could be dealt to its reputation by association. This is evidenced by films such as *Spider-Man 3* (Raimi, 2007) being the highest-grossing film (worldwide) in that series ($890 million, compared to *Spider-Man*: $821 million and *Spider-Man 2* (Raimi, 2004): $783 million),[11] but having the poorest critical and popular reception (63 per cent on critic aggregator Rotten Tomatoes,[12] compared to *Spider-Man's* 89 per cent and *Spider-Man 2's* 93 per cent). The diminishing response was a damaging development for the franchise and a factor in its dormancy for five years; the antithesis of the stability Marvel required. Further, Marvel reeled from the severely damaged reputation of less immediately recognizable characters, typified in the release of *Elektra* (Rob Bowman, 2005) – a spin off from

Daredevil (Mark Johnson, 2003), itself recipient of a muted critical reaction – which was crushed with a 10 per cent Rotten Tomatoes rating. So although, on the whole, Marvel's identity benefited from the global recognition that its characters could take a place among cinema's highest-grossing, most thrilling properties, it was not in the long-term interest of Marvel for its characters – particularly those with potential but small fanbases – to be produced under conditions dictated by the short-term incentives of temporary licensing arrangements. The negative reaction to these films was not conducive to the story of success and resurgence that Marvel was trying to dictate. In fact, in 2015, Marvel's continued disadvantage due to such, still active, licensing deals is evident, as the Fox-produced *Fantastic Four* (Josh Trank, 2015) put a severe dent in the reputation of those prominent Marvel characters; its 8 per cent Rotten Tomatoes rating marks it as possibly the worst reviewed superhero film of all time.

The mixed success of the film licences from the first half of the decade still supported Arad's view that its characters – particularly its 'A' list – were suitable investment properties. A proposal was made that Marvel should put the cinematic rights to characters on the line as collateral, in order to acquire the finance it needed to produce its own films, bringing the characters to which it still held – or had regained – the cinematic rights, into the controlled environment of a newly formed Marvel Cinematic Universe (MCU). Arguably this development was both reflective of, and fuelled Marvel's continuing return to core principles, and thus significantly contributes to Marvel's current industrial standing and the de facto existence of 'Marvel Studios'. Therefore, in the next section, Marvel's originary identifying features highlighted throughout this chapter – the balance between art and commerce; the establishment of a shared universe; the cultivation of a sense of inclusivity derived from fan engagement; and the stability that allowed the identity around such features to form – will be rationalized within the context the of MCU's development. Aiding this, Marvel's use of various public relations tools (more specifically, what Derek Johnson (2012) terms 'trade narratives') will be emphasized. In his comprehensive article, particularly focusing on the brief period of MS's independence prior to its purchase by Disney, Johnson defines trade narratives as 'the self-reflexive trade stories that Marvel executives have deployed to legitimate their incursion into Hollywood production communities' (2012: 4), and adds that they have 'constructed Marvel's cinematic independence as commonsense – even as "destiny"' (2). He emphasizes that the ways in which Marvel executives have influenced the narrative telling of its resurgence should be paid serious attention:

> To understand the impact of these self-reflexive utterances, it is important to recognize them not as meaningless hot air spewing forth from the executive suite but rather as discursive acts rich with semiotic utility that had a significant impact on how Marvel could be imagined within the culture industries.

(2012: 15)

Taking control: Stability and a long-term focus

Marvel took control of producing its own films under the sign of stability reintroduced during Perlmutter's reign. It could control release schedules to better coordinate with other areas of the organization (see Chapter 6); it could also control the quality of production; and it could control the character traits scripted into the films, policing inconsistency which would help to increase long-term sustainability of characters' reputations. The instability present under The Townhouse's stewardship of Marvel made the development of even a single feature film unlikely, but in 2016, under its rejuvenated long-term approach to strategic planning, Marvel can impose its longevity by announcing features to be released up to five years into the future,[13] as well as hinting at development plans stretching further still.[14] Such stability harks back to the Lee/Kirby *Fantastic Four* run as well as other long-running creative continuities upon which that first Marvel Comics decade was built, and can be construed as a version of those days under Lee as EIC: a core, (mostly) trusted team enabled to make healthy decisions on characters' behalf, because given leave to do this by a lead creative with access to, and the trust of, the money men. Throughout the MCU's development, the ever-present Kevin Feige looks more and more like a film producer in the mould of an EIC. Like Lee, Feige is a strong, charismatic figurehead, whose image and patter lends itself to publicity, with a primary stated focus of channelling the creative abilities of others; yet is associated with elements of a creative – or at least creatively sympathetic – force. Mark Graser (2014a) highlights this stability within the studio, adding that it flows through Feige and the creative team assembled around him. Referring to Marvel's efforts to craft its public identity in the mould of its originary era (raising the 'Bullpen' camaraderie, real or imagined, that is synonymous with it), Graser subscribes to this historical view, in opining that MS's success has resulted from 'the consistency of having a core team of executives'. He cites MS Executive VP of Visual Effects and Post Production, Victoria Alonso: 'It's like having a family'.

Striking the balance: Art versus commerce

Akin to Goodman's rule, the stability within MS that is now provided by Perlmutter, is attributed to a hands-off, long-term business approach. Creative individuals are afforded the freedom they require, so long as the financial implications balance. Johnson believes that this reconciliation of art and commerce is a major thrust of the trade narratives created by MS, stating that its 'promise of imminent success ... hinged on making meaningful its expertise as a force of corporate management and control as much as its creative acumen' (2012: 16–7). This balance is at the root of Marvel's decision to move its cinematic endeavours, wherever possible, from licensing to independent production. Not only does Marvel profit more from the policy,[15] but it can also protect itself creatively, so that films based on its characters are not produced hastily, but fit into the well-planned architecture of a lasting franchise. The MCU allows – *requires* – Marvel to put the same level of investment, effort and care into more obscure characters as it would its established ones, because it benefits from their long-term viability[16] (see Chapter 6 for more on MS initiatives introducing, and investing in, different characters).

This balance can also be seen in the way that partnerships between executives and creatives function within MS. The nature of such a partnership is defined on an executive level by Feige: 'When we're looking for a partner in a director, writer or actor, it's to come into our sandbox and share in the temporary stewardship in whatever we're making' (Feige, cited in Graser 2014a). Echoing support of the creative value residing in this 'partnership' model, *Guardians of the Galaxy* (*GOTG*) director James Gunn remarks, in interview, of the experience he had with Marvel during the film's production: 'I felt, and I do to this day, feel unbelievably blessed, and truly truly grateful to Marvel. … Because I feel like I was able to make something that has that independent spirit to it. And I can't believe that Marvel allowed me to do that' (Gunn in Goldsmith, 2014). Yet, it must be stressed that despite efforts to craft its identity as one that is in harmony with creative personalities, it seems that Marvel still cannot fully rise above entangling issues of creative credit and freedom (recalling one of the rare negatives of the Stan Lee days), suggesting the selective and constructed nature of talk about creative-financial reconciliation and balance. Even the image struck in Feige's 'sandbox' metaphor – inviting others into *its* sandbox, implying ownership and a gatekeeping stance to what surely only makes sense as a place of spontaneity and the absence of rules – feeds ideas of control exerted in the name of maintaining coveted stability. Criticism of MS's relationship with creators, while not reaching crisis level and playing out mainly in knowledgeable fan/trade discourse, is nonetheless visible throughout its endeavours so far. Marvel has approached the cases of Edward Norton, Jon Favreau, Edgar Wright and others[17] not through denial, but by tolerating – to an extent – that artists will occasionally go off-message, and trusting in its *industrial storytelling* to control the narratives built around such developments, and manage the impressions they make. As can be seen in Feige's statement, MS supplies a message that individuals' creativity, although welcomed, must comply with house style as they 'share' temporary stewardship of these Marvel characters. On another view, of course, Feige's responsibility for the characters is enormous, and the lessons of the recent past advise caution. This forms the grounds on which MS defends such actions; as Johnson notes, the spectres of failures such as *Elektra*'s (or, to extrapolate beyond Johnson, that of the 2015 *Fantastic Four*) proving, in this sense, to be useful after all: 'Marvel's ability to manage the creative enterprise of filmmaking was framed as a necessity for commercial and critical success rather than as meddling by an outside executive office without filmmaking expertise' (Johnson, 2012: 17). The fact that Gunn's public comments noted above support this idea of partnership, and that the policies paid off in a film that was a success on all counts (see Chapter 6), helps Marvel to renew the narrative of dedication to creativity.

It is such iterations in the press that show how Marvel, as an organization of storytellers, understands the power of perception, and views the narrative built around industrial developments as a tool to mitigate some of the negative feedback faced in the past, and carve the desired identity as it becomes more established and moves away from early naivety. The mass exposure of MS releases, especially when pre-release indications are favourable, has afforded an extra platform on which to control such a public narrative, extending this not just to include comics operations, but even to retrospectively address negative press of the past. Accompanying the release of *GOTG*, Marvel made a specific point of acknowledging the contribution of Bill Mantlo, whose comic scripts first introduced the film's breakout star Rocket Raccoon (voiced by Bradley Cooper).[18] Mantlo was severely debilitated due to a traffic accident in 1992, which drew further attention to the public relations story that was circulated. This highlighted that Marvel had not only agreed a generous financial deal with Mantlo's brother and carer Michael, but also, working around legal barriers – thus, assisting the emergence of an image where Marvel seemed less rigid an organization – arranged a private family screening at Mantlo's care facility. Marvel's success at circulating the story can be measured by the amount of print and online publications using the same citations and press images,[19] alluding to a coordinated strategy on projecting a cohesive, favourable 'feel-good' story to the public. This is a feature of Marvel's public relations machine identified by Johnson: 'With the press reproducing one another's stories, statements made in one publication echoed in another' (2012: 15). The positivity reflected back onto Marvel's identity, and the discourses to which it could provide a corrective, emerged when an article from Dave Itzkoff (2014) appeared in *The New York Times,* criticizing Marvel and the comic book industry for the lack of credit afforded to creators. At this, Michael Mantlo struck out at the way he had been misrepresented, as reported by Graeme McMillan (2014): '[Michael] Mantlo contested the framing of the *Times* article in a Facebook post and wrote that the *Times* piece "made it seem as though Marvel has been unfair. … On behalf of Bill, Marvel and I have developed a solid, trusting, open, honest and more often than not an extremely compassionate relationship"'. At a time when it has been folded into Disney, a corporation so dominantly in charge of its meanings that critics speak of 'a destructive apparatus of control' (Budd, 2005: 12), MS's success may strengthen resources, but it also drives up costs and, perhaps, expectations; sympathy, in some cases, may be reduced. Although many other factors are at play, the studio attracts risks that could repeat history: becoming distanced from the source of creativity; losing the tag of 'underdog' that is common to both Howe's tale of early Marvel Comics and Johnson's scrutiny of trade narratives at the start of Marvel Studios. The benefits of succeeding in controlling such a narrative around the organization, syncing with positive mass exposure for *GOTG*, a relatively unheralded cinematic release bespeaking new depths in the creativity reserves (see Chapter 6), allows for the identity that Marvel desires to rebuild with global audiences. In branding terms, Ries and Ries (2000) stress the importance to an organization of telling its story through such an avenue, asserting that 'what others say about your brand is so much more powerful than what you can say about it yourself' (28).

Owning a concept: The shared universe

The strength of Marvel's 1960s system, of allowing creative individuals to create, resulted in a plethora of characters and stylistic innovations, but its signature achievement, and Marvel's lasting contribution to superhero comics, was the formation of the interconnected Marvel Universe (MU). At the time, this was a unique creative approach that singled Marvel out as significant among its competition. Now, the MCU is its cinematic equivalent, currently earning MS a defining feature and source for competitive advantage; an advantage that, although prone to emulation, requires a huge commitment to be taken on by rivals. The likes of filmmakers Jon Favreau, Shane Black, Joss Whedon and James Gunn have been able to use their imagination – albeit, as was the case in the 1960s, within the confines of Marvel's controlled 'sandbox' – to stoke innovation and thus add artistic legitimacy to Marvel's image. To recall Ries and Ries's (2000) overriding message identified earlier in this chapter, it appears that, as first to achieve the feat (at least, in superhero narrative), Marvel can 'own' the category of a large-scale shared cinematic 'universe', and therefore its brand can benefit from this commanding identification. The conscious emphasis on dominating that term and trait is evident in the very naming of the Marvel Cinematic *Universe*, as well as in the fact that at the earliest sign of intention becoming reality, a character – Nick Fury (Samuel L. Jackson), in the post-credits scene of *Iron Man*, explicitly announces the plan, informing Tony Stark: 'You've become part of a bigger *universe*. You just don't know it yet'. Such dominance is then reflected and supported in the unfurling trade narrative, as Kim Masters (2014) asserts that MS has 'prompted nearly every major studio to mimic its "universe" strategy for building franchises'.

Stan's Soapbox for the digital age: Fan engagement

Individual cinematic texts do not define the limits of Marvel's activities in crafting identity, as a look at the company's management of social media illustrates. A contemporary iteration of Lee's fourth wall-breaking address to consumers can be seen here, with the Women of Marvel Podcast[20] promoting itself, just as did Lee's 'Soapbox' columns and letter pages, as a dialogue between the organization and fans, and thus participating in Marvel self-narrativizing. The podcast is a regularly updated audio programme, hosted by various women within Marvel, including Adri Cowan (Social Media Manager), Emily Shaw (Comics Editor), Sana Amanat (Director of Content and Character Development), among others. The podcast's self-proclaimed aim is to 'talk all things Marvel'; it does so through running themed shows, covering conventions and interviewing guests both within and outside of Marvel. These have included Clark Gregg, who plays Agent Coulson in the MCU (ep 39); *Captain Marvel* author Kelly Sue Deconnick (eps 11 and 52); Cosplay artists such as Yaya Han (ep 27) and even particle physicists working on the Atlas Experiment, part of the Large Hadron Collider, who were brought on to talk about 'Marvel science' (ep 18). The mode of address used, although more collective, echoes Lee's, due to the hosts' jovial, self-deprecating admissions of fallibility and an informal tone that reduces distance between fans and professionals. Clearly, there are differences: media norms would not allow the method of interaction to stand still from print in the 1960s to podcasts today, however, a similar ethos exists. The show frequently encourages contact via social media with the individual hosts, and the show's many guests; this engaging inclusivity is embodied in the show's sign-off slogan: 'This is Marvel, *your* universe' (note once again the use of the word '*universe*', further compounding a belief within Marvel that its brand image particularly expresses dominance in this concept). One episode in particular (ep 11) is dedicated to an act of Marvel fan engagement, as it spotlights the fan-instigated, fan-led phenomenon known as the 'Carol Corps'. This is an instance of fandom that has grown around the character of Carol Danvers, since adopting the 'Captain Marvel' moniker (in *Captain Marvel* Vol.7, #1, 2012).[21] Showing Marvel's conscious cultivation of such a fan-derived activity and understanding of the contribution it can make to perpetuating a desirable story of an in-touch, fan-appreciative organization, series writer Kelly Sue Deconnick, elsewhere in interview with Rachel Edidin, discusses Marvel's handling of the title:

> Somebody somewhere [in Marvel] has made a call that they're backing this up. ... The book got a relaunch, and they kept me on it. That's not a thing that generally happens, you know? The Carol Corps is addressed specifically in the letter columns, in their social media outreach. Merchandise is starting to appear with Carol on it.

> (Deconnick cited in Edidin 2014)

The fact that this message – that such acts of fandom can be recognized by the organization – is projected to the public, assists Marvel in constructing an image of inclusivity. The Women of Marvel Podcast, along with the example of how Marvel has handled the development of the Carol Corps, is an example of how such a large organization can maintain an intimate, personable identity.

Conclusion

The above examples intend to illustrate that since the recovery from bankruptcy, Marvel has systematically deployed its storytelling resources and experience to redress the factors that led to a drift from its core principles, threatening its reputation, financial performance, and long-term viability. Marvel's inherent capacity to tell stories (and to tell stories about its storytelling) typifies the organizational approach as well as the product. The advent of the MCU shows that, once settling its business and proving anew its stability, the company has found ways to more effectively involve returning and new consumers in its extensive shared universe; but on an industrial level, Marvel has used the platform afforded by this to forge a narrative of its renewal, and ensure that the identity that served it well during the 1960s is perceived as having been restored. This scenario suggests that the underlying, originary identity of an organization is so strong that it can function as a homing beacon for it to retrace its steps after such a tumultuous period. The constantly circulating rise-and-fall narratives of superheroes in the texts, where classic identities are divested and then returned to (see Chapter 4), sets the pattern; it would seem that once core principles were reinstated (albeit adapted to suit the contemporary environment), Marvel's fortunes resurged.

Marvel's sustainability draws upon the competence with which its organizational affairs have been tended, but just as Webb, Turner and others attest, organizations are much more socially complicated than the 'muck and brass' view would imply. Further, as Ryan notes, an organization that operates in the culture industries has to negotiate the dichotomy between art and commerce in order to benefit from the creativity it produces, and to sustain the appropriate platform from which to reinvest in further creativity. When the policy choices of management led Marvel to weigh too heavily on one side of this relation – when, as an organization, it downplayed or even forgot about storytelling – it severed its recognized identity, disengaged fans, and drifted from its core principles into a mode of decline. We make this point allowing for the fact that *story* itself is a value that has a certain fictive, constructed and not innate quality (see Chapter 7). Marvel's recognition and re-embracing of its own tradition of storytelling played a major role in its recrafting of identity, created distinction within its competitive environment, and in the current phase, continues to provide the type of stability that guarantees a position as market leader, continuing to define this not only in business but also in creative terms.

CHAPTER 3
'DOTH MOTHER KNOW YOU WEARETH HER DRAPES?': THE GENRE TACTICS OF MARVEL STUDIOS

Introduction: 'Stark choices'

Looking back upon the moment of release of *Iron Man*, into an active (see Appendix: Timeline) but disconnected field for superhero cinema, one of the interesting elements to analyse is the opportunity to set new generic boundaries that was presented to MS, which, taking advantage of the vacuum of true shared universe superhero production, went ahead and inscribed such innovation as cornerstone to its own reputation. As we saw in the first two chapters, MS's combination of innovation and history seems to justify a reading in terms of allegorical 'studio stories'[1]: its texts/paratexts often revisiting its own creation and development, replicating in fiction its 'initiative' of bringing old and new Hollywood logics together. It is now time to turn to genre, in order to understand how Marvel's content and decision making come into focus through narratives which show an awareness of needing to situate the whole project within the landscape of cinematic superhero fiction.

With a connected story universe across platforms, it is obvious that while some consumers will engage with the full sweep of the MCU, the experience of others will be more partial and intermittent (the serial *Agents of S.H.I.E.L.D.*, for instance, adds nearly seventeen real-time hours to the body of the macro-narrative per season; a very different proposition from engaging with a summer blockbuster or two. See Chapter 8). Yet MS must appeal to both types of viewer profiles. Allied to this, certain desirable segments of the audience may not be aware of the lexicon and lore of superhero culture, Marvel-style, or attuned to ways of responding to texts that deliberately read for open-ended, explorable universes. This chapter argues that 'genres-within-genres', operating in a 'fractal' manner, can play a significant role in keeping this enterprise together and making it available for different levels of consumer engagement.

The recurrent themes and formal elements of a broader, historically informed action and adventure cinema structure become evident in MCU texts from the first exciting ambush of Tony Stark's Humvee in the Afghan desert, which comes shortly after the genre cue of hard rock music signals mayhem in *Iron Man*.[2] We begin, then, by examining how this film and franchise constituted an important textual statement of intent, and played on ideas of innovation diegetically and industrially. Setting aside, for the moment, the unavailability in 2008 of other well-known properties (tied up in franchise deals to competing studios), there were still choices from a considerable character repertoire. What made this property so fit for this purpose, and what did *Iron Man* do to embed the first signs of the emergence of MS as producer?

'I am Iron Man'

Progress in the MCU seems to involve deepening and expanding a kind of all-encompassing media virtuality. In a world-building sense, this furnishes an impressive level of detail, right down to the possession of an 'in-house' diegetic media network that consistently features in the margins of 'main' texts[3]; 'bulletins' from the WHiH 'network' (available on the web) round out the narrative prehistories of characters like *Ant-Man*'s Scott Lang and construct easily sharable narrative linkages between summer film releases (during a season when Marvel's TV shows like *AoS* are off-air). It is, then, fitting to begin with a vignette that feeds off the intense conviction in MCU textuality.

Born with a partially developed right arm, Alex Pring was seven years old when Iron Man came to visit in 2015. Presenting Alex with a 'Mk II' upgrade to his prosthetic limb was none other than his favourite 'superhero'. As Robert Downey Jr (sporting the trademark, pristine Stark facial hair) brandished two steel cases imprinted with 'Stark Industries' logo (another in-MCU organization), two matching Iron Man technology 'gauntlets' were eventually revealed. The difference, of course, is that one of these is a movie prop from the franchise that established MS, while the other is a fully-functioning 3D-printed bionic limb. Even Downey Jr is forced to admit that Pring's gauntlet 'might be better than [his]' (Office Videos, 2015). Before the limbs are field-tested, Pring is asked if he knows who his expensively suited benefactor is, and replies without hesitation: 'That's Iron Man'. The declaration cannot help but remind us of the finale of the character's introductory film, where Stark confesses to the world 'I am Iron Man'. Both lines invoke an intent of identifying with this character that Downey Jr regularly repeats offscreen in the social media realm (Kimble, 2015). 'I am Iron Man' was a significant textual moment in enabling later developments where Stark's notoriety complicates Iron Man's job, but also marked MS – before it had barely even started – dispensing with two things: a considerable part of the history of Tony Stark as rendered in the stock of Marvel Comics stories where, for decades, Iron Man was explained – even to his fellow Avengers – as the bodyguard of Tony Stark; and the previous principle that superhero narratives followed in privileging the 'duality' of the hero and civilian identity, or making risk of exposure of the latter into a plot point (as in various Superman, Batman and Spider-Man films).

In the Pring video, Downey Jr's 'portrayal' of Tony Stark and inclusion of his distinctive style and mannerisms leads to an apparent misidentification of the actor for the character he portrays; Downey Jr expresses palpable glee at this, although, when pushed, the child names the man as 'Robert'. Apart from the obvious financial gain of being indelibly associated with one the most visible icons of twenty-first-century popular cinema, this deliberate ambiguity of identity is an aspect of Downey's public persona that appears organic in how it connects up PR opportunity, publicity for a well-deserving cause (the low-cost production of bionic prosthetics), but also the breathing of extra life into the character which inevitably extends the Iron Man text. The filmed meeting, massively shared on social media, becomes an automatic performance for Downey Jr. As 'textually privileged assertions of superheroic identity' go (Koh, 2014: 485), the *IM* movie scene, although signalling that is MS going its own way, is somewhat consistent with other superhero narratives that place emphasis on heroic self-possession and the acceptance of destiny's call (although this is commonly done in visual, not verbal terms, as the closing shots of various superhero films attest).[4] As a startling moment of honesty, it also plays with the intertextual meanings of Downey Jr in a way that is somewhat rare for an MCU, the films of which tend to avoid 'lengthy pre-existing star narrative[s]' (2014: 486). However, the conscious blurring of identity in the Pring video is just as interesting as the movie scene, as a star seems to comment on their own surrender to the stronger meanings of a fictional world. The clip also functions to, perhaps, obscure or reframe some other associations of the Stark character – with the harnessing of research that supports (and formerly, exploits) defence policies in the name of private capitalist profitmaking in a hegemonic US-led security sector – for a use of science that is uncontroversially philanthropic in nature. Pring is clearly delighted, but to be more cynical, this is also an excellent way to crystallize the fact that MS holds a monopoly on superheroic meanings; dominates its competition, even, having the redeemed, formerly irresponsible 'Robert' or 'Iron Man' show up and spell out for a huge viral audience the power of identification, crossing over from viewer to star.[5]

Do MS texts present more than the usual levels of intentionality to genre assignation? A tendency to playfully combine genres, and even to make genre play legible within narratives, was not new even to classical Hollywood. However, the corporate atmosphere of the 1980s 'New Hollywood' phase (when we use Thomas Schatz's sense of this term)[6] seems to have contributed to style and signature becoming profoundly fused, whether a strong conventional *auteur* was present or not. This era saw the studio identity stretch across 'unauthored' genre products and convert them into messages on behalf of a particular company. Connor describes Paramount during the period when it became the home of 'High Concept' in the 1980s, remarking that it indulged in 'hyperstylization' of its own products as a way of assuming increased control: films that may have floated among the spaces of different genres became Paramount films 'because, and only because, of the work done to them by creative executives, crucial technical personnel, casts, directors and marketers' (2015: 186). These ripples are still felt today and perhaps tell us something about the conscious blurring of lines in terms of self-referentiality and the application of 'genre' within the MCU. *Iron Man* – marketed and distributed by Paramount for 'independent' neophyte producer MS – was important to this process.

'The weapon you only have to fire once'

The narrative of Jon Favreau's film commences with a tone that condemns risky, individualistic capitalism, as the convoy carrying Stark from his Afghanistan arms deal is attacked, just at the peak of his complacency.[7] Tony Stark seems to float outside social convention, and, to facilitate this, is deliberately (but, as a developer of arms, plausibly) set against the discipline and dutifulness of his Defence Department liaison James Rhodes (Terrence Howard; in later films Rhodes assumes the additional guise of War Machine and there is a casting change to Don Cheadle). In these early scenes, Stark is portrayed as an untrammelled, but soulful alpha-capitalist – confident that his products cannot be beaten, but spending his downtime tinkering with vintage cars. His is a new generation of capitalism; opposing Stark's swagger is the elder statesman of his company, Obadiah Stane (Jeff Bridges). From his first scene (faux-bashfully covering for Tony who has failed to turn up for an award presentation), Stane is presented as the old-school capitalist. A friend of Howard Stark, he appears a paternal figure but is quickly revealed to be intent on ousting Stark's son. With his front of acting in Tony's interests as surrogate father, he intends to entrench his control of the business for another generation by manipulating both Tony and ostensible terrorist group the 'Ten Rings', and weaponizing Tony's incredible innovation of the 'Arc Reactor'. This would take the company irrevocably into the moral quagmire of supplying international terrorism.

As the film intended to trademark MS's new genre offering, *Iron Man* wants to set innovation in a particular frame. Marvel's origin for Iron Man dates from 1963,[8] and saw Stark kidnapped and coerced by North Vietnamese forces into building high-tech weaponry; but, as in Favreau's film, he turns his technological genius against them. What worked as a straightforward intersection of narrative and theme and 'entertaining medium through which to address … American insecurities' (Fellman, 2010: 12) for Marvel Comics in 1963 requires adjustment for an Iron Man origin, 2008-style: the idea that the United States needs to suppress Communism and weapons are needed to do this will no longer cover it. A master of innovation and enterprise is ordered to make weapons of mass destruction, the likes of which his captors have been freely buying anyway; this notion can only be brought off with a lot more hedging qualification. Thus, Stark's work on defence contracts is made ambivalent, with an honourably represented media even enlisted, calling Stark out on his warmongering[9] and opening up a narrative thread that sustains throughout the MCU. This holds that corporations (as well as unelected institutions with huge power like S.H.I.E.L.D. – see Chapter 5) must have their internal processes brought into the light, which applies to Stark's firm, Cross Technologies in *Ant-Man*, or one of several more featured under untrustworthy oligarch figures like Wilson Fisk (Vincent D'Onofrio) or Ian Quinn (David Conrad) in the television shows.

The boardroom battle or intrigue has in fact solidified its status as a generic preoccupation of the superhero narrative, with heroes like Stark, Hank Pym (*Ant-Man*), Bruce Wayne (Christian Bale – *Batman Begins*, 2005) and even villains like Norman Osborn (Willem Dafoe – *Spider-Man*) having to respond to hostile takeovers. At some level, however much the superhero film refuses to trust the paternalistic, smiling guardians of power like Obadiah Stane, the question of replacing their position with something completely different is never seriously broached.[10] With even more ambivalence, evidencing what producers calculate as requirements for popular entertainment, the politics of such anti-business discourses are kept carefully balanced. In MCU terms, a telling example exists in the Wikileaks-style hacker/alternative media group 'Rising Tide', prominently featured in *AoS*. Such a group could be positioned as the natural contemporary opponent of military-industrial complex venality, but the text ensures that it is just as vulnerable to corruption and the temptation to sell to the highest bidder (S1E5, 'Girl in the Flower Dress'). A more extreme version of anti-globalization and anti-US hegemony, the 'Ten Rings' organization that is responsible for unrest in Afghanistan (achieved using Stark Industries weaponry), and which originally attacks and captures Stark, hypocritically feeds off and allows itself to be used by the form of ultra-capitalism represented by the treasonous Stane. Private enterprise and the appearance of terrorist threat are interwoven throughout the franchise and generally throughout MCU texts; acutely so in *Iron Man 3*, where a sinister research corporation successfully pins its malpractice upon a fictionalized incarnation of the 'Ten Rings'. It is hard not to see this shift in terms of popular cinema's turn to the 'theme of corporate greed operating behind the visible menace' (Calbreath-Frasieur, 2014: 26), an often unconvincing but nevertheless visible liberal strand in a blockbuster format that, when it turns to more progressive agendas, tends to find only parts of the state and the capitalist system responsible, rather than the whole.[11]

Stane's capitalism is confused and particularly hostile to the moral spirit of innovation. At one point he happily paints himself as the unfair thief of IP: 'Do you really think that because you have an idea, it belongs to you?', as he addresses the (by implication) creative but naïve Stark. Stane's will to steal is positioned as his chief force, but at other times, he is a cruel downsizing manager (telling employee Pepper Potts (Gwyneth Paltrow), 'Your services are no longer required'). Tony Stark's conversion to the ways of peace is doubled up with the triumph of one form of capitalism over another (the latter, Stane's, is one which will do business with anyone, including terrorists). An individualist character journey to redemption, and restitution for the damage he has caused, is provided for Stark, but only in a very narrow sense can the film be said to enact liberal takes on business and the military. The Department of Defence collaborated with MS on the production, and *Iron Man*'s energizing of the concept of American innovation (allied to the sympathetic depiction of Colonel Rhodes) proved an opportune moment for the cross-promotion of Air Force technologies around communications and protective combat exoskeletons (years later, the Falcon would sport a different model of exoskeleton in *CA:TWS*). As our main priority is genre, we shall not pursue further discussion of the ideological implications of this close, 'militainment'-style relationship, but these aspects receive close consideration in Mirrlees (2013: 7–9).

Connected to this, though, the film does explore the notion of empire building, looking critically at those with ambitions to form them (an apparent leader of the Ten Rings, played by Faran Tahir, lionizes Genghis Khan for controlling lands 'four times the size of the Roman Empire'), but enjoying the spectacle of Stark breezily rejecting the notion of steady payment of what is due: 'Render unto Caesar that which is Caesar's', he quips to a colourfully garbed employee, while exiting the famed casino, and giving away his 'Apogee Award' without a thought. This follows a scene where the audience at the Apogee awards ceremony is shown a hagiographic montage of Stark (Stane lurks in the wings) that explicitly associates him with the flag of the United States. The video even uses the phrase 'the passing of a titan' in relation to Stark's father, solidifying a distinct referential connection to a similar montage in another examination of American individualistic industry: *Citizen Kane* (Orson Welles, 1941). Like the hubristic Kane, Stark controls an empire; although Stane's manipulations are masked by business-as-usual when the film starts, his opponent is left in a position of mastery – albeit with new ideals – by the end. The size and dominance of empires are not in themselves bad, but who is doing the building needs to be watched. There is no clear objection (one with which audiences might sympathize) to the individualistic journey which Stark is on, until he encounters Captain America in *The Avengers*. What is perhaps most important about *Iron Man*, as the first MCU release, is letting Stark/Downey Jr's 'voice' ring out. Less straight-laced and self-evidently noble, more comedically narcissistic than previous superhero alter-egos, MS used Stark as a friendly global entertainment weapon with which to present itself to the world. By smart, precise 'challenges to the superhero movie formula' it helped 'set the stage' for later imperial developments (Calbreath-Frasieur, 2014: 28).

Genre raiding

We will spend a little time returning to some genre 'basics' before going any further. This will be beneficial, since the situation as it applies to the superhero text is not straightforward, and clarity of terminology and position is needed. The genre among which MCU superhero films nestle is the action-adventure genre.[12] Films in this area – at least, the high-budgeted ones – carry huge expectations and assumptions stemming from the notion that they are closer to the sources of studio economic power than are other traditions, and that the regularity with which they multiply into franchises can level audience tastes, ultimately leading to a stifling of the variety of cinema. It is rare, therefore, for 'action' as a term to be discussed without 'blockbuster' attending closely behind. Matt Hills affirms that where blockbuster classification is concerned, questions of value seem inextricable from economic definitions: 'Blockbuster status is indeed conferred and contested in struggles over cultural status' (2003: 180). Barry Langford points out serious limitations to the idea of the 'action blockbuster' as supplying the consistent shape necessary for a genre attribution; among very valid reasons he cites are that 'excessive scale … and consumption' are neither iconographic nor thematic properties (Film Studies usually looks for genre in terms of these criteria and how they become coded into narrative designs which are stable and repeatable enough to transcend individual cases – Maltby, 1996: 114). Langford goes on to pinpoint the 'rampant generic hybridity' often exhibited in the tradition as further complicating matters, suggesting that it is difficult to locate 'action' because it is so prone to merge with its close genre neighbours such as science-fiction, fantasy and the crime film (2005: 233–4). We will shortly see the point about innate hybridity echoed from within comic practitioners' commentary on superhero fiction. Nevertheless, Langford settles on the position that 'reliable constants' can be found in the textuality of large-scale action films, indicating that these comprise of: spectacular action sequences (supplying iconographic requirements); stable, repeatable narrative structures (a 'thin' spine leading off into weakly connected set-pieces), and a lack of emotional and psychological depth, squeezed out by lack of 'space', if not interest (234).

Tasker (2004) applies more of a historicized sense to how action/adventure have become contested terms with a flexible set of meanings; they may not form 'secure generic objects' but do allow for a series of nuanced designations that remain open enough to make use of, not be threatened by, that hybridity of which Langford speaks (action/fantasy, action thriller and so on – 2004: 3–4). Here is the territory where we might find productive clues to bolster our sense of where superhero films sit, particularly as in passing throughout this book, we note that different MS texts clearly position themselves with a relevance that is counted in genre values: *AoS* as high-tech espionage procedural; *CA:TWS* as a paranoid 'New Hollywood'-style conspiracy thriller; *Agent Carter* as period, semi-*noir* 'buddy' show with a feminist slant; *Ant-Man* as 'family-adventure'[13] with heist elements, and so on.

Tasker returns to definitions of action-adventure in a more recent work (Tasker, 2015). Still respecting the broad and numerous palette of sub-genres residing within action-adventure, Tasker sets out more superhero cinema-specific commentary (its increased exposure in her account reflecting the rising priority of the superhero cycle in the Hollywood environment). Her findings add a few pertinent nuances, such as a need to organize narrative in a way which will justify 'fascinating sites of action' (2015: 181), reflective of a thematic drive towards exploring the transformed body (allowing for digital FX to be shown off). The superhero narrative partakes of action's general fixation on 'the quest for freedom from oppression … the hero's ability to use his/her body … physical conflicts or challenge, whether battling human or alien opponents or even hostile natural environments [all of which] are fundamental to the genre in all its manifestations' (2015: 2).

Tasker continues by saying that, linked to this, the superhero body carries more ambivalent meanings in terms of the narrative functions released by super powers (often via the once-ubiquitous[14] origin story trope, where this ambivalence marks 'relationships to authority and society', and sees the new hero struggle to return to previous relationships with family and community (181)). Fidelity to the visual traditions of comics, as well as the need for clear character incarnations for ancillary marketing, demands a certain typicality in depictions of the superhero physique. Radical costume changes don't always go down well with fans, but, although figure-hugging costumes remain in vogue in the MCU for men and women, the most generically centred iconographic feature of superhero dress – the cape – has played a limited part so far (so long as we accept that Asgardian fashion codes dictate that Thor's garment is a cloak, and it is true that they are worn widely across Asgardian citizenry and do not have seem to have an identity-related function).[15] The sites at which Marvel sanctions a certain deviation from conventional genre associations, as in costuming, keys in to the idea of seeking to control or reshape expectations. Another way of looking at this invokes the idea of Hollywood studios homogenizing superhero adaptations in a way that brings them into line with those norms of 'realism' which obtain in action-adventure. Here, the insertion of Captain America into more combat-friendly garb (which follows the sending up of his traditional appearance in comics, in *CA:TFA*)[16] and other adjustments for realism also can be read as compensation for the insecurity about an inherent silliness to these narratives. Tony Stark's ridiculing of Thor for his 'Shakespeare in the Park' appearance and for wearing his 'mother's drapes' as battle attire in *The Avengers* thus follows such as *X-Men* (2000), where characters joke about being expected to wear spandex.[17] Yet, there may be other motives to the attempt to link superheroes to figureheads from more normative sectors of the action-adventure family, as we shall explore later.

Although the specific role of the body and other genre textures are noted by Tasker, and we will find them and many others in the course of this work, they are – obviously – versions of things that apply to other strands of a broader action tradition, too (notably the Western, many elements of which migrate into science-fiction in the 1970s). All this reminds us that the action template integrates narrative in a limited, fixed and repetitive way. The way that time and space interrelate to generate plot in the action tradition is abstractly formal (see Flanagan, 2004b), designed to privilege ritualized motifs which – allowing for variance of factors like the intended audience – permit degrees of violence, spectacle, and FX. Occasionally, this simplicity in the action form has been seen in a slightly more positive historical light as a modern persistence of qualities dating back to the earliest magical appeal of cinema (Bather, 2004: 41).

As well as their linear force and pace, action's abstract formalism often dictates matters where characterological motive and 'depth' are concerned (although a surface/depth model of regarding meaning, comparatively, across types of film presents a range of problems). The reputation of action films has perhaps moved on from being classed as the textual epicentre of modern Hollywood's structural 'incoherence' (Schatz, 1993: 32–4), reflecting how films in the tradition tended to be seen in the 1980s and 1990s, but the genre situation certainly remains cloudy. Superheroes are inarguably the biggest news in action-adventure since the turn of the millennium, and some of the recent narrative cycles which centralize them could justifiably form evidence of a contribution to extending the rather one-dimensional parameters defining the action genre as outlined above. Christopher Nolan's Batman cycle, Sam Raimi's Spider-Man films, and – arguably – some of the MCU films could all be offered up here, whether on the basis of narrative innovation (or, at least, added narrative density, often worked through, consciously, over the course of multiple films and hence expressing industrial discourses of franchise-based convergence), or their increased thematic engagement towards social realities (see Chapters 3 and 7). We could also look at the extension of cinematic ideas of masculinity in some of the above examples, and in M. Night Shyamalan's original yet hugely archetypal superhero feature *Unbreakable* (2000), among others. Yet, what would it mean to offer them in this way? Popularity, critical endorsement and box office can serve to take a film away from the natural genre placement conferred by its textual features; increasing the legitimacy of the genre frame by arguing for a repositioning because a text is endowed with qualities of maturity, irony, innovation or genre self-examination is not an automatic boon for the popular filmic product (Jancovich, 2001, *passim*). Genre distinctions are constantly opening up to new calibrations in popular film taste, making any genre or sub-genre a moving target.

Hooked on a blissed-out feeling…

The question deserving attention is not whether superhero films have *value*, but how we can best situate the MCU films' functions in terms of recognized ideas of genre, and how this contributes to the viewer's making sense of the text. Our position is that it is not possible to be entirely comfortable with the constitution of superhero cinema as a 'genre', yet we can still isolate its features in a way that is useful for our overarching project: the demonstration both of continuities and breaks in MS's articulation of blockbuster practice.

As Langford notes, it is not uncommon for action cinema to embrace multiple genres simultaneously into its textuality, to the extent that flux becomes naturally embedded in the genre's definition. A degree of hybridity has been a systematic feature of Hollywood's attitude to genre production since the 1970s, with examples of mixing also found further back (Collins, 1993: 244–5). Perhaps we need to adjust the whole frame for looking at the MCU in terms of genre. Instead of isolating the differences which introduce hybrid genre flavours, or trouble the assumed constraints of superhero cinema, or serve agendas of 'legitimising' the field by speaking of formal maturation, perhaps we should appreciate what it is that *grounds* these texts, cutting inexhaustibly across types of platform, but also referential periods, and sectors of audience (see the discussion of Netflix in Chapters 1 and 8).

The trick that MS has performed so well is to build a considerable shared universe and let genre, and the insertion of referential material, provide a map to the shifts in tone that must be negotiated to get the best from it. This, we would propose, occurs via a complex combination of elements and discourses, interacting in a way that can be summed up in the notion of a 'genre fractal'. A fractal version of something is a miniaturized replica, a repeat of the pattern in a scaled-down form; in the sense of genre, we apply it as a way of imaging the content of one genre, reduced and nestling in the territory of another one. Showing that film genre behaves in a recursive fashion, the fractal genre element is like a miniature 'sample' (the musical sense of the word applies), or encapsulation of another genre, used – in its specific deployment by MS – to help carry the meaning of a text derived from superhero fiction in a way that meshes it with filmic value. That MS has experienced success in this practice seems to be underlined by ecstatic social media responses like those that greeted a popular image of *CA:TWS*. The poster by erstwhile Marvel Comics artist Paolo Rivera applies a 1970s painted realism to Cap and other characters of the film, constructing a 'fractal' relationship with slanted genre precursors like *Chinatown* (Roman Polanski, 1974) and, particularly, *Three Days of the Condor* (Sidney Pollack, 1975, and which shares a star, Robert Redford, with the MS film).[18] In this reference to a much-admired period of film history, the words 'Captain America' are interestingly left off Rivera's version, suggesting an embarrassment about superheroics – seen as the thing holding Marvel productions back from true film classic status – that we discuss elsewhere in this chapter. Yet, Marvel commissioned the poster, showing, perhaps, an awareness of these issues.

Fractal genre instances replay in microcosmic form the 'world-building' labour that has gone on in constructing the MCU, where tonally disparate texts are shown to nevertheless be related (just as was always the case with the universe in comics). This will clearly be the case when the *Defenders* miniseries arrives on Netflix, to unite the 'street level' heroes of New York (see Chapter 8) in a scaled-down replica of the process that generated the first Avengers extravaganza. But genre play in the MCU is not limited to self-reflection. Perhaps the key text in the MCU releases so far to bring into play values from elsewhere in genre history, while respecting what has gone on in other corners of the shared universe, is *GOTG*. This film loops enthusiastically and effectively between genres and eras, and although we look at it through a different lens in Chapter 6 (since it contains a rich seam of ideas surrounding originality and differentiation at various levels), a brief reading now follows with the aim of showing that the genre product that exhibits self-knowledge could as easily be seen as following, not breaking orthodoxy.

Quill in the genre playground

Among many interesting moments during the sojourn of Peter Quill, AKA 'Star-Lord' (Chris Pratt) on the planet 'Morag' near to the beginning of *GOTG* is the glimpse we get of the tech which Quill possesses. Where Stark has to fight off the deadening hand of old-school capitalist and Oedipal competition to innovate, Quill (whose own 'daddy issues' are present but seem to be being teed up for a future film) boasts devices which explicitly conjure the past. Superficially, we might note his boot jets, which would probably satisfy a child's hopes for space exploratory equipment, but he also wields some kind of compass/tracker device which sweeps the empty landscape and immediately projects for him the living past of this desolate place. Little vignettes open up to his view in three-dimensions, such as a small girl petting a dog. It is interesting that Quill navigates his scavenging of space treasures by use of technology that collapses time and allows two zones to be experienced at once in the same place. The real biographies of those who were once citizens of Morags are thus rerun for viewer Quill in terms of tropes and units of narrative from a selection of history that can be experienced again. Not to labour the point, but here in microcosm is a similar blurring of life-into-entertainment (and vice versa) seen earlier with Alex Pring's story. This will not be the only occasion in the film that Quill feels the pain and pleasure of nostalgia, and indeed uses it to map his mission.

Mere film minutes earlier, the craft which abducts the juvenile Quill is presented for audience admiration via a spectacle of hovering metal and pulsating lasers reminiscent of the Spielbergian 'motherships' of 1970s/80s cinema seen, to great effect, in *E.T.: The Extra-Terrestrial* (1982) and *Close Encounters of the Third Kind*. More than the ship design, the lighting and Quill's response cues the audience to reproduce his stare in wonder (his initial attraction to the empty space where the ship manifests works only in the logic of his flight from the emotional devastation of his mother's approaching death). Nigel Morris discusses Spielbergian cinema's distinctive use of a light that cues spectacle for viewers, but also sets up a transcendent experience for the character who receives an address from the metaphysical realm:

> Having evolved this visual style, called 'God Lights' after childhood experiences of similar emanations in a synagogue, Spielberg continues using it in conjunction with protagonists' desires. ... Characters are repeatedly attracted to light, awestruck, their faces illuminated by their projected vision.
>
> (Morris, 2007: 13)

Morris goes on to cite Richard Combs' connection of the fascination of Roy Neary (Richard Dreyfuss), whose visions interact with 'God Lights' in *Close Encounters*, to the address to viewers of Spielberg's film, noting that the spectacular light which 'draws audiences' in also fixes the film's self-reflexive discourse: 'What the film is "about", in a way, is its own illusionism' (Combs, cited in Morris, 2007: 13). *GOTG* is meant to be a fun entertainment, no doubt, but the way in which it connects the emotional shock and gravity of family and Quill's apparent orphaning with the heightened pleasure of a contemporary Hollywood special effects extravaganza cannot fail to conjure Spielbergian cinema (and it is notable that other directors of James Gunn's generation have also been busy 'remixing' this in recent years).[19]

When the action cuts suddenly to a starscape, in orbit of Morag, possible viewer distress or confusion at Quill's bereavement or abduction has been assuaged – as mentioned in the Introduction – by the famous MS logo sequence. The change in terms of environment is drastic (as MCU watchers, we visit space for the first time since *The Avengers* and *Thor: The Dark World*, but this time the sense is that we are going to get to know it properly, through the eyes of somebody like us), and quickly accompanied by a caption that alerts us to the temporal jump ('26 years later') from the 1988 of the hospital scene. Again, a collapse of time that could be jarring is soothed away by a reassuring brand promise, which helps embed a transition from a traumatized boy of maybe ten years old to a self-confident, slightly clowning, but physically skilled man. If there is something familiar about the switched tone, the bridge provided by trusted branding, and the feeling of slightly adolescent joy that soon undercuts the mystery of the first moments on Morag, it is because the exact form of cinematic time zone which is being invoked is that of Spielberg and Lucas; one which many of us have experienced before. The filmic worlds of those directors and of some of their collaborators (Joe Dante, John Landis, Ron Howard) defined a blockbuster paradigm for a generation. Yet, the works of Lucas and Spielberg came with a critical admonition that a 'bliss-out' cinema was the entertainment industry's mollifying solution to the social anxieties of the 1980s – the decade that Quill has left back on Earth.[20]

That may not be completely obvious as the film gets underway, but the presence of totems of 1980s culture soon becomes hard to miss since Quill's human cultural references are locked into the period predating 1988: the prologue scene and the existence of the 'Awesome Mix volume 1' music cassette he carries into space suggest that this period has been heavily mediated for Quill by his mother. A subtle awareness of ideas of cross-generational enjoyment of pop culture, further cementing links to the Spielbergian 'family-adventure' prototype (as outlined in Chapter 7), is thus detectable. Further, it serves to declare MS, subsidiary of Disney, as staking a claim on a certain family entertainment space on which the following year's explicitly family-oriented *Ant-Man* will seek to build. Quill's Walkman cassette is his most prized possession, and the music on this consciously antiquated-yet-hip retro format also helps lend an identity to *GOTG* in a way that helps the film carve out its particular pop culture-commercial space. In narrative terms, the tape is a link not only to his mother – music chosen for him, it seems, a special, durable bond created paradoxically through supposedly ephemeral pop – but also to the culture of his lost Terran upbringing. This way of culturally freezing time, we can imagine, assuaged some feelings of terror upon the boy's initial abduction. The playlist contained on the tape exceeds the diegetic space as a major portion of the film's soundtrack, however. The appearance of the 'Awesome Mix' cassette became an icon of marketing materials, and the related album – released through Disney Music Group's Hollywood Records – was said to have sold 2.5 million copies worldwide in 2014 alone (IFPI, 2015: 12). The album reached #1 in the overall Billboard album sales chart in August that year (Caulfield, 2014), amusingly equalling the achievement of the soundtrack album for one 1980s Paramount production specifically referenced by Quill several times as part of his personal pop culture imaginary: *Footloose* (Herbert Ross, 1984).

While elsewhere in the MCU, Captain America struggles with his teammates' modern references, and works proactively to find shared cultural ground, the galaxy's wild frontiers pose a specific existential challenge that inclines Quill to ground himself retrospectively, via his earthbound possessions and reverentially preserved memories, from his mother's bubble gum pop to the *Alf* trading cards seen on his craft.[21] Ambiguously going to work alongside mercs 'the Reavers', equipped with a genre-respecting cowboy duster, gunmanship and a self-image of 'legendary outlaw', Quill finds himself in a universe not too dissimilar from that of *Star Wars*, or the *Firefly* universe of Joss Whedon himself,[22] signalling affinities between *GOTG*, the space opera, and the Western and Samurai echoes that are trailed by that science-fiction sub-genre (see Chapter 6).

As Quill explores Morag, the mist, low levels of light, distance of the camera and slightly obscure framing (as well as Quill's possession of a protective space-faring mask not too dissimilar in function and appearance to that worn by Iron Man) consciously conjure memories of a similarly vague introduction to a franchise hero: that of Indiana Jones in the talismanic *Raiders of the Lost Ark*. That film carefully holds Harrison Ford's face back from the audience until the object of his pursuit is in sight, forcing identification both with the star and also with the mission. After its generically uncertain start – atmospherically but moodily keying the powerful, lonely emotions of Spielbergian protagonists even to the inclusion of 'God Lights' – the older Quill is suddenly being depicted as the star, emphasizing a change from the distraught and helpless boy of the opening. Yet, Quill will always have something of the kid about him.

Heightening our awareness that 1980s genre cinema will be a bountiful source in framing this text (also in saying something about Gunn's tastes, and, beyond this, how MS plugs itself into the genre terrain), the pleasures being rekindled or adapted here solidify around two types of choreography, consisting of a sort of blend between the tense artefact pursuit of the aforementioned opening of *Raiders*, and the dance scenes of *Footloose*. As Quill hits 'play' on his Walkman, his dancing sequence floats relatively free of narrative weight (surprisingly successfully given the nature of the hospital scene), just as the featured songs of *Footloose* were not diegetically sung by cast members (breaking with film musical tradition), and were pre-designed to be sold via an association with the text that could be reassembled into music videos, yet defined the film in a strange kind of performativity (Connor, 2015: 180–1). The heroes of both Paramount blockbusters echo in Quill's persona (*Footloose* star Kevin Bacon is mentioned twice in *GOTG*): this is a persona that is capable but undisciplined, Peter Pan-like in its indeterminate age (this applies to the often selfish and clumsy Jones in particular), heroic but drenched in camp pop significance. Beyond being characterological touchstones for Quill, the references are also thematic signposts of content. Beyond genre, even, the play of references indicates where this film should be filed in terms of its wider industrial family tree: self-justifying its *bricolage* of '80s favourites with reference to Quill's situation, and what he might cling to, to remind him of a lost mother.

The film and music references are, perhaps, there to do more than amuse one demographic, to shift albums for Disney, or to send parents home keen to replay beloved movies for their kids. In an MCU-wide context, Quill's entire situation carries a slight sadness in that, just like that other genre and period wanderer Steve Rogers (Captain America), profound dislocation in narrative time and space renders him unable to participate in his contemporary community (or at least would if he visited Earth, and it is difficult to imagine that he will not).[23] This is captured well by the free-and-easy, 'everyman' associations, and sitcom-gauche performance style of Chris Pratt, a striking piece of casting with a sense of more writers/star-interaction creating the character than many other Marvel heroes.[24] These elements neatly give Quill narrative justification. He is a throwback: robbed of a family and a historical experience, but still able to have fun with it; a man out-of-genre.

Quill's new 'family' is the Guardians, for whom he forsakes the Reavers; but in an allegorical sense, his family will be the MCU and its library of misfits. Interesting, then, that so much in the parts of the film dealing with Benicio del Toro's Taneleer Tivan/'Collector' reflects on the sadness in the idea of trapping and containing one-offs. Tivan – for no particular good reason – removes creatures from their ambient cultures and inserts them into a rambling library of species (see the discussion of Howard the Duck in Chapter 6). Tivan is a figure – if we wish to make connections across the studio landscape – for the conglomerate raider hell-bent on preserving behind glass what is special about the independent (this can be noted as part of a series: we see exactly the same function in the role of villainous Al (voiced by Wayne Knight) in *Toy Story 2* – see Chapter 7).

This idea of being against hermetic segregation and for interference and play could be applied to the idea of how living specimens of genre can thrive. But of course, cultural orphan Quill starts out as a thief of precious artefacts, greedy like his role model Indiana Jones (or the pre-redemption Tony Stark), so the activity is not fully condemned. There is something to the cheeky coexistence of two time zones in this film's aesthetics and diegesis (accentuated by the signifiers of Earth pop culture ephemera adorning Quill's craft the Milano,[25] and the Walkman's 1970s/80s playlist), that seems to anxiously justify but also narrativize a process of pleasure-through-nostalgia. Koh notes an 'ahistorical climate' as a feature that accompanies the increased Hollywood prioritization of what he terms the superhero 'metagenre' (2014: 496), and thinking as we are about the genre-jukebox approach in popular film, it is unwise to neglect Frederick Jameson's observations of 1980s cinema. Jameson (1992) cites several films (including *Raiders of the Lost Ark*) wherein what is communicated by nostalgia is the shape of the art of a quoted period, not the period (in any sense of lived socio-historical 'reality') itself. This does seem apposite for the way that Gunn's film – with its comic musical sequences, reconstructed 1980s hero and heavy use of pop music now on its third 'lease of life' (such as 'Hooked on a Feeling', a song which gained its first major revival via a Quentin Tarantino film), is positioned in relation to genre forerunners.[26] It can incorporate them as 'fractals' and consume their value without being obliged to invest energy in a structure that reflects their sources. All this is not to say, though, that the film does not present a combination that is fresh in a MS context; *GOTG* steps away from superheroics to form a strategy that opens the MCU to contain more genre diversity. We would not expect *Captain America: Civil War*, say, to follow its referential lead. Indeed, generally speaking, reviews met the film as a 'risky' gamble that paid off, and we contextualize its rather surprised reception with a discussion of the element of risk in Chapter 6.

Conclusion: Continuing Marvel's genre story

Approaching the superhero texts presented under the MCU banner through the lens of genre requires care. MS has imparted a definite stratification that sets *GOTG* apart from *Captain America: The First Avenger*, say, or *Agents of S.H.I.E.L.D.* from *Jessica Jones*, but keeps the potential pathways between them open. The messages coming from within Marvel (or in the example that follows, Disney management) sometimes make interesting reading, emphasizing that MS wants to operate across genre fields but is unwilling to relinquish primacy of its superheroic 'strategic group' (see Chapter 2). Walt Disney Studios' Chairman Alan Horn discusses Marvel's genre profile:

> HORN: I think there are delineations. *Captain America* [*The Winter Soldier*] is
>   a spy movie to us, in many respects. *Thor* is a Shakespearean drama in some
>   respects.
> INTERVIEWER: And what is *Iron Man*?
> HORN: *Iron Man* is a superhero movie. (*Laughs*.)
>
> (McClintock and Masters, 2014)

'Iron Man is a superhero movie': the line, applied to Marvel, uncannily recalls the character's own definition of self ('I am Iron Man'). The tendency to apply the label of superhero to anything sourced from a Marvel comic must recognize that superhero-based meanings contain their own distinctions; as we have said elsewhere, many (but not all) aspects of the MCU cleave to an era when superhero comics, though striving for 'relevance', were less informed by the fractal genre strategies that are now established as an organic part of contemporary comics.[27] Grant Morrison, a renowned comic practitioner and one-time Marvel author with decided leanings towards the revisionist in terms of his own approach to superheroics, offers 'costumed superheroes' in a further level of delineation:

> I'm not even sure if there is a superhero genre or if the idea of the superhero is a special chilli pepper-like ingredient designed to energize other genres. The costumed superhero has survived since 1938, constantly shifting in tone from decade to decade to reflect the fears and the needs of the audience.
>
> (Morrison, cited in Anders, 2009)

Morrison's comment posits that superhero genre boundaries are open in ways that promote vibrancy and the evolutionary process. The MCU is, of course populated by superheroes, but the terminology breaks down when texts like *Agent Carter* come into focus; considered as a whole, the absence of Captain America was just one aspect of the show, and a clever way was found to reflect Carter's emotional state for her off-screen lost love, while slowly building up material on the early days of S.H.I.E.L.D. and priming the idea of a world that would need to develop an infrastructure for dealing with a powered community (see Chapters 4 and 5).

If pronouncing the superhero film a 'genre' is not satisfactory, then action-adventure appears our best recourse to describe in established film genre language what it is that MS offers. However, this does not tell the whole story. The self-reflexive image of cinematic cataloguing that is the library – standing out from the diegesis in the form of Tivan in *GOTG*, but also, as Connor points out (2012: 525–32), present in *The Incredible Hulk* – points to the high place still held by genre within Hollywood film's symbol system. Elements of Jim Collins' discussion of hybridity versus 'sincerity' in Hollywood's genre logic of the early 1990s remain prescient for the current era as, via the 'shared universe', Marvel's dominance shapes practice beyond the superheroic field, into popular film as a whole. Back then, Collins mused on what effect 'massive recategorization … [in the form of an] ever-increasing number of entertainment options and the fragmentation of what was once thought to be a mass audience into a cluster of "target" audiences' (1993: 243) might have had on notions of genre. Those genre texts of the late 1980s/early 1990s which Collins had in mind demonstrated a 'sophisticated hyperconsciousness concerning not just narrative formulae but the conditions of their own circulation and reception' (1993: 248); this is updated in the readings of allegorical storytelling presented by Connor. We certainly see the kind of 'intensified production consciousness' symptomatic of allegorical popular cinema in both of the films discussed within this chapter (Connor, 2015: 322). This is the 'consciousness' that seeps through *Iron Man*, the film that attempted to find a narrative solution to the problem of containing innovation within respectful, proven structures; to light an 'arc reactor' that could power a universe. That film broke as many rules (such as Stark's sensational identity reveal at the climactic press conference and the announcement of the 'Avengers Initiative') as it observed. Contemporary Hollywood narrative, for Connor, 'works through cataloguing and recall', with MS, often privileging imagery of just that, specifically projecting an 'aggressive self-understanding' that powers a renegotiation of identity uniting 'producers and audiences' (2012: 527). As we saw in the first chapter, following the logic articulated in Johnson's (2012) view of the MS project, the company wished to boldly venture onto territory to which it may not have seemed automatically entitled (at least, prior to 2009 and purchase by the more credentialled Disney). The journey from *Iron Man* to *Guardians of the Galaxy* gives a vivid picture of how traditions of genre have supported an incursion towards new lands. The later film is able to plunder past blueprints, and retroactively incorporate 'fractal' lineages stretching back to the late 1970s, which it nestles within itself. At times the reference to specific films is explicit, as we have seen, but the tonal effect sought is one that places special effects, high emotion and pop culture in a specific combination – an 'Awesome Mix', perhaps. At a very different stage in the MCU, the innovatory brief of *Iron Man* was accordingly different: to establish 'Marvel's new typology of the superhero film' (Calbreath-Frasieur, 2014: 27) and redefine the expectations that went with it. The more MCU texts we see, the more it seems the case that those superhero elements are reforming and enlarging to accommodate a range of epic contemporary Hollywood genre moments. Another way to look at it might be that the raw codes of the superhero entertainment become more transparent, fading – deliberately – into a broader, familiar, connected textuality that brings MS to the heart of event filmmaking.

CHAPTER 4
CAPTAINS AMERICA

Introduction

In these current, exciting times for Marvel, the studio seems confident that its audience has a sure grasp of its characters and, where necessary, of the lore from the comics in which their adventures initially appeared. This supports the branching out into multiple forms, franchises and platforms detailed earlier in this work, culminating in the expansion announcement of October 2014. To look at contemporary iterations of those same comic series', gigantic, fluid casts of characters, extended storylines and spreading formats are in vogue. The 'event' – offspring of 'one-offs' like Shooter's *Secret Wars* – brings together several titles (or suspends them until consequences are revealed) and is the driver of current canon formation; whole families of ongoing comics are liable to be temporarily retired to suit current interests.[1] One interlocking event may overlap into the next, leaving the single issue adventure or developing series (with noble exceptions) in a forgotten cul-de-sac. As if in recognition of the riches at its disposal, yet strategically focusing on the life beyond a solid continuity established many decades ago (and most important to an ageing fandom), Marvel editorial fiats and writers' wishes to explore new ground peel branded identities away from established characters. Such characters become like 'actors' stepping into the star roles of hero identities, while other players move around the chessboard.[2] As of summer 2015, Carol Danvers is the current Captain Marvel (there have been several others); she was replaced in her former role Ms Marvel by the recent creation Kamala Khan; Spider-Man's body only recently evicted the consciousness of his arch-villain, Otto Octavius, allowing Peter Parker to move back in; Marvel's movie star of the summer, Ant-Man, is himself a 'Mark II'; and Sam 'Falcon' Wilson currently wears the famed mantle of Captain America, among numerous other examples.[3]

Such character 'shake ups', with others stepping into and occupying superhero identities if only temporarily, is a proven sales device[4] used by Marvel Comics many times. At the time of writing, Steve Rogers has just directed one group of heroes against another (in a rather confusing crossover storyline),[5] while eschewing his familiar, bright star-spangled uniform (Dittmer, 2005: 629) for a purposely muted and practical 'soldier' outfit (as also seen on Chris Evans in some sequences of *Captain America: The Winter Soldier*). As we have seen (in Chapter 1), film policy and the direction taken by MU comics are not indivisible, but are moving in a direction of synchronization and links certainly go far beyond a sharing of costume.

Yet, any MU that did not in some way pivot around Steve Rogers as moral compass is difficult to imagine, whatever the medium. Created by Joe Simon and Jack Kirby as an explicitly patriotic embodiment of ideals deemed close to the national heart, 'Captain America's image and origin mirror the American identity/dream of 1941' but, as many scholars have observed, are not limited to it (Dittmer, 2005: 629). A few choice adjectives from Dittmer's analysis add light to various attributes of Cap: responsible; reluctant as a warrior but a keen patriot; a leader; athletic; innocent; hard-working; and democratic (2005: 629–30). All of these are accurate, yet the character has gone far beyond them in accruing sixty years' worth of narrative.[6] From his propaganda origins as 'the meridian example of pro-war attitudes in World War II era comic books' (Yanes, 2009: 53), Cap has always been chiefly symbolic, despite efforts to ground him in specific conflicts and political positions. This 'old-fashioned' character's purpose, post-1964 resurrection in the pages of *The Avengers*, arguably has been not to check or reverse the flow of American time, but to provide a reference point for analysing its effects. That ideological problems come along with this function is unquestionable, although it is also true that what the character reflects at a given time tends to be not immanent, but rather imposed by analysis. Dittmer (2005: 628) settles on Cap as a 'politically important' figure, and subject to a similar 'battle' of meaning as other contested objects of popular culture in an atmosphere of 'Culture Wars'; some argue that a special confusion has fallen across the character since 9/11 (Evans, 2010: 120), but even when Cap fights in the midst of government-implicated hypocrisy and national malaise, various crises, like those of the early 1970s discussed by Matthew Pustz, serve to refocus his attention on what needs to be done to bolster fragile American ideals, and to make reality better conform to them (2012: 140).

In this chapter, Captain America (as far as the MCU is concerned, a role still inhabited by Steve Rogers) will be examined as the character at the centre of MS's most politically charged saga. To understand the importance of various distinct iterations of the character, Cap's continuing, fluid relevance through eras, incarnations and, indeed, surrogates shall be reckoned with.

The meanings of a legend

Sean Cubitt maintains that, 'Contemporary Hollywood often finds it difficult to picture the good, but the evil is a constant' (2015). Superhero films in the past perhaps saved their most intense acting and writing energies for villainous characters (which as much as anything can be viewed as indicative of their observance of broader action film traditions). It could be said that it takes some effort, in film narrative terms, to open up the substance of most upstanding superheroes, and on the face of it, Captain America's meanings may seem pretty secure, when we encounter him pounding a punchbag and talking to Nick Fury (Samuel L. Jackson) in *The Avengers*. By the conclusion of that film, which has shown him ascend to the strategic and motivational (as well as hearts-and-minds) focal point for that strange team, he rides off from Central Park on the Harley-Davidson brand in which he has kept faith since his war issue (Anon., 2015a).[7] Already inspired by Fury's manipulation of the death of Agent Phil Coulson (see Chapter 5), the Avengers still require organization into an effective, disciplined team by Cap's leadership[8]; indeed, Cap's effect on various authority figures is made a point of in Whedon's film. However, the more intangible inspirational symbolism is also accentuated when we see him through the eyes of an 'ordinary' citizen (Ashley Johnson) caught up in the events of the battle.[9]

That first sight of him in the gym enforces continuity with the previous year's *Captain America: The First Avenger* (*CA:TFA*) by emphasizing his alienation at waking up in a new century, as he opens up to Fury. More important to Cap's accepting the role of leader, despite the chaos of his personal situation, is a vignette that in a larger way, represents something key to the MCU, and its chronology. In *The Avengers* sequence where Loki, main villain and motive force in the invasion of space beings the Chitauri,[10] attempts to subjugate the city of Stuttgart, Cap defends an elderly German man who stands up to the Asgardian. The moment would appear to be intended to revise early uncompromising, 'ultra-American' propaganda versions of the hero (Wright, 2003: 30–6; see also Scott, 2011, ch. 2). In the context of the ambiguous representation of the 'team', already established by this stage of the film, the sequence neatly affirms that what Captain America defends is freedom; unlike the arrangements between nations (or those between fractious, egotistical heroes), this is not subject to change. The greater good will always be present, but it is the rare superhero who can be trusted to identify it; this ties into a sense that a world experiencing superheroes for the first time would be wary, and seek to first regulate, then exploit, them (as is seen across the MCU, from General 'Thunderbolt' Ross' attempts to subdue the Hulk, to congressional moves to limit Tony Stark's power, and the fallout from the Captain's own second movie). As A. David Lewis has pointed out, Captain America himself verbalizes this position during the highly significant *Civil War* miniseries (2006–7): 'Superheroes need to stay above [politics] or Washington starts telling us who the supervillains are' (cited in Lewis, 2012: 229). As the premise of *Civil War* comics migrates into MCU plans, this idea becomes central to the Captain America film saga at the end of the second instalment: developments around government monitoring of superhumans are signposted and Natasha Romanoff/Black Widow (Scarlet Johannsen) is seen facing an inquiry after the collapse of S.H.I.E.L.D.

Staying with the reference to Germany, the Stuttgart sequence and Cap's encounter with the old man's heroism have a wider significance in underlining the importance of the Second World War (and attitudes to it then, as well as subsequent revisions to those attitudes and how they regard views of the global order) to this MCU. In comics, the MU established an undisputed place whereby the Second World War generated not only Golden Age stars like Cap (and his 'rogues gallery' of villains like the Red Skull, Master Man and so on) but also the familiar settings of mainstays like Sergeant Nicholas J. Fury, the Invaders (a Cap-led Allied team that included the original 'Human Torch' and anti-hero Namor/The Sub-Mariner among its ranks) and many others. The first identifiably 'Marvel' comic series, *Marvel Comics* Vol.1, #1 (published by Timely in October 1939), quickly developed war, or at least anti-Nazi themes. Namor first aids the Allied effort in issue #3 in early 1940. This centrality of war material may seem unsurprising; after all, *Captain America Comics* (1941–9) were freely distributed to troops by the War Department 'without scrutiny of [its] political content' (Lawrence, 2009: 2), so taken for granted was the comic's synchronization of war aims with audience-pleasing adventure. Beyond this, however, comics' fixation with Second World War tropes sufficiently outlasted the first burst of popularity of superheroes to strongly resurge, when Stan Lee led the return of costumed crime fighters into the pages of the newly named publishing group as of late 1961. Marvel writers consequently worked the war into the origin stories of so many heroes that it eventually had to be 'retconned' out of some, as their ages in 'Marvel Time' started to contradict their origins (although shown in combat in *Fantastic Four*, Vol.1, #11 (1963), and later suggested to have fought alongside Fury, this temporal origin disappeared for Reed Richards and Ben Grimm, for instance). The tight correspondence – between the emergence of the Marvel heroes, post-FF, and the memory and ongoing relevance of the war (not least in those who produced the comics, like Jack Kirby,[11] and those who paid for young readers to own them) that had ended just sixteen years previously seems understandable, but it is another thing to consider how MS's cinematic universe has come to rely upon the same conflict.

Not only is the origin of Captain America reproduced more or less intact and his introductory film given an entirely Second World War setting (a brief coda, aside), but also key plotlines of *AoS* tie in with the fight against HYDRA (a terrorist organization with world-ruling plans, which began as an offshoot of Third Reich scientific research) and the *Agent Carter* miniseries sets its sights on the immediate postwar society. The growth of intelligence and peacekeeping force S.H.I.E.L.D. itself – in many ways the cement holding this universe together – is shown to stem from the collaboration of figures brought together by the war: the Howling Commandos, an elite combat infantry unit that fights alongside Cap; Peggy Carter (Hayley Atwell), and Howard Stark (Dominic Cooper), genius inventor father of Tony. The parallel rise of HYDRA is masterminded by the warped Nazi scientist Arnim Zola (Toby Jones).[12] These battles, forged in the Second World War, still rage in the present-day MCU. In terms of the foundations of the MCU excavated by Phase II texts, the war remains important in underpinning and anchoring that universe in time (*Agent Carter* begins in 1946; a HYDRA foe, Daniel Whitehall (Reed Diamond), has defied nature to menace Coulson's team in Season Two of *AoS*; the Avengers fight Nazi-styled Baron Strucker in *Avengers: Age of Ultron* (*A:AOU*), and so on). The temporal implications, alone, of this may yet damage the MCU in the future, although plot fixes have been conjured up to show how characters like Whitehall may have been able to defy time (and some, such as Thor, do not face this problem). Much as Marvel Comics had to rearrange the pasts of Reed Richards and Tony Stark to tidy up historical and ideological slippage (and the MU has always featured a lot of time travel), the MCU will continue to require solutions as it drifts, chronologically, away from the Second World War. Acknowledging this issue, a generation gap has been projected between characters who are born decades after the fallout of the conflict, and those who comprehend it; the ambiguous Inhuman Rayna (Ruth Negga) expresses exasperation with the outmoded worldview of the HYDRA organization she has been working with: 'World domination ... it's so 1945' (in *AoS* S2E2 'Heavy is the Head').

Part of the mission of Joe Johnston, director of *CA:TFA* was to sink a shared universe anchor in a Second World War setting that could – with the economy of a two-hour feature – reflect the conflict's status as imaginative fountainhead for a comics universe. The Timely period may have been over, but the Second World War was hugely important to early Silver Age Marvel. When *Fantastic Four* #1 announced the 'Marvel Age', a wide selection of war titles was still being offered by the DC and Charlton companies. This testified to the health of that section of the comics market in 1961 (McClelland-Nugent, 2010: 138; Scott, 2011: 106, 116). War adventure would remain a staple (bordering, for certain publishers, on an obsession) well into the 1980s (Scott, 2011: 122–3). Today, comics continue to explore war in numerous ways, though not always through ostensibly shallow adventure. The importance, in a time of war, even of this can be attested, as in sometime Marvel scriptwriter Michael Chabon's novel *The Amazing Adventures of Kavalier and Clay* (2000).[13] It is clear, then, that where the MU once led in terms of laying roots in a Second World War-informed mythology, the modern MCU follows, placing a similar value on the same motifs and events in generating themes and plotlines. Most of these characters and plot points are first glimpsed[14] in the sole period film of 'Marvel Phase I', a film we shall now consider in detail.

A singular avenger/*The First Avenger*

In August 2011, *CA:TFA* followed *Thor*, released three months earlier, in paving the continuity road towards *The Avengers*, planned as MS's big 2012 release. Yet, despite its place in this fabric, Joe Johnston's film is as interesting for the ways in which it differs from the four MCU films issued previously as for its similarities and connections with them. This is not to overlook the fact that *CA:TFA* takes some of the narrative strain of the shared MCU. Among the things seeded are the Stark empire, S.H.I.E.L.D., and characters for potential franchise expansion. The most important of these – villain Arnim Zola, James 'Bucky' Barnes (Sebastian Stan), and Peggy Carter – make good on the promise of further involvement in *CA:TWS* three years later, with Carter's return in her 2015 TV miniseries underlining the character's importance. Yet, in comparison to *Thor,* with a storyline that prepares the *Avengers'* major villain, *CA:TFA* lacks a dedicated narrative line leading to the subsequent film, thus justifying a consideration of how it stands alone as well as represents a piece of a more ambitious jigsaw puzzle.

Preceded by the other core solo movies making up the road to *The Avengers*, *CA:TFA* has limited obligations to already presented continuity. This leaves room for playfulness; in a manner that resembles other fresh point-of-view exercises in retelling the genesis of the comic universe (such as *Marvels*, Busiek and Ross 2004, originally published 1994; *The Marvels Project*, Brubaker and Epting 2011, originally published 2009–10), *CA:TFA* makes some important future plotlines sideshow glimpses for the eagle-eyed fan. While such narrative layering falls short of constituting an extensive, coordinated effort to pull back corners of the universe, and not every plotline shows signs of taking root in the MCU,[15] it does hint at the riches to be mined from already published Marvel storylines. Also notable in the centrality of characters like Peggy Carter, the Howling Commandos, and Howard Stark is MS's strategy of developing secondary (and especially, de-powered) characters like Carter and S.H.I.E.L.D.'s Phil Coulson as a way of introducing continuing television projects. It may also be noted that the third MCU television project to arrive on screens – *Daredevil* – also boasts a character whose abilities require less investment in time-consuming special FX.

With a brief to situate Captain America's moral development outside of the modern context, Joe Johnston, while respectful to existing comics, was essentially given a chance to construct his own 'Golden Age', without contradicting any ideas already held by the general movie audience. The director, a proven *pasticheur* (particularly in *The Rocketeer*, 1991), skilled in fusing 'Golden Age' style period atmosphere with action-filled, idealistic heroics, faced a twofold task: to address the application of formula needed to extend the franchise (at that point, standing only at four films), and set up elements of *The Avengers*; yet, at the same time, retain the somewhat opposing notion of unrepeatability. Fittingly then, the notion of breaking the mould resides at the heart of Johnston's film, as the emergence of Captain America simultaneously heralds a new beginning for US efforts in the Second World War, and – with the death of scientist Abraham Erskine (Stanley Tucci) at Nazi hands – the disappearance of a promised future army of Super-Soldiers. In Marvel comics, the status of Cap as a one-off is regularly foregrounded in the dynamic of his relations with other heroes: he stands as the exemplar of a brand of heroism that even the most powerful heroes can only admire, the (relative) inferiority of his power set being balanced out by his moral superiority (and a tactical command honed in situations like those presented in this film). His origin as an instrument to fight a specific war is developed by Johnston and screenwriters Christopher Markus and Stephen McFeely, in a way that represents the notion of singularity in terms of existential loneliness (in the concluding sequence where Rogers emerges into a disorientating present day), as well as the matchless virtues of heart and courage.

Cap's unifying qualities – etched into legend, the film implies, during his absence while buried under Arctic ice – qualify Rogers for Agent Coulson's hero worship in *The Avengers*, even as the 'team' he is supposed to lead is beset by petty squabbles. These strands in Rogers' character can be summed up in the notion of 'a little old fashioned' (as Cap is dubbed by Coulson): 'old fashioned' in this universe comes to represent decency, hope, preparation for the future, but also a moral framing to the vision of that future which sets Rogers apart not only from fellow heroes but also from ambiguous spymaster Fury. At the end of Whedon's film, Fury's response to a question about what could possibly motivate such a disparate collection of super-beings to reunite once more ('because we'll need them to') projects his realization that everything about the Avengers is improbable and nebulous, aside from the moral imperative behind their existence. Steve Rogers drives this moral imperative.

Dr Erskine is the man who transforms the Steve Rogers of the MCU into Captain America. The film locates the good heart of scientific exploration – and its military application – in this figure, alienated German creator of the 'Super-Soldier' serum and the only man to spot the potential in a scrawny Brooklyn kid. Erskine combines scientific brilliance with a moral wisdom – borne of the experience of seeing his country stolen by Fascism – unmatched elsewhere in the film. The prospect of a utopian, peaceful future hinges on the encounter between Dr Erskine,[16] who rejects nationalism, and Rogers, who believes that flags 'are in his future' (setting him against the Red Skull's vision of a stateless world).

Although sabotaged by HYDRA, it is made clear that Erskine's experiment – the production of a super-strength serum that will be delivered to legions of soldiers – should be viewed as a necessary, responsible use of technology. That the serum will only work properly with a good man is established in Erskine's quirky choice of Rogers, and his repeated message that it is Rogers' noble heart and bravery that make him the best candidate to inspire the nation. The similarly enhanced Johann Schmidt/Red Skull (Hugo Weaving) doubles Rogers as the twisted reminder of the high consequence of failure; this, a classic instance of the comic book villain as essentially the negative version of the good qualities in the hero. The formula echoes through MCU episodes with Hulk and Thor possessing their own twisted reflections such as Emil 'Abomination' Blonsky (Tim Roth) and Loki. Tony Stark confronts opponents who employ twisted takes on his technology (played by Jeff Bridges and Mickey Rourke, respectively, in the first two *Iron Man* films). Stark then faces the spoiled product of it – Ultron (James Spader) – in *A:AOU* (more the offspring of Stark's actions, perhaps, than a mirror image).[17] If Cap thinks the Red Skull will be the last such distorted counterpart he must face, he is mistaken.

Rogers' transformation underneath the unassuming 'Brooklyn Antiques' shop – rendered in a kitschy sci-fi lab with genius-industrialist Howard Stark at the controls – fails to result in the expected production line of supermen, instead marking the beginning of a short career as a propaganda machine. *CA:TFA* occasionally toys with a more cynical vision of war, and the propaganda/United Service Organization's show scenes have a suitably corny feel. Cut adrift from his planned purpose with the loss of Erskine's formula, the nation's best use for Rogers is to make him a shill for the industrial and economic effort. In scenes of fund-raising events that recall the manipulated Iwo Jima vets of Clint Eastwood's *Flags of Our Fathers* (2006), Rogers is put on display in a gaudy outfit and alienated from 'real' G.I.'s: the once puny Rogers may have gained the dimensions of the ideal fighting man, but here is put once again into the position of freak. This is a classic lesson for Marvel protagonists – famed for their outsider status – to absorb, and again points up notions of singularity and uniqueness, which can confer a burden of alienation as much as an aura of specialness upon the hero.

The film flirts with a modern attitude to the conduct of war as more oriented around political control of public perception, although the critique is light. As with so much US action-adventure cinema, bureaucracy and a preference to cut deals rather than fight presents one kind of enemy; when overbearing Senator Brandt (Michael Brandon) pulls one string too many, the movie replaces him as Rogers' mentor with salt-of-the-earth Colonel Philips. However, it takes time for Philips to come around to Erskine's high valuation of Rogers. In general, *CA:TFA* elects to present a sanitized version of the European theatre of the Second World War, despite the fact that comic continuity confirms that Captain America and Bucky experienced concentration camps (Brubaker, Andreyko and Samnee, 2011). Tight historical and geographical parameters on this war prevent Cap from encountering the Holocaust, even in montage sequences (see Lee, 2011). This may seem a harsh criticism of a nascent franchise bearing the Marvel (and, ultimately, Disney) branding, although a film from the same summer – the non-MCU *X-Men: First Class* (Matthew Vaughn, 2011) – explicitly presented its villain as a death camp authority figure. In a way, *CA:TFA* is only a war film in the sense that is *Raiders of the Lost Ark* (Spielberg's 1981 film is an obvious model for Johnston's nostalgic adventure): the Tesseract that obsesses the Skull represents the 'Ultimate Weapon' – structurally important but intrinsically meaningless – found in every episode of the Indiana Jones series (1981–2008). *Raiders* itself, on which Johnston worked, is of course an excavation of beloved genres/conventions, in the same way that the director would like his MCU film to be.

The First Avenger relishes opportunities to suggest a hidden layer of technological influence on both Allied and Axis/HYDRA sides that could only transpire in an MCU where authorities turn to science to provide Vibranium shields before A-bombs (the serum can be seen as a sort of MCU antidote to the A-bomb).[18] Such substitutions represent Markus and McFeely's attempts to make sense of Captain America's brand of natural heroism and self-sacrifice for a mass audience grown used to the conflicted, reluctant and anguished men of action fronting films from the early part of the 2000s (see Flanagan, 2009: 171–2, and Chapter 7). The nobility of Rogers thus necessitates a different treatment from the struggles of characters such as Stark and Bruce Banner (whether the struggle is that of self-identification as a hero, or a progression from experiencing powers as a curse to recognizing them as a tool that can benefit society). Along these lines, Steve's obvious affection for Erskine, 'good German' (prefiguring the old man in Stuttgart) and honourable figure of science, leads us directly, and logically, into Cap's first intervention in the Avengers' mission against Loki, as discussed above.

The symbol

> Without a stable external Other against which to define itself, America's identity increasingly came under scrutiny.
>
> (Darowski J., 2014: 93)

Battles, and adversaries, change of course. Cap appeared to have an ability to hold the projections of divergent political groups in divided times; perhaps the ultimate tribute paid to this was the naming of Peter Fonda's character for him in *Easy Rider* (Dennis Hopper, 1968). This, just at the point when Marvel, under Lee, was negotiating the uncomfortable topic of US involvement in Vietnam, charting a tentative path that avoided censorship of the issue (see Introduction). In a way, Lee/Kirby, and particularly later Cap writers like Steve Englehart (1972–5), were fortunate that Cap spent his spell in the ice, for when he was revived into the ranks of the Avengers in 1964, they could use him as a fresh pair of eyes onto a dynamically changing social scene in which other characters (like Tony Stark) were more embroiled.[19] However, it is also important that Cap re-enters a world where a legend has grown to fill the vacuum left by the man (an ambiguous notion nevertheless celebrated in a romantic shot of children empowering themselves at play as Cap in the intervening years after his 'death' is postulated near the end of *CA:TFA*). This removes control of the meaning of 'Captain America' from Steve Rogers, a person who must now compete with a symbolism the momentum of which has surged without him. This idea has fuelled storylines for many decades since; one of Rogers' agonies, revealed in a monologue in Ed Brubaker's very last issue, is 'Knowing I couldn't control what people *thought* I stood for'.[20]

It is standard to acknowledge that the meaning of Captain America varies with 'the meaning of America and the role of the state' (Dittmer, 2007: 256), and selected comic runs from 1970 to 2005 strongly suggest that Marvel was very aware of Cap's meanings as unfixed and provisional (one, the 'Grand Director' storyline, is discussed later). Despite the reputation of superhero comics as juvenile and trivial, this discourse was perhaps supported by the very production dynamics of the medium. John Darowski contends that the monthly comic book format ideally positions it to function as a kind of rolling cultural commentary: 'When the very nature of what is right comes into debate, such stories become a way to evaluate societal morals, preserving those which are beneficial, adopting the new as they prove valid, and discarding the old as they become obsolete' (2014: 95). Captain America's meanings could be adapted to throw light onto new circumstances – but not, arguably, without some hollowing out of the essential 'Americanness' that the character is thought to, outwardly, represent (Dittmer, 2007: 257). Far from shying away from confronting social issues, runs of *Captain America*, particularly with writer Steve Englehart at the controls (1972–5), took them on, with race prominent (Nama, 2011: 72). Englehart himself expresses pride at manoeuvring Falcon, Cap's African American partner, into the spotlight of the book, with Rogers retiring for a period in the 1970s (Englehart, 2015).

Various creators have tended to invoke Rogers' military background when explaining Cap's frequent difficulty in accepting how American democracy is implemented by politics.[21] Forcing identification with him, Rogers' conviction that soldiers are alienated by politics resounds in the craven depiction of the MCU's World Security Council (WSC), a United Nations-like organization that seems expressly set up to oversee S.H.I.E.L.D. In hastening to restrict Nick Fury, the interfering WSC almost brings about the complete destruction of Manhattan Island in *The Avengers*. Yet, Fury is a government employee in a way that Thor or Hulk certainly are not. Although teamwork is definitely achieved in confronting Loki and the Chitauri, and it is established that both Black Widow and Hawkeye have a grasp of paramilitary command structure and have experienced the moral agonies of service, it is stressed that Rogers is the only one in the team who has genuinely served his time as a soldier. This will remain the case until War Machine and Falcon join in the closing moments of *A:AOU*; the significance here is in the sense that Cap has formed a team containing more military figures as the unpredictable elements (Stark and Hulk) and those beyond humanity (Thor) depart.

The team dynamic is the focus of our next chapter, but for now, with reference to *The Avengers*, Tasker points out that in any cinematic team individuals need harnessing, and that the generic formula of the war movie shapes how this usually occurs: 'Results are achieved when individuals operate as one' (2015: 189). That the otherworldliness and instability of the other Avengers might be accompanied by uncertain moral paradigms perhaps helps to explain, in narrative terms, the quasi-governmental oversight of S.H.I.E.L.D. However, there is far more to know about S.H.I.E.L.D., as the second Captain America movie spells out, and as we shall discuss later.

Ultimately, Cap's efforts are not decisive in this MCU take on the Second World War, with the extent of the Skull's threat remaining classified, and the Tesseract coming into the custody of Howard Stark and S.H.I.E.L.D. A HYDRA ship, boarded in pursuit of the Skull, crashes off the coast of Greenland with Rogers on board (the unstable Tesseract has neutralized the Skull, perhaps jumping him to another dimension, although this is not clarified by the film). Following the rescue glimpsed in the film's framing device, Rogers wakes to find himself held by S.H.I.E.L.D. as well. On discovering Fury's fabricated 1940s (intended to let him adapt to the length of his absence), Rogers breaks out of his illusory quarters and storms into the heart of present day Times Square. It is no accident that Cap emerges into the famous location of so many V-J Day images from popular culture, celebrations that Rogers – poignantly – has missed. Underlining this – and reminding us of how Erskine pinpointed Rogers' humanity as a source of strength – Cap tells Fury of his regret at missing a date with Peggy, his British military liaison since the early days (arranged in the previous scene). A triumphal ending is avoided, but it would have been difficult to engineer in any case, with MCU continuity making it necessary that Cap spends a spell in the Greenland ice. The film finds a simple and affecting way to convey Rogers' loss, while refuting the Skull's assertion that these two very different sons of Erskine have 'left humanity behind'. Thus, the singular Captain is reintegrated into the ranks of humanity via his values and moral code: his defining character elements in place, Cap progresses into *The Avengers*. However, in *CA:TWS*, while he does not quite become the 'enemy of the state' he has sometimes appeared in Marvel comics, those values become strained as Cap deals with a corrupted S.H.I.E.L.D.,[22] a resurgent HYDRA – and his own sense of personal responsibility for the tragic fate of Bucky Barnes.

Interlude (1946): *Agent Carter*

Johnston's *The First Avenger* enjoys referencing the tradition of filmic war adventure, and before Cap is lost to the ice, a final reference is pressed into service; it is one which underscores the essentially romantic vision of the Second World War in *CA:TFA*. The most blatant piece of intertextuality in the film is a reference to Michael Powell and Emeric Pressburger's British favourite *A Matter of Life and Death* (1946). Officially a propaganda film, this film first showed the scene of a radio operator speaking to her doomed love as the seconds count down to their ship crashing as re-created by Carter and Cap. Commissioned to smooth 'tensions with England's American allies' and promote cooperation between the nations (Lazar, 2003: xv), here, its presence crystallizes Rogers' sense of duty-as-sacrifice, while showing that before the inspirational public icon stood a human being, capable of connecting to others, of making plans towards his own, private, future. As Howard Stark realizes, in 1946, finally understanding Erskine's initial regard for Rogers: 'He was good before [Project Rebirth] got hold of him' (*Agent Carter*, S1E8 – 'Valediction').

With Rogers apparently denied his future, the woman who must forge ahead into her own is Peggy Carter. ABC's miniseries *Agent Carter* ran in January and February 2015, ostensibly designed to fill the hiatus of *Agents of S.H.I.E.L.D.* (then at the midpoint of its second season). Hayley Atwell made guest appearances (in period flashbacks) in two *AoS* episodes (S2E1 'Shadows' and S2E8 'The Things We Bury') to heighten audience awareness and, in diegetic terms, line up various developments around HYDRA that fed into the idea of a rebuilt S.H.I.E.L.D., with new priorities, after the events of *CA:TWS*. Although the *AoS* flashbacks show that Peggy has been active for the Strategic Science Reserve in the period between V-E Day and 1946, her own show picks up in that year, focusing upon her struggles to reattain the influence and respect she held while fighting alongside Steve Rogers. Carter's male colleagues' view of her as little more than window-dressing to the presumed-dead Super-Soldier suggests a bridge from the arduous yet hopeful Second World War world to the world of mistrust and gender envy explored by American *film noir* (the dynamics of which have yet to be explored in the MCU), and the Strategic Scientific Reserve (SSR) in which she must establish herself. When understanding Carter's alienation within SSR ranks, a certain circularity is encountered: if the seeds of HYDRA are always within

S.H.I.E.L.D., necessitating the storyline that sees S.H.I.E.L.D. dismantled across the first season of *AoS* and *CA:TWS*, then American heroes and other representatives of good have fundamentally misread postwar optimism. A peacekeeping organization sanctioned by government, rotten with anti-capitalist traitors: that seed of disquiet planted by the United States itself, in allowing S.H.I.E.L.D. to boost its science efforts by recruiting the cream of German technicians.[23] The other way of looking at this is that the rottenness within S.H.I.E.L.D. was only designed in once the story ideas for *CA:TWS* and the TV show had been developed, and that the roots of the corruption, as they affect Carter, merely represent a pragmatic instance of wider narrative retro-fitting. To whatever extent this is all planned, the notion of an anti-freedom HYDRA time bomb is evident in *CA:TFA*, where it is clear that Arnim Zola has tampered with the mental and physical being of Bucky Barnes.

Trust – as earned by the integrity and decency of servicemen and women's actions, and as that which is granted to political leadership in the hope that it shall be treated responsibly – emerges as a key issue linking the – at face value – disparate subject matters and styles of the two Captain America films (the distinctive structure of the MCU allows certain thematic lines of *The Avengers* and then, more centrally, *AoS* to mature across the three-year spell between releases). The Cap of *The First Avenger* loses his most trusted partner to HYDRA machinations (HYDRA's hypocritical rhetoric defends its actions in terms of the banishment of lies from society). Story events mean that Rogers wakes up in a world where he is immediately lied to by S.H.I.E.L.D. (on the pretext of calming his culture shock at reawakening), and finds the first offer of allegiance to present itself is Fury's ambivalent, controlling one.[24] While serving S.H.I.E.L.D. missions, and believing himself among 'friends' (a belief gently mocked by the more hardened Romanoff), Cap starts to doubt the motives of those working on his own 'side' as early as the raid on the Lemurian Star satellite ship, early in *CA:TWS*. To fall on the right side of trust for a hero in these texts is, interestingly, often the same as opposing the official line[25]: this is the position that Cap himself finds himself in when S.H.I.E.L.D. – the puppet for a huge, government-sanctioned investment in defence, 'Project Insight' – collapses. In the end, an all-out display of trust based on Rogers' instincts, and the personal history he experienced prior to Project Rebirth, saves both Bucky and Cap: Cap refuses to fight his one-time friend, accepting the consequences, meaning that both men survive once the three 'Project Insight' warships have been downed.

The notion that the good in honourable people will out, even when their public image suggests traitorous or anti-American agendas, picks up a thread from *Agent Carter*, where the same applies to Howard Stark, framed government enemy. The real honour within Stark is expressed by his deepened respect for the reality of Peggy Carter's feelings for Steve Rogers, and also his responsible decision to arrange the destruction of recent weapon designs – the only way to prevent them from government exploitation. Both *CA:TWS* and elements of *AoS* make clear that artificially provoked fear is distorting people's experience of American reality (in another instance either of retro-fitting or master-planning, *Agent Carter* shows the 1940s roots of this villainous manoeuvre with its inclusion of the rage-producing 'Madbomb' weapon, dubbed 'Midnight Oil' in the episode). Yet despite that hedging, *CA:TWS* does not suggest that a diagnosis of genuine decline is completely wide of the mark. Romanoff is a useful character complementing Cap here, as her utilitarian blood-letting past – a source of regret, but not disavowal – had been established in key scenes in *The Avengers* (and returns in *A:AOU*). Steve Rogers puts a brave face on decline (keeping a catch-up notebook to familiarize himself with key moments in the culture that has rocketed past him), and would never share this, we suspect, with Fury.[26] However, what Fury fails to comprehend is how much the HYDRA view haunts ways of responding to such decline. Their top man in S.H.I.E.L.D., Alexander Pierce (Robert Redford), sees the removal of democracy as the key to order, and so seeks to unfetter S.H.I.E.L.D.'s power; Arnim Zola wants to help Pierce pacify society through the destruction of free thought – a societal reboot, the HYDRA way. At this point, Zola is a disembodied consciousness running through an ancient computer in a lost bunker, data gone mad. Pierce believes that freedom damages the public, who cannot be trusted with it. Fitting into discourses seen widely in Hollywood over the last fifteen years, his scenes emphasize the view that freedom and security are each other's cost, and his side is clear.

Bureaucracy and information-stockpiling remain the enemy: deal-cutting, red tape and cover-up spinning the methods that make stand-up fights look increasingly civilized. Back in 1946, when Zola is still flesh and blood, Peggy Carter's legacy from her friendship with Steve Rogers is to remain the individual who keeps the system in check by asserting their own messy existence. Carter feels the need to remake officialdom – reforming the SSR into S.H.I.E.L.D. (a process not yet shown, but inevitable from information given). Her reasons to do this are to preserve the sacrifices and lessons of the war (not least, that of Rogers), and also to ensure that her personal contribution, as thousands of other women's, cannot be undervalued because of her gender. Perhaps the saddest point made in *CA:TWS* (in which an aged Peggy Carter has a cameo) is that the good intentions of Stark and Carter fail to derail HYDRA's plans.

'Trouble Man' – *Captain America: The Winter Soldier*[27]

Government is not the solution to our problem, government is the problem.

(Ronald Reagan in Darowski J., 2014: 94)

The degree to which the founders of S.H.I.E.L.D. get it wrong is fully explored in *CA:TWS* (we take another perspective on this in Chapter 5). Just as a concern of the *Agent Carter* show is the changed way in which individuals are regarded by institutions once their service, in a crisis, is over, Cap himself is the next hero from the Second World War contingent of the MCU to experience a harsh and disorienting 'peacetime'. The Russos' film signals a shift in the concerns of MCU fictions in various ways (Radford, 2014). *The Avengers* seeded this change, exposing Cap to a new set of rules and a new global vulnerability that shocks even relatively similarly inclined allies like Coulson. Cap has more in common with the defiant, honest old man in Stuttgart – who refuses to tell Loki what the Asgardian wants to hear – than some of his new heroic colleagues. The nature of the new threat in *CA:TWS* – HYDRA, hiding in plain sight within edifices of stability and control – challenge the rules of collective valour even more, forcing Cap to form his own small team and go on the run.

Not to bypass *Iron Man 3*, which has something to say on these issues,[28] but *CA:TWS* stands as the first MCU film to carry through the full consequences of Whedon's *Avengers* premise: that the world contains multiple 'enhanced' people of different powers, allegiances and worldviews, who are now aware of each other. That is one of the ways in which *CA:TWS* shifts the gravity of the centre of the MCU; another is by advancing two significant narrative issues: the belief of Avengers figurehead Cap in the independent, self-guided moral interpretation of right as any superhero sees it (demonstrated in the trust he shows towards Bucky/Winter Soldier, and the reassessment (and possible redemption from) a murky, deceitful past that he engenders in Romanoff); second, and branching from the first, the fact that a secretive, information-hungry S.H.I.E.L.D. cannot protect the interests of the public from the abuse of super powers (whether located in individuals or developed by science), and that its political handlers cannot or will not competently or honourably control it. Alongside these, the major thematic dynamic explored by the film (and as we shall see in the next chapter, carried into Phase II as a whole) concerns trust.

S.H.I.E.L.D's 'Triskelion' administrative base looms prominently over the Potomac, as Rogers is relocated into present-day Washington, DC, the better to serve the agency. The general spatial language of the film is tuned in to Rogers' continued disconcerted experience of the present day. The 1930s Brooklyn boy in him seems to struggle in an entrapping DC, represented as a gridlike bureaucracy with the algorithm-controlled sentinels of the 'Project Insight' warships. Rogers is literally overlooked; he possesses a barely lived in apartment (soon gatecrashed by Fury, wounded by the mysterious HYDRA weapon the 'Winter Soldier' – actually a resurrected, mind-enslaved Bucky Barnes) with an ersatz neighbour who is actually Agent 13 (Emily Van Camp), an undercover S.H.I.E.L.D. minder. Just as when he awoke in the fake '1940s room' in the first film, Cap is being watched, contained, and feared, by the institution entrusted with American and global security.

On more than one occasion the overly rationalized environment forces Cap to break through its conforming and fictitious lines – once, using technology to cut through the ground to evade arrest, and once smashing through an elevator window and out of the Triskelion to a bruising landing, below, to escape the attentions of S.H.I.E.L.D's 'STRIKE' subdivision. The challenge of STRIKE's leader, HYDRA sleeper agent Brock Rumlow (Frank Grillo), keeps the film busy with action sequences, but while the spatial and narrative design piles pressure on Rogers, the generic language the film 'speaks' aims to add textural fluency to the MCU (see Chapters 3 and 6). Take away the costumes (there are no alien or mutated super-characters in the film proper, although the mid-credits scene is an exception), and a backing off from superhero conventions is evident. The convention of a paranoid individualist working for truth and openness in an alienating American urban landscape quite deliberately recalls a cycle of 'New Hollywood'-era thrillers that have provided the referential and paratextual framework in which *CA:TWS* has been read. Among others, these include *The Parallax View* (Alan J. Pakula, 1974), and the Robert Redford starring *All the President's Men* (Pakula, 1976) and *Three Days of the Condor* (Sydney Pollack, 1975). Narrative components of subterfuge, double-crossing and life-on-the-run are strong, and thematic philosophies are given vent in dialogue; however, we might ask if the structure of the film itself is notably different from that described in classic action genre terms by Tasker (see Chapter 3), particularly when we think of the different and escalating fight sequence opportunities afforded both Cap and Bucky: a close quarters clash with martial-arts style moves; an expertly edited mass brawl in a glass elevator; a city street battle with rocket launchers and automatic weapons. The 'paranoid 1970s spy thriller' label often attached to the film in reviews, and in the framing paratextual words, both of the Russos themselves and even Disney executive Alan Horn (Radford, 2014; McClintock and Masters, 2014), show this to be an atmosphere imported more as a calculated referential risk, addressing the hip consumption patterns of an audience able to recognize codes of post-Cold War films. The political-conspiracy thriller elements are themselves a kind of smokescreen or genre cloak, successfully encouraging an interpretation as a 'revisionist' superhero fiction (Radford, 2014). One minor reference, though, is particularly interesting. The Lake View Cemetery Dam area of Cleveland, used in the film (Sangiacomo, 2014), hosts a marker indicating where the ashes of Elliot Ness were scattered. Ness, an icon of honest American crime fighting turned into a larger-than-life genre hero by television series and film,[29] was a key figure of a 1930s struggle against not only organized crime but also the police corruption that supported it, and would certainly have been known to the young Steve Rogers.

Alternate versions: Shadows, surrogates, 'sidekicks'

A running source of humour in *Agent Carter* pinpoints the immediacy with which Captain America passes into a (distorted) myth after his apparent wartime death. This is conveyed via a sensationalized 'pulp' translation in the form of a popular radio serial, *The Captain America Adventure Program* ('brought to you by Roxxon motor oil'). In this show, diegetically embedded in several episodes, Peggy Carter's (meta) fictional analogue 'Betty' epitomizes the soppy damsel of a popular culture before feminism's second wave. Betty perpetually requires rescue, much to the chagrin of the far more formidable SSR agent. This is an unusually comedic treatment, but a certain multiplicity to Captain América is consistent with his comics' mythology. Koh (2014: 490) points out that around the summer 2011 release of *CA:TFA*, Marvel issued a prequel comic, which tied directly into MCU continuity, in addition to starting a reprint line of original 1940s adventures, all the while maintaining Cap's regular presence in the mainstream MU, showing the publisher trading on 'similar-enough markers of familiarity' to bridge the disruptions between bodies of continuity.

The supposedly unrepeatable Super-Soldier form of Rogers becomes almost a provocation to his enemies, so that occupancy, not just of the symbolic costume but of Rogers' very body, is subject to contestation. Super-villains, and others with reasons to become Cap's opponents, cannot resist the idea of discrediting the incumbent, then replacing and installing their own candidate in Cap's station, which makes for a long list of surrogates, doubles and dark reflections. Additionally, Steve Rogers' tempestuous relationship to the governance of the day has led to a number of occasions where he has vacated the role by choice.[30] Rogers' disillusionment with the state and politics was never more pronounced than within the events of *Civil War*, after which the character was 'assassinated' in a notorious, bestselling issue, only to come back when yet another body/mind-swap ploy (dreamed up, of course, by the Red Skull) was revealed.[31] As already mentioned, rotating the characters who 'play' the star heroes stokes sales, while also providing writers with narrative opportunities to explore established characters in out-of-costume drama (the FF inaugurated a whole era, yet only received costumes in their third issue). It now seems that the MCU may be seeking to adapt this kind of strategy to a film production model where the rewards built into star actors' contracts have an inflationary effect on budgets as series' progress (see Chapter 6). Various narrative plans could be speculated upon, but it did not seem purely a story development that a new team of Avengers (minus Hulk, Iron Man, Thor and Hawkeye) was introduced in the final shot of *A:AOU*.

As mentioned, Captain America's series historically held the position of carrying the greatest political stamp of almost any major Marvel title (with the strongest competition, perhaps, coming from the X-Men – see Fawaz, 2011). This aspect follows through into his MCU presence. From an editorial point of view, many comic revisions were designed to reconcile or invalidate outdated or newly sensitive associations of Cap's brand of patriotism. J. D. Connor views the cinema reboot as the purging of older stories 'of whatever might have become problematic in them – whether ... problems of politics, narrative balancing, pacing or, more generally, style' (2012: 530), a description that, in at least one or two functions, matches the comic retcon as it applies to the Captain. In these revisions, as well as the times when Captain America identities have proliferated, individual writers address earlier periods where the character's past ideological aims undercut those of the present. This is particularly true with the problematic 1950s legacy of Cold War Captain America.

The Cold War history surrounding Cap's supporting cast has famously manifested in the storylines associated with 'Winter Soldier' Bucky Barnes (see below), with a huge impact on the MCU as already described. However it was also visited by writer J. M. DeMatteis in the 1980s, who envisaged Cap and the Red Skull as representative of the 'deadlocked Superpower' protagonists of the Cold War (Walton, 2009: 167). As changed times saw Nazism ebb away as a clear and present threat, this was reflected in the Skull's ideology morphing into a more general totalitarianism (Donovan, 2014: 77), or, at times, a nihilistic terrorist tendency borne of no precise political viewpoint other than a desire to bring down capitalist normalcy.[32] The Cold War sometimes plunged Cap's history into confusion. One of his key opponents in the 1970s was a character, William Burnside, whose values made him another distorted echo of Rogers. Seeking to fill the breach when Cap was thought dead, Burnside blackmails the government into letting him serve as a new Captain America; but his entire existence is that of an embodied 'retcon', pressed into action by 1970s writers to attempt to straighten out the continuity hampering existence of Timely comics of the 1950s.

Overseen by Stan Lee, the stories predated the Marvel phase of the company and allowed comics' purest American symbol to fight Communism (and a Red Skull rewritten to serve Moscow) in the era of the Korean War. At a time when explicit reference to shared textual worlds was rare, the Human Torch, Namor and Captain America all interacted in Timely's *Young Men* (a title which at the time had a heavy war emphasis) during this short-lived superhero revival phase that fell, essentially, between the Golden and Silver Ages. This helped to solidify the shared world of the company's superheroes (Sweeney, 2013: 134–5).[33] Later on, however, *Avengers* Vol.1, #4 (1964) asserted that Steve Rogers had laid in the ice since 1945, creating conflict. Two decades from the original publication, Cap's 'Commie Smashing' run of adventures had become a continuity based and ideological embarrassment, as Marvel acknowledged that Nazism and Communism were not, in fact, comparable (Moss, 2014). In the 1970s, Burnside became the instrument to wipe those stories from the legacy of Steve Rogers. Increasingly discredited, Burnside ended up as the brainwashed leader of a neo-Nazi hate group, dubbed 'the Grand Director'.[34] If having a counterfeit Rogers exposed as the mentally controlled puppet leader of a Fascist group failed to sufficiently contradict the stain on the authentic Captain America ethos, subsequent comics found new approaches to extend and analyse Cap's meanings. An interesting story from more recent times (but one that as part of Marvel's *What If?* line is notably bracketed out of 'normal' continuity),[35] sees a parallel universe 1863 tale of 'General America's ancestor, Stephen Rogers. Rogers is the 'Union Man' who, once a naïve corporal, shows inner worthiness and resists corruption to be awarded supernatural powers by a Shamanic Sam Wilson (this world's surrogate for Erskine). Here, Wilson is made an overdetermined hybrid figure, a Black man serving in an all-volunteer Native American regiment. The choice of Rogers to be elevated into the required unification figure by the powers (which include the insight to see men as equals) is at least pragmatically explained by Wilson: 'You think white folks are ready to follow someone who looks like me?' Whichever the dimension, race is an issue. The comic, studied by Barbour (2015), strains to find a level of hybridity in the Captain America–Falcon relationship without seeming to expend the value of the non-White American once their wisdom is transmitted into a palatable figurehead (it also could be construed as pushing Wilson into the familiar, essentialized Black magical figure of filmic culture as discussed by Audrey Colombe (2002)). HYDRA (and other race groups featured in Marvel comics) may divide society, but the recurrence of the racial issue cannot all be put down to them.

The Falcon's relationship with Cap is one of two that stand out from a large supporting cast associated with the superhero. From a host of sidekicks, Bucky Barnes and the Falcon are the two partners who indelibly define stages in Cap's fictional universe: the Second World War period/ensuing Cold War; the pessimistic American 1970s of 'malaise', and Cap's rebirth into a new politics with chilling echoes of older times in writer Ed Brubaker's run (2005–12). With histories that are similarly rich – or, equally chequered – as Steve Rogers' own, each warrants some consideration here.

*****

With Bucky and Peggy familiar from *CA:TFA*, the major MCU debut in *CA:TWS* is that of Sam Wilson (Anthony Mackie), another main player in the distinguished comic history of Captain America. As Adilifu Nama points out, a controversial 'retcon' aside,[36] the Falcon's genesis had him indebted to Captain America for identity and purpose (2011: 70). The pairing as seen in comics is usually discussed in terms of Marvel's vision of racial reconciliation in a chaotic 1970s (the character's importance is said to seep away when the political winds changed – Nama, 2011: 78). But Falcon was frequently used to negotiate arguments around Black militancy and the means of violence (2011: 72). In the 1970s, Wilson was accompanied by a lover, Leila, who critiqued his support role to Captain America, questioning its veiled replication of structural racial subservience. The film tries to hold this in check via a more personally defined sense of help shared by the two characters. The opening scene paints a chance relationship that can develop equally, drawing on a military bond that is an MCU invention. Two soldiers, struggling to adjust to civilian life, out for a run around the Mall in Washington, DC; however, one has super-strength and speed while the other has to suffer being recurrently lapped by the jogger who patronisingly utters 'On your left' on every pass. Recovering afterwards, Wilson introduces himself to the man who he has already worked out is Steve Rogers. Bonding over service talk, Wilson's note that he lost his partner Riley on a mission strikes a particular chord with Cap. Later, when Rogers and Romanoff become S.H.I.E.L.D. targets and turn to Wilson for help, it comes to light that he and Riley were in fact part of a 'pararescue' team utilizing cutting-edge stealth technology in the form of flying suits. The film develops the notion that Wilson in fact brings Rogers back to a place where duty can be reconciled with the need to live a life (discussed in a scene they share at the Veterans Association), but by the postscript – when Wilson refuses Fury's offer to join him in hunting the remnants of HYDRA in Europe – it is Wilson's identity as a useful soldier that has been reconstructed, and it is on this basis, and that of his loyalty to Cap, that he finds his way to the Avengers team seen in the closing moments of *A:AOU*.

Doubt about his own worthiness has long attended the comics Falcon, and is not limited to the starker racial conversation unfolding in Marvel pages of the 1970s; it was seen again as recently as 2012 in a storyline where a 'Madbomb'[37] brainwashing draws (what may be) repressed feelings of social dispossession out of him. When he leads a chemically altered mob to riot against 'the Man', Cap is implicitly associated with the latter.[38] Minds and bodies are crawled into by interlopers with such regularity in the pages of various *Captain America* arcs published over the years, that for this to happen to Rogers' closest ally is hardly a shocking development; yet, in Falcon's case, a specific dimension of his self-critical ponderings and identity doubts always recalls the questions around racial politics, and how a superhero might genuinely represent and improve things for the Black community, once posed by the sceptical Laila.

Sam Wilson's conscientiousness (as a civilian he supports his Harlem community as a social worker; translated in the MCU to fit the military theme, he instead becomes a VA worker) only seems to exacerbate the pressure of working alongside an icon such as Cap, leading to the character often displaying anxiety about being a 'second-rate sidekick' in Cap's shadow (Nama, 2011: 70). An interesting possibility that remains open for the MCU connects Wilson to arguably Marvel's most well-developed – in character terms – male Black superhero: the African Black Panther, a character whose feature is set for 2018. A notable move to upgrade his power so as to cut a figure more equal to Cap saw the Panther bestow new technological wings – and upward mobility – upon Falcon (in *Captain America* Vol.1, #170, 1974). The Panther is rated as one of Marvel's 'seminal black superheroes' (Nama, 2011: 73).

For Wilson's part, he has had to look on as the Captain America identity is hijacked by white supremacists like the Grand Director, highlighting the fight to control the meanings of the role (and amplifying the moment when Wilson assumes the identity himself in 2014's *Captain America* Vol.7, #25). In the MCU, by the end of *CA:TWS*, the trials of the battle against Alexander Pierce have served only to intensify Wilson's sense of identity with (non-governmental) service and thus with Cap: they are a team, and in turning down Fury's offer, Wilson identifies as a 'soldier' only. Once positioned in comics in an ambiguous state between 'ghetto' criminal and activist for social justice, the MCU rewriting tweaks Wilson's meanings in a way that recognizes the different configurations of Black authority in an MCU that is ruled by Nick Fury – himself, no longer the white Second World War veteran of war comics, but the African American grandson of a lift operator. In a way, Fury is another Cap reflection (made clear in their conversation down in the 'Insight' warship bay), but one who advocates 'compartmentalisation' as a way to morally manage the compromises of the modern form of 'war'. Like Romanoff earlier in the film, Fury claims the privilege of clear-sightedness. However, she gradually takes Rogers' example that this amounts to a cynical, dehumanizing distrust of people.

Wilson is not the ambivalent figure that Fury is. His sense of honour and satisfaction at fighting a true and morally acceptable fight – whether this places him on the government 'side' or not – shows that the character falls on the 'correct' side of trust, distinguishing him from S.H.I.E.L.D. values and preparing the way further for the cinematic *Civil War*. Where the MCU version comes full circle into conformity with the source is that Wilson's decision is shown to be due to the example of Captain America; thus the question of agency returns and Cap, again, is responsible for what Sam Wilson 'needs to hear'.[39]

The history of the 'Winter Soldier' is much more compressed in comics (because of the truncated existence of Bucky), and so requires less space to outline. This is not to suggest that it is simple; a product of the mid-2000s Ed Brubaker shake-up of Captain America's comic, which extended it into the murkier tonal territory of realistic spy adventure (reflecting the different ways in which a modern Steve Rogers might conduct himself, but also jarring with the more traditional function given the character in *Avengers* comics), this is the era that inspires the genre atmosphere of the Russos' film. Before the 'Winter Soldier' identity, Bucky Barnes was one of the few who gave the lie to the axiomatic assumption that comic heroes never stay dead, having never been successfully resurrected. An 'army brat' who is orphaned by the death of his military father, early comics showed Bucky growing up as mascot at Camp Lehigh (seen in both MCU Cap movies). His pairing with the newly christened 'Captain America' – just out of Project Rebirth – is as much about straightening out the feisty young James Barnes as countering images of the Hitler Youth with an icon of young American rectitude (Brubaker and Epting, 2011). Bucky joins Cap in both the genuine fight and the propaganda effort. After his assumed death at the end of the war, his body is retrieved by agents of the USSR and after an interval, he is remade into the perfect political assassin during the 1950s, operating at the whim of his masters over the next few decades and spending non-active periods in a cryogenic state.[40] In the MCU, Bucky's resurrection is at the hands of HYDRA, not the Soviets, and seen to be anticipated by Arnim Zola. It should also be noted that contrary to comics, there is no age gap between the two friends, with the opening scenes of *CA:TFA* portraying Barnes as the more worldly, a decided skew away from the source (at least, prior to the revisionist tendencies of later comic arcs that posit a more complicated Bucky).[41] One of the resulting changes to their dynamic is that Rogers' sense of guilt at losing his friend has a different tenor.

The next few adventures of the returned Bucky, who is deprogrammed and regains trust with Rogers' allies and S.H.I.E.L.D., took a very different turn, one which may yet furnish new story points for the MCU.[42] In comics, the Winter Soldier opened up a new vista within 'Marvel Time' for Bucky's exploits to be recounted, since tapped into by different creators[43]; more importantly, Brubaker gave mainstream MU continuity a valid reason to reabsorb the era that had become a retcon-necessitating embarrassment: confirming, that is, that a dark Cap double 'shaped the century' (as Peirce puts it) in the heights of the Cold War, even if the exigencies of comic continuity and the image of Captain America insisted otherwise. Reworking this 'cover-up' in comics actually fits quite well with the 'trust' thematic that has become a bedrock of the MCU take on Captain America. Rogers' basic and unshakeable honesty will not allow him to dismiss or repress Bucky's return, whatever the sins that were performed under HYDRA mind-control; convenient political solutions are not how he thinks. The HYDRA way of wiping memories (as is excruciatingly performed on Bucky between missions to ensure compliance) and burying data places an artificial seal on history. *CA:TWS* contains a portentous shot of the Watergate building (to the left of the Triskelion as Cap rides the elevator, just before STRIKE's attack). Even with his back to the wall, hypocrisy and cover-ups appal Rogers; the people he serves can be trusted with the truth.

Conclusion

Captain America as a character once seemed to inhabit the dead centre of US comics understood as jingoistic, nation-binding fantasy. In fact, Steve Rogers is worthy of sustained study because his evolution charts many of the changes in Big Two comic publishing's relation to 'relevance', and how this could affect sales, over decades. The MCU takes up the gauntlet of reflecting on Captain America's burdens, values and occasional identity crises. The 'splitting' of Steve Rogers is referenced in an exchange at the end of *A:AOU*, when Tony Stark teases Cap about his 'dark side', to Rogers' reply:

> Family, stability … the guy who wanted all that went in the ice … I think someone else came out.

> (Steve Rogers, *Avengers: Age of Ultron*)

As well as reflecting the idea of a broken continuity separating different iterations of Cap (as we've discussed with the 'Commie Smasher' era, rendered in a complex form in comics), the moment compounds something the film raised earlier. On Ultron's orders, the Scarlet Witch invades Rogers' mind (the familiar trope) and creates there a horrifying vision akin to ones that have already unsettled Stark and Thor. The image depicts a celebratory dance for servicemen and women, and the realization of the unfulfilled date that Rogers had arranged with Carter; however, Rogers' experiences of combat, all the wartime aggression and death he saw and in which he participated, are mixed in with the dance. As the hallucinatory Peggy figure offers the reassurance that they are 'home', the dancehall empties. What is interesting is that Rogers shrugs this vision off, and returns to the fight without becoming destabilized like Stark and Thor; his threat to Ultron is unimpaired (in fact, in one sense poorly matched, the all-too-human Cap has more one-to-one combat with Ultron in the film than any Avenger). This is because a socially empty world – his peers almost gone – and the removal of a future with Carter was simply the reality that Steve Rogers met on escaping the ice. He has experienced it, thus it cannot be his worst fear. One of a kind, and alone, once again: his curse, and motivating strength.

CHAPTER 5
TEAMS/SCREENS

Introduction

Everything really started with a team. Although heroes from earlier 'Golden Age' Timely comics were later adapted and reintegrated, the new 'Marvel Age' was prompted, as we know, by Martin Goodman's 1961 command. In gradually unfurling its 'universe', several superheroes (or villains) were always better than one, as far as Marvel was concerned, and the Timely era was jettisoned rapidly after the debut of the Fantastic Four (FF) in November of that year. Even before a dynasty of super-teams was established (the X-Men arriving in the same month as the Avengers in 1963, to be later joined by the Guardians of the Galaxy [Mark I] in 1969; the Defenders [1971]; the Champions [1975], and thereafter, many others), Lee's editorial judgement in this early period was inseparable from his promotional instinct, leading to the regular conjoining of characters and the use of established stars to publicize newer ones. Hence, the FF guest in the premiere issue of Spider-Man's solo title[1] via the familiar Marvel narrative motif of heroes first meeting in aggressive circumstances (the FF were heavily promoted on the issue cover, but played only a modest story role in the issue's secondary strip). A villains' collective was evident as early as March 1964 (the Brotherhood of Evil Mutants in the pages of *X-Men*), the FF regularly battled nemesis group the 'Frightful Four', and Marvel combined Doctor Doom and Namor the Sub-Mariner in an extra-value bad guy title that mirrored the established heroic *Marvel Team-Up*, first launched in 1972.[2] The revived Captain America walked straight into a team (in fact, having to rescue the other Avengers hours after his defrosting in *Avengers* Vol.1, #4, 1964), and found his natural leadership almost immediately accepted, once the obligatory initial clash with future team-mates was dispensed with. As good feedback from Cap's re-emergence as an Avenger started to come in, Cap guested in an anthology title alongside Iron Man (*Tales of Suspense* Vol.1, #59, 1964), before that title morphed into a 'double feature' showcase with an Iron Man story alongside one starring Rogers. Marvel, then, always specialized in bumper treats, envisaging heroes scrapping and socializing (often during the same issue) in a shared universe virtually from day one.

The idea of the team was catalytic for the Marvel Age, seeming to amplify the general traits of superheroes in the company style. When differentially powered heroes from radically different social environments come together, the problem of the existential loneliness and detachment of the superhero as god-figure, the Thor type, can be worked out in narrative terms. Arguably, this theme was explored to its ultimate conclusion outside Marvel, in Alan Moore and Dave Gibbons' character Dr Manhattan (Moore and Gibbons, 1987); however, the Avengers first explored the idea from various perspectives, including a few storylines wherein resentment of how power dictates standing among peers drove unsettling conflict (over the years many of these involved founder member Henry 'Hank' Pym – see Lee, 2014: 67). When power levels among team memberships is more equal, as in the MCU's mostly human/non-mutant S.H.I.E.L.D. team under Agent Coulson, professionalism, loyalty, friendship and personal secrets become the focus of drama. The existence of teams has also always thrown into relief the splendid isolation of superheroes who really did belong apart from everyone else: Spider-Man and Daredevil being exemplary in this.[3] The brooding presence of the Hulk within the famous 'non-team' the Defenders in the 1970s was a source for fertile story points in that series, and the X-Men's Wolverine – a go-to team player for many Marvel titles – is another non-settler, whose ironic presence brings special drama. Even heroes created to be existentially alone, such as demigod Adam Warlock, found themselves with an entourage (Warlock's initial following included Gamora, who would evolve into the warrior who later joins the fun in MS's *GOTG*, played by Zoe Saldana).[4] In Marvel, some of the heroes who most often crave solitude to ponder life's injustices are those who find themselves forced to get along in a colourful melange of egos that could stand – as an exaggerated version, certainly – for any workplace. The paradigmatic example, again, came from the FF: the self-doubts attending Ben Grimm's value to his team were ironically compounded by his need to work alongside a new hero every month in the *Two-in-One* series. It is the Marvel way to remind sulky heroes of the inviolable importance of their civic/social purpose: Hulk, the X-Men, Spider-Man and Grimm, in particular, are rarely thanked for setting aside their feelings of alienation, swallowing their pride and contributing to society.[5]

As Goodman noted in relation to the *Justice League of America* comic in 1961, there was also a solid business case for concentrating on team books. In terms of Marvel's planning around the ebb and flow of character popularity, teams were also a way of preserving certain characters in a degree of the spotlight at times when they were not popular enough to merit a solo title (the fitful publishing history of Hawkeye – as played by Jeremy Renner, a popular cinematic Avenger – is a good case in point. Now, in MCU terms, we see the Hulk treated in a similar way, with the exposure received in team films helping to support his primary role in ancillary marketing, and other iterations like his animated show *Hulk and the Agents of S.M.A.S.H,* (2013–)). Lee's salesman instincts turned the shared universe concept into an injunction to buy more comics.[6] In any given Marvel comic, a true believer might get lucky with some new, weird or combustible superhero combination – 'Treasury Editions', oversized and costlier cardboard-backed comics that came out at holidays, were even referred to as 'Grab-Bags'.[7] The notorious 1984 *Secret Wars* crossover was essentially a special grab-bag with more lasting consequences for the MU. But of course, the more heroes that joined teams and experienced the same battles, often off-planet or in alternate timelines, the more continuity headaches were presented for resolution by the poor editors of those characters with parallel solo titles. When this worked well, it arguably improved the character: Spider-Man returned from the changes of *Secret Wars* with a new alien costume that – for a while – invigorated the character (but was eventually dispensed with, although that is another story). At other times, avoiding contradiction with the character's current iteration and relevant status quo (their location, supporting characters and the status of their powers) involved cooking up a narrative reason for them to skip a crossover.[8]

Marvel's flagship team was the FF, setting terms for not only the later dynamics of teams (and families) in house style, but also providing a hybrid sci-fi-and-soap premise that spawned almost everything interesting from the MU's first decade. The way that magazine accomplished this deserves brief attention (film adaptations of the team itself are outside the bounds of our book, falling outside of the MCU; however, see Chapter 7).[9] As Yockey has affirmed, the initial impetus for the FF comes from the space race and the national need for dominance in technological progress (2005: 59), a premise that informs the representation of not just the team but the New York City community and the city itself as a 'transformed' vertical space pointing to the next frontier (epitomized in their headquarters, the skyscraper Baxter Building). The Four are explorer-adventurers, and they experience many things after their experimental rocket flight is hit by cosmic rays: regularly traversing other dimensions, and, from an early stage, alternate times. Needed by the public but not always appreciated (a Marvel trait), the Four regularly display ego and fractiousness; facing financial pressure, even avarice (seeking better paying careers, in a memorable issue).[10] However, that they – in their individual ways – are morally correct is a safe proposition, shown, for instance, in a recurring trope of the Lee/Kirby days, that being a liberal belief that people can reform; hence the hostilities with the anti-hero Prince Namor never boil over into serious anguish, and several characters that fight the team are eventually accepted as allies or members (such as Sandman and Medusa of the Inhumans). The four members, however, are individuals. From the first treatment (a bare sketch of characters and the team origin written by Lee and given to Kirby to turn into story), disagreements borne out of different 'ethical' points of view were written into them, Lee initially imagining that the other three would unite to subdue the Thing when his mind turned to using their powers strictly for personal gain (Lee, 2007: 351). In practice and with time, and the softening effects of popularity, Ben Grimm began to seem merely ornery rather than Lee's vision of a sometime 'heavy' (351), but the important precedent had been set that Marvel teams would have to work hard merely to stay *as* a team: they would easily, if temporarily, disintegrate (opponents would rapidly catch on to this), and even the best of them would experience disharmonious interpersonal situations with people they nevertheless loved. The FF was more like a family (with a pair of siblings and, a few years into the run, a married couple within the group) than the Avengers, although they would acquire their own sibling pair and also host various couples in their ranks in time.

Another part of the template laid in by the FF is that the superheroes' extended family of loved ones and non-powered associates serves as a sort of recruitment stream for the good fight. In the magazine's early days, it was Ben Grimm's girlfriend Alicia – step-daughter to a super-villain – who was often dragged into adventures, but in the right (or wrong) circumstances, many others joined the effort against villainy, becoming part of an expanded collective: Johnny Storm's college roommate; principals from the African land of Wakanda and 'the Great Refuge', home of the Inhumans[11] – both places visited by the Four; even the regular postman of their Baxter Building headquarters participated in a number of adventures.[12] Observation of the non-heroic life of superheroes has always been a Marvel signature, but this is accompanied by an interest in their relationships, as new powers change how they are seen by others, sometimes tragically (a 'genre'-defining staple for Tasker, 2015: 180). The first words uttered by Peter Parker's Aunt May to her nephew after his origin incident (a radioactive spider bite) remark on a perceived physical change: 'You looked a little tired, Petey …'.[13] Aunt May is a famous example of how supporting casts sustained a continuity friendly 'status quo' around a hero, locking in certain relationship tensions for longer stories, enhancing the Marvel style.

Readers of Marvel comics became conditioned to expect outlandish events and super-crises to appear as disruptive intervals in the course of lives that had to be lived out as regularly as possible (Sanderson, 1992: 72) – and, the latter could be just as testing. From the earliest point in their team career, the Avengers were attended by eternal 'sidekick' and teen identificatory figure Rick Jones (who later gained powers), as well as stoic butler Edwin Jarvis. Although often kidnapped, used and tortured, Jarvis has proved to be a constant among the shifting rosters of that team. Occasionally given the limelight in comics, this figure's existence in the MCU is twofold: transmuted into an Artificial Intelligence version in *Iron Man* films, Jarvis serves as the personality basis of android the Vision (Paul Bettany), in this form defeating villain Ultron's intentions to use the Vision as an improved duplicate bodily vessel for his own consciousness. The 'Jarvis' system is simultaneously an emotional piece of Stark family heritage, based on a very real butler (James D'Arcy), aide to Howard Stark and Peggy Carter in their postwar adventures (see Chapter 4). It is this human incarnation that is given a significant piece of dialogue about the support system needed by Marvel crimefighters, whether they want – or acknowledge – it or not, in *Carter* S1E2 ('Bridge and Tunnel'). Over Peggy's protestations, Jarvis reminds her that she must accept support, or make a mockery of the extremely effective and mutual way in which she and Steve Rogers worked together: 'You were his support. Your desire to help others is noble. But I doubt you'll find much success unless you allow others to help you'.

Recent Marvel comics have returned to this tendency to involve supporting cast members, even turn them into spin-off heroes who reflect the main character and thereby extend their internal universes alongside multiplying opportunities for franchise extension.[14] In the MCU, similarly, we arguably see a sub-team form around each lead character, constituted of family or co-workers. Thor's Asgardian crew the 'Warriors Three' is mirrored, on Earth, by the scientists around Jane Foster (Natalie Portman), who use their expertise in Astrophysics and Norse legend to also support the Thunder God; Tony Stark acknowledges the personal, emotional and business support given by girlfriend Pepper Potts (Gwyneth Paltrow) long before her literal 'suiting up' in *Iron Man 3*, and the same film sees his bodyguard Happy Hogan (Jon Favreau) turn detective to aid Stark. Captain America runs with the elite fighting unit the 'Howling Commandos' in wartime, and is supported by the Falcon, Black Widow and Agent 13/Sharon Carter (Emily VanCamp) in *Captain America: The Winter Soldier*. The mid-credit tease of *Ant-Man* shows another character being granted a powered suit, suggesting another team readying around Scott Lang (Paul Rudd).

Striking instant success with the formula presented by the FF, Marvel comics did not simply give up on further innovating the team concept. Even less was it the case that a static conception of the team concept resulted once Lee backed away from writing and the different groupings started to move through the hands of writers directed by a 'house style' pattern, yet keen to assert individual styles and preoccupations.[15] Marvel heroes are people, and readers of Marvel spend more time with heroes *as* people, arguably, than do those faithful to other publishers. As Roger Stern – who has a strong association with the Avengers but has also written the FF and X-Men – notes, people come together in different circumstances that, naturally, dictate different ways of conducting relationships:

> The thing about the Avengers [is t]he team is always changing. See, the Avengers is an alliance, an organization with a charter and bylaws and an elected chairperson and formal meetings. In contrast, the FF is an extended family, and the X-Men … well, they started out as a school and training facility, and became an underground movement and support group. … But the Avengers? They're the varsity squad.

> (Stern, cited in Thomas and Trodglen, 2015: 48)

Although government pressure did tell on the Avengers, who – for a time – became a highly organized, official entity (with some sound principles: keeping a detailed database of records, running training programmes and having rules for membership), stories suggested that excessive regulation denuded the spirit behind their formation and sapped the team of (political) will, allowing them to be made an instrument. Hence, Whedon's *The Avengers* gives frequent textual reminders that the team is together as a response to a specific need (Loki's alliance with the Chitauri), and that their unity of purpose transcends the behind-the-scenes manipulation of Nick Fury (Samuel L. Jackson), director of security and peacekeeping agency S.H.I.E.L.D. Even if the component egos, personalities and demons prevent any permanent gelling, chafing against the desired containment in governmental structures, they will assemble again when a need on the same scale arises. The film thus contains something of the truth of the 1963 comics Avengers, who were responding to an out-of-the-blue provocation by Loki, directed at half-brother Thor but with the unwanted side-effect of drawing together a powerful group of heroes in common purpose.

As its universe matured (eventually becoming a 'multiverse'), and hierarchies of heroes and the internal stratification across Marvel's wide constellation of earthly and unearthly dimensions became more codified, different forms of team were needed (as per Stern's observation). Thus, when in 2008, writers Dan Abnett and Andy Lanning assembled a new Guardians of the Galaxy from a loose grouping, the members of which had been brought together by a wider comics event, the motivating force was different (see Chapter 6).[16] Consciously proactive, this new model Guardians would pre-empt threats to galactic stability before they occur, rather than accept the collateral damage of a more reactive position. This origin line does not quite survive into their MCU incarnation,[17] but other differences helping to position the Guardians as a new type of team with a different ethos and purpose from the Avengers do manifest in the film.

Before we move into greater detail on team texts, we should look outside the diegesis, where the formation of a team of superheroes has presented Marvel – which owns neither the FF nor X-Men movie rights – with specific industrial and contractual challenges.[18] Marvel's plan recognized not only that narrative capital had to be carefully built to trigger an audience view of a progressive superhero team film as a desirable thing (a 'six-in-one ... super-movie', Stork, 2014: 79), but that the behind-the-scenes work would take years and have to be planned just as carefully. Nevertheless, there were breaks: The Avengers could never have happened in the same way if New Line had been successful in producing an Iron Man film before 2005; negotiations for continuing rights would no doubt have gone differently had that been the case, as sequel options would have been included in original contracts. Now that MS is established as a trusted producer – and moreover, a big league blockbuster performer now outshining those studios with experience of sustaining superhero franchises (Fox, Sony, even the horizontally integrated Warner Bros./DC partnership – Johnson, 2007: 68) – the once unthinkable is made to happen: a character whose cinematic existence is not actually controlled by Marvel will swing into the MCU (Spider-Man, due in a 2017 feature if not earlier). Sony retains the right to distribute the film, and Marvel gets a Cinematic Universe that includes their far and away most popular and marketable solo character.

A day unlike any other ... The Avengers

Chapter 1 argued that the residue of older Hollywood practices lay beneath the process by which MS's policies of production and brand were crafted; that convergence tactics seeking to expedite the escalation of a shared universe rested alongside risk-assuaging blockbuster methodologies and an insistence on house style (such as the quasi-classical reining-in of authorship). What does the team narrative contribute to that which is distinctively 'Marvel Studios'? The build-up to a team of heroes – the first its universe had known[19] – was promised way back in the closing moments of *Iron Man*, a marker laid down to ostentatiously signify that the studios managing rival superhero franchises were about to be eclipsed by Marvel's massive expansion. Delivery on this plan required an 'initiative' called the Avengers. At a narrative level, a team forged in fraternal betrayal and emphasizing typical Marvel divisions (forming only after the usual misunderstandings between heroic parties, with Fury pulling the strings unbeknownst to the World Security Council (WSC)) becomes, as an industrial project, a doomsday weapon of convergence strategy: the 'zenith of a transmedia franchise ... four years in the making' and 'apotheosis' of the MCU sequence (Taylor, 2014: 6). Whedon's film is the payoff of a plan, uniting and retrospectively justifying (as a subtitle like 'The First Avenger' makes clear) the convoluted route started in the solo Phase I films.

The Avengers is the spectacular product of the logic of the whole narrative experiment, carrying with it and within it the idea of escalation, of being bigger and better: 'The superhero action film writ large' (Tasker, 2015: 185). Despite this mandate, Whedon's storytelling imparts a sense of precise economy drafted straight from the source material – the same thing that apparently inspired the rushed production of *Avengers* (Vol.1) #1 in 1963: the lack of need to recount origin stories (Darowski J. J., 2014: 1).[20] Every principal had been at least glimpsed before (and the two characters who have had least play in the Phase I movies – Black Widow and Hawkeye – are the most secretive in background terms). This facilitates classical simplicity of storytelling in the first film that is notably less evident in the unwieldy *A:AOU*.[21]

Bringing into play advantages of the 'connective tissue' principle (see Chapter 8), the first film presents Whedon with a diabolical device (the 'Tesseract'), a villain who covets it, his earthly helper (Erik Selvig/Stellan Skarsgard, from the *Thor* series), and some shadowy cosmic forces already laid out in events of the earlier MS releases of 2011. Such factors allow the film to begin *in media res* with the Tesseract established as an awesome, coveted object. With few introductions needed, the first half-hour of the film is mainly turned over to outlining the mission (really an excuse to peer into the antagonistic relationship between S.H.I.E.L.D. and the ruling WSC), the gathering of the team and the recruitment of Steve Rogers: character stuff, essentially, but written with Whedon's typical verve. Gaps in character development caused by scheduling are acknowledged: of the established heroes, Downey Jr's Iron Man, whose status quo has changed little since *Iron Man 2* (*IM2*), receives less attention than Mark Ruffalo's Bruce Banner (Hulk). Offscreen since 2008, Banner receives an extended recruitment scene with Scarlet Johannson's Black Widow. The scene contains no FX or spectacle, yet was excerpted and made focus for publicity in the weeks prior to the release of the film (Brevet, 2012), showing that MS appreciated that which Whedon – a veteran of team narratives with intimate and dramatic emotional beats a speciality[22] – could bring to the table. The minimal honesty which Widow/Romanoff – Fury's top spy – trades with Banner (invoking the cruelty of her own upbringing in Soviet security service custody as context to her involvement of a child who helps to trick Banner into this meeting) is enough to underwrite a close bond that is developed in *A:AOU*. In that film, Renner's Clint Barton (Hawkeye) is revealed – in a nice surprise inspired by the *Ultimates 2* series – to have secret and blissful domestic roots, leaving Widow and Banner to come together in the realization that they are the only real 'outsiders' left (even man-out-of-time Rogers has acquired a partner, Sam Wilson, by this point).

'Pulled apart like cotton candy'

The amount of planning that went in to the uniting of the Iron Man, Thor and Captain America series' casts *The Avengers* as a product of calculation; this is a little ironic, as their intrinsic diegetic character, built over decades, has more to do with chaos and circumstance. The issue of how the members of this team fit together (usually badly) cannot be ignored, as the literature around the Avengers in comics testifies (see for instance Wright, 2003: 215; Darowski J., 2014; Sacks, 2014). Suitably then, dysfunctionality is shot through a film which repeatedly questions whether a team ethos is really just a temporary state of ego suppression: 'We're a chemical mixture that makes chaos' is Bruce Banner's evaluation of the combustible assemblage of loners, banished gods and assassins around him. The language is interesting, given an analogy extended to the partnership of the team's co-creators[23] Kirby and Lee. Gerard Jones notes that it was their 'chemical combustion' of personal, stylistic and experiential differences that lent an originary spark to the MU (2002: 228). The idea of a violent yet creative collision would mark Marvel forever, sowing the presence of conflict into fiction as an almost permanent fixture (with plenty of background tension in the Bullpen too, of course).

Such tension did not evade the notice of the team itself; in a Steve Englehart-authored issue (Vol.1, #109, March, 1973), Thor predicts that 'internal dissension' will cost the group its existence and, later, Captain America explicitly jockeys for the leadership, such inadequacy does he perceive in how Iron Man carries out the role (Vol.1, #164, October, 1977; #168, February 1978). For the reader, though, the in-fighting barely required such commentary, as the characters so regularly stormed out of the group. So it is that a key aspect of the narrative of *The Avengers*, as Yvonne Tasker notes, is how events turn '... on the disparate group's ability to overcome their disagreements and come together as a team; a "handful of freaks" to a protective force' (2015: 188). Whedon sets up extended scenes to reflect this, most memorably a three-way battle ostensibly over the custody of Loki but reflecting the different styles and priorities of Thor, Cap and Iron Man; and the helicarrier scene, from which Banner's team motto ('a chemical mixture that makes chaos') comes.

As Stork intimates, the assembling of the Avengers (the film went by the title *Avengers Assemble* in the United Kingdom and Ireland)[24] – the union – is the promise of both MS and the Phase I suite of films. It is also the metaphor for what MS is best at doing (connected storytelling). So the first half of *The Avengers* introduces the narrative complication that keeps this from happening until the optimal time, with Loki – as in the original *Avengers* comics – instrumental in sowing discord. The effect of Loki's sceptre is to pour out bad vibes, touching personalities and radiating discord; or does it merely add more of it to the already wary and unstable congress? Thor loftily mocks the idea that a team of mortals could surmount and responsibly control powerful forces; Rogers accuses Stark of selfishness; Stark counters that Cap is only special because of the experimentation of smart guys like himself. No one can call the Avengers imprecise judges of each other's character. The squabbling, in-fighting, and Hawkeye's recovery back to his heroic self from a Tesseract-induced brainwashing all deliberately work to intensify the moment when team, film narrative and transmedia sequence actually do tie together: 'All this antagonism … defers the very action image promised by the promotional materials' (Tasker, 2015: 188). Hence, the lack of fit among the heroes themselves is a useful narrative component; the absence of this, perhaps, in *A:AOU* (which begins with the group already reconstituted and closing in on HYDRA villain Baron Strucker (Thomas Kretschmann)), contributes to a feeling that a little purpose has been lost in the franchise even as the team (temporarily) appears more solid. That the producers may be aware of this, as well as such creeping financial and logistical considerations as star availability, desire and remuneration going forward (see Chapter 6), is signalled by the conclusion of the sequel, where a new or parallel team has been 'assembled' by Captain America.[25] In more diegetic terms, the scene is not just a positive announcement of new heroes; a secondary meaning available is that a schism between members has swelled again – this time, without Loki's interference, suggesting something deep-rooted. Here we detect Marvel's plans for 2016's *Captain America: Civil War* and the playing out of Stark and Rogers' different philosophies in relation to how superheroes can best contribute to national and global security. The impression of a planned new era is capped by the inclusion of a (narratively, fairly spurious) encounter between Falcon and Scott Lang in *Ant-Man*, leading to a recruitment scene at the end of Peyton Reed's film.

Three years previously in 2012,[26] the saviour of team and New York had been Tony Stark, who proved Cap wrong by making the 'sacrifice play' that allows the city to be saved and the invading Chitauri sealed off from Earth's dimension. As the saga progresses, it connects with concerns from the mature *Avengers* comic run of the 1970s–90s, including those relating to how our feelings and responses confirm us as human. Using Hammontree's work, John Darowski comments on how changes to the team's environment followed naturally on from earlier anxieties in the 'malaise'-stricken 1970s:

> The early nineties was the dawn of the information age … The Avengers seemed to embrace this change. Their previously-destroyed base, a brownstone mansion, had been replaced with a sleek postmodern building filled with rooms crammed with as much technology as possible. But accompanying the convenience of portability arose concerns about the dehumanizing affect … on people's lives … New modes of communication increasingly isolated the individual and could result in fragmenting social cohesion (Hammontree, 168). How soon before everyone became as impersonal as The Vision?
>
> (2014: 96)

Reflecting such concerns, and how grasping for security increases the temptation to trust technology beyond common sense, *A:AOU* sees 'murderbot' Ultron spring from Stark's paranoia. Stark has been seen (in *Iron Man 3*) to suffer a form of post-traumatic stress from laying down his life for the team and the planet in *The Avengers*. In *A:AOU*, Stark is bewitched into experiencing a vision of letting his comrades down – which he interprets as a paucity of decision making and strength rather than anything else – and this appears key in his later actions. The continually upgrading Ultron then gathers resources to begin a process that will birth the entity known as the Vision. The creation scenario plays out rather differently in the comics (we shall not go into this for reasons of space), but the MCU Vision bears little of Stark's personality; Ultron, however, displays the arrogance, quick wit and problem-solving pragmatism of his mercurial creator[27]: so much so that their similarity is noted as one which Whedon 'went to great pains' on. The programme's 'megalomaniac egotism, overriding ambition, obsessive focus on a "logical" goal were all distorted, magnified versions of Stark's own qualities', amplified by having the robot use 'Stark-like language and [make] Stark-like comments' (Hawkes, 2015). Ultron thus grows out of components of Stark's own personality, another radical metallic remaking of his irresponsible old self (as seen in the first Iron Man film and early *Avengers* scenes). A man whose fortunes are changed by a tiny piece of metal becoming embedded near his heart in *Iron Man* reaches for the goal of manufacturing Iron Avengers – a 'suit of armour around the world'. Though partial redemption comes in the noble (yet, unintended) creation that is the Vision, this is after Stark has seen his own Oedipal nightmare assume sentient, mobile form and terrify the world. Stark's presumption is overriding human instinct for over-rationalized, morally remote technology; a fear-borne misjudgement which, of course, could be argued to reinforce his humanity until one realizes that his method inadvertently places him in the company of the veiled HYDRA plan to create Project Insight in *CA:TWS*. This sinister plan is justified by Fury to an unconvinced Captain America in terms of necessity to 'neutralise … threats before they happen' (see Chapter 4).

In the MCU, teams which in some form keep in touch with the inner chaos and contingency that keeps them fluid, honest and looking for purpose are those which audiences are directed to accept as valid. The Avengers, and Coulson's S.H.I.E.L.D. unit fall on the right side of this; Stark's hawkish Iron Avenger plan, Project Insight and 'The Real S.H.I.E.L.D.' faction (to be discussed shortly) do not, since they escalate trouble by attempting to take measures against 'what won't be' (as the Vision says of Stark).[28] The tension between camaraderie and common morality versus a bigger, politically dictated but indiscriminate, distantly human form of strategic control seems destined to come to a head in *Captain America: Civil War*. In terms of the role of teams in the MCU, it shall be interesting to see where the Defenders sit in relation to this, when the Netflix show airs. One thing that can be noted at this point is that it is a team where professions – one expert lawyer, one hired but socially conscious strongman, one detective and one billionaire – will be important in defining either the unity of the group, or, more likely and this being Marvel, the estrangement (with this team having the reputation of being populated by heroes who don't believe in teams).[29]

S.H.I.E.L.D.: Avengers aftershocks

Join S.H.I.E.L.D. Travel to distant lands. Meet exciting and unusual people … and kill them.

> (Lance Hunter (Nick Blood), characterizing Coulson's
> recruitment pitch in *Agents of S.H.I.E.L.D.* S2E10, 'What They Become')

Marvel teams are emotional oddities, and sometimes little more than loosely assembled refuges for various angry types (as in the Defenders of comics). As already pointed out regarding the FF, teams tend to believe in second chances (beneficiaries of this policy in the MCU alone include all of the following who are redeemed from criminal or 'enemy' pasts: Hawkeye, Black Widow, Bucky, Scott 'Ant-Man' Lang). As of Summer 2015, the hungry rumour mill for Marvel news was speculating that ambiguously reformed all-villain team the Thunderbolts could be being lined up for the Netflix treatment (Cassidy, 2015). Whether this materializes or not, a Marvel team is certainly a channel for atoning for regrettable decisions; when Spider-Man enters the MCU, we assume the careworn youngster will join in. Despite the motif of the team marking Marvel's signature work from the FF's debut onward, the difficult singularity felt by the hugely popular Spider-Man showed creators' interests around individual identity. The compulsion to follow one's inner nature, with difficult moral lessons as the cost of exploring a free destiny was most classically seen in that character and the death of his uncle and girlfriend, but also expressed in key *Avengers* runs (such as their battle with ambivalent cosmic force Korvac).[30]

The emotional maturity found in the MU treated young readers with respect. Renegades and sinners were allowed to find a place in teams from an early stage, leaving them vulnerable but dramatically enhanced. The MCU version of Hank Pym (Michael Douglas) – the first Ant-Man – is imbued with one key regret about falling short in helping his wife avoid oblivion on a mission. The character in comics, however, while a founding Avenger, has an incredibly chequered history of being easily corrupted from outside (leading him to join villain teams), insecurity, jealousness and – controversially for readers – even domestic violence (see Lee, 2014). The inclusivity, and, sometimes, the excessive respect heroes show for each other's civilian privacy lets in malign influences. Corrosive, controlling figures infiltrate teams. Coulson's S.H.I.E.L.D. team has to deal with the betrayal of the hugely effective but apparently amoral 'mole' Grant Ward (Brett Dalton) – turned by his abusive HYDRA controller John Garrett (Bill Paxton).

Any gathering of heroes is threatened by another damaging tendency: that of reading strengths as weaknesses, and vice versa. This reverberates through Phase II via the core issue of trust. In Chapter 4, we argued this to be the defining moral dynamic of the run of films from *CA:TWS*, taking in much of *Agents of S.H.I.E.L.D.* (*AoS*) and even aspects of *Agent Carter* (e.g., Carter's guilt at maintaining a duplicitous front with loved ones; the ambiguous rumours of Howard Stark's anti-Americanism). The theme is frequently distilled into a confrontation of the values of individual versus organization. The events of *A:AOU* can be interpreted as a lesson in humility demonstrated to Iron Man – strength lies in togetherness and trust; yet the acceptance of others into our lives carries risk. When humanity starts to encounter gods, synthetic people, mutates like the Hulk, and genetic 'miracles', the gateway to acceptance is suddenly blocked to some (a problem deeply embedded in Marvel from the earliest issues of *Fantastic Four*: three members of that group carried on public lives with no secret identities, suffering little due to this, whereas the Thing, the sole member physically transformed beyond 'normal' standards, grew ever more bitter at his change in social standing).

Season One (2013–14) of *AoS* shows that Phil Coulson, like his idol Captain America, trusts his instincts that wrongdoers can reform. The pilot, transmitted in the US in September 2013, brings us to the team *in media res*, with the role of viewer's proxy being taken by new recruit Skye (later known as 'Daisy Johnson'), played by Chloe Bennet. In time Skye becomes the team's unofficial communications expert and later a field agent, before the further revelation that she is an 'Inhuman' in the second season; but she is originally picked up as a hacker against S.H.I.E.L.D., working on proving that events involving 'enhanced' people have happened. Coulson welcomes Skye, yet, misses the Grant Ward rift within his own ranks. Indeed, Coulson himself, or rather his existence,[31] is a major Nick Fury lie made (remade) flesh. The cover-up of his return enables the Avengers to continue to be used by Fury, who exploited Coulson's 'death' as a cause for their rallying together. Just as in comics, Marvel heroes can never enjoy paragon status, as someone calling them out on their hypocrisy is always around the corner. The resurrection process leaves an alien message implanted in Coulson's mind which does, however, lead to a deepening of his trusting relationship with his key lieutenant, Melinda May (Ming-Na Wen), as she helps him cope with its strain (S2E2, 'Heavy is the Head').

The presence of the S.H.I.E.L.D. agency runs throughout the MCU. It evolved from the Strategic Science Reserve (those important post-Second World War connections, again), which employed Peggy Carter; her service is covered in parts of *Captain America: The First Avenger* and Season One (2015) of her series. As previously mentioned, flashbacks reveal Carter's role in relieving HYDRA of the object (the 'obelisk')[32] that drives the 'Inhumans' plot for much of *AoS*' second season. The surveillance function – and S.H.I.E.L.D.'s neutrality to 'good' and 'bad' – that will come to define it is mentioned even back then, with Carter opining that the SSR must evolve not just to play custodian to such deadly, barely understood technology, but to watch over those who are needed to 'toy' with it, to understand it but also to find ways to exploit it (in this case, Howard Stark).[33] With honourable intentions, the notion of (governmentally sanctioned) oversight – later to cause untold problems, from 'Project Insight' to the coming 'civil war' – was there in the first SSR days. The dilemma is that the absence of this kind of oversight risks a nightmarish Ultron: a genuinely amoral monster whose rampage will ironically bring superheroes' activities fully, harshly into the examining light of the political world.[34]

Understood as a narrative device or universal 'glue' (Oldham, 2014),[35] S.H.I.E.L.D. helps to professionalize heroics – Widow, Hawkeye, Peggy Carter and Fury are all effectively employees, at different levels; Cap's Army history draws him to service; Stark and Banner are 'consultants' (as a side note, this flags up the fact that surprisingly few of the MCU's leading heroes are fully masked, or maintain secret identities, the issue being effectively boxed off as early as the final scene of *Iron Man*). Marvel comics have always been interested in *why* heroes serve. The notion of *noblesse oblige* will be introduced to the MCU as a further complication of the basic idea of responsibility with two upcoming releases: *Black Panther* (lead character T'Challa balances adventuring with serving as King of the Wakandans, the African nation mentioned in *A:AOU*); and, *Inhumans* (more of which shortly). The far less traditional power structures of S.H.I.E.L.D. are turned upside down by the revelations of its long-term, fatal compromising by HYDRA agents and leadership. In response, Coulson's previously specialist team[36] takes the lead of the rump of the organization as, invited by Fury, he seeks to rebuild it in the image of his beliefs. As Chapter 8 examines in further detail, Phil Coulson's journey to a major, storied character is synonymous with the gradual textual expansion of the MCU. A character created specially for it, he is uniquely placed to represent continuity, where Tony Stark represents innovation (the first hero to receive a solo film – see Chapter 3), and Captain America represents singularity. In *Iron Man*, the shorthand used for Coulson is of a 'man in black' shell representing a faceless but presumably benign bureaucracy. As Nick Fury pulls more screen time in subsequent films, Coulson undergoes a transition into the human face of a murky organization. By the time viewers are reacquainted with Coulson in *AoS*, the tension between the all-seeing corporate atmosphere of the S.H.I.E.L.D.

machine – running on surveillance and clearance levels – and the quirky, forgiving environment of Coulson's unit – running on the presence of trust, and Coulson's (not infallible) judgement – has become an evident theme. Within a few episodes – synced in, impressively, with the events of *CA:TWS* (Oldham, 2014) – the main S.H.I.E.L.D. organization dissolves.

Coulson's renegades

Is S.H.I.E.L.D. good at protecting the world? It can be recalled that it held the Tesseract in custody at the beginning of *The Avengers*, but proved vulnerable to Loki (who psychologically commands Selvig into being his thrall). At this point, the organization is bloated but, worse, Fury's plans (to weaponize the power of the Tesseract, as discovered by Cap), cast it in an untrustworthily hawkish light. Fury rationalizes about the discovery of Asgardians upping the security stakes and still has the chutzpah to stand on a pedestal at the movie's climax to deflect an upbraiding from the WSC, which questions the wisdom of entrusting the Tesseract to one of those Asgardians. S.H.I.E.L.D. carries on into MCU Phase II surrounded by a sense of ineffectuality alongside the revealed rottenness. *CA:TWS* and the first seasons of *AoS* and *Agent Carter* retrospectively show that since 1946, whatever its achievements, it has most likely been working to unintended agendas (though loyal to S.H.I.E.L.D., Fury's own career was advanced by bigwig traitor Alexander Pierce). This places the 'big organization', again, in a critical spotlight that is escaped by the improvised, chaotic group (a strength of television work from *AoS* co-creator Joss Whedon – Oldham, 2014). The tendency to institutionalized secrecy is presented as ruinous, but in the context of the bigger picture of the MCU it is the attitude to control of a wildly changing world that is presented as flawed (the point that Thor made, under Loki's influence, in *The Avengers*). At the same time, a readymade answer of giving the 'enhanced' community, superheroes, freedom to deploy their powers as they wish is not proffered. S.H.I.E.L.D. – and whatever may replace it to effect the direct regulation of superheroes in *CA:CW* – is a bureaucracy that will inevitably corrupt, keeping the answer to this problem out of reach and in the realms of 'better the devil you know'.

Why S.H.I.E.L.D.? With all this distrust, treachery and incompetence, *AoS* may seem a strange choice for the MCU's first television venture. Individuals with tracking, intelligence and combat skills sometimes need to come together in the name of world defence, just as do the 'enhanced'; but the housing of this within the politically accountable S.H.I.E.L.D. is ambivalent. It supplies drama, however, developing viewer intrigue about the in-MCU world – a world gradually turning superhuman. Where superheroes are the problem, S.H.I.E.L.D. clears up their mess but also tracks and tags them; in some ways aspiring to *manage*, not aid, the rising superhuman population. Lists of dangerous or alien objects ('0-8-4's) or beings ('the Index') to be investigated – and ideally obtained/recruited – are kept. The need to vet everyone reduces honour and diminishes the trust of any such enterprise; it clearly does not sit well with Captain America and grates with Coulson. Yet, the programme makers are emphasizing another perspective here. The storytellers approach Coulson's team as a window onto how society reacts to a strange new super-powered reality.[37] That the creative team can only selectively explore this reality due to star contracts with proliferating costs unrealistic for TV budgets[38] only validates the logic of retaining this premise and perspective. This can work both for and against perceptions of the strength of the show's meaning and value in relation to MCU films (Oldham, 2014; Hadas, 2014: 9). Part of the creative strategy to manage this relies on those very same narrative ploys of '0-8-4s' and 'the Index', while the subject of the One-Shot *Item 47* – the bridge from *The Avengers* to *Iron Man 3* – consolidates the message (see Chapter 8 for more on 'One-Shots' and this film specifically).

Although a shadowy organization, a goal pursued across Season One and embodied in the sympathetic, Wikileaks-type figure of Skye is to make S.H.I.E.L.D., if not transparent, then more honest. This goal is consistent with *CA:TWS* and its attitude to free information (contrasting Zola's bizarre existence in HYDRA's electronic systems with Romanoff's intention to turn the data from the 'Lemurian Star' flash drive into a weapon against their foes by releasing it onto the web, no matter the consequences for herself and S.H.I.E.L.D.), evidence of the thematic planning extending across platforms. The theme is further explored as the public image of S.H.I.E.L.D. becomes a focus of Season Two. After HYDRA is exposed, its opponents like Brigadier General Glenn Talbot (Adrian Pasdar) and Senator Christian Ward (Tim DeKay) attempt to define public opinion around S.H.I.E.L.D. – an obstruction to both the regular military and politics – as a terrorist organization.[39] The type of organization S.H.I.E.L.D. could be to work as television also seems to factor into its breaking down: it needed to be swiftly reduced from a bloated organization into a fast-moving, relatable team (in harmony with the established strengths of previous Whedon projects such as 'the creation of a "family" unit from an oddball cast of characters' – Oldham, 2014). Thus, this becomes the precise task of Season One: episodes set in the enormous, hierarchical 'Hub' or training academy[40] convey an institutional lack of soul and tendency to absorb individualism, while – officially licensed by Nick Fury – Coulson's unit enjoys autonomy and a country-hopping global remit on its 'Bus'. Compared to remote, scary, hard to understand superheroes, Coulson's black-ops agents ironically become a sort of beacon of light as they try to reconstruct a better S.H.I.E.L.D., based on Coulson's more compassionate values (rather than Fury's subterfuge, where keeping secrets from official watchmen like the WSC, from enemies and from allies all became the same thing).[41] The S.H.I.E.L.D. agents suffer from their own problems with trust and treachery; it could be said that dramatically, the show over-relies on these ingredients. However, *AoS* is a spy show after all (in this, closing a feedback loop in relation to TV genre, as Oldham (2014) contests: 'The programme's actual generic category is best conceptualized as a revival of the light-hearted spy-fi adventure series of the 1960s, such *as The Man from UNCLE* (1964–8) … an entirely appropriate model, as the comics version of SHIELD originally emerged from the 1960s vogue for utopian international spy organisations with catchy acronyms'). The emphasis on S.H.I.E.L.D.'s capacity to pursue utilitarian ends at high moral cost makes labelling as 'utopian' problematic, but mirrors the frequently opaque moral vision guiding the S.H.I.E.L.D. of comics.[42] Fury's way is not shown as the only conceivable way to operate a peacekeeping force. Although accompanied by a certain ambivalence, Coulson – the embodiment of the MCU's capacity for growth – promises change.

Conclusion

At the time of writing, *AoS* had run forty-five episodes. Our limited space allows only a brief report of two unfurling storylines that are germane both to this chapter's theme, and the future of the MCU. An interesting direction taken in the second half of Season Two of the show, amid the post-collapse paranoia, where infiltration is revealed as endemic to the organization's ruling structures, is that Coulson's Fury-anointed team is not the only group to claim the identity of S.H.I.E.L.D. Another faction – with (the by now inevitable) moles within Coulson's team – arises, dubbing itself 'the real S.H.I.E.L.D.', as a struggle to compromise in the face of the newest, potentially threating unknown (the presence of Skye's people, the Inhumans) ensues. The explicit 'civil war' connotations of the idea not only stay true to Marvel traditions of the good guys disagreeing on method and principle, but also anticipate the clash between points of view that will see Iron Man and Captain America on sharply opposed sides. With the notion that part of the brief of *AoS* is to delineate a ground-level view of a world where superhuman threats multiply, its third season has cleared room to explore values from different sides during its run (its episodes will air until May 2016, with the *Civil War* movie scheduled for 6th May).

Just as S.H.I.E.L.D. has its 'index', the ancient race of the Inhumans has 'the diviner'/'obelisk' – an object that scans humans for stored genetic potential which is released using a special chemical agent. Where S.H.I.E.L.D. uses the index to track down and manage potential trouble, the Inhumans use the diviner to identify and add to their 'family' – with the downside of this being that their social system has already ratified a decision to live in total isolation (meaning that newly transformed Inhumans must forsake the regular world). Treated badly by humanity when exposed in the past,[43] this policy is presumably driven by the council of 'elders', kept offscreen but referenced in the show.[44] Little is known about the upcoming *Inhumans* film, slated for 2018, but *AoS* has set a significant amount of groundwork for understanding their role in the MCU as well as establishing Skye (now 'Daisy Johnson') as a prominent figure: Skye/Daisy is the daughter of villainous Calvin Zabo (Kyle McLachlan) and Jiaying (Dichen Lachman), an Inhuman extremist who angles to lead their society.

The recognizable Inhuman team from comics, showcased in the *Fantastic Four* (interrelating with that team in various ways) before two well-remembered 1970s runs steered by Kirby[45] and writer Doug Moench, as well as a popular 1990s revival, is actually a royal family. Ruled by silent monarch Black Bolt and including his wife, her sister, his cousin and so on, we assume that these are the 'elders' so far unseen. Just as interesting to this development as the addition of a fresh team dynamic – one caught up in blood, kingship and responsibility for a threatened people but also built on customs of respect and obedience, unlike other groups – is the notion of potential Inhumans spread worldwide, only needing to be activated: this being the real thrust of the damage that Jiaying plans to inflict on the human world (an unsuccessful 'terrigenesis' process kills the subject). The finale of Season Two suggested that she may still pull this off. The MCU moves to a world where potential to be powered can reside within anyone; the distinction between powers that are bestowed or innate has often been a point of interest in Marvel.[46] Many people seem set to unwillingly go through this 'divining' process (and S.H.I.E.L.D.'s actions are implicated, again). Will the field be levelled, or the amount of social division and death simply escalate? Whatever the answer to this, the ingrainedness of teams in Marvel company heritage – the tradition of dramatically investing in the 'chaotic' chemistry of superhero relations – will undoubtedly be reaffirmed and expanded by the film slate and complementary third season of *Agents of S.H.I.E.L.D.*

CHAPTER 6

STAR-LORD, WHO?: *GUARDIANS OF THE GALAXY* – RAIDING THE 'B-LIST' FOR NEW LEGENDS

Introduction

In 2014, already nine films into its shared cinematic universe, Marvel Studios (MS) took what appeared to be a great risk, drawing upon relatively obscure source material to launch a seemingly new franchise in the form of the James Gunn-directed *Guardians of the Galaxy* (*GOTG*). Unlike the previous Avengers-centric sequence (hereafter, collectively referred to as the Avengers Franchise (AF),[1] this next feature would include a cast of characters that, upon the film's announcement, had not been teased in previous MCU releases; could not be found prominently in existing videogames, animated series, toys or miscellaneous merchandise; and, compared to the multi-title publishing franchise that is the Avengers, barely even had a recognizable comic book series on which to base the film. The characters that would appear in *GOTG* were about as obscure as Marvel could possibly still make marketable, yet had been selected to embark upon the studio's next phase of expansion, as it pushed its universe into a more cosmic setting than had been seen in the (mostly) earthbound AF. The risk of assembling this specific cast of characters, relatively new even to their own comic title, can be rationalized by considering the desire of MS for them to occupy a strategic position within its burgeoning film universe. The film initiates a 'brand' that is separate and differentiated from the Avengers, while still being a part of the complex narrative matrix represented by the MCU. This chapter will propose that this perception of risk, although not discouraged by Marvel (indeed, set up as a theme in promotional discourse)[2] actually masks careful calculation designed to minimize the challenges of expanding the universe's potential scope. For, although in the eyes of the popular and trade press this film is identified as a risk, the emergence of *GOTG* is in fact the result of an astute, long-term focused organizational decision, combating the more pertinent threat of over-reliance on a single prominent property such as the AF, with its mounting talent costs (elaborated upon later). This decision has been somewhat vindicated by both *GOTG*'s success, and the immediate – possibly earlier than expected – signs of fatigue in the AF, evidenced by a relatively underwhelming reception of *Avengers: Age of Ultron* (*A:AOU*).[3]

Organizational theory, particularly the work of Graham Hooley et al. (2012) and Richard Lynch (2006), will inform this chapter, with specific attention paid to how an organization's corporate strategy aims to maintain a sustainable competitive advantage. A reading of the popular and trade presses will illuminate such theory by offering insight into the popular reception of *GOTG*, within the meaning of the overall development of the MCU plan, as seen by these sources. Further, the organizational significance of *GOTG*'s release will be supported by instances of textual analysis that will show how ideas surrounding differentiation, strategic planning and calculated risks are narrativized, bleeding into the film's diegesis. The film can thus be seen as a further instance of strategic and creative aims and intentions intertwining.

How the risk was received

Since *GOTG* was released in July 2014, a year before the aforementioned signs of Avengers fatigue surrounding *A:AOU*, Marvel's pre-emptive decision to risk diverging from such a successful franchise at that point can be read as proactive strategic marketing: taking the early decisions necessary in order to maintain a sustainable competitive advantage. The necessity of such proactive risk-taking is emphasized by Hooley et al., when stressing the importance of innovation to an organization seeking to secure or maintain such an advantage:

> The heart of radical innovation is the search for big ideas, rather than settling for small ideas. To stay relevant and to succeed, companies need bold innovative strategies. But this relies on the ability to create and resource big ideas, and to overcome inertia, narrow-mindedness and risk aversion that provide barriers to true innovation.

> (2012: 333)

Marvel's risk of expending valuable, finite resources on a seemingly untested property, rather than channelling these resources into a product already in peak condition, can be read as an extension of the type of 'big idea' that MS showcased throughout the early stages of building the MCU. Marc Graser (2014a) subscribes to this notion of revisiting risk, explaining that many of MS's initial moves were met with scepticism: '*Iron Man* was considered too obscure. *Captain America* too American. And *Thor* too much of a fantasy figure'. The sentiment is echoed by Devin Leonard (2014b), who states that MS has 'shown in its first phase that it would take superheroes once considered B-listers in the pages of comics … and meld them into the Avengers, a multibillion-dollar franchise'. The touch of Kevin Feige is again implicated on a personal creative level, as Graser adds that through such risk-taking, Feige 'has proved his critics wrong, launching some of Hollywood's biggest franchises', then turns to the then imminent *GOTG* release, explaining that it invites 'even more raised eyebrows'. Once again, the same point is highlighted by Leonard: 'Now Marvel hopes to [... form a multibillion-dollar franchise] with the Guardians, using even less famous characters. Before the standard blockbuster ad blitz, members of this new superhero team had almost zero penetration into mainstream pop culture'. Feige himself emphasizes that the level of risk presented by this release is comparable with previous points in the development of the MCU, showing a tendency to contextualize the new with reference to an existing track record: 'While we were selling (the first) *Iron Man* to the outside world, it was met with skepticism. "Why would anyone want to see a movie with a character they've never heard of?" (With *Guardians*) it was exciting for us to be in this position again' (Feige cited in Graser 2014a). The way attention is placed here is not accidental, with Feige foreseeing a benefit from the cultural cache that being associated with adventurous propositions can attain.[4] Even with such emphasis placed on the risk being taken, Marvel's confidence in the strategic necessity of this film's release is acknowledged by Pamela McClintock (2014), who states that *GOTG* was the 'widest August release in history', opening in 4,080 theatres during a month that has in the past been considered a barren time at the box office.[5] Ray Subers (2014) was typical in calibrating the instant success of *GOTG* to have surpassed expectations, stating that the film 'ruled the box office this weekend with a fantastic $94.3 million. That's easily the biggest debut ever for an August release'.

Many in the popular and trade press reappraised the apparent risk in the light of this powerful start. Bilge Ebiri (2014) declared that the numbers validate 'the filmmakers and executives who took a chance on a tongue-in-cheek, big-budget sci-fi adventure based on a lesser-known cult title'. To add further perspective to MS's confidence in this perceived risk, an examination of *GOTG*'s 'big budget' can offer insight.[6] At $170 million, *GOTG* had the same advertised production budget as *Captain America: The Winter Soldier* (*CA:TWS*), released that same year, which is a direct sequel to a film based on the already more recognizable character of Captain America. Further, *GOTG* had the highest budget of any non-sequel MCU film (with the exception of *The Avengers*, which is difficult to define as not, at least, a pseudo-sequel to previous AF films, costing $220 million). *Iron Man* and *Captain America: The First Avenger* (*CA:TFA*) had production budgets of $140 million, while *Thor* and *The Incredible Hulk* each cost $150 million. For the Guardians to be invested in as heavily as a known quantity such as Captain America illustrates the intentions within MS to not only take this new franchise seriously and give it a chance by conferring on it the status and prestige of other properties (stressing industrial continuities, that is, even where there is an intention to vary the textual product), but to also serve as a declaration of Marvel's belief that characters drawn from deep within its catalogue can be both entertaining, and worthy investment.

Guardians on the page

> Guardians assem… Oh, it's not the same!

(Rocket Raccoon, Guardians Team-Up #2, 2015)

Some context to the page-based origins of the characters may be required. Although the Guardians have appeared in comics since 1969,[7] the line-up of heroes seen in 2014's cinematic incarnation have only been involved in the franchise since Dan Abnett and Andy Lanning's 2008 story arc, initially illustrated by Paul Pelletier.[8] The 1969 line-up were thirty-first-century adventurers, a team comprising a handful of heroes fighting an intergalactic guerrilla war against a race known as the Badoon, who had all but conquered the galaxy. The title found its way back to a twenty-first-century setting in Abnett, Lanning and Pelletier's reboot of the series, where, building upon the narrative constructed in a major 2007 event in the Marvel Universe (MU) known as 'Annihilation: Conquest',[9] the already established character of Star-Lord (Peter Quill) sought to form a team that would anticipate threats to intergalactic peace. This twenty-first-century team draws much of its resonance from The Avengers; using a time travel narrative and referring to the plot device of Marvel's 'multiverse' (see Introduction), a mysterious individual, frozen in ice and bearing a star-spangled shield arrives in the path of the newly formed (and not yet named) Guardians. With the characters, and the reader, led into thinking that this could be some version of Captain America, it is then revealed to be an individual called Major Victory/Vance Astro, member of a team called the 'Guardians of the Galaxy' from the thirty-first century. In his own era, Astro acted as custodian of the shield made famous by Steve Rogers' Captain America, therefore his significant contribution to the origin of this team symbolically transfers the values of Captain America (as discussed in Chapter 4), and by extension The Avengers, onto the newly forming Guardians. This legacy idea – pertaining to the team, but also the Marvel team book tradition – is emphasized within the narrative, where themes of destiny and cosmic symbolism are raised. Quill asks, referring to Astro's/Captain America's shield: 'Is it just me or is this a little too perfect? We're trying to build a team of 'mighty heroes' and day one we find … *That* in a block of ice'.[10] Abnett et al. also include self-deprecating jokes about the team's struggle to live up to expectations set by the Avengers. One such example sees Quill, isolated from the rest of the Guardians, explaining to a group of thuggish villains – who at this point in the narrative are the lesser of two evils – that 'his team' will come to rescue them. When he refers to the Guardians by name, Gorilla Man (described in the comic as 'an old-school freak villain') dismisses the team as a joke, compared to their more famous counterparts: 'Who? What the ****? I thought you meant the Avengers or something' (**** in original as skull and crossbones).[11] Two comic franchises were here being connected on a meta-level, just as, in a cinematic context, *GOTG* would later be connected to the AF, with a comic undercutting of stature helping to sell the idea of a diverse heroic firmament.

GOTG would be elevated by association with its MCU stablemates, yet – consistent with the 'risk' notion – this would bring inflated audience and studio expectations set by those films, in particular the first crossover/team title, *The Avengers*.[12] Here lies the balance that Marvel seeks to achieve: to create a fresh and differentiated offering, featuring a much less typically 'heroic' band of rogues and outlaws in a 'cosmic' setting far removed from the (mostly) earthbound Avengers heroes, while bracketing the extension in with the prestige and loyalty attracted by the existing success of the Marvel brand, thus strengthening shared universe continuity.

After Abnett et al.'s run on the title ended in 2010, it wasn't until the 2013 'Marvel Now' reboot that the ongoing monthly title restarted with a new issue #1.[13] This run on the comic was illustrated by Steve McNiven and written by one of Marvel's loyal writers Brian Michael Bendis, who has a say in MCU creative affairs as a member of the Marvel Creative Committee (MCC).[14] The pair stripped away the characters from Abnett et al.'s line-up that weren't to feature in the team's cinematic outing. Around the already mentioned Star-Lord (Chris Pratt), the team members that made it from comic to screen were the warrior-brute Drax the Destroyer (Dave Batista); sleek assassin, daughter of ominous villain Thanos (Josh Brolin) and 'most dangerous woman in the galaxy' Gamora (Zoe Saldana); genetically enhanced creature and master tactician, Rocket Raccoon (voiced by Bradley Cooper); and his partner in crime, the tree-like humanoid, and royalty among his own people, Groot (voiced by Vin Diesel). A further choice of Bendis and McNiven's run aligned this team with the established MCU, as it welcomed aboard a new – yet temporary – member; an individual that wasn't to feature in their cinematic debut, but carried great weight in that universe already: Iron Man/Tony Stark. As well as drawing attention from fans of the comic mainstream who might have been reluctant to give the (still, fairly uncelebrated with wider MU readers) title a chance, Stark's presence significantly bears on character development in the team, and especially that of Quill. The fact that Quill's 'leader' role within the team is not remotely challenged by the presence of such a prominent, established and charismatic figure, adds to his reputation and brings the Guardians further equality with Marvel's ultimate team, the Avengers, reiterating the balance whereby they are presented as separate and distinct, yet can benefit from that brand's reputation. Bendis and McNiven's story picks up as though the team is settled, with brief biographies of the characters given in the form of Infinite Comics,[15] apart from Quill's Star-Lord, whose more in-depth, and emotionally evocative origin features in an issue #0.1 prelude. The emotional resonance in this telling of Quill's origin survives into the film, as it opens with his mother (Laura Haddock) on her death bed, and a young Quill (Wyatt Oleff) hesitating, because afraid, then missing his opportunity to take her hand before she dies. The risk of featuring such an intense and tonally unusual start for a summer adventure movie reflects the confidence to be gained in risky narrative choices that have already been successfully deployed in a less capital-intensive, and less scrutinized, medium. As much is confirmed by Feige, who accepted that the printed storytelling has a strong influence on the films 'because it's a hell of a lot less expensive to take a chance in a comic than it is [to – sic] take a chance in a movie. … It's the cheapest R&D there is, but the best R&D there is' (Feige cited in Dave Itzkoff, 2011).

Strategic marketing and the sustainable competitive advantage

Marvel's decision to open a new window showcasing its expanding cinematic universe through the Guardians of the Galaxy property can be understood by applying the frame of strategic marketing. Both Lynch and Hooley et al. provide a holistic view of business, believing in a totally integrated approach to marketing and corporate strategy, with the latter work stressing that 'the marketing process should be seen as interfunctional and cross-disciplinary' (Hooley et al. 2012: 9). They stress that marketing's total integration makes it intrinsic to the development of corporate strategy, which, as defined by Lynch, pertains to 'fundamental decisions about the future direction of an organisation: its purpose, its resources and how it interacts with the world in which it operates' (2006: 2). It is Lynch's view that for any organization, such a strategy needs to be 'the match between its internal capabilities and its external relationships' (6), adding that this can be separated into two distinct levels: the 'corporate level' and the 'business level'. The 'corporate level', which is responsible for overarching leadership and inherent internal culture, seeks to guide 'what business the company is in or is to be in and the kind of company it is or is to be' (6). The 'business level', which utilizes this leadership and corporate culture to focus on the specific requirements needed to take the organization in its desired direction, encompasses 'competing for customers, generating value from the resources and the underlying principle of the sustainable competitive advantages of those resources over rival companies' (6). Lynch and Hooley et al. each place a great deal of emphasis on the importance of the sustainability of such a competitive advantage, with Lynch explaining that the most efficient way of ensuring sustainability is to ensure that the advantage 'cannot easily be imitated' (78). This chapter largely focuses on the 'business level' decisions made in order to attain an inimitable advantage, while Chapter 2 has previously provided context for how, on a 'corporate level', Marvel's cultivated organizational identity is the bedrock from which such decisions can be made. The connection between the two is important to bear in mind, considering Lynch's assertion that in order to remain sustainable and inimitable, 'competitive advantage needs to be more deeply embedded in the organisation – its resources, skills, culture and investment over time' (117).

These general definitions allow us to extrapolate a view of Marvel's corporate strategy. Since moving into film production, sustainable competitive advantage has been pursued via a strategy centring on the MCU. At the 'corporate level', Marvel hopes to excel at the creation of characters and stories that can exist within various and overlapping fictional universes, in order to entertain, inform and inspire, all the while becoming lucrative commodities that can earn the organization and its owners financial remuneration, producing further capital to reinvest into this strategy. Therefore, a relationship between art and commerce must be successfully managed (again, Chapter 2 discusses this in detail). On a 'business level', in order to maximize the value generated from its resources, and therefore increase its competitive advantage, Marvel has expanded its focus from publishing and licensing only, to the production of its own cinematic/televisual incarnations of its characters.[16] In order to achieve this cinematic expansion, Marvel has exploited a number of unique and relatively inimitable properties. Hooley et al. class such properties as 'organizational resources', which they explain 'include both tangible and intangible assets, capabilities and competences. This is the base from which organisations build their competitive position' (2012: 130). Such organizational resources for Marvel, in the context of film production, would include: the bank of potentially strong intellectual property (IP) from which to draw inspiration; an existing, and so far successful, shared cinematic universe in which to explore its characters; an efficient process of film production; a strong, recognizable and consistent brand image; departmental cohesion within the same organization, and therefore a fully integrated research and development function in the form of less capital-intensive mediums (particularly comic books); and as an extension of this, further synergistic links throughout its corporate structure, through the aegis of parent Disney.

Departmental cohesion: An internal capability

To single out one of the above-mentioned strategic resources salient to the context of *GOTG*, *departmental cohesion* encompasses the relationship between two departments within the same organization, that are individually responsible for the production of the comic book and the cinematic adaptation. This is a notable departure from the traditional process of licensed film production based on a Marvel comic, carried out by a fee-paying external studio (the pre-MCU norm; see Appendix: Timeline for some examples). Abnett et al.'s work exposed the twenty-first-century interpretation of the Guardians to audiences and alerted studio decision makers and strategists to the potential of these characters. Nicola Perlman, the original scriptwriter on *GOTG*, has stated as much: said by interviewer Marc Strom (2014) to have 'instantly [taken] to the quirky, space-operatic nature of writers Dan Abnett and Andy Lanning's 2008 series', Perlman explains that when she joined MS's writers program in 2009, she chose to develop this team over many other available properties because Abnett and Lanning's interpretation was 'a very funny, sarcastic and tongue-in-cheek version of this kind of genre' (Perlman cited in Strom, 2014). Following James Gunn's September 2012 appointment to direct the film and adapt Perlman's script (see Zakarin, 2012), Bendis's position within the MCC meant that he could ensure his run on the comics, which began within six months of Gunn's appointment, could depict these characters in such a way as to prepare audience expectations for the film's release. This coordinating process exemplifies Marvel's utilization of the relatively unique capability of having direct and cohesive control of both its publishing and film production departments. Put another way, to have publishing feed into film with no outside parties to obstruct this, as would be the case where Marvel has presold the rights, such as with Fox's X-Men or Fantastic Four productions (FF productions). It must be noted that some of these organizational resources are not uniquely held by Marvel and thus characterize ways of working elsewhere: a synergistic corporate structure is comparable with that of DC's integration within Time Warner; an efficient production process has been mastered by many entertainment studios; and other organizations have the resources to acquire exploitable IP – even if obtaining it requires cost and negotiation, as is no longer the case for Marvel's operation (save for a few heroes; only Spider-Man has been negotiated 'back' into the MCU, from a position of rights being held by an outsider). Yet, it is the combination in which these organizational resources and external relationships exist that is more difficult to imitate, and which allows the MCU greater strategic differentiation, resulting in the coveted sustainable competitive advantage.

External relationships I: The competitive environment

Further to an organization's internal capabilities, its external relationships – with such as, but not limited to, competitors, complementors,[17] customers and suppliers – have a meaningful effect upon its competitive position. Chapter 2 touched upon how Marvel understands and communicates with customers, but the context of *GOTG*'s release helps us to throw a spotlight on some of Marvel's other external relationships, and how it derives value from them. Thus, the film's strategic worth can be understood.

When considering an organization's competition, Hooley et al. promote the use of the term 'strategic group'. They explain that rather than losing focus within sometimes arbitrary industry boundaries, strategic groups are specifically comprised of 'firms within an industry following similar strategies aimed at similar customers or customer groups' (2012: 74). With this consideration, MS must consider several avenues of competition: that from studios producing films based on characters belonging to Marvel's comic book publishing rivals[18]; from film studios such as Fox and Sony attempting to bring Marvel's own characters to the screen, and also, due to overlapping customer groups, any of the other major film studios releasing big-budget tentpole event films.[19] Hooley et al. also add that although members of the same strategic group are in competition, they also, where similarities are stark, actually complement one another; they can raise the awareness of a strategic group as a whole or they can adversely affect its reputation, which is a factor Marvel must strategically negotiate since it cannot be outright controlled. For example, on the one hand, positive reception of *Star Trek* (J. J. Abrams, 2009) and its sequel *Star Trek Into Darkness* (J. J. Abrams, 2013) could enhance audience anticipation and acceptance of *GOTG*, due to the nostalgic, space opera genre features the films share – both of which can also be compared favourably to the Star Wars franchise. Yet, negative reaction to a cinematic interpretation of a cosmically associated superhero property such as DC's *Green Lantern* (Martin Campbell, 2011) – which has a mere 26 per cent Rotten Tomatoes rating – could harm preconceptions of *GOTG*. There is a need, then, to negotiate this, courting favourable association where beneficial, while flexibly distancing the MS product from toxic elements. This can be seen by comparing reports of the reception of *GOTG*: Kenneth Turan (2014) states that 'the scruffy *Guardians* is irreverent in a way that can bring the first *Star Wars* to mind', while Kim Newman (2014) asserts that '*Guardians of the Galaxy* bests Warner/DC's *Green Lantern* movie in finding a bridge between superheroics and space opera'. Both comparisons plunge directly into *GOTG's* strategic group: one reflects the glory of a much-loved property, the other frames *GOTG* by distancing it from a toxic one. How Marvel might seek to effect such favourable relationships will be returned to shortly.

External relationships II: Backed by Disney

An important external force to consider is Marvel's parent company Disney, for even though the two are part of the same business family, the structuring of both the chronology (MS remaining 'independent' until late 2009 – see Chapter 1) and the corporate hierarchy that is in place mean that Disney's influence over strategic decisions regarding MCU development should be considered from an external, rather than internal perspective. Such a relationship could potentially restrict the studio's freedom by exerting pressure on decision making, a situation that Marvel has negotiated with mixed success in past corporate relationships (see Chapter 2). As reports have indicated, there seems to be a certain amount of flux in the way that the top levels of the Marvel executive (Feige as production head, Perlmutter as CEO) relate to Disney (see Conclusion). Yet, the increased security afforded by having a corporate parent of Disney's means could significantly aid Marvel in its entertainment ambitions. For instance, it enables the 'risk' of using the barely recognized Guardians of the Galaxy brand to take the MCU in a new direction. Subers (2014), on this subject, specifically highlights Disney's contribution to familiarizing the film-going public with *GOTG's* previously unseen and – on this scale – untested characters: 'Disney's stellar marketing campaign addressed that issue early and often: from the teaser trailer on, the focus was squarely on building a connection between the audience and this bizarre group'. He specifically notes how the most unique characters were singled out: 'Characters that initially seemed like liabilities – Rocket Raccoon and Groot, specifically – wound up being a major draw'.[20] This 'stellar marketing campaign' included the promotion of ancillary products such as playable character figures within the videogame 'Disney Infinity'.[21] Such ancillary products are often a feature of large-scale action-adventure films, but in this example, MS's proven track record, strong brand and integration within Disney, have bolstered its exploitation of this. Graser (2014a) explains that Disney's industrial power is such that 'while merchandise partners typically steer clear of an unproven property, Disney Consumer Products was able to line up an array of licensees to produce toys and apparel around the film and its characters, especially Rocket Raccoon'. It is evident that the industrial momentum instigated by prior MS releases aided this development, as John Blackburn, senior Vice President and General Manager of Disney Infinity describes the decision to promote the Guardians before the film's release as 'really easy … Marvel's batting a thousand. It's easy to get behind anything they're doing' (Blackburn cited in Graser 2014b). Through such promotion, Disney embraced Rocket Raccoon among its own prestigious (animal) characters, and it attracted huge pre-sales, at one point reported to be 'selling nearly twice as much as the game's bestselling characters last year, which were *Monsters Inc.*'s Mike Wazowski and *Frozen*'s Elsa' (Graser 2014b). This clearly denotes the kind of ballpark in which Disney believes a Marvel character such as Rocket belongs. It is this type of mutual benefit – Marvel's film strategy reinforced, alongside Disney gaining a new iconic character to associate with its brand – that vindicates the strategy to align the organizations' fortunes. The source of Disney's confidence in the MS strategy being brand-based is something that has been publically acknowledged at a senior level by Disney's president and CEO Bob Iger in an interview conducted by Jon Erlichman (2014) for *Bloomberg*. His final comment interestingly takes in the 'strategic group' concept by acknowledging how the same policy is open to use by competitors.

> You have to make great content, you have to create or nurture great brands and franchises. … Brands are very important; *Guardians of the Galaxy* is a great example of that. People said it came out of nowhere, because those characters were not well known; that title was not well known. But the Marvel brand has become something that, at least in the consumer's eyes, really means something, and that should be trusted, because they have a track record of making good films. … In today's world, that serves Marvel well, it serves Disney well, and it will continue to serve companies in this space well.
>
> (Iger in Erlichman, 2014)

External relationships III: Actors, directors and stars as suppliers

Expounding his 'five competitive forces that shape strategy' model, organizational theorist Michael E. Porter (2008) suggests that when analysing an organization's competitive position, one main consideration should be the 'bargaining power of suppliers' (4), stating that 'powerful suppliers capture more of the value for themselves' (13). Organizations must manage this bargaining power to ensure that too much of this value is not diverted. Exemplified by *GOTG*, MS can be seen to have historically taken a distinct strategy, hiring creative talent (its suppliers) with less exposure than more typically 'bankable' stars, but lining this strategy with a certain credibility, associating itself with before-and-behind camera individuals identified as independent, distinctive and imbued with creativity (a process that is not without risk and ambiguity, as discussed in Chapter 1). Newman (2014) characterizes the hiring of Gunn in such a way, setting it alongside a pattern of previous MS creative appointments, by identifying him as 'like Joss Whedon, an interesting genre filmmaker who could do with a movie hit'. Similarly, Graser (2014a) places the appointment of Pratt – formerly recognized (see Adalian, 2015) as emerging from the ensemble of niche television comedy *Parks and Recreation* (2009–15) – as Star-Lord within a legacy of creative hiring decisions: '[Marvel] re-launched the career of Robert Downey Jr. with *Iron Man*, and recently surprised Hollywood with the directing abilities of the Russo brothers, a duo mostly known for helming episodes of comedies like *Arrested Development*, but who showed off their action chops with *Captain America: The Winter Soldier*'. He batches this 'surprise' with the appointment of Gunn: 'Marvel also took a gamble by handing the reins of a $170 million production to a director, James Gunn, previously known for helming low-budget films such as the $2.5 million comedy *Super* and the $15 million horror pic *Slither*'. Strategically, this reinforces Marvel's proposed identity as 'hip', attuned to current trends, and in possession of cultural capital. It is seen to monitor creative but less heralded zones of entertainment, allowing it to 'make' stars, and seem less interested in retreading the careers of long-standing ones (Koh, 2014: 485).[22]

Such a strategy of attracting lesser-known potential stars supports Marvel's ability to build its universe. Due to their limited star power at the point of entering contracts, Marvel is able to secure the long-term deals necessary to have characters recur in various media across the MCU. Further, securing new and emerging creative talent mitigates reliance on those whose growing star status would have otherwise increased their bargaining power, constructing a star base which is flexible and renewable to match the identity of superheroes (see Chapter 4). This again brings to attention the strategic significance of *GOTG*, as the possibility of Pratt as Star-Lord supplanting Downey Jr's Iron Man as the charismatic, masculine figure at the centre of the MCU, alleviates pressure on Marvel to appease Downey Jr, a 'supplier' whose bargaining position has increased since first entering the MCU. In financial terms, Graser (2014c) highlights what Downey Jr has cost Marvel: 'He's reaped between $250 million and $300 million for the *Iron Man* trilogy, his role in *The Avengers* films, and a brief appearance in *The Incredible Hulk*'. Such reports will not exactly discourage other stars from wanting to be involved with MS, although this is true of the strategic group.

Naturally, this ever-evolving requirement of a steady flow of potential breakout stars, with limits placed on star pay, must be prepared for if the shared universe is to continue with no breaks or unplanned reboots. Ben Child (2014) notes a similar significance to the appointment of Benedict Cumberbatch as the eponymous Doctor Strange in the upcoming (due 2016) solo feature, specifying that he 'has the potential to take over from Tony Stark as the central figure in the Marvel [Cinematic] universe should Downey Jr decide not to return for further solo outings'.

What is the *real* risk?: Taking the long-term view

This strategy of elevating the Guardians of the Galaxy property in order to promote new characters and rotate their significance within the MCU can be rationalized by considering the organizational 'product mix'. Despite the frequent characterization as a risk, both by the press and by Marvel itself, the strategy of evolving the character portfolio while expanding into a distinctly different (cosmic) setting, is in fact a diversification of risk. On the necessity of the pursuit of such diversification by organizations, Lynch states that 'to be reliant on one product or customer clearly carries immense risks if, for any reason, that product or service should fail or the customer should go elsewhere' (2006: 130). So should the AF falter – as has been, perhaps precipitously, noted following the release of *A:AOU* – having an alternative, differentiated franchise keeps studio momentum on course, and stretches audience ideas of what 'counts' or is valid, aesthetically, within the MCU, which could inform a freshening of the weaker or declining performers. Lynch advises that 'the key strategy is to produce a *balanced portfolio of products*' (130; emphasis in original),[23] therefore the idea is to diversify each product so that it suits a slightly different purpose, while not deviating far from the organization's capabilities. If the products are diversified in such a way as to not saturate their specific purpose, but do not trouble strategic group boundaries, the organization has a greater chance of dominating the group. As Hooley et al. explain: 'Even though there may be numerous products on the market, consumers are rarely able to name more than a few' (2012: 276). The more Marvel heroes to become synonymous with big-budget action-adventure cinema – including, but not limited to, superheroes – the less space for its competition to prosper. The fact that the release schedule for key event films is so constricted, with predictable seasonal milestones, and years of lead-in time, increases Marvel's chance of such dominance; hence its attempts to 'own' key dates in the calendar. Along these lines, Marvel postured on an industrial level following the buoyant reception of *CA:TWS*, as it announced the third Captain America film would be released over the same weekend that would see Warner Bros./ DC's *Batman Vs Superman: Dawn of Justice* (Zack Snyder, 2016) released (see Kroll 2014): a direct historical challenge between the publishers, and a clear assertion of dominance. The momentum that the Captain America brand had generated forced Warner Bros. to change its plans, despite the global recognition of Batman and Superman (let alone the prospect of their first big-screen team-up). This one episode illustrates what possession of Marvel has done for Disney in the strategic group of event film (specifically, the segment of this that, in the next chapter, and after Peter Krämer (1998b), we can term the 'Family-Adventure' category). In the 2000s, the long-running mega-tentpole of the Harry Potter series (2001–11) gave Warner Bros. dominance in a category and at times of the year in which Disney had always prospered. Disney put up rivals to little avail, from the Chronicles of Narnia series (2005–8 with Disney, thereafter with Fox) to *The Sorcerer's Apprentice*

(Jon Turteltaub, 2010); but, effectively, Warner Bros. 'owned' the family-adventure fantasy spot in the market at this time.

Further to the consideration of specific characters, a transition from an Avengers brand to a Guardians of the Galaxy brand, with its 'cosmic' setting and its lack of superhero iconography, means that the team is not bound to the superhero 'genre', other than originating with a producer synonymous with superheroes, and the promotional material consciously tying it to *The Avengers* (see Chapter 1). Where *GOTG* varies is consciously acknowledged by Gunn, who asserts that the film is 'much more of a space opera than a superhero movie' (Gunn cited in McClintock, 2014). The slight diversification – from overt superheroics, to science-fiction adventure with a hint of classic mercenary team-up (shades of *The Dirty Dozen* (Robert Aldrich, 1967) or even *Shichinin no samurai* (*Seven Samurai*) (Akira Kurosawa, 1954), an indirect influence on space opera *Star Wars*) – extends the portfolio of character types, while staying within the same strategic group as previous AF releases, meaning that new characters assist in dominating that market sector. Chapter 3 addressed the playfulness with which Marvel has been approaching genre within films throughout the MCU, but pertinent here is that the space opera setting has given *GOTG* a way to be both spatially and thematically distant enough from other AF releases to be distinguished as a fresh approach. The move to a cosmic setting has been characterized as a point of separation and innovation from other MCU films, although not every observer agrees (Cubitt (2015) spends time discussing its common genre structures with other sci-fi outlaw narratives). However, in MCU terms, there is differentiation speaking to a carefully planned logic, which can be understood by considering the favourable comparisons made earlier in this chapter: to the recent Star Trek franchise reboot, and the relaunching of the Star Wars franchise as of late 2015. Hooley et al. explain that when preparing to launch a new product, 'business analysis considers the attractiveness of the market for the proposed new product' (2012: 344). The successful relaunch of the dormant Star Trek franchise in 2009 would have evidenced the appetite for such space-operatic action, providing encouragement to pursue the script that Perlman was working on at the time. Further, one could speculate that Marvel's decision makers were aware of preparations for Disney's purchase of Lucasfilm (and its cross-marketing possibilities for comic publishing – see Chapter 1); the October 2012 announcement of this deal followed only a few months after the announcement of *GOTG's* production in July 2012, enabling awareness of the publicity burst from which the space opera genre was about to benefit. The courting of such comparisons and its preference over an association with existing superhero films can be seen in the construction of Marvel's 'trade narratives'[24] via the vocal auspices of Feige, as noted by Graser (2014a): 'As a child of the '80s and a fan of *Star Trek* and *Star Wars*, *Guardians* scratches his itch to make a big space opera'. Considering the implications of specifically describing Feige as a 'child of the '80s', it is not only the cosmic association that reflects favourably on *GOTG*, but also the link to other staples of 1980s popular culture. Such descriptions of Feige chime with instances such as Turan (2014): in the same article which likens *GOTG* to *Star Wars*, he describes the former as having 'a loose, anarchic B-picture soul'. These comparisons encourage a bracketing of this franchise within nostalgia-fuelled popular genre cycles like those produced by George Lucas and Steven Spielberg, providing a further grip for audiences on genre designation (see Chapter 7). The Indiana Jones series (1981–2008) is referenced with various degrees of subtlety throughout the film[25]: From one of the earliest scenes being the recovery of a mysterious artefact, to a direct reference by Quill to 'The Ark of the Covenant', to elements of *mise-en-scène* (for instance the outburst of energy when the main villain of the film Ronan (Lee Pace) infuses the power of an Infinity Stone with his Warhammer). Non-superhero associations can be additionally made with the mercenary westerns and war movies mentioned earlier, from directors like Kurosawa, Aldrich and Sam Peckinpah, which fed into the 'New Hollywood' moment generative of Lucas and Spielberg's careers (as well as those of mavericks like John Sayles, writer of the similar *Battle Beyond the Stars* (Jimmy T. Murakami, 1980)); the lineage of this genre territory arguably extends to James Gunn and takes in Joss Whedon's *Serenity* (2005) (see Cubitt, 2015). Furthermore, its comic nature derives from too many 'buddy'/odd couple pictures to mention. The film, then, can be – *wants* to be – seen as a playful 'outlaw' brew of various genre associations. Yet, its success is not solely due to diverging from the elements of the AF, but from holding this divergence in combination with a simultaneous replication of what has proved successful in the MS release formula to date. This balance can be seen in the *GOTG* comics that sit alongside this film's release, as the subtitle of the collected first run (Bendis and McNiven, 2013) reads: 'Cosmic Avengers'. This phrase is the fusion of established superhero conventions, represented by Marvel's flagship franchise, with more overt elements of pulp/homage/space opera of the 'cosmic' trajectory Marvel seeks to pursue within its cinematic universe. This fusion can be appreciated through analysis of a number of instances within the diegesis of *GOTG*, as compared to other AF films, chiefly *The Avengers*.

One of the most apparent similarities is the coming together of a 'team'[26] (which is privileged by both the film's title and promotional images, before even considering the narrative). Something that ties together the teams of the Avengers and the Guardians, is that many characteristics represented by members of one team can be seen in members of the other, such as Drax's comical misunderstandings of his teammates' colloquialisms being a similar, albeit exaggerated, version of Norse god Thor (Chris Hemsworth), and man-out-of-time Steve Rogers/Captain America often being off-pace amidst combat banter. Both teams feature a charismatic, petulant white male at their centre (Stark and Quill); a fierce female warrior (Black Widow and Gamora) and an inarticulate or minimally verbal, loveable but devastatingly powerful creature (Hulk (Mark Ruffalo) and Groot). With respect to these two characters, one scene in *GOTG* particularly matches the *mise-en-scène* of *The Avengers*: during the final act's action scene, Groot brutally smashes a host of Ronan's guards repeatedly against the wall, before dropping their bodies to the floor. With comic flair, there is a pause as he then turns right into the barrel of the camera (as implied, to his teammates) with a charming, naive smile. During a similar point in *The Avengers'* final act, Hulk swings the film's chief villain Loki (Tom Hiddleston) by his legs, pounding him repeatedly into the ground; a similar beat passes, before a comical whimper from Loki. Yet, despite the similarities to the make-up of teams, there are telling differences that mark *GOTG* as an alternative. These include the fact that the Guardians come together through coincidence, aligned incentives and cosmic destiny, rather than are coerced into forming as are the Avengers (by S.H.I.E.L.D.). A further difference is that while most of the constituent members of *The Avengers* received an origin story prior to their team-up, *GOTG* depicts the immediate coming together of the team; a team origin as opposed to many individual origins coming together. This is a significant differentiation, considering that despite both teams being depicted as chaotic, the Guardians' disagreements seem more petty than ideologically fractious, and the team complete the narrative as a more stable property than the Avengers, confidently standing by their clear leader, Star-Lord, as they triumphantly fly towards their future. The Avengers, as discussed in Chapter 5, are characterized rather differently, with each of their films emphasizing separation in their closing scenes (the replacement, possibly, of one team with another in *A:AOU*), their temporariness accented. Grey areas when it comes to leadership are pointed up, setting out a schism of ideology between Steve Rogers and Tony Stark that prepares *Captain America: Civil War*.[27]

Both films depict heroism, but in very different ways. *GOTG* ends with a statement that lends a specialized moral standing to this project, not a simple reproduction of the more overtly heroic dimensions of the MCU, or of expectations around superheroes. Quill asks his team: 'What shall we do next? Something good? Something bad? Bit of both?'; deciding: '[a] bit of both!' Supporting this characterization of the Guardians as 'a bit of both', is that they are portrayed as accidental heroes with apparently unheroic traits, separating them from the embodiment of heroic duty seen in Avengers members like Thor and Captain America. Rocket's first action is to mock a toddler: 'What is this thing? Look at how it thinks it's so cool. It's not cool to get help; walk by yourself you little gargoyle!' Drax ends the film still struggling to understand why the Nova Corps considers him committing murder – even if the target has 'irked' him – as a bad thing; and Quill is palpably surprised when a moment of heroism overcomes him to save Gamora: 'I found something inside of myself; something incredibly heroic – I mean, not to brag'. But despite the different treatment, heroism is still a central theme; the Guardians' heroism wells up surprisingly from self-assured confidence in their own actions and skills, and their willingness to come together for nothing more than 'a chance to give a shit'.

The balance between difference and similarity is embodied within the central characters. Although the similarities between Stark and Quill have been identified, *GOTG* has a special swagger that is captured in the nonchalant, childlike abandon with which Quill throws himself into space-adventuring even when ostensible benefits of self-interest have been removed. In contrast to this, grandiosity and self-doubt seem interlocked in the AF, and are stitched into it: Stark is seen throughout *Iron Man 3* and *A:AOU* struggling to come to terms with the potential ramifications of threats posed by intelligent life outside of Earth, his heroic responsibility to prepare for it, and self-doubt – he is frivolous Tony Stark, after all – of meeting such responsibility. These are not negatives in representation, they are elements of Stark's character. This intensity of morality is absent in Quill's almost infantilized confidence in his own moral standing, a difference that can be tracked in genre terms by the depicted relationships between protagonists and antagonists in both franchises. The moral ambiguity evoked by pairing heroes with mirror-image or negative villains in AF films (several examples were given in Chapter 4) is absent from *GOTG*. On the other hand, Ronan, a radical zealot of the Kree race obsessed with purity, tyrannically throwing his power around even before obtaining the Infinity Stone, is defined as totally 'other' to Quill, who is almost entirely de-powered,[28] and wholly accepting of racial difference (ascertained throughout the film via his frequent mention of sexual encounters with various, notably diverse – particularly around the 'Knowhere' community glimpsed in the film – inhabitants of the galaxy). Although the inevitable crossover of these franchises is cheekily hinted at via Drax remarking that he would like to visit Earth, after hearing Quill speak of its 'outlaws' – and, indeed, the background presence of Ronan's sponsor, Thanos (who has more screen time in *GOTG* than any AF entry to date) – the Guardians' settled nature, and current relative isolation from the rest of the MCU, allows the franchise a little more freedom to explore different notions of being a heroic team. Thus, audiences can make sense of it with reference to the Avengers, but the film is not restricted to the same aesthetic or thematic palette.

A pre-emptive strike: Understanding the product life cycle

Regarding the rationale behind differentiation, Lynch states that 'many organisations will not wish to risk having all their products in the same markets and at the same stages of development' (2006: 130). Relatedly, Hooley et al. refer to a product life cycle encompassing the stages of 'introduction', 'growth', 'maturity' and 'decline' (see Figure 1). To understand the AF as a product – formed from an amalgamation of character series that stand as franchises/products in their own right – it helps to gauge how the films stack up in terms of total worldwide gross.[29] *Iron Man* ($585 million), *The Incredible Hulk* ($263 million), *Iron Man 2* ($623 million), *Thor* ($449 million) and *Captain America: The First Avenger* ($370 million) could be seen as the franchise moving through the 'introduction' stage. Hooley et al. explain that in this phase, a product thrives on the basis of uniqueness (72). The 'unique' property in this example is the shared universe concept, which was exploited to clearly set a Marvel 'way' apart from its competition. In the 'growth' stage, sales see a 'rapid increase' (73), which can be seen in the release of *The Avengers* ($1.519 billion) and *Iron Man 3* ($1.215 billion). Hooley et al. explain that at this stage, the competition typically figures out a way to

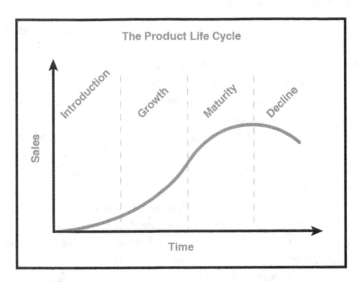

Figure 1 The Product Life Cycle (adapted from Hooley *et al.*, 2012: 72).

imitate what is unique, and forms a plan to compete within its bounds (73). In this respect, Fox's X-Men films and DC's forthcoming 'Justice League' property have shown signs of forming their own respective shared universes in the same mould.[30] Following this, a product enters a 'maturity' stage where growth 'slows down significantly' (73); here we see *Thor: The Dark World* ($644 million) *CA:TWS* ($714 million), *A:AOU* ($1.395 billion) and *Ant-Man* ($519 million). These are all still reasonable values, and generally still increasing in sales volume, with the second solo outings for Captain America and Thor being improvements on their debuts, but showing signs of a decreasing growth rate in the franchise as a whole[31] (of course, a complication here is whether to treat all releases in the AF sequence as equally valuable; with Iron Man and Avengers entries established as the 'A' properties, it may not be fair to treat figures with a broad brush). It is the anticipation of such 'maturity' that led to MS taking the strategic risk of bringing *GOTG* into play to lend a differentiation factor. Failure to recognize and pre-emptively address a product's shortcomings while in that 'maturity' stage, could see a product forced to reach the damaging 'decline' stage. Here, worse than a product diminishing in value, its downward trajectory can damage its reputation, and that of associated brands. Such a decline in brand value can be recognized in the third instalments of Sony's Spider-Man or Fox's X-Men franchises.[32] Despite worldwide grosses both exceeding their respective franchise's previous release, with *Spider-Man 3*'s $890 million, up from *Spider-Man* ($821 million) and *Spider-Man 2*: ($783 million). While *X-Men: The Last Stand*'s $459 million improved from *X-Men* ($296 million) and *X-Men 2* ($407 million). Yet, critical and audience reception threatened to damage the sustainability of these properties: *Spider-Man 3* has a Rotten Tomatoes rating of 63 per cent, down from *Spider-Man* (89 per cent) and *Spider-Man 2* (93 per cent).

Similarly *X-Men: The Last Stand* has a rating of 58 per cent, down from *X-Men* (83 per cent) and *X-Men 2* (86 per cent). Such a decrease in critical enthusiasm, no doubt attributable to mixed factors, precipitated years of absence from the screen. Thus, the short-term gain in sales for those third entries was at the expense of long-term sustainability, and – thinking of critical response – character reputation. This outcome resulted because the studios handling these properties were not incentivized by the same long-term goals held by MS, as owner of its own IP. In fact, when both series were 'rebooted', the greater success was experienced by Fox's approach to the X-Men series, as it strategized for the long term via a limited emulation of the shared universe concept, doing this by innovatively constructing *First Class* as a quasi-reboot-cum-prequel, set decades prior to the events of the initial films and mixing partly fresh and previously seen elements.[33] *Days of Future Past* went on to merge the two waves via its time travel plot (also beneficially, Fox's cycle had already established a wider universe by allowing characters Wolverine and Deadpool to branch off into reasonably discrete solo features). By comparison, Sony's simple recasting and retelling of Spider-Man's origin in *The Amazing Spider-Man* failed to reignite the franchise, with a muted box office ($757 million – lower than all prior instalments) and critical response (72 per cent); this was compounded by an even lower performing sequel ($708 million/53 per cent). Sony had publicized plans for a wider Spider-Man universe, but such poor performance seems to have propelled the studio into negotiation with Marvel, leading to an MCU reintroduction for the character (see Chapter 1). This appears to be Sony's one option to regain value in the character, and shows MS's dominance within its strategic group in terms of the perceived infallibility of its creativity, relative to other producers.

Crude as some of the measurements are, the above examples show the challenge in maintaining a film franchise beyond a limited number of releases. The unique nature of the MCU has meant that the AF has thrived beyond the span of the other examples given. Where a problem has occurred, as can be argued was the case with the immediate sign of decline following *The Incredible Hulk*'s release in 2008, due to a unique benefit of the shared universe, the Hulk has been resituated as a major draw among the Avengers, with no immediate need to showcase him in further solo films. The initial decline is absorbed into the greater success, and the character can stay relevant and visible for his considerable marketing value. This act of repurposing a product is highlighted by Hooley et al. (2012: 301) as a way to refresh or reposition it within its life cycle, circling back to the introduction or growth stage, and thus avoiding the decline stage.

A further way of refreshing the purpose of elements within the AF is to show stylistic or thematic differentiation within the separate character series in order to influence their product life cycle. As much is claimed to be the case by Kim Masters (2014), who explains that MS 'manage to not just change the outfits of their superheroes. They've actually created a Captain America brand versus a Thor brand versus an Iron Man brand'. Yet, even with such stylistic differences, the characters can still interact, with the believability of the shared universe, even when connectors are only in the form of dialogue or minor characters, accumulating in layers that bind the franchises together. Within the AF portfolio, there is a distinct difference between the grim heroics demanded by *CA:TWS*, and the light and morally clear-cut comedic adventure of *Ant-Man*, so much so that the presence of Falcon/Sam Wilson in both films can seem somewhat jarring, but is a step needed to enable entry of Ant-Man into future Avengers plans.

'I told you I had a plan'

The repurposing, tweaking and repositioning of a character or franchise within the MCU, as well as the wholesale opening up of new franchises, as represented by *GOTG*, requires a great deal of planning. In addition to the foresight required to make proactive decisions, the handling of *The Incredible Hulk* aftermath illustrates that planning must be nimble, reactive and adapt itself to developing events. Such strategizing is jovially represented within the diegesis of *GOTG*, enabling a reading of the film as meta-statement on how MS's planning might be perceived.

As was noted in the earlier comparison between *GOTG* and the AF films, the 'Avengers Initiative' – Nick Fury's diegetic shadow of Marvel's industrial plan to assemble a crossover super-franchise – was meticulous, while the Guardians happened upon each other, a team thrown together and making the best of it. Yet, of course, we know that this is simply a narrative tool; a scripted facade of happenstance and destiny that invokes shambolic roguery and the lovable chaos of 'anarchic B-Picture' subversion. This binds diegetic narrative together with MS's industrial narrative (what Johnson (2012) also terms 'destiny'), allowing a precise execution to be covered by a perceived organic nature. Here, two constituents of Marvel's dual approach to identity creation, as addressed in Chapter 2, return to view.

The theme of planning is brought to the fore in *GOTG* via the device of a prison breakout which the newly acquainted characters must come together to organize. Rocket recites a well thought-out plan, but Groot, only listening to the first step before going off half-cocked with the best of intentions, collects an object without knowing that this action will set off the alarms; unbeknownst to the already active Groot, Rocket concludes his explanation: this part absolutely must be left until last. Once this action has already been taken, Rocket exclaims: 'Or, we could just get that first and improvise'. This comically represents how difficult it is to control so many moving parts, irrespective of how effective each element is, how well-intentioned a participant's actions are, or how well-thought out the plan is. This process renders Marvel's experience on an industrial level: many moving parts must be organized, but the structure must allow them to perform with agency and autonomy. This is especially the case considering that MS's success has derived, in part, from giving (unpredictable) creative individuals access to the Marvel 'sandbox' (see Chapter 2), with most outcomes that could go well having done so. Towards the end of the *GOTG* scene, as the audience has just witnessed anarchy quickly transform into a spectacle-laden, innovative approach to a prison-break, Rocket says: 'I told you I had a plan'; Quill concedes in reply: 'that was a pretty good plan'. The audience is encouraged to marvel at Rocket's plan coming together, against the odds, just as the financial and critical success of this film points to Marvel's industrial plan coming together. Hence, as the ramshackle escape pod launches out of the space-prison, so too, a new franchise sails forth into the bigger MCU.

Regarding flexibility in the strategic planning of the universe, when asked why *Ant-Man* was announced in 2006 as part of the first round of films, but was not realized until 2015, Feige responded: 'If the stars had aligned, we would have made it earlier' (Feige cited in Kilday, 2015). In another instance, Feige acknowledges that the *Captain Marvel* film 'has been in the works almost as long as *Doctor Strange* or *Guardians of the Galaxy* before it came out, and one of the key things was figuring out what we wanted to do with it' (Feige cited in Graser, 2014d). Both examples stick to the line often communicated, that MS is more likely to wait and capitalize on momentary opportunities, when the mix of elements is right, than force a rigid course of action to happen. Of course, the strategic group of superhero films can offer examples of what the latter approach can lead to.

The theme of planning returns in the film's final act, via Quill's plan to retrieve the Infinity Stone from Ronan. Again, the recurring comic emphasis on 'plan' actually having a meaning among the group of 'ad-hoc improvisation', and certainly not something micro-managed and precise to the last degree, is evident. When pushed on how much of a plan Quill has, he concedes: 'I don't know; twelve per cent'. A comical, arbitrary figure, only offered because he was pushed. MS's industrial reality is being mythologized, again, here. Quill recognizes that what matters is convincing their captor Yondu of the thoughtfulness of this 'big plan of ours' – confidence and posturing, buying time to put things in place. There is a sense that the Yondu-style bigger, uglier fish of the Hollywood firmament – including some that might be called 'parents' (a relation Yondu has had to Quill) – might need to be sold some story that masks contingent, anarchic elements at the heart of the plan.

Conclusion

Marvel's MCU plan has now been thriving for the best part of a decade, and it has already been publically acknowledged that there is at least another twelve years laid out.[34] This chapter has involved apprehending the introduction of the Guardians of the Galaxy property as a move supporting MS in vital areas of strategy: the main one being the maintenance of a sustainable competitive advantage. It makes for a more exciting story to characterize this decision in terms of risk, whereas, in fact, by diversifying the studio's offering, risk is probably being diluted as much as possible in a shifting arena (the viability of franchises) that any analyst must accept is fraught with unpredictability.

It appears that throughout MS's deployment of characters and properties that launch new story worlds, the studio can manage risk, and control – not with ease, but with a plan – several strands of a universe that can be snapped together wherever the organization glimpses a strategic fit. The positive commercial and critical response that *GOTG* met with shows that by successfully integrating some of its most obscure characters – even when compared to the previously considered fringe characters such as Thor and Iron Man – Marvel's confidence that it needn't simply rely on its most recognizable characters is well founded. Audience acceptance of only a known sample of its vast IP is not the condition for success; a 'signature' must be sought elsewhere, not only among diegetic elements but also in the product mix and the studio narrative. A comment upon this feat can be read in *GOTG*'s post-credits scene, news of which was shared widely by fans immediately on release. The scene introduces Howard the Duck, a shock inclusion of a leftfield Marvel character, infamous for having been the centre of one of the worst commercial flops of the licensing days.[35] This symbolic gesture can be read as refuting claims that Marvel's use of characters from outside its upper tiers would result in the same fate. With this point emphatically made, *GOTG* will have added a great deal of confidence with regards to the taking of similarly calculated risks on other characters in the future. As a look through Johnson's early history of MS as figured through trade narratives shows us, in Hollywood, sometimes it is necessary to appear as if nothing is left to chance and self-possession is total; on other occasions, 12 per cent of a plan can swing it.

CHAPTER 7
'A LITTLE OLD-FASHIONED…': MARVEL STUDIOS AND PIXAR

Introduction

In a sequence of *Toy Story 2* (John Lasseter/Ash Brannon, 1999), Buzz Lightyear (voiced by Tim Allen), sentient space toy hero, comes to painfully face the reality of his peculiar ontological state. As the toy crew investigates villainous Al's 'Toy Barn' store, Buzz happens upon the 'Buzz Lightyear' aisle, where he encounters row after row of identical (unsold) Buzzes, set behind pristine plastic windows, waiting to have their strings pulled and identities activated. The film (and later chapter *Toy Story 3*, Lee Unkrich, 2010) – make a number of interesting, even poignant points abut Buzz's existential uncertainty on discovering this mass-market purgatory of Buzz units, but the sequence might invoke any Disney or generic toy store stocking a Pixar – or, these days, Marvel – range of products. As for MS's part, no character has quite had Buzz's experience, but Tony Stark – his Iron Man technology endlessly remade and replicated either by himself or others (Obadiah Stane/Iron Monger; the Ultron drones; one spectacle in *Iron Man 3* is even expressly designed around an army of empty Iron Men) – comes closest. Thinking of Buzz's ontological anxiety, no wonder the shot in *Iron Man 3* where Stark slacks off on a couch next to his idling metal shell raises an uncanny *frisson* as well as a laugh.

For all the humour about genericity that goes into Buzz's representation, like the Marvel superheroes (those heroes who had their antecedents lumped together as undifferentiated 'long underwear characters' in the opening narration of *Amazing Fantasy* Vol.1, #15, (1962)), he can lay claim, by now, to be a beloved character, with well-known foibles. One of the most interesting points of comparison between MS and Pixar Animation Studios is precisely the relationship of both organizations, as creative and industrial entities constructed through self but also external discourses, to notions of the *generic*. Pixar is a byword for smart success in the field of computer-generated film,[1] with the credit drawn by its achievements increasingly wrapping around consecutive fields (animation, films-for-children, cross-generational family viewing) which help it to openly converge on the identity territory for so long controlled by its parent, Disney. Hailed as the 'most reliable family brand' in Hollywood (Goldstein, 2008), effortlessly able to connect with audiences, critics like Richard McCulloch (2014), Brookey and Westerfelhaus (2006) and others identify a combination of discourses used to prop up the circulation of Pixar's brand meanings and values. Over two decades Pixar has undergone something of a 'meta-branding' project (Rehak, 2008), going about this in a way not dissimilar to the one we observed as MS recast its own rawness as a Hollywood entity with the accumulated entertainment and character experience of half a century of Marvel Comics (see Chapter 1).

Pixar's goal was to secure a 'classic', Old Hollywood-style studio identity, building this around the veneration of a certain attitude to story, as constantly reinforced in materials around the films (McCulloch, 2014: 184). Appropriate to its field, Pixar's self-mythologizing deliberately revives those Disney classic animation principles articulated by Wells (2002: 26), prioritizing the relationship between 'realism' and what the studio's creative figurehead John Lasseter calls 'story power' (quoted in Anon., 2004b; see also Iwerks, 2007). Narrative, after all, is 'what the Disney name is famous for' (Hebdige, 2005: 39). Common perceptions of the virtues of Pixar films from critics and commentators tend to reflect this line (Brookey and Westerfelhaus, 2006: 125). While musing on how its reputation powers Pixar's productions as much as the other way round, McCulloch (2014: 184) notes that critics often stay on-message – accepting the shaping line of the company's self-promotion and press releases – something we have observed around MS also (see Chapter 2). Championing the old-fashioned application of *story* (see Keane, 2007: 64–5) as a way to contain the disorientating novelty of technology, Pixar solicits a specific validation and view of their sequence of films as going through a progressive *maturing*, and setting evaluative limits for the whole form. Keenly cooperating in reading the films and accepting this stated ethos, critics often home in on story as the prime quality that is said to separate Pixar's productions from general perceptions of digital animation (which, back in its emergent days of the late 1990s and early 2000s – replaying how earlier innovatory cycles were received in Hollywood – came fraught with worrisome connotations of enervating, soulless technology that were posited as negating warm, fuzzy story values).[2]

Those same observers adopt common tactics in approaching the task of deconstructing Pixar. As McCulloch affirms, such commentary involves looking for the heart of a mystery – the 'secret' to Pixar's success, the ingredient that makes the company 'special', their products a more personal experience than provided by its rivals, and so forth (2014: 174). Critics actively become co-authors in a re-mystifying process (by advertising the notion that Pixar is different and singular – unlike poor old generic Buzz). The success of the track record and body of work – the naturalness of *this* company making *these* 'labour-of-love' entertainments (Brereton, 2012: 143) – colours any process of making sense of fresh releases.

Something similar seems to be at work around MS. Johnson's (2012) work gives the most coherent account of this process. MS manipulates trade reporting of its self-professed 'destiny' to succeed in the film business; more than simply an effort to procure critical compliance, for Johnson this is a case of Marvel giving 'cultural meaning to the cinematic agency that it pursued' (2012: 23–4). He goes so far as to say that in the studio's initial drive to use publicity to explain itself, 'management discourses' were 'reproduced' by industry analysts (2012: 17). Johnson reads this as evidence that the commentators are already won over to 'Marvel models of textuality', which is precisely what has happened with Pixar, too, as McCulloch notes (2014: 185).

Johnson concentrates on one very specific message; a wider message but one that is just as vital in authenticating the project is found shot through commentary on MS. A typical article ('Why Marvel Studios Succeeds (And How It Will Fail If It Doesn't Diversify)') couches its criticism in a sense, elaborated in the article, that consistency of style and purpose has been Marvel's winning feature up to now (Wheeler, 2014a). Further, language that is highly similar to Goldstein's ('reliable family brand') is used to underscore MS's 'trustworthy' offer to audiences. A slightly more august *Variety* piece (albeit with a general take on things very similar to that of Wheeler) quotes a Hollywood analyst (Jeff Bock of Exhibitor Relations), as saying that 'the media expects a lot, maybe too much, from Marvel movies' (cited in Lang, 2015), while the article seems to bracket out its own part in the excitement around Marvel's trustworthiness, staying power and audience connection.

Added to this, of course, both companies must negotiate the road to success and blue-chip media brand status while operating within the controls, and to the general strategic aims, of the same gigantic media parent. The circumscription and compromise necessary to operate in a horizontally integrated relationship within Disney is one that Pixar negotiated before Marvel did. Although the relationship frayed when Pixar was servicing distribution partner Disney with movies between 1991 and 2006,[3] once the purchase went through, on-the-record pronouncements coming from Pixar stressed harmony ('Everything they've said they would do they have lived up to', said co-founder Ed Catmull (cited in Barnes, 2008)). Disney CEO Bob Iger could calmingly assure MS: 'We didn't touch Pixar, We're not touching you' (cited in Johnson, 2013: 103). Disney's concession of certain facets of brand supremacy – that it is number one in family entertainment, or has the most beloved and potent library of characters – becomes understandable, when we look at what Pixar and Marvel contribute to the parent corporation.

This chapter contends that Pixar, like MS, should be understood via 'an argument about rebranding, self-presentation, and self-reflexive legitimization', and that the attempts of both to concentrate a studio identity draw on extremely similar tactics (those which 'shore up, and give industrial meaning to a strategic course of action already engaged' – Johnson, 2012: 4). Among many connections, the most intriguing point on the Disney-Marvel-Pixar nexus comes in 2004, with Brad Bird's *The Incredibles*, Pixar's only superhero narrative to date and something of a visual nostalgia trip into comics' Silver Age. At the same time, the movie locked into contemporaneous preoccupations bubbling through Hollywood (including the live-action superhero film). A reading of this film will be provided to support our case.

Origin story: of Pixar and the 'New Hollywood'

First, it will be helpful to set out some points which shall justify why we see fit to compare MS's strategies to those of Pixar. Here, we concentrate on perceptions of the studios' success as expressed in a selection of measures that indicate common approaches (though other measures could certainly be consulted).

- *A profound connection to moviegoers, often underscored as 'natural' in criticism and commentary.* Christensen (2012: 339) denotes the Pixar record of success by using the term 'institutional capital'. How might this be defined? Whether the measure used is critical approval (e.g. Rotten Tomatoes),[4] or linked to audience feedback (e.g. Cinemascore),[5] reports underline how the Pixar textual address impresses critics (and surely must have been important to securing investment at an earlier stage). A report of the reception of the most recent Pixar release (*Inside Out*, Pete Docter 2015) is illustrative: 'Pixar films have a 4.1 multiple when it comes to their opening-to-final cume, and everyone loves [*Inside Out*] with an "A" CinemaScore (Pixar's ninth A) and a 98 per cent Rotten Tomatoes' (D'allesandro 2015). The bundling together of audience approval and box office evidence here is not uncommon in reporting. The data suggests a strong continuity of audience, with this loyalty supporting expansion of the brand even when new or unrequested entries are released (sequels such as *Cars 2* were accused of a lack of innovation – see Lussier, 2012). Marvel's 'institutional capital' has been covered throughout this book.[6]

- *Creative regimes under long-term, benevolent (and well-publicized) leaders.* For Pixar, current Chief Creative Officer of Disney Studios and director of both *Toy Story* and, significantly, of Pixar *ur-text*, *Luxo Jr.* (1986),[7] John Lasseter. For Marvel, Kevin Feige, who replaced Avi Arad as the creative focal point in the setting up of the studio (both men's images, as discussed earlier, are informed by Marvel history and the creative leadership of Stan Lee).

- *Involvement of strong in-house creators.* The senior creatives employed, like Joss Whedon, James Gunn and Brad Bird bring (unthreatening) hipness and records of quality, translating this under studio guidance into well-crafted popular cinema. They have reputations for 'smart' approaches to low-rated genres (including stigmatized 'kids only' animations – McCulloch, 2014: 185), although the process by which creatives are brought in must be qualified with Pixar (as most directors have been promoted from within the company). Related to this:

- *An innovative approach to development.* Pixar boasts an 'artisanal' culture (referring to its own studio premises as a 'campus' – McCulloch, 2014: 174–5) where an important milestone of process is to allow untried directors feature-level resources to realize short films. Since said shorts still achieve a public release (either theatrical, accompanying a feature, as a DVD supplement, or both; certain shorts can also be viewed on Pixar's Youtube channel) the films must attain a pre-set standard. Marvel's matching tradition is the 'One-Shot', a full explanation of which can be found in Chapter 8. For Marvel's part, Beckett and Apperley (2014) state: 'The One-Shots create another platform for the [MS] brand to reach fans and provides a risk free environment for experimentation. This diminishes the possibility of damaging the brand by releasing an under-developed film' (this is one more form taken by the amelioration of risk discussed in Chapter 6). There are two slightly divergent types of Pixar short. One is tied into a feature, serving to shine light on offscreen plot issues or bump up the DVD package (*Jack-Jack Attack*, Brad Bird, 2005, which accompanied *The Incredibles*, is exemplary here). This kind of short resembles, in a limited way, the Marvel 'One-Shot'. The other type has an original premise with no connection to the host feature (examples: *Geri's Game*, Jan Pinkava, 1997; *Presto*, Doug Sweetland, 2008), seeming to serve as a technical and narrative try-out for less experienced filmmakers.

- *Extensive character libraries in a universe in which distinct narratives take place in a shared space ...?*: Our take on the MS 'shared universe' needs no reiteration; Pixar is a little more complicated. Occasionally elements from shorts recur in later features to suggest a unified universe, such as the physical resemblance (and connection to chess) of a character in *Toy Story 2* to the protagonist of *Geri's Game*. The fictional restaurant chain 'Pizza Planet' plays a significant role in *Toy Story* and a string of features suggest that all of the Pixar worlds contain a 'Pizza Planet' restaurant. Yet, ontological issues prevent firmer connections (the characters of *Cars*, for instance, seem to transpire in a car-only ontology where human involvement would create considerable confusion). Many such links are subtle, play to the initiated, and understanding of texts is not dependent on them; thus, it is perhaps best to approach the Pixar 'universe' as a coordinated, authorially managed environment, rich with 'Easter Eggs' as fan rewards, but foregoing explicit narrative connections. On this point, J. D. Connor scrutinizes *Wall-E*'s teaser trailer to note how Pixar has continued to return for inspiration to a group of projects. Self-consciously burnishing a studio legend, the trailer encourages consumers in a view that

> the films pitched [at a 1994 meeting mentioned in the trailer] belonged together.... They constituted a unified sensibility, a library waiting to be born. The trailer fosters that continuity linking one filmscape to another: the *Bug's Life* grass island, *Monsters, Inc.*'s vault of doors, and *Nemo*'s jellyfish. All of Pixar is available to us, the viewers, and all at once.
>
> (Connor, 2012: 525)

Connor's 'unified sensibility' captures the Pixar approach to diegetic 'connective tissue' perfectly.

*****

> We believe there are only two significant brands in the film industry: 'Disney' and 'Steven Spielberg'. We would like to establish 'Pixar' as the third.
>
> (Steve Jobs, cited in Grainge, 2008: 186)

Pixar was originally a division of Lucasfilm. Amid a plethora of connections and inter-references between the entertainment philosophy, as well as specific content, engaged by Lucas and his peer and sometime collaborator Spielberg (see Chapters 3 and 6), the sense of common practice linking Pixar, Lucasfilm, Marvel – new *Star Wars* comic publisher – and Disney (which now owns all three) is powerful. More than a mere cameo role in Pixar's industrial biography, the presence of Lucasfilm reveals the web of influence and emulation running between studios and across histories (fusing 'old' and 'new' studio practices) that we discussed in relation to MS in Chapter 1, allowing correspondences to come into full view. We shall spend a little time considering these.

The kind of aesthetic and structural changes that the cinema of Lucas and Spielberg presaged indelibly shaped modern event film logic (Schatz, 1993: 17–25), and this in turn determines the form taken by MS. Joe Johnston, supplier of visual FX to three Star Wars episodes and Spielberg's protégé as effects designer on *Raiders of the Lost Ark*, brought this experience to MS when dashing period adventure was required for *Captain America: The First Avenger* (tellingly, both *Toy Story* and *GOTG* etch the comic overconfidence of protagonists Buzz and Quill via homages to Indiana Jones). *Raiders* was the first formal collaboration between Lucas (as producer) and Spielberg, and Connor regards it as 'a triumph of deal-making [... because] Lucas and Spielberg received nearly half of the gross, ... participated in the music and merchandising ... had control over the poster and trailers; and Paramount reduced its distribution fee' (2012: 522). This recipe, a kind of late refashioning of 'New Hollywood'-era directorial privilege, may have dealt studios a blow in self-confidence terms, but it delivered a monster hit to Paramount in 1981.

Connor argues that *Raiders* self-reflexively meshed the profiles of its authors with its 'content', allowing it to exemplify the kind of 'intensified production consciousness' that is often found in the allegorical operations of what he calls 'neoclassical' Hollywood (2015: 322). The uniqueness of the *Raiders* deal saturates its narrative, the film '[elevating] auteurist play to the level of corporate identity' (2015: 51). Whatever considerable profit to Paramount, ownership clearly lay with its producer/director combo, and Lucas' company. Where *Raiders* self-consciously displayed mastery of a kind of storytelling that revived once-popular dramatic forms (comic strips and movie serials[8] – Buckland, 1998: 169–71), the films of MS would remediate 1960s comic storytelling for a digital FX age. And, just as had been achieved by Pixar (McCulloch, 2014: 174), the feedback solicited by Marvel's PR would, again and again, refer to this in characterizing a natural studio-author, wielding a warm tradition of Hollywood story-making. Paratexts carrying the Disney/Pixar seal of approval confirm this as an active theme. A documentary released a year after the purchase features a montage that carefully places Pixar in the American animation pantheon running from Winsor McCay to *Looney Tunes*, but notably slotting in fragments of Disney classics (*Steamboat Willie*, Ub Iwerks and Walt Disney, 1928; *The Old Mill*, Wilfred Jackson, 1937; *Snow White and the Seven Dwarfs*, David Hand, 1938) – with the only sign of special effects' modern era reserved for computer graphics breakthrough *Tron* (Steven Lisberger, 1982). Conversely, in the same documentary, the 1970s period during which John Lasseter worked in-house as a Disney animator is presented as a time of retreat from such landmarks, with lessened artistic quality dictated by an economically anxious management.[9]

Lucas and Spielberg's fortunes were rising during that very period; aspects of the practice of each, crossing aesthetics and business, were informed by Disney (as both admitted; see Krämer, 2006: 190). However, Pixar – in 1986, looking more like an unprofitable software company than a maker of feature films – was let go by Lucas, with Apple's Steve Jobs coming on board as majority investor and, by 1995, CEO. This is surprising. Lucas was close to Francis Coppola, a key 1970s filmmaker whom critics loved to frame as dramatizing the antagonism of a generation of 'boomer' directors towards studios; at an early stage, both Lucas and Spielberg were associated with the same creative energy as 'romantic *auteur*' (Buckland, 2003: 84–5) figures like Coppola (Lewis, 2008: 319). The importance of *Jaws* (Spielberg, 1975), *Star Wars*, *Raiders* and others does not need to be put forward again, any more than does the influence of Disney, from *Snow White* to *The Lion King* (Roger Allers and Rob Minkoff, 1994); but the significance of Lucas' efforts was not in uncovering a new revolutionary terrain but in the 'restabilisation' (Schatz, 1993: 10) of the old studio one. It is barely contentious to say that Hollywood's blockbuster practice today fits almost exclusively into three zones: Disney-type family entertainment, the FX-filled Lucas-Spielberg-style 'family-adventure' film (Krämer, 1998b) and what Larry Gross has termed the 'Big, Loud Action Movie' (1995). These days, 1980s action icons once of R-rated[10] territory trade their blows in PG-13-land, slotting comfortably in summer or Christmas theatres alongside *Transformers*, *Frozen* and *Jurassic World*[11]; textbooks batch Marvel superhero films alongside standards of the action/adventure canon (see Tasker, 2015). Both Pixar, with its increasing excursions into adventures – such as *Up* and *Brave*[12] – fronted by the human characters that once posed such a challenge to their systems, and MS, on the trajectory that produced *Captain America: The Winter Soldier* on the one hand, and the family-friendly *Ant-Man* caper on the other, have walked the same paths crossing these zones.[13] This is not a US-only phenomenon, which should be stressed; the effects on studio revenues of international takings is significant, and used to make production and greenlighting decisions including those of MS (an example can be found in the involvement of *Iron Man 3* with Chinese locations and Beijing co-producers, resulting in scenes included solely for Chinese theatrical audiences; see Brzeski, 2012; Tsui, 2013).

Pixar homes in on a philosophy of audience that has been seen as the terrain of Disney and the Lucas/Spielberg axis. Grainge terms this 'the "Disney Model" [... in which] Disney has been attuned ... to wider transitions in the ... construction of the domestic and international movie audience' (2008: 49). Peter Krämer extends the credit for tapping into this directly to trends set by Spielberg and Lucas, suggesting that most of Hollywood's biggest post-1970 hits should be understood as 'family-adventure' movies: films which are designed to address children and their parents as well as teenagers and young adults. The end of the studio system and the crisis of early 1960s Hollywood pulled youth and adult markets apart.[14] Krämer places Spielberg and Disney together at the heart of reuniting them, defining major studio practice as the 1970s wore on.[15] Prioritizing a combination of new effects and exhibition technologies with nostalgic play with older forms (the 'B' movie, serials, comics) – keying into the juvenile genre tastes of the 'baby boomer' parental generation – the expanded sense of 'family film' which was engendered collapsed certain boundaries that had separated genre offers for audience sectors. Narratives revolved around the spectacular adventures of familial groups (which did not have to be traditional nuclear families), and the median Hollywood product, in terms of age, was remade into something that excluded no one.

One interesting point about this interpretation of the nexus of cinema taste and demography moving in the direction of juvenility is that at around the same period, American comic publishing strategy seemed to be passing in the opposite direction. For many commentators, in both its formats and its approaches to technique and subject, for the first time, the comics industry was calculating an ideal reader who was out of their teenaged years (Wright, 2003: 277–80). As Douglas Brode points out, the cultivation of 'an immature audience, whatever its age' that was sometimes attributed to Spielberg and Lucas by unhappy critics was not the same thing as a mass lowering of the actual age of attendees (2000: 339–40). However, the challenging of the MPAA age-rating system which was posed implicitly by films like the Spielberg-produced *Gremlins* (Joe Dante, 1984) and directly by *Indiana Jones and the Temple of Doom* (1984)[16] is a significant issue, with a bearing on contemporary Hollywood that requires far more space than is available. For now, returning to Pixar, it is enough to relate that critics have registered the orientation towards a blurred child/adult audience – what Gant (2015) calls, in relation to the appeal of *Inside Out*, a 'strong adult skew' – and, that through diegetic and paratextual discourses (such as reports of how development and production processes are conducted at Pixar's Emeryville headquarters), that this is reconstructed as a positive element.

In this vein, McCulloch sees Pixar as rewriting 'stigmas' of the audience associations carried by the animated form, stating that because such discourses 'collapse notions of age', Pixar is empowered 'to create films that connect with as many people as possible' (2014: 178). This aspect of how Pixar is discussed transcends the effective identification of target audiences and touches on the construction of those audiences as social and ideological beings, which means not only cultivating what is good for the institution, but also validating topics and positions in which audiences are already invested. Pixar films are placed among the canon of computer-animated children's productions said to undertake a 'thematic engagement with [issues of] consumerism' (Hinkins, 2007: 44). Some are specifically namechecked for their eco-credentials which 'tease out important global issues for contemporary civilization (Brereton, 2012: 158 and *passim*). Again, here, careful brand management actions help reduce conflict with other goals, since Disney still has a 'universe' of characters to manage. The relatively slow bleed of Marvel characters into Disney-branded commercial and aesthetic space (discussed in Chapter 6 in terms of the successful introduction of Rocket Raccoon into the *Disney Infinity* game) seems to show Disney's awareness of the damaging consequences of contradicting – in the eyes of Marvel fans – Iger's word to not 'rebrand [the company] as Disney' (cited in Rasmussen, 2009: 6). It is in keeping with the more recent approach to accepting non-traditional characters into its stable[17], provided that potential value to someone in the audience can be demonstrated.

Pat Brereton goes further, suggesting that Disney's approval of Pixar characters like Wall-E (titular eco-robot of Andrew Stanton's romcom-adventure, 2008) is a brand-modification opportunity that the parent conglomerate gratefully seizes. Providing a 'smarter variety ... of anthropomorphic engagement' (2012: 147), *Wall-E* helps to dilute the more 'cutesy' and 'sentimental' qualities associated with other Disney characters, as well as contributing to a social discourse that softens or (to adapt Brereton's term) 'smartens' the didactic edge of earlier, criticized texts that were more recognizably 'Disney' (2012: 148). The company may not be known for cultural opposition to capitalist practices like the consumerism that *Wall-E* targets (along with, arguably, the Buzz scene mentioned earlier), but such mild critique – channelled through Pixar, not the 'pure' Disney brand – is consistent with views of recent children's films as 'offering diagnoses of culture for adults even as they enculturate children' (Freeman, cited in Hinkins, 2007: 43). Thus, a sub-brand whose products almost unfailingly reaffirm community – whether this is uniting scattered groups of toys, bringing aquatic parents back together with their children, or many other examples – is used to heal rifts between Disney and the 'real world' of a critically and socially informed consumer engagement.

The economic and corporate conditions that have set the current terms on which the studio-brand value is managed across texts engender dynamics of authorship as surely as any film-school wave or taste constellation could. When dealing with Marvel, we have already argued that the studio signature is framed as the guarantee of quality (a point which we return to examine in the Conclusion). No matter what the official message says about creators and their freedom, the studio is the 'personality' that each success builds up (if a person absolutely must be invoked, studio embodiment and ruling creative agent Feige is chosen). Similarly, McCulloch notes that cumulatively, the messages, paratexts and critiques emerging from and applying to Pixar assert a special case where the exercise of authorial command is shown to issue from 'a group rather than a single person' (2014: 177). In the light of information released from Pixar's top echelon[18] about its decision-making process, Holliday elaborates: 'Pixar have outwardly (re)negotiated authorship in contemporary Hollywood cinema as a strongly collective enterprise. Since Walt Disney's $7.4 billion acquisition … this collaborative model for creativity has even proved to be a game-changer for Pixar's parent company' (2014) – by which Holliday means the influence of Pixar methods (and importantly, the personnel that instituted them) upon Disney.[19] One problem an earlier regime of Disney had was a perception that an initial reputation as friendly to the finest craftsmen, such as its famous 'Nine Old Men',[20] was squandered through boardroom wars, punitive labour relations (a problem that has also dogged Pixar), and a reputation for overzealous protection – rather than creative proliferation of – IP.[21] As branding becomes ever more important, one remedy to this is to maintain a more circumspect image when it comes to the question of harbouring and nurturing artistic talent, and the 'Pixar Braintrust' is offered up as an example of good practice; providing a structure infused with the ethos of supporting novice artists with assistance and a steer from colleagues who are directly connected to hallowed story traditions (see Holliday, 2014). The comparison to MS's controversial committee or MCC,[22] formed to steer creative control towards mutual understanding between proven comic and filmic practitioners (and away from 'outside producers' – Leonard, 2014a), is tantalizing. Pixar claims that such methods as the Braintrust govern story policy; mention is not made that the technologies used to bring productions to the screen are similarly governed. Thus, *story* is reinforced as a sacred component, that which carries quality movie-making DNA. The responsible application of it transcends the rights of an individual filmmaker. Like Marvel, not every director who originates a Pixar production is left to see it through.[23] The 'Braintrust' thus appears not just a way of coordinating authentic expression, but an internal safeguarding mechanism blocking extensions to or contradictions of styles and tastes.[24]

One Pixar filmmaker, who is very much in the 'classical *auteur*' Spielbergian mould when it comes to maintaining individuality in a commercially sound approach to style, is Brad Bird. The smartly populist Bird, schooled in Disney tradition as a CalArts graduate, spent time on *The Simpsons* (a show with a highly critical stance towards Disney's monolithic presence in animation). Nevertheless it was his responsibility to re-mythologize Disney's cinematic identity by constructing an effects-filled live action-adventure from one of its symbolic 'texts': 'Tomorrowland', a themed futuristic leisure park zone. Several weeks after its US-wide release in 2015, the film was showing no signs of making back its money in the theatrical window; almost proving that Pixar is a better bet than its parent in defending values that signify classic Disney, this was a rare box office and critical misfire for Bird (McClintock, 2015). However, Bird had already proven his ability to connect the pop-cultural preoccupations of his youth with Pixar's technological excellence in *The Incredibles* (2004). The film is, in some ways, a love letter to the Marvel Silver Age style.

Pixar does Marvel: the finest Fantastic Four movie ever made

If the apotheosis of early Pixar style is *Finding Nemo* (Andrew Stanton, 2003) – coupling specialized new undersea computer textures with a sentimental 'family-adventure' narrative – *The Incredibles* seemed to show the studio changing gears. A prominent shift from Pixar norms was that for the first time, its work directly engaged with the (live action) cinema *zeitgeist*, entering what was, by 2004 (and before the MCU) already a crowded marketplace for superhero films.[25] Bob Parr/'Mr. Incredible' (voiced by Craig T. Nelson) is a retired costumed fighter, who lives in deep suburban cover with similarly superheroic wife Helen (voiced by Holly Hunter, and formerly 'Elastigirl') and their powered kids: Dash (voiced by Spencer Fox) possesses super-speed, while Violet (voiced by Sarah Vowell) can turn invisible and project forcefields. Their anonymity is a necessary condition of the wholesale withdrawal of 'supers' years before. This is blamed on unmanageable property damage bills, and an ungrateful public obsessed with litigation, leading the government to insist that the supers end their exploits and step down.

The former supers adopt normal jobs and a cover story of mediocrity to hide their talents; the kids have never expressed their abilities for fear of 'outing' themselves. The clear point of comparison from Marvel's catalogue is the FF (although the visual environments and narrative tropes used draw on superhero culture more generally). The main difference between the 'Incredibles' and the FF is that the FF do not hide their identities and thus have to deal with the issues of celebrity, whereas the Incredibles (specifically Bob and Dash) have a hard time dealing with the cover story the family has to wear, yearning to be released in their (very American) exceptionality (Meinel, 2014: 183).[26] It is interesting that, with the rights to the FF and their supporting cast residing outside MS as already mentioned, Fox is yet to produce a cinematic incarnation of the team that satisfies fans. With the notably light tone of Tim Story's brace of films sacrificed in the still less popular 2015 'reboot', Fox seems stricken by awkwardness in settling on a tone for the famous characters, needing, it seems, to engender both familiarity and suitability for genre norms. Rumours even swirled of desperate attempts to draw out of fans what manner of approach might please them.[27] While There are differences (although a familial group, the FF are all adults, with the team's junior member, Johnny Storm, attending college a few years into the Lee/Kirby run), the CG register used by Pixar seemed to free Bird and his team into a way to imaginatively adapt the *spirit* of FF adventures, while circumventing the need to be clunkily modern, 'relevant', or to differentiate itself from other genre entries on emotional or psychological grounds.

Pixar's high standards are an inevitable reference point in assessing any new movie's strengths (McCulloch, 2014: 184), and *The Incredibles* was no different: ironically given the superhero premise, reviewers focused on the cueing of material towards adult spectators and the resulting unification of the intergenerational audience (Newman, 2005: 56; McCulloch, 2014: 185). Reconciling some of the problems of authenticity posed by digital methods, a mature 'fusing of narrative and spectacle', deriving from the focus on human characters and 'adult' concerns, was attributed to the film (Keane, 2007: 65). The diegesis itself harbours tropes of growth and progression, yet in its thematic scope – larger than previous Pixar projects – also considers the temptations of fantasy lives and irresponsibility. At the start of the film, Bob misses the 'glory days'. Trying to expurgate this by seeking discreet crime fighting kicks with his friend Lucius Best/Frozone (voiced by Sam Jackson, MS's Nick Fury), Bob is drawn into a shadowy operation testing combat robots on a secluded island. This is a set-up that brings him back into contact with Syndrome (voiced by Jason Lee; formerly Buddy Pine, aka 'Incredi-Boy'), an infatuated would-be 'sidekick' that Bob rejected years before. Now a science villain obsessed with Bob's demise, Syndrome's plot forces the family to reform, both as an expanded fighting team, and emotionally. Helen will need to forgive Bob for the mid-life crisis that has disrupted their stable life; Bob will learn that watching his family grow can also be a source of thrills and mystery; the children learn to exercise their powers responsibly. Cold War cultural discourses, coded into the design of the film (as we shall see) and amplified by the Silver Age comic references, linked the stability of 'traditional [family] roles' with American 'political security' (Darowski J., 2014: 100); there is a little confusion in how messages from that time are brought into the era of the audience, and the predominant ideologies of the culture in which *The Incredibles* participates. Sometimes this is played for comic irony, and a fun take on nostalgia is evident, but does not totally resolve this tension.

After the prologue scenes showing the Parrs and Lucius in action before the curb on supers, we join the present, where a stolid, stable world has been attained at the cost of the more exciting but unpredictable era of supers. Helen can handle this; Bob cannot. Floundering in his soul-destroying insurance job, he misses action, finding it difficult to 'grow up' and out of his self-identification with his powers and costume. From Bob's superhuman viewpoint, the vacuum created by the end of the supers represents a culture of celebrating mediocrity. A certain idea of 'common sense' and 'back to basics' echoes in Bob's conviction that strength should be exercised and applauded; the film does not strictly discount this view (this culture, after all, has permitted Syndrome's threat to rise). The influence of popular psychology and an apologetic, liberal therapeutic culture (there are references to family and marital counselling, educational and child-rearing styles) is indicted; because Bob is capable of looking after his family, he sees the modern culture that prevents this as selfish and trivial. At the same time, Bob's psychological resources are clearly weaker than Helen's; the new adventure ends up serving as a kind of therapeutic role-play for him, even helping him come to a recognition (confessed to Helen) that his greatest weakness is the fear that his family will be hurt. However, Bob has a funny way of showing it; only by placing himself and his family in danger does he properly shake off his ennui and reconnect with the inner strength to truly 'intervene' (as Helen implores of him while the kids run rings round her at dinner time). This draws Bob into a mirror relation with Syndrome, who sets up a theatrical public attack of his 'Omnidroid' robot. In defeating the Omnidroid in this set-up or personal reality show, the much more modern Syndrome will secure coveted hero status.

Bob makes sense if seen within a series of conflicted heroes in films of the time, who struggle with the fact that their powers can save the world, but who eventually exorcise this doubt after positive reaffirmation from the community. In a similar scenario, Peter Parker (Tobey Maguire) tries to walk away from his powers in *Spider-Man 2*, and the motif recurs in many texts.[28] In many cases, the heroes deal with their own fears along the way to dispatching the villainous threat; in some of them, the threat *is* the climate of fear. Fear is an important trope for popular cinema after September 11 and the 'War on Terror', suggesting a wish on the part of filmmakers to retain a purpose for films that posit (fantasy) violence as a solution, but a desire to frame this within a more liberal context that refuses fixed definitions of evil. Villains like Henri Ducard (Liam Neeson) in *Batman Begins* (Christopher Nolan, 2005) and Mr Linderman (Malcolm McDowell) in the ABC superhero serial *Heroes* (2006–10) explicitly discuss their mission as the artificial incubation of fear, which they believe will lead society to destroy itself in extreme responses. The same theme has been discussed in relation to the *Iron Man* series (see Chapter 3), and the machinations of HYDRA which combine mass distraction and mass destruction (see Chapters 4 and 5).

Weak, mundane reality cannot rival the vivid fantasy life of a super: this is something which Bob and Syndrome seem to share. The constraints on Bob of an overdetermined domestic normality are represented in desaturated colour and special space-flattening long lens settings (on the production's 'virtual camera').[29] When the action kicks in, Bob can run rampant on Syndrome's island, or the city of Metroville. Resembling the 1960s 'idealized' Manhattan of the FF, Marvel's 'First Family', Metroville basks in the nostalgia of a clean utopianism, less of the moment than Kirby's Manhattan, a place of 'abstract and intricate' form reflective of capitalist progress (Yockey, 2005: 65). This is probably to undersell its specificity: Metroville is visually coded to convey a meeting point between Jacques Tati-style modernist critique and 'World's Fair' utopianism. Pixar's tools are used highly effectively in creating not only the buildings, but also technologies, objects and transport modes of a retrofuturist age. Part cartoon, part spy-movie, the detail that has gone into balancing Metroville's archetypicality and fictionality with felt architectural histories (keying in to 1950s pulp adventure environments, classic superheroics/Bond-style spy fiction and the Silver Age) has attracted recognition (Edelson, 2013). It is probably no accident that the super-team is banished because of the inability of the likes of them to refrain from wrecking the city.

The nostalgia impulse embodied in Metroville's design is an important clue to divining Pixar's goals: desirous of winning a place on the cutting-edge, the company simultaneously wishes to establish itself in the inclusive heart of filmic tradition. Jonathan Romney is aware of this when he appraises nostalgia as long 'a central factor in Pixar narratives … Pixar's writers have been adept at resolving the contradiction between its cults of old and hyper-new, which in other studios' films comes across simply as glaring hypocrisy' (2006: 46). Part of how nostalgia brackets, but does not eradicate, other tensions addresses scholars' concerns over digital representation cited earlier; presenting David Rodowick's argument, Brereton writes that 'the most productive response to the gradual erasing of cinema's photomechanical basis is a combination of mournful nostalgia and forward-looking optimism' (Brereton, 2012: 153). As indicated earlier, temporal cues are oddly mixed up in *The Incredibles*[30]; the search for an authentic, communal past (which is typically Pixar) constructs an out-of-reach fantasy world characterized by an illogical temporality. The nostalgia here tweaks temporal bounds so that more 'innocent' adventures can remain unencumbered from selected aspects of cynical modernity; in this, functioning rather like Raimi's 2002–7 Spider-Man trilogy where the innocence of Marvel Comics' Silver Age phase is visually and thematically invoked (see Flanagan, 2007: 146–8). Pixar-style nostalgia self-reflexively acknowledges a dimension of its own 'meta-branding': wherein old and new is set into a dialogue just as is 'young' and 'old' in spectatorship. *Toy Story 2* gives the launch of Sputnik (i.e. late 1957) an important position in the history of cowboy toy Woody (voiced by Tom Hanks); but from the toy protagonists' perspective, Sputnik signifies changes in the audience for toys, as space travel becomes the rage (from cowboy Woody to spaceman Buzz, one frontier exchanged for another). The Cold War is held in the background, but the historical reference is enlarged in *The Incredibles*. Through intertextual design and music cues that conjure the early James Bond films (from *Dr No*, Terence Young, 1962), the 'golden age' of retired superheroes – despite some signs to the contrary – does appear to transpire in the late 1950s or very early 1960s. Tellingly for the Disney connection, 'authentic values' for Pixar films seem to be located at a time of 'New Frontier' political optimism (and buoyant consumerism).

When Pixar tells its own history it is clear that the studio views its own contribution to popular film as another kind of valiant frontier crossing: blasting wide the sub-genre of CGI animation by bravely demystifying artist and audience anxieties about incorporating computers into craft.[31] This validates the 'studio allegory' approaches of critics like Connor (2012, 2015) and Christensen (2012).[32] *The Incredibles* might be considered a post-9/11 film, in that it has an interest in working through problematic new inflections on the concept of 'might is right'. Although, in national terms, it has been received as an 'apologia' (Anon., 2004b) for hawkish foreign policy choices that require sacrifice in the name of preserving stability (connecting it to *Iron Man*), it shares with other popular films a mature idea that new ideological weapons call into being a different kind of response from the good guys. This involves engaging with that little used part of the heroic skillset, humility; Bob goes through this process as he waits, agonized, for his family to save him. Earlier, the idea of *balance* was cited in terms of the need to regulate digital representation through appealing to the values of 'story'; here, balance is applied as a mild political theme. Showing weakness (as Bob is ultimately prepared to do in front of Helen) is an appropriate index of strength, because it implies value for life. Like other superhero narratives, *The Incredibles* thinks about the heroic imperative in terms of stark choices, but does so with greater critical acumen than many films revolving around similar material.

Conclusion

Complementary, equally instructive lessons about the modern forms taken by American studio filmmaking and industrial culture are there to be drawn from studying the reputations of MS and Pixar Animation Studios. Pixar led the way, and Marvel surely noted many of its findings. Marked by the 'maverick' business codes promoted by owners Lucas and later Steve Jobs, Pixar took note of the successes of Disney, but also of the way that the bigger company allowed itself to be framed as representing business logic above all else. When Pixar was the independent and contracted with Disney from 1991 to 1996, it was forced to construct and stand behind its own independence, through this, continuing to make films that pleased audiences even as the working relationship declined (Eller, 2003). The fact that Pixar and MS both managed to parlay their initial track records into prized values of independence proved priceless, as critics and investors came on board. Today, the studios continue to be acclaimed with an intense dedication to getting creative processes right, and this helps to revamp impressions of the whole Disney infrastructure under Iger. 'Diplomatic, deferential' compared to the 'combative' Eisner (Leonard, 2014a), Iger uses Pixar to exemplify Disney's recent record of artistic non-interference, and binds Marvel and Pixar together in the name of quality in public comments: '[The MCC] live and breathe Marvel full time just like the Pixar folks live and breathe Pixar full time,' (cited in Leonard 2014a). Pixar's official bio-documentary frames the 2006 acquisition as the symbolic mainspring in a transition marking Eisner's uncompromising and self-destructive regime passing into that of Iger (Iwerks, 2007). Shades here of the outsider-amateurs of Toy Biz, Arad and Perlmutter, interceding when Marvel's fortunes declined: the ones who could match smarter ways of doing business with a deep understanding of the spirit of the company, and its inventory.

Lasseter – shown by promo materials to once sleep in his car or under his work desk as the first wave of Pixar employees struggled to arrive at a breakthrough that would energize the company's work and bring financial stability – was cast out by a change-averse 1980s Disney regime – one that had lost the pulse of shifts in the direction of family entertainment, as evidenced by the 'turn[ing] down [of] proposals for *Raiders of the Lost Ark* and *E.T. the Extra-Terrestrial*' (Wasko, 2007: 31). Thus Disney missed out on the first great boon of 'family-adventure'. Lasseter is now the company's overall creative head, redeeming the Disney tradition and selecting new accents and priorities for it. The brand value that he presents to Disney refreshes and refocuses values that were once perceived as key to company practice, but had faded into a lost era when Disney's focus on business allowed belief in their 'Magic Kingdom' of folk-entertainment production to dwindle.

Nothing is left to chance in Disney's sealing of its status as 'global entertainment juggernaut' (Grainge, 2008: 49). On a wider view of studio strategy, J. D. Connor considers the Marvel and Pixar acquisitions 'crucial' for a company like Disney at a time of general studio retreat from an older, expansionist approach to the market (2012: 523). Often criticized for a lack of imagination in production in the 1970s and early 2000s, Disney's swag is not just a library of characters of immense potential and value, but – because of how both studios are reported and framed in commentary – the credit for those characters' effectiveness. In terms of supporting the Disney reputation, and pumping value in through transmedia zones that have become key to the family entertainment arena (such as their theme parks or the Infinity game), it is difficult to imagine how another acquisition could have brought the cachet of 'indie smartness' that is attributed to Pixar's *Wall-E* (Brereton, 2012: 141). Disney need not relinquish the standing of a 'trustworthy' name in smart, popular cinema to Pixar or Marvel as it owns them; but to maintain the benefits requires careful management of how the parent brand interacts with sub-brand (the real import of Iger's public statements and implied promise to secure Marvel's brand as distinct to that of Disney). Again, the process of imprinting a studio with a meaningful signature[33] looks back: older forms of studio reputational culture once depended on circulating brand imagery, feeding press and publicity circuits with slogans and value statements, and fusing all of these into a 'house style' ready to be given textual form (Schatz, 1998: 6–7).

Pixar's 'reification' (McCulloch's apt term) of story, through the discourses we have examined, works towards the same end: a freewheeling, wacky (even 'childlike', and not 'normal' – McCulloch, 2014: 175, 178 and 180) culture of creative chaos harnessed into the stuff of a 'reliable family brand'. Pixar's founding myths echo through their most important, tone-setting works, as Connor notes: 'The implicit appeal of [… the first *Wall-E*] trailer was to our nostalgia for the founding moments of Pixar as a production company, and for its independence' (2012: 525). The natural creativity and understanding of story – summarized as a painstaking approach to craft, preference for innovation over formula, and a well-publicized progressive labour policy centring on an artisan, apprentice-style culture (Brereton, 2012: 142) – that is associated with Pixar resembles the aura that surrounds 'storyteller' Marvel, as we saw in Chapter 2. In Marvel's case, it is the oft-cited long history of publication and experience of universe-building, roadmap of a Johnsonian cinematic 'destiny', which mark the key points to which commentary responds. For both, a specific 'production culture', as much as the implementation of specific aesthetic choices in given texts by particular creative agents, is what is really being acclaimed when success is noted (McCulloch, 2014: 174).

The traditional Disney zone of influence, obviously, is the family film. There have been – arguably – two clear examples of Disney, through MS or under the aegis of Disney Animation Studios, attempting to navigate Marvel properties into this market.[34] *Ant-Man* is a clear tilt at the family-adventure narrative, sweeping up young Cassie Lang (Abbie Ryder Fortson) into the redemption narrative of her father. Cassie gets the chance to see Scott Lang – whom so many others have given up on – act like the hero he has always been in her eyes, and is at hand for the climactic battle. Released the same summer as *Age of Ultron*, *Ant-Man* earned a lower-than-Marvel-average $57,000,000 opening weekend gross (US), but by September 2015, its performance was shaping up like a successful contemporary family release. On course to achieve a steady 'multiple' (total box office divided by opening weekend) of 3.1 – indicative of reasonable box office 'legs' – the film was looking at a likely endpoint of $175–180 million US gross.[35] (It was noted earlier that one indicator of satisfied Pixar audiences is the high average multiple figure of 4.1 attracted by their films – D'Allesandro, 2015). Speaking for Disney, distribution executive Dave Hollis explained that *Ant-Man*'s address had connected with women and families to a greater degree than previous Marvel releases (Gensler, 2015).

More obviously functioning as a mixture of Pixar and Marvel approaches is the computer-animated hit *Big Hero 6* (John Hall and Chris Williams, 2014). John Lasseter's Feige-like presence in any discussion of Disney animation demonstrates how the Pixar ethos has come to define the tone and scope of Disney's animated output; accordingly, the film's British release enlisted Lasseter to provide promotional context for this adaptation of a little known Marvel title (the *Telegraph* profile tied in to the film including the inevitable reference to respect for 'storytelling traditions [Disney had …] helped set down the best part of a century ago' (Collin, 2015)). The adaptation is looser than other Marvel works, with the core movie audience far outnumbering readers of the original comic – presumably, a fact regarded positively in the production of the film.[36] Consequently, Hiro (voiced by Ryan Potter) and Baymax (voiced by Scott Adsit) are treated as completely new characters, with a strong Spielbergian emotional arc of Hiro discovering a father-surrogate and working through grief in his adventures with the caring Baymax, and the super-team throwing off disappointments to form a 'family', learning to respect each other's skills and feelings, much as in Pixar narratives like *A Bug's Life* (John Lasseter and Andrew Stanton, 1998), *Up* and – classically – *Toy Story*. Connections that loosely linked the source to MU comics are more or less eradicated, and in MCU terms, no diegetic suggestion that narrative events take place there is included. There is no Marvel branding around the film's paratextual existence, and no tie-in comic.[37] Given Iger's reassurances, it is obvious that this kind of case – where the Marvel brand fades and the Disney one, buttressed by Pixar-like approaches to story and visuals, takes precedence, could only occur with a property that will not draw out fans' protective loyalties.

Perhaps the final point to make about their similarities concerns genre: Pixar can reasonably claim to have annexed the meanings of 'computer-generated animated film' – if not 'animated film' – into its own domain by the way it has preserved its institutional capital. As standard-bearer for a form (just as Disney was in the 1930s in leading animation away from its more abstract expressive potentialities and into a register of 'realism' anchored to classical, live action narrative), Pixar defines the sector's expressive norms. Over at Marvel, superhero films issue easily from its system: shared universe coordination and the careful matching of creatives and other partners to strategic needs are the market-leading tactics that set the 'genre' idiom. Competitors both 'horizontal' (the Fox franchises like *Fantastic Four*) and 'vertical' (DC–Warner Brothers) can only emulate – not change – this vernacular.

CHAPTER 8
TIE-INS, TIE-UPS AND LET-DOWNS: MARVEL'S TRANSMEDIA EMPIRE

Introduction

With a catalogue of characters as large and diverse as Marvel's, it was inevitable that slow-moving theatrical film production would soon be deemed unable to contain them. Marvel has a rich history of trying to exploit this catalogue of intellectual property (IP), with Stan Lee, in a 1977 attempt to stoke an extended licensing strategy, stating:

> Considering the vast influence and appeal Marvel and I seem to have with today's so-called 'youth market', it seems a shame not to be harnessing this tremendous asset in areas other than the sale of comic books alone.

> (Lee cited in Howe, 2013: 190)

As this chapter will illuminate, Marvel saw variable success in such activity throughout that decade via licensing and merchandising exploits, its full potential remaining unexpressed. Only in the last decade has the movement towards exploiting this potential in the vast catalogue been sustained, beyond a handful of characters, and the argument will be made that the improvement is due to the adoption of a genuine transmedia approach to storytelling. This has provided the difference between simply having the same recognized characters exist in different media, but also in different (or at least, not implied as connected) story universes, as compared to a single, cohesive story universe 'told' across different media. In evaluating this process, the meaning of transmedia as concept, and how it should be understood in the context of the current work, will be elaborated. As has been noted throughout our discussion, changes arising from industrial affairs have enabled the increasing freedom with which Marvel has been able to deploy its own IP across different media. The continued use of the term Marvel *Cinematic* Universe, as opposed to a Marvel *Transmedia* Universe, begs an explanation of how the transmedia approach taken by Marvel Studios (MS) can be understood as fully utilizing a range of platforms, generating 'connective tissue' that nevertheless leads back to that central, privileged cinematic hub in the web of content.[1] Following our definition of transmedia, the different approaches taken and their attendant media will in turn be analysed for the 'connective tissue'[1] function (what Feige, speaking in terms of the address to audiences, has termed 'breadcrumbs' meant to lead a viewer through the associated parts (cited in Philibrick, 2010)).

Some scrutiny of network TV show *Agents of S.H.I.E.L.D.* (*AoS*), will examine how that show functions, not only as an expansion of the 'main narrative' constructed within the cinematic properties, but also its continuing influence on the continuity of the MCU as a 'world-building' device.[2] We will consider how it may have struggled to live up to its promise in the early stages of its development, only taking from the wider universe, without giving back, and how such issues were transcended as the second season progressed. This approach will then be compared to one of the other MCU forays into the small screen, by which we have in mind the tonally more mature shows appearing on Netflix on-demand streaming, which commenced with 2015's *Daredevil*.

Predating *AoS*, we will look at how Marvel used the series' lead character, non-powered S.H.I.E.L.D. mainstay Phil Coulson (Clark Gregg), to build familiarity and indicate connection points between heroes' narratives, both across the individual cinematic releases, and through a number of standalone mini-episode 'One-Shots'. Similar to these seemingly self-sufficient, yet connective short films, MS's use of post-credit scenes will be marked as significant within a wider deployment of 'Easter Eggs'. Another instance of connective tissue at work relates to tie-in comic books, often titled 'Preludes', which describe events leading up to the starting points of MCU films.[3] Finally, a look at MCU tie-in videogames will reveal how credulity can be stretched by remediation of an ongoing continuity into a medium within which successful functioning depends on vastly different tenets. The ambiguous evidence presenting itself regarding the videogames' true validity and import within MCU canon, and Marvel's apparent withdrawal from the sector following poor reception (and possibly, not unrelated to the Disney purchase) make this struggling case worth looking at.

Early attempts: The limits of licensing

For decades, despite obvious ambition, when it came to showcasing its characters in other media, Marvel stuttered time and again. Proposals circulated for live-action movies (including an X-Men film scripted by Roy Thomas and legendary Spider-Man scribe Gerry Conway in 1984),[4] as well as television series and syndicated cartoons (Howe even recounts work undertaken to launch an animated show teaming respectable – if not A-list – heroes with canine allies – 2013: 231). Most of these attempts were abandoned, with few being realized with any degree of success; a true transmedia empire built on Marvel creativity remained frustratingly out of reach for decades. As discussed in Chapter 2, even when licensing deals proved vital to the post-bankruptcy financial restabilization, Marvel wielded little control over the characters' depictions.

While the majority of attempts fell short of the commercial success they were designed to yield, projects such as CBS's *The Incredible Hulk* (1978–82) TV show created lasting pop-cultural legacies, not only exposing elements of, but even adding to, the Hulk character (the image of an ennui-filled Banner hitchhiking along a highway, as made famous by the series, has entrenched itself within public consciousness; as was recognized by its invocation in 2008's MCU-based *The Incredible Hulk*). Another 1970s attempt to branch into television, *The Amazing Spider-Man* (1977–9), represents a further significant milestone despite lasting only a modest two seasons. Although plans to bring the two properties together for a standalone movie were thwarted (see Ferrigno, 2003: 182), this illustrated that the ambition to suture two (or more) separate properties together – and show that, under the Marvel banner, they were not in fact separate – was always there. Yet, as these characters were simply licensed to external commercial interests (in this instance, CBS), such decisions were out of Marvel's hands. Indeed, it was a branding issue, internal to CBS, that pulled *The Amazing Spider-Man* from screens so early: with it already alongside *The Incredible Hulk* and (DC property) *Wonder Woman* (1975–9) in its schedules, a newly arrived CEO at the station was said to object to being defined as a 'cartoon network' (Howe, 2013: 215). As CBS interest cooled, half-hearted efforts like the unsuccessful made-for-TV movie, *Dr Strange* (1978) and an undistinguished pair of *Captain America* adaptations (both 1979) showed that the network's strategies did not seem to be serving blue-chip Marvel characters well. At this stage in its history, Marvel's position justified Johnson's later description as a content 'development farm' (2012: 9): surrendering rights cheaply, cut out of revenue streams, and excluded from creative processes. This was in a late-1970s moment when Warner Bros./DC's Superman was performing in the manner of an orthodox blockbuster series. Refraining (at least in its first two instalments, *Superman* (Richard Donner, 1978) and *Superman II* (Richard Lester, 1980)), from disguising aspects of its 'comic book world' through an apologetic attitude of camp (very much in line with other fantasy successes of this post-*Star Wars* era), the Superman films were entertaining huge audiences. The sums involved illustrate Marvel's squandered chance, as Howe reports that the live-action TV rights for twelve Marvel characters went to Universal for little over one thousand dollars per head in 1976–7 (2013: 195), whereas *Superman*, although budgeted at a pricey $55 million, eventually reaped over $300 million at the worldwide box office.[5] The integration of Warner Bros. and DC seemed to give Marvel's competition the advantage, as Marvel, in its contemporaneous industrial structure, was unable to emulate such success. In the late 1970s, Stan Lee and Magazine Management president Jim Galton, tried to convince parent Cadence Industries to actually buy a 'small studio' to effect a proper, controlled schedule of Marvel moving image production, but to no avail (Howe, 2013: 215).

Despite earlier reservations, someone within CBS could clearly conceive those possible rewards. The network exercised its options again, attempting to revive its Hulk show several years after its cancellation, with *The Incredible Hulk Returns*

(Nicholas Corea, 1988). Although only produced at the level of a TV movie, it portended Marvel's ambition to weave premium characters together in a shared space. During the film, Marvel's Asgardian god Thor (Eric Kramer) appears alongside Lou Ferrigno's Hulk, in what was not only the first successful live-action crossover of a Marvel comics character, but also the first and only live-action depiction of Thor until the MCU films almost twenty years later. The movie was both a way of bringing the Hulk back onscreen, and a kind of back-door pilot for Thor. CBS then followed this up with the production of a second TV movie within a year: *The Trial of the Incredible Hulk* (Bill Bixby, 1989). Once again, CBS introduced another Marvel character to support the Hulk, this time in the form of lawyer-by-day, crime fighter-by-night Daredevil/Matt Murdoch (Rex Smith). Indifferently produced back-door pilots for CBS shows that never occurred though these were, the developments would have alerted Marvel to the possibilities of further character overlap: a situation wherein an Asgardian god meeting a gamma radiation-enhanced giant would feel like a pay-off of careful storytelling, rather than a fleeting market-testing experiment. However, Marvel had to be in a very different industrial and organizational position before it could construct a true transmedia story universe. Before considering the MCU as constituting such a transmedia approach to storytelling, we will first introduce the notion and outline how it is to be understood in the current context.

What is transmedia storytelling?

The academic literature for 'transmedia storytelling' has grown around Henry Jenkins' (2003) seminal article for *MIT Technology Review*, the succinctly titled 'Transmedia Storytelling'. Note that this refers to transmedia *storytelling*; Jenkins (2011) specifically takes pains to emphasize that there is a discourse around other forms of transmedia, noting the scholar Marsha Kinder's seminal role within this. He contends that the principles around transmedia *storytelling* are more specific than a general cross-media approach to creative content; the telling contribution is that throughout the span of media, a single cohesive story is constructed, albeit out of multiple smaller stories. In his book *Convergence Culture* (first published in 2006), he clearly defines transmedia storytelling as:

> Stories that unfold across multiple media platforms, with each medium making distinctive contributions to our understanding of the world, a more integrated approach to franchise development than models based on urtexts and ancillary products.

(Jenkins, 2008: 334)

The notion of consistency throughout a single universe holds the key to why the term is so perfectly applicable in the case of the MCU. As alluded to earlier, though, one might wonder: Why not Marvel *Transmedia* Universe? Such nomenclature shows a certain bias, a hierarchy organized around the *cinematic*. As per such an understanding of transmedia storytelling, this cinematic-centrality needn't detract from its transmedia credentials, so long as, essentially, the constituent parts contribute to the universe. Jenkins explains that 'each franchise entry needs to be self-contained so you don't need to have seen the film to enjoy the [video]game, and vice versa. Any given product is a point of entry into the franchise as a whole' (2008: 98). As will be articulated throughout this chapter, this is not entirely accurate, in every MCU case; some of the texts do constitute 'connective tissue' built to support that central stream. As for such connective elements of the story universe, particularly the One-Shots, a qualifying criterion of Jenkins' definition is still met: 'In the ideal form of transmedia storytelling, each medium does what it does best' (2008: 98). Even if these additions to the story universe are not created to be consumed alone, they do serve a unique purpose, and each one 'does what it does best', ultimately leading to a situation where 'reading across the media sustains a depth of experience that motivates more consumption' (2008: 98).

Transmedia storytelling has been addressed comprehensively by Elizabeth Evans (2011). Writing from a specifically televisual context, Evans' insights are nevertheless germane to the very nature of the transmedia topic as we shall apply it. She takes care to delineate a complete view of transmedia storytelling, along the lines established by Jenkins, debunking versions that simply apply to promotional ends. Unlike promotional tie-ins, or even instances such as Marvel's many prior forays into licensed non-comics media, which acted as adaptational, rather than transmedial, Evans clarifies that 'transmedia elements do not involve the telling of the same events on different platforms; they involve the telling of *new* events from the *same* storyworld' (2011: 27; emphasis in original).[6] She proposes that there are three elements that constitute a truly transmedia story: narrative, authorship and temporality, insisting that 'their combined presence offers the key ways in which texts become transmedia, rather than function as marketing spin-offs or adaptations' (2011: 28). To introduce each of these three in light of the examples at issue in this chapter will enable a better understanding of how MS enacts the strategy.

On the subject of narrative, Evans notes that 'elements of the text are not produced as secondary to a primary source; they are instead part of a synergistic whole, with each contributing to the experience of the viewer in different ways' (2011: 28). In a softening of Jenkins' supposition that each text must be a standalone entity, this definition more readily suits MCU usage, as each element, including the post-credits scenes, One-Shots and tie-in comics, have a distinct narrative purpose, with their own depth that adds synergistically to the whole. The TV shows can then be more readily conceived as potentially standalone texts, that also add to the whole (with *AoS* and *Daredevil* achieving this in different ways).

With regards to authorship, Evans states that transmedia story universes come from 'a coherence that emerges from the point of production; more specifically, transmedia texts have a unified "author"' (2011: 31). Her elaboration of this chimes with what Jenkins declares as pivotal to transmedia storytelling – that is, 'collaborative authorship' (Jenkins, 2008: 110) – as she clarifies that 'for many examples of transmedia storytelling the situation is more complex [than personal authorship], with the position of "author" attributed to an institutional, rather than personal, level' (Evans, 2011: 32). This point on collaborative authorship – or, as we have approached it, studio authorship – has been made frequently throughout the course of this book, and is specifically addressed in the Conclusion; aptly, then, it is centralized in Jenkins' and Evans' readings of the creation of successful and cohesive transmedia stories. On this point, Jenkins affirms that 'storytellers are developing a more collaborative model of authorship, co-creating content with artists with different visions and experiences' (2008: 98). This can refer simply to different filmmakers collaborating with the same studio on a single character,[7] or how an organization such as S.H.I.E.L.D. is treated as a consistent entity, but utilized differently in separate media.[8] Such controlled collaboration and institutional authorship factors in to Evans' final element of transmedia storytelling: temporality. She cautions that 'the different production processes associated with different media platforms can interfere with the potential creation of coherent, integrated transmedia texts' (Evans, 2011: 36). The fact that temporal cohesion of texts is difficult to achieve, means that a very strong and coherent organizational presence commonly accompanies the production of transmedia stories. On such control, Evans refers to the difficulty of arranging other media alongside network television schedules, clarifying that 'an authorial coherence and creation of such texts from the point of commissioning is necessary in order for a transmedia element to appear within the appropriate moment of an episode's lifespan' (Evans, 2011: 38). The status-quo-altering revelation that is HYDRA's infiltration of S.H.I.E.L.D., centre stage in *Captain America: The Winter Soldier* (*CA:TWS*) but in tune with the plot developments in the *AoS* episode that aired in the week of the film's release (in the United States), testifies to a strong organizational arrangement underlying the MCU.

Jenkins couples his notions of transmedia storytelling closely with his conception of 'convergence culture', but care must be taken to distinguish between the two. He specifically intimates that convergence culture is more ephemeral; that it 'represents a paradigm shift' (2008: 254), and is more specifically about moving 'toward ever more complex relations between top-down corporate media and bottom-up participatory culture' (254). As it was noted above that the transmedia universe being constructed by MS utilizes a certain level of collaborative authorship – and given the character of the parent conglomerate – it might still be a stretch to mark the MCU as 'participatory culture'. As we unwrap the notion of Easter Eggs, it will be clear that fan communities are welcomed to engage in an interpretative process, but the tight control administered by Marvel, as this book has often dwelt upon, leaves little room for bottom-up meaning creation; despite this, signs of collaboration within 'its' sandbox are genuine (see Chapter 2), rendering the situation more complex. It is in relation to this point that our final inclusion in this chapter – that of the failed state of the MCU's videogame wing – contributes. The field of transmedia storytelling is rife with examples of 'new media', and its relative prominence in the field of study has been enhanced by proliferations of digital content; yet this is arguably not a real strength of the MCU, except in ways which supplement the theatrical film experience.[9] Digital platforms have surely been used to support the universe's development, but only in so much as the kind of branching ancillary products and relatively lightweight story shards that are exactly those conceived by Evans as not being a full part of the transmedia story; they do not *add* anything of great importance to the narrative of that universe. The successes that are charted below all reside in 'old' forms of media: TV, film, print publications, even where they are administered in new ways (on-demand viewing, digitally downloadable versions of the print-comic).[10] Perhaps 'new' forms of media – as evidenced by Marvel's failure to grasp gaming – move too far from the control required by the above-mentioned coherence. In fact, it is such control that Jenkins identifies as forming the most successful transmedia experiences, which he explains via an example that has been frequently invoked throughout the present study:

> So far, the most successful transmedia franchises have emerged when a single creator or creative unit maintains control. Hollywood might well study the ways that Lucasfilm has managed and cultivated its *Indiana Jones* (1981) and *Star Wars* (1977) franchises.
>
> (Jenkins, 2008: 108)

This level of control is arguably essential to the creation of a new universe such as the MCU: it must function as a new slate for inscription, benefitting from being aligned within volumes of chronicled myth and saga, drawing prestige from that, but avoiding being compromised by over-adherence to a seventy-five year body of continuity. In order to create a transmedia universe that is capable of impacting upon itself, the execution of a shared continuity is a vital component. The control and cohesion highlighted above is pivotal because the MCU's own narrative history is growing with a seemingly exponential momentum, increasingly requiring careful management and monitoring. As franchise elements entail such varying production and deployment methods, their execution rests on a kind of internal fidelity, as they interlock to not just inhabit a shared universe but help build the universe they share.

Hunting Easter Eggs: Post-credits scenes

Iron Man, while only the first film of the newly re-purposed MS, boldly made clear exactly what those longer term studio intentions meant to build through use of the post-credits sequence. In this scene, Nick Fury (Samuel L. Jackson) chastises Tony

Stark (Robert Downey Jr) for the hubris of revealing his identity to the public, before announcing: 'You're not the only superhero out there, you know'. The phrasing is laden with obvious purpose: the newly established hero isn't going to face future adventures alone. Hardly unique to the MCU, but handled so well and consistently that they have become emblematic of the continuous and branching, specifically MS macronarrative, such scenes have become a calling card, and the most recognizable Easter Egg associated with the studio.[11] Named as such because it requires a certain amount of hunting in order to activate, an Easter Egg is a piece of additional information that traditionally presents itself as a reward for inquisitive minds. With its etymology in computing, an Easter Egg was often an undocumented function hidden within the coding of a program that (with the requisite knowledge) could present the user with some form of additional content, denied to the uninitiated, and often requiring some manner of active participation to find. Alternatively, it could be simply hidden in plain sight, in which case the knowledge required to activate the content is referential, depending on existing familiarity. Despite the technical nature of its origins, many of these principles flow directly into the manner in which MS deploys the referential device, and examples that reward such existing familiarity can be seen throughout the MCU. In a film as early in the universe's development as *The Incredible Hulk*, mere months after *Iron Man*, a modified version of Super Soldier Serum is used to 'enhance' Emil Blonsky (Tim Roth). This comes before the cinematic audience is introduced to the serum's originary use during the Second World War: to transform the scrawny Steve Rogers (and, as planned but not realized, many others) into the Super-Soldier he is known as in 2011's *Captain America: The First Avenger* and subsequent films. A reference that is thrown out in 2014's *CA:TWS* sees the passing mention of a 'Stephen Strange' who is identified as a threat to HYDRA; the initiated will recognize this individual as Doctor Strange, whose own MCU feature is set for November 2016. Further, 2015's *Ant-Man* features a particularly tongue-in-cheek reference to the powered beings known to reside within the MCU: 'We got a guy who jumps; we got a guy who swings; we got guy who crawls up the walls', which overtly refers to MS's industrial coup of that year: the agreement with Sony to co-produce a new iteration of Spider-Man that will bring Marvel Comics' flagship character into the MCU. A particularly meta-textual example is the cameo from Howard the Duck at the end of *Guardians of the Galaxy (GOTG)* after the complete credits have rolled; Howard being a character famed for having flopped at the box office. This can be read as a rejoinder to those that might have believed a film such as *GOTG*, delving into unfamiliar characters, would inevitably be visited with a similar fate (see Chapter 6). Other post-credit scenes have been used to introduce upcoming characters – Thanos (Josh Brolin) was first revealed as the mastermind behind the events of *The Avengers* in its post-credits scene; Scarlet Witch (Elizabeth Olsen) and Quicksilver (Aaron Taylor-Johnson), lined up to feature in *Avengers: Age of Ultron*, were teased after the credits of *CA:TWS*. Character developments can simultaneously be signals of franchise expansion: Hope van Dyne (Evangeline Lilly) finds her Wasp suit in a mid-credits scene at the end of *Ant-Man*, and in Autumn 2015, MS announced that a 2018 sequel would give *Ant-Man and the Wasp* equal billing.

These post-credits scenes, among other Easter Eggs found throughout the MCU, fabricate connective tissue, not only between other texts throughout the transmedia story universe, but also as a way of calling out to fan communities, and thus they denote the closest point where the MCU approaches Jenkins' hopes for a convergence culture featuring the destabilization of strictly top-down production in a classical guise. He emphasizes that a 'growing number of consumers may be choosing their popular culture because of the opportunities it offers them to explore complex worlds and compare notes with others' (2008: 134), and uses the term 'knowledge cultures' which form around consumers 'discovering what it is like to expand one's comprehension by tapping the combined expertise of these grassroots communities' (134).

Reloading the One-Shot: Agent Coulson

Post-credits teases, while salient to the narratives they are embedded within, as discussed above, allow filmmakers to depart from, or hold in abeyance, the consequential effects of the main narrative. MS's 'One-Shots' – direct-to-video short films included as extras on the DVD/Blu-ray release of some MCU features, thus courting the collectors within the Marvel fanbase – also demonstrate the identification of an opportunity not only to provide bridging narrative material for other properties, but also to signpost their forthcoming development. As early hype generators, any character or plot element that finds itself the focus of a post-credits sequence or a One-Shot 'teasing' a future release is somewhat instinctively attributed significance, a claim on the attention of the audience. With a vast catalogue of comics attached to Marvel, any plot-object offered, need only raise awareness of its existence within this new universe, to engage fan approval. The reference can be real but lightweight and self-contained, showing respect for tradition but not shackling the story logic of future releases, or the detail of character presentation, to the body of continuity mentioned earlier. For those intrigued enough to learn more, comics exist as a vast research archive for the curious, even when details have been adjusted (the MCU's 'Tesseract' for the MU's 'Cosmic Cube', say).

The most prominent character to have been designed specifically for the MCU is Agent Phil Coulson, who, throughout MS's Phase I cinematic releases, often exists just offscreen of the main action. Coulson, therefore, logically assumes the role of most frequently invoked primary character in the One-Shots, showing how what may look like a 'bridge' from one perspective can embody the dead centre of narrative in another moment. During its Phase I, at least, Coulson is perhaps the lynchpin of the entire MCU.

In his early incarnations, the appearances and actions of Coulson were catalytic to the alignment of the texts, being invoked almost as an omnipresent guiding hand, segueing from one text to another and referencing simultaneous activity that grounds its audience not only spatially, but also chronologically. In fact, the term *grounded* is applicable in another sense: it is an unmistakable component of Coulson's character that in this world of superheroes and the occasional god, he is an ordinary looking guy, with a governmental, bureaucratic ambiance. As such, when Coulson makes a swift departure from Stark's semi-destroyed Malibu penthouse in *IM2*, he makes his excuses – 'I've been reassigned. Director Fury wants me in New Mexico' – and leaves, which at this point is presented as an oblique but curious statement of some intended significance. In the film's post-credits sequence, we witness Coulson arriving in the New Mexico desert to find a mysterious, immovable hammer within a crater. For the initiated, the message is once again obvious: the hammer is Mjolnir, the weapon of Thor, who at that time was upcoming in the MCU development plan. For non-comic readers, or the general event movie audience, there is still the effect of teasing an eccentric new character, and the thematic cliff-hanger that the powered community is still more varied than possibly even Fury had bargained for. Despite the almost twelve months between the releases of *IM2* and *Thor*, the narrative of the latter (which begins with the titular hero still in possession of his fabled hammer, only to face banishment to Earth at the climax of the first act) testifies that these two adventures occur roughly simultaneously (Thor's ostracization being enacted roughly halfway through the events of *IM2*).

With these two films drawn together by Coulson, connections are advanced further with the Coulson-showcasing One-Shot, *The Consultant* (Leythum, 2011), which was presented as a special feature on the *Thor* DVD release. This short film unites the rest of the MCU with *The Incredible Hulk* – specifically a pre-end credits sequence, designed to arouse interest in the franchise plan, therein, where Tony Stark approaches the Hulk-hunting General Thaddeus 'Thunderbolt' Ross (William Hurt), regarding the putting together of this 'team'. *The Consultant* sees S.H.I.E.L.D. agents Coulson and Jasper Sitwell (Maximiliano Hernández) express discontent with their current assignment: to negotiate terms with Ross, for the appropriation of his protégé: Emil Blonsky, who – through genetic experimentation intended to replicate the Hulk's creation – transformed himself into a malignant force of destruction, known as 'The Abomination'. The two agents plan what could be construed as a minor act of mutiny: the assigning of wild card Stark (the titular consultant) to negotiate with the general (the S.H.I.E.L.D. men betting on their belief that the incompatibility of this pair will scupper the arrangement to lease the unhinged and unwanted Blonsky, as has been requested by a World Security Council (WSC) that is not fully abreast with Blonsky's destructive nature, wishing rather to blame his rampage – as seen during *The Incredible Hulk* – on Banner). In addition to the spatial and temporal links made by such One-Shots, they provide thematic development, such as Coulson's curation of the 'powered' universe, and further development of Stark's character as a loose cannon, who will likely disrupt the gravity of any unit (a theme that recurs with increasing intensity throughout the MCU). The film also foreshadows that S.H.I.E.L.D.

operations clash with other government agencies, and demonstrates that S.H.I.E.L.D. understands it must appear to do the bidding of organizations such as the WSC, while in fact implementing actions to the contrary (another theme further developed in later instalments of the MCU). The fresh narrative offered within the short addresses unresolved questions on the outcome of the Stark/Ross meeting as it was to be understood during *The Incredible Hulk*; details which emerge about Blonsky, and the now apparent manipulation of Stark, can be seen as correcting previous readings, since a fair interpretation of the scene in its original context would be that the pair were actually discussing Banner/Hulk and not Blonsky. So Ross, Stark, Sitwell and Coulson receive useful character development, Blonsky is 'tabled' for potential future use, and the parameters of the 'Avengers Initiative' are expanded. The One-Shot also tidies up a temporal ambiguity, since Stark is apparently dismissed from the Avengers programme and given a new role as 'consultant' in the events of *IM2*, a film which, as explained above, runs concurrent to the events of *Thor*. *The Consultant* then, ties together the narrative action of *Thor, The Incredible Hulk* and *IM2*.

The later, Phase II One-Shots appear to function in a slightly different way, either as self-contained adventures, such as *Item 47* (Louis D'Esposito, 2012), or explicit try-outs for longer forms, like *Agent Carter* (Louis D'Esposito, 2013), showcasing the character's individual potential ahead of her own show. Yet, *All Hail the King* (Drew Pearce, 2014), in some ways, operated akin to *The Consultant*: not in the reassessment of a previous narrative point, or the tying-together function, but in stowing away a useful antagonist for further MCU use, as well as adding depth to the universe by developing the presence of the 'Ten Rings' organization (see Chapter 3). *All Hail the King* plays a double bluff regarding the character of The Mandarin (Ben Kingsley), for in *Iron Man 3*, this villain of great stature in the comics is revealed to be a theatrical ruse, linking to the ongoing thematic of the nature of fear and its media reflections. The Mandarin is revisited in jail after the events of *Iron Man 3*, where it is revealed that the character upon which the diegetic actor based his sinister role is in fact real, and much more malevolent than this charade. The presence of the Oscar-winning Kingsley, as well as the successful Sam Rockwell (Justin Hammer in *IM2*) in the short shows Marvel's determination to run a story universe where characters of any standing have continuing narratives.

With the sheer scope of the current MCU, the specific functions of these elaborate shorts seem to have been suspended (*All Hail the King* being the final one, as of the time of writing), or, rather, transferred into the material of a number of simultaneous television series unrolling throughout the year. The purpose of One-Shots as 'catch up' episodes or arousing interest for the future is less required to perpetuate continuity when, since 2013, there is an MS show on most weeks of the television calendar, and when 'box sets' of such as *Daredevil* can be consumed at any time. The status of the post-credits tease does not appear to have suffered in the same way, but to locate where the 'connective tissue' principle is at its most vigorous, we need look no further than to the first remediation of the MCU's cinematic logic into the realm of television: that is, *AoS*.

First forays into television: *Agents of S.H.I.E.L.D.*

Ever since the creation of Marvel Television in 2010, following the 2009 Disney purchase, Marvel has worked hard to develop TV projects, including two co-productions with ABC Studios that significantly enhance the MCU (*Agent Carter* is discussed in Chapter 4). Premiering in the Autumn of 2013, over a year after Coulson's 'death' in *The Avengers*, *AoS* 'revived' the character and made him central to a specific tactical team within S.H.I.E.L.D. With knowledge of his survival exposed to prospective operative Grant Ward (Brett Dalton) as a 'level seven secret',[12] his death and resurrection remain a plot-powering mystery – even to Coulson himself – for much of the first season. The show is ostensibly a supernatural spy procedural following a specialty team within the peacekeeping organization (see Chapter 5); yet, the narrative's frequent reference back to Coulson's death within *The Avengers* functions both as a narrative anchor and as a constant reminder of affiliation through proximity, and the enhancement of 'unmissability' for a greater audience by a relatively direct link to MCU cinema releases (reinforcing the 'hierarchy' that has been alluded to in this chapter and also in Chapter 1). The show can thus retain a position of connectedness, even where – particularly throughout its first season – its action has little impact outside its immediate sphere of influence.

Consisting of forty-five minute episodes, the first two seasons of *AoS* have already contributed over thirty hours of screen time to the body of the MCU narrative. The intention appears to be for the show to convey a sort of hyperdiegetic mode of storytelling that, through synergistic cross-reference, suggestion and elaboration, establishes a vivid landscape grounded in a shared continuity reflective of the film entries. In terms of Easter Eggs, and other connective tissue, the prospect that any and all background elements could be potential signposts for further plot details represents a veritable hunting ground of referential material, and thus increases engagement with initiated 'fans' and 'knowledge communities'. The series is made 'world-builder' by virtue of the added screen time and the need to depict detail serving two levels of necessity: for the show to function both with its own internal interest, and its wider supportive role. During its first season, after the establishing dynamics of its early episodes, *AoS* functioned primarily to expand upon the events of its connected films (foregrounding the mystery of Coulson's death and the infiltration of HYDRA).

As a character created for the MCU, Coulson remains at the centre of the tension between world threat level events deemed only suitable for major superheroes, and the more human eye level continuing narrative within his S.H.I.E.L.D. team (see Chapter 5). His privileged position as the character that unifies the television to the cinematic franchises allows focus to be drawn to larger transmedia events without a sense of disappointment at the lack of star heroes. While irregular characters are able to emerge and ebb away as necessary (sometimes with a likely return ahead, such as the casting of the well-known Ian Hart as Dr Franklin Hall – a major comics villain in 'Graviton' – in an early episode (S1E3, 'The Asset'), whose potential remains to be explored), Coulson's every move is automatically scrutinized against earlier appearances, creating the opportunity for inter-referentiality that rarely goes unexploited. A seemingly throw-away line during *The Avengers* spoken by Stark, making reference to 'a cellist in Portland', becomes the basis of the episode 'The Only Light in the Darkness' (S1E19), in which Coulson is ambiguously reunited with his former lover (now wiped of her memory of him).

While capable of directly addressing the impact of other narratives, *AoS* demonstrates a capability of world-building through its exploration of the tenets and structure of the titular organization itself. S.H.I.E.L.D. is presented as a global taskforce, an expansion and upgrade from contemporary NATO that also embraces espionage and tactical black ops. Intended as a defence component, the existence of 'powered beings' changes the organization's mandate towards the surveillance of, interaction with, and ultimately recruitment/neutralization/storage of such characters (see Chapter 5). Here, the narrative opens up the eventual cinematic appropriation of the Superhero Registration Act featured in Marvel Comics' *Civil War* (Millar et al., 2007).

As the first season of *AoS* took narrative cues from the films, but seemingly without reciprocation, its main contribution was by way of its world-building, supporting the wider unfolding transmedia story rather than forging new ones. It could still 'do what it does best', and contribute to fleshing out the universe, but there appeared a hierarchy of agency that raises notions of contested or conflicting interests; a type of hierarchy that Derek Johnson believes exists in the construction of franchises:

> As franchise worlds have been shared across media boundaries, critics, audiences, and creators alike have privileged notions of continuity, legitimacy, integrality, and especially centralized authorship in assessing use of creative resources. ... Quality and creativity, in this case, are constructed by proximity to privileged production identities at the center of the franchise.
>
> (2013: 140)

As we have seen, the Marvel *Cinematic* Universe – in various ways – asks to be taken with the theatrical film experience at its centre. Yet, Johnson elaborates that such a situation often derives from issues in licensing, which is fundamentally not the case throughout the MCU, where the relationship between media might better be understood, rather than along the inter-industrial situation that it actually is, but intra-industrially, due to Marvel's unique arrangement of this shared universe, and its internal control of each node. In such intra-industrial arrangements, Johnson states that 'discrete production teams and communities within the same industry make negotiated claims to creative identity in relation to the shared use of resources in spin-off production' (2013: 122). It is precisely such negotiation – albeit in the slightly divergent industries of TV and film – that is evident in public statements such as that of Marvel Television head Jeph Loeb, emphasizing that: 'The television division is its own division; it has to have its own identity. The shows that we've done at ABC, *Agent Carter* and *S.H.I.E.L.D.*, absolutely came from that [cinematic] world, but I think really have cut their own little mold out as spy, espionage' (cited in Casey, 2015). This statement encapsulates Johnson's assertion that such 'peers' 'establish their own unique identities and subjective viewpoints [… in] practices that acknowledge the use of shared worlds while also pushing … to make meaningful claims to creative and professional distinction' (2013: 123).

In such an attempt to establish distinction, *AoS* builds on first-season hints of powers and forces outside of what had been experienced in the films (specifically involving the alien race known as the Kree)[13] to, in the second season, overtly introduce entirely new concepts of how powered individuals come about. It first teased, then explicitly announced, the existence of a society of 'Inhumans', a Marvel property deriving from a Kree military experiment for weaponizing organic beings. The most well-known Inhumans are yet to feature in any of the MCU's cinematic releases, but their cinematic debut has been announced for 2019. That this development has been primed by *AoS* shifts the hierarchical gravity of the universe's narrative, redefining the supporting role and showing that the various media in orbit of the cinematic texts are just as able to offer new developments as those previously considered to reside at the centre.

MCU on-demand: *Daredevil*

Heroes and their consequences is why we have our current opportunities.

(Leland Owlsley (Bob Gunton) in *Daredevil*, S1E1, 'Into the Ring')

Further to Marvel's co-productions with Disney television stablemates ABC Studios, in April 2015, it teamed with on-demand streaming service Netflix to launch a new TV series in an entirely different manner; *Daredevil*'s full first season, in line with Netflix's 'box-set' release strategy, was made available in one drop, inviting audiences to 'binge' on its totality immediately. This show is also linked into the MCU, but with a different remit to that of *AoS*. The immediate significance here for any potential synergy with the wider universe, is that unlike *AoS*, which to be synchronized with filmic developments has to be meticulously planned (such as those that occurred in *CA:TWS*, as noted above), Marvel will know precisely when the series will become available, and therefore precisely how the universe will look at that point in time, provided that communication is good throughout. Up to 2015, Marvel had put in place the Marvel Creative Committee (MCC)[14] to facilitate this. Where *AoS*'s first season often drifted with respect to its narrative focus, dictated by cinematic needs that coincided with its release pattern and required 'filler' material to hold off plot-spoiling developments, *Daredevil* can select a narrow theme and stay focused on that. This distancing from the universe, paradoxically, emerges as a strength with regards to its transmedia storytelling capacity, and for its contribution to the universe as a whole. As a different kind of world builder, the show is much more grounded in the everyday lives of people in a specific geographic location: Hell's Kitchen, New York. Described by Loeb as prioritizing the 'street-level heroes' (cited in Casey, 2015) it specifically distances itself from the high-flying superheroics of characters such as Thor and Iron Man. Yet, despite such distance, its relationship with the events of the films drives the narrative focus, only to then specifically play this out on the 'street level'. It is stated in the first episode ('Into the Ring') during a meeting of what appears to be a governing group of representatives from several criminal organizations based in the district, that their nefarious, successful activities – particularly with respect to rife corruption in real estate – have come about as a result of the actions of these super-powered beings. When discussing their operatives being attacked by a 'man in a black mask', Leland Owlsley declares: 'Why do we care? Every time one of these guys punches someone through a building our margins go up three per cent'. Such a reference specifically bears upon the destruction caused in the final action set-piece in *The Avengers*, and, like we have argued of *AoS*, takes the view of a non-powered individual at the changes coming to this world.

A notable difference that separates these texts from those found elsewhere within this transmedia universe is the distinctly more mature tone. The TV-MA (15 in the United Kingdom) rating, with visceral scenes of violence that aren't to be found in the PG-13/12A realm of the comic book violence seen in the cinematic releases allows this addition to the transmedia story universe to both 'do what it does best', as per Jenkins' assertion of successful transmedia texts, as well as carve its own distinctive identity among its 'peers', as per Johnson's above contention. This distancing in tone, as opposed to moving away from being considered a universe-contributing form of transmedia storytelling, actually achieves something that Jenkins stresses: 'A good transmedia franchise works to attract multiple constituencies by pitching the content somewhat differently in the different media' (Jenkins, 2008: 98). This supports his proposal that any given text in the bigger narrative can be a 'jumping on' point, which although not necessarily true for all the story portals discussed in this chapter (One-Shots, for instance), is possibly most true of this series, with its own 'corner' of the universe set to expand in content richness as it is joined by several other 'street-level' heroes. *Daredevil*'s first successor was *Jessica Jones* in November 2015, with other shows due to centre around Luke Cage and Iron Fist, respectively. Showing a mini-convergence 'fractal' principle at play, the huge expansion that led to *The Avengers* will be replicated for television when the characters, established by their own series', eventually come together in *The Defenders*.

Back to basics: Tie-in comics

Appropriately, given its print origins, Marvel Comics produces a series of prologue, or 'tie-in' comics relating to the major films that MS releases. These not only serve as a cinematic primer, but also fill in key plot details that effectively mask what could otherwise be considered story inconsistencies without burdening the films with the encumbrance of exposition. An example would be *Marvel's Thor: The Dark World Prelude*,[15] a comic which explains how the Bifrost (Asgardians' primary means of interdimensional travel) is repaired following the events of *Thor*, explaining how the titular hero is able to once more return to Earth for a new adventure. These comics create preview opportunities for audience members (fans), as they feature the re-introduction of characters, signalling not only their presence in the forthcoming film, but often deepening a sense of their motivation. Should they be inclined, a prospective audience member can be primed and pre-engaged with an upcoming film, and perhaps experience a sense of advantage over other audience members in terms of competence and successful Easter Egg hunting. However, such techniques do come with risks, as previous Hollywood transmedia texts such as the *Matrix* trilogy alienated viewers with complicated references to videogame sub-plots about which the majority of audiences were unaware.

Tie-in comics, while still maintaining a paratextual status in terms of their validation within MCU continuity, are tasked with catering to a much smaller portion of the total audience. The boon to the comic industry and the overall impression that Marvel comics and MCU movies are synchronized (see Chapter 1) is perhaps the overriding objective here. Offering tie-ins for consumption in a way that avoids the risks experienced by other franchises requires participants to remain intertextually organized in order to make sense of the unfolding narrative (Gray, 2010: 120). Therefore, this addition to the transmedia storytelling arsenal makes a contribution, but the constraints that the hierarchal relationship produces on the comics' ability to participate with a level of parity in terms of other MCU texts cannot be dismissed.

Losing control: The MCU in videogames

If, like the tie-in comics, the MCU videogames sought to participate in the construction of the universe by elaborating connective tissue around the films' content, it is somewhat harder to appraise them as having met anywhere near the same level of success. Having travelled successfully through many portals into different media, videogames are where the MCU expansion has become unstuck by the failure to negotiate medium specificity. Behind this story, the relinquishment of more creative control than is typically the case with MCU productions features, suggesting one area where more traditional operating conditions of franchise licensing could not be renegotiated, with a result that the smooth running of the MS machine was hampered.

Derek Johnson suggests that Marvel's relationship with videogame design studios has been cordial and un-obstructive, albeit structured by legal boundaries. Although not an MCU-based example, he notes that Raven Software – developers behind a number of X-Men-based videogames – held more kinship with Marvel than with publisher Activision, to whom Raven was actually accountable, and that the identification was 'based on common "geekness"' (2013: 99). This does not suggest reduced professionalism, however, with Johnson also finding that Marvel retains a high level of scrutiny over the development of such licensed properties: former Vice President of Marvel Interactive, Justin Lambros, is presented as feeling it 'crucial for him to take a hand in production, working closely and collaboratively with licensed collaborators' (2013: 97). Such collaboration extended to the creation of MCU-based videogames, with games developer Matt Powers describing how working closely with MS yielded valuable access to the production of *Thor* when designing the tie-in game *Thor: God of Thunder* (Sega, 2011): 'The Marvel guys were a tremendous help. Like with the cape, they sent us actual swatches of the cloth so we can make sure the game matched up with the film. ... We're constantly getting new designs in' (Powers cited in Fillipponi, 2010). But despite such interaction being possible, the games were still licensed productions, and therefore putting them together differed fundamentally to the production process involved in any other aspect of the transmedia puzzle looked at by this chapter. Marvel lacked the level of cohesion and control that it experienced in those other instances.

Only the first five MCU films were supported by a tie-in videogame, with publishing licensed to prestigious industry giant Sega. The games were released in conjunction with, or even slightly before, their corresponding film, with the intention of creating hype for the cinematic release; this can itself cause issues with plotting, regarding how much of the film's narrative material the games are able to meaningfully invoke. The first release, *Iron Man* (2008), is far from a cohesive addition to the transmedia story universe, as it seeks simply to translate the events of the film into a videogame experience. In fact, worse than this, it adds additional narrative events and characters that not only fail to add depth or interest, but also actively contradict the events of the film. With the focus on combat and gameplay, there was a necessity to add extra action scenes, which led to the introduction of new antagonists from the (MU) in the form of research/terrorist group Advanced Idea Mechanics(A.I.M.). The changed meaning – failing to stack up with what is seen in the film – suggested that villain Obadiah Stane (Jeff Bridges) had been in collaboration with A.I.M. throughout. This resulted in a continuity calamity, confusingly renegotiating details of the film that made matching the properties together as a cohesive district of the shared universe impossible.

With the largely negative critical reception that the *Iron Man* game earned,[16] Marvel revisited strategy on MCU-based videogames, adopting a preference to create narratives that occur around the fringes of the film's plot, but avoid recreating the action itself. Thus, the games were meant to come further in line with a truer contribution to transmedia story operating. Not only does this tactic sidestep the tricky onus of fidelity to the onscreen action, it also (as with the One-Shots and tie-in comics) creates the opportunity for the videogames to contribute unique sub-narratives, that can support the universe, expanding upon plot details or clearing up inconsistencies. As such, the gameplay of other Sega-published productions *Iron Man 2* (2010), the aforementioned *Thor: God of Thunder* and particularly 2011's *Captain America: Super Solider* (*CA:SS*) takes the player outside the specific events of their associated films, creating new and relatively unconnected storylines that fit within the universe and conform with other information given, while retaining the feel of complete properties in their own right. *CA:SS*, for example, situates itself somewhere within the events of *Captain America: The First Avenger*, following a particular mission wherein Cap fights to save his team, the Howling Commandos, from a HYDRA-controlled castle, after their plane is shot down. As the film features a montage sequence depicting various missions carried out by this team in quick succession, it is no stretch to consider this adventure as one of those instances. The game takes careful steps to avoid conflict with the events of the film, even managing to feature its antagonist, the Red Skull (Hugo Weaving), but contriving so that he never actually crosses paths with Captain America (which would dampen the impact of their encounters in the film).

Despite this move towards a more integrated form of transmedia storytelling, these videogames were not offering any significant developments back into the wider universe (the same problem we identified with the initial episodes of *AoS*). In fact, a videogame's only narrative impact upon the wider MCU actually owes a debt to a deleted film scene. During one of the many heated debates during *The Avengers*, Bruce Banner (Mark Ruffalo) explains that in a suicide attempt: 'I put a bullet in my mouth, and the other guy spat it out'. Footage exists of a deleted scene from *The Incredible Hulk* that sees Banner (then played by Edward Norton) holding a revolver before transforming into the Hulk – but with no shot fired – and smashing the gun. It is only in the opening sequence of the game, *The Incredible Hulk* (Sega, 2008), where a near enactment of this scene can be found; what is actually depicted corresponds to the instance described in *The Avengers* (Banner kneels in the snow; a blank screen is shown as the gun is fired, then the Hulk is seen in Banner's place, as he physically spits the bullet into his hand). The fact that such a scene never featured in the film, and even the deleted scene lacks the bullet, renders the line present in *The Avengers* as a form of explicit reference to the episode within the game; even if the filmic authors did not intend this, competent fans can put it together, thus enhancing the game's legitimacy.

Despite such a contribution, and despite *CA:SS* showing signs of guiding the MCU's videogame content into a more integrated and cohesive approach to transmedia storytelling, there were no follow-ups of this kind.[17] The next logical instalment would have been a tie-in with 2012's highly anticipated *The Avengers*, but by then, MCU operations in this area had seemingly been abandoned. When TQ Jefferson, VP of games production for Marvel, was asked by John Gaudiosi (2012) specifically about a videogame connected to *The Avengers*, he referred only to the Facebook-based *Marvel: Avengers Alliance* (Playdom, 2012); this is an Avengers property true enough, but very much in the vein of the many other licensed Marvel character awareness-raising products, with no connection to the MCU. A straighter answer to such a question came years later in 2014, during the build-up to *Avengers: Age of Ultron*. In this instance, Jefferson seemed to offer back-up to the reading above: that any failure of these games to comply with Marvel's expanding transmedia universe highlights an issue of control.

> The Avengers game will come when we have the right partner, that has the right vision, that has the time to develop a strong, competitive triple-A title and wants to do it right. ... It has to hit our three pillars: Fun and engaging gameplay, true to the characters, compelling story. Without hitting those notes, we shouldn't do it. Gamers, they know better. They're not going to flock to something that's sub-par.
>
> (Jefferson cited in Dyer, 2014)

When asked if this was caution brought about by negative reactions to previous MCU games, particularly *CA:SS* and *Thor: God of Thunder*, Jefferson replied: 'Absolutely, absolutely. We got a bloody nose on both of those' (cited in Dyer, 2014).

As Jefferson's aforementioned framing of *Marvel: Avengers Alliance* suggests, Marvel has not totally abandoned production in this area. As part of Disney, certain characters – often chiming with those with a profile in MCU film and television – were given significant exposure in 2014 as the headline addition to *Disney Infinity 2.0* (see Chapter 6), the so-called 'sandbox' gaming experience with an added-on collectible toy feature produced by Disney Interactive. A strategy of exposing a broad audience of gamers to the breadth of Marvel's character catalogue can also be seen in *Lego: Marvel Super Heroes* (Warner Bros. Interactive, 2013), an example of licensing where the character iterations are 'blurred' with the recognized dimensions of Lego protagonists (and in which, Marvel becomes merely one content provider under the Lego umbrella, taking a place alongside DC Comics, Pirates of the Caribbean and many other entertainment properties). Despite these, as well as other successful licensing deals including Marvel characters, the account presented above illustrates how a licensing-focused approach to videogame creation does not appear to be compatible with the kind of cohesive transmedia story universe that Marvel seeks to build, and for the time being, an alternative that would be fully controlled 'in-house' has not been possible. Unlike with television, where MS combines with Netflix or ABC, this appears to be down to the nature of collaboration and the significance of the games developer in the production process.

Conclusion

For decades, Marvel characters have been presented to a popular audience that transcended their comic book readership by way of licensing deals with external producers. As noted in the 1970s instance of CBS's *The Incredible Hulk*, this has at times been useful for raising public awareness of Marvel characters. Another such instance, that of the Fox-produced *X-Men* animated series (1992–7), no doubt primed a generation ready for the 2000 cinematic debut *X-Men* (Bryan Singer), itself a licensed Fox production, the revenues from which were significant to Marvel. Videogames, too, have played a significant part in this; due to their expansive and immersive nature, videogames such as Capcom's various 'Marvel Vs Capcom' titles (1996–2012),[18] *Marvel: Ultimate Alliance* (Activision) and the aforementioned *Lego: Marvel Super Heroes* have been able to include a much more varied and diverse roster of characters than those typically seen in licensed TV and film productions. Even where Marvel lacked control, this enabled the public to experience characters that Marvel has, for decades, argued were ripe for exploitation (see Introduction). The capacity of such licensing deals to showcase Marvel's fringe characters is sure to help the MCU's development, just as does the Marvel Television-produced but non-canon animated universe, encompassing *Ultimate Spider-Man* (2012–), *Hulk and the Agents of S.M.A.S.H.*, *Avengers Assemble* (both 2013–) and *GOTG* (2015–). The shows bring into play a massive range of MU characters, and not only those who fit the designs of MCU exploitation or those who have recently figured in comic storylines. But even when such non-MCU successes boost knowledge of a wealth of characters and help the general lead-in to MS texts, they are not bound to conform with the same iterations of characters, and their exploitation can pose a challenge to the consistency of shared transmedia universe that is the MCU's main appeal. It is only when the tenets outlined by Jenkins and Evans earlier in this chapter are in place that a series of texts deployed in various media can collaboratively contribute to the development of a single story universe. The level of control exerted by Marvel, in industrial terms, has led to the development of the MCU's (mostly) coherent transmedia story universe and removed the dependency of the company in earlier times upon licensing (not exactly a moot point under Disney, but certainly a reduced financial priority). However, as the industrial picture changes, forcing working practices and communication channels throughout the organization to be reassessed, the situation must be closely scrutinized. Loeb's assertion noted above – that Marvel Television needs its own identity, distinct from that of MS – raises a spectre of discontent and even differing objectives between departments, each holding a stake in the MCU. A fixed hierarchy favouring theatrical film may be good for discipline, but is highly complex in production and unhelpful, perhaps, to morale and the politics of collaboration. In such a case, will transmedial cohesiveness always be able to be maintained throughout the universe?

CONCLUSION

Studio authorship: No strings?

As Hollywood adjusted after the demise of the 'Studio System', some historic companies faced major change or were swallowed by unrelated conglomerate businesses (sometimes, with only a brand logo being spat out, as with the legendary MGM). With the migration of studios to intangible digital 'backlots', and their need to address the challenges but also opportunities of the internet, an inevitable impact is felt on the very ways in which we conceptualize the studio. This means that recent Hollywood eras are read in 'post-industrial' terms (Naficy, 2001: 40), revising older ideas of a certain industrial set-up that defined who was worked for, and what – and who – was worked on. In such readings, textual change is frequently, and rightly taken as symptom of structural transformations encapsulating labour, consumption and global flows of power and capital.

Such a view invites readings that stress breaks and fragmentation. No doubt this has partly been imprinted onto the object of study by authors wishing to understand and – as we have seen with Pixar – validate external theories and positions. As authors like Connor (2012) note, the term *independence* is more important to defining mainstream film practice than ever, even as a 'reflection' (524). The way 'a studio' coalesces around power is undoubtedly different today, and the most successful modern studio identities are exactly this: *identities*. As is often pointed out, they are contingent boundaries placed around a flow of images, capital, creative labour, and meaning. Yet, as Wasko points out, we still think in terms of 'Hollywood' (1995: 4), meaning a cadre of legendary companies. The image still has a residual power. If we seem to want to make contemporary studios tangible, MS – a company with a strong vision in pursuit of a clear house style, dominant in its 'genre' zone, and expressing all this through a USP (the shared universe) that has its competitors scrambling in emulation – would appear to fit that bill. A 'factory' may not stand there, but certain top-down relations are acceptable parts of Marvel's success story (arguably, are a part of company DNA). A certain amount of iconoclasm has also been part of the Marvel identity for a long time. A major component of the promotion of *Avengers: Age of Ultron* sounded a very ambiguous note about control, rebellion, and going with one's own vision. The teaser trailer wittily incorporated echoes of an animation classic into Ultron's revolt against his 'father' Tony Stark, setting the refrain 'I've got no strings to hold me down … Now I'm free' against a, by turns, haunting and pummelling 'industrial' soundtrack. The source, of course, is Disney's *Pinocchio* (Ben Sharpsteen and Hamilton Luske, 1940), though the recency of our viewing may determine how strongly we recall that the moral tale sees Pinocchio's overconfidence at becoming animate lead him into danger at every turn; he struggles with every free step, unless his conscience is there to guide, or remonstrate, with him.[1] A curbing of agency and a recommendation to turn back to authority figures is hardly new ground for a Disney text, even in 1940.

This kind of mirroring is often enjoyable to figure out, probably tolerated by institutional powers, and a release for artists. The spectrum of meaning populated by an 'industrially reflexive' Hollywood (Connor, 2012) is far from limited, and it seems as if continuity can be found more readily in textual products than anywhere else in the process. Continuities abound in the modern Hollywood, existing alongside the industrial shifts (Smith, 1998: 14–16; Connor, 2015: 247). Warren Buckland (1998) uses *Raiders of the Lost Ark* – a film cited in this work often, viewed by us as a sort of stylistic time machine for 'Old Hollywood' thrills, a textual hub for many criss-crossings of the last thirty-five years of practice – to make a case that classical narrative DNA was still running in the filmmaking grammars of the 1980s. These grammars, as Chapter 7 and its discussion of developments around the family film and event cinema, are seriously influential on current event film practice. To say that textual style can be one of the factors that pulls Hollywood's diffuse values together is not to seek to quell expressions of the need for variety; any student of Hollywood is automatically a student of genre (i.e. we look for what is the same as a way of understanding what is before us). Who or what is the agent behind the imposition of these effects?

'Follow those breadcrumbs'

In policy terms, the way Marvel handles itself seemingly shows the effects of an analysis and absorption of how aspects of 'old' and 'new' might work together in filmmaking logics. This reminds of where Disney went before, across the 1930s to the 1960s – from niche outsider to main player via a cycle of tough management, innovation, protecting key properties from dilution, risk (expanding into TV, for instance) and also, perhaps, a shrewd ability to spot when someone was beating it at its own game (Pixar is perhaps the best example, but there are others).[2] Defined broadly, as a body of IP as well as the company's major outlet in certain forms (e.g. comics), Marvel is now a hub through which many different commercial activities and aspirations of Disney can link: from the series of non-MCU animated shows going out on Disney X-D channels in various territories[3] to *Big Hero 6*, which has kept alive a John Lasseter-inspired run of animation hits for the features division, to the 'Infinity' game, and the *Star Wars* comics triumph. There are many, many departments to service. Within the more specific and autonomous MS domain, initial dealings with proven creators like Whedon seemed to speak to an awareness in management of the advantage of utilizing 'authorship ... as a guarantor of consistency and authenticity' (Hadas, 2014: 7). However, Marvel is aware of the need for limits and so reverts to a classical bearing in checking authorial power more generally (this assuring continuity with the not uncontroversial history of management/creative relations in the publisher). In raising films from properties that already have a vivid, specific life in the minds of one segment of the target audience, there is a careful balance to be struck regarding fan approval. Hence, the notion of valid, authentic artists who 'get' Marvel and even when they are construed as 'edgy', adapt their style to it (like James Gunn). Yet, not every artist who believes that having their own say is in the best interests of the project can be shown the door in the way that it appears Edgar Wright, Patty Jenkins,[4] Ed Norton (and, perhaps, Whedon and Jon Favreau) have been. For almost a decade, the MCC appeared purpose-built to arbitrate the process by which many different inputs combined to generate a successful product, and – aside from some notable exceptions – this was delivered without being attended by poisonous stories or crises of personnel. However, as we have alluded to in the chapters, all of a sudden, as of late 2015, the future seems less certain. Online and trade reports in September prevent us from closing the book on assumptions about internal MS structures – and about how the whole relates to Disney-on-high.

As our chapters have shown, the speciality of MS has been to innovate a little in the relatively small area afforded around a very carefully worked-out plan, but even the current writers were surprised that a summer which began with creeping signs of change (Whedon's dissatisfaction with Marvel's process, speaking out about the difficulties of working in film, while the television canvas clouded narrative options – Tilly, 2015), ended in September with credible rumblings that Feige was reaching a point beyond reconciliation with Perlmutter. This situation, and its associated questions regarding the MCC, holds important ramifications; we shall return to these shortly. Whedon moving on could suddenly seem less like a solution for preventing things from getting stale, and more a Favreau-like moment of an artist reaching the limits of how much they feel they can engage with a particular definition of the process.

Classic takes and new horizons

We have taken stock of what has transpired up to now, but also hope to have shown how MS has engineered a way to sustain an escalation of transmedia opportunities. Recently, the different rhythm of television has allowed the MCU canon to splinter off into open-ended sagas in the image of how Lee, Kirby and others generated the MU. In the 'mix' of looking at MS must always remain the issue of Disney oversight. There is a considerable comics business to maintain there, accentuating notions of fidelity. The current, stable Marvel Comics was in a good shape before the Disney purchase, and prior to the existence of the MCU was attracting some of its best reviews for years, as Chapter 2 confirmed.[5] However, the comics side moves increasingly into synchronization with iterations of characters that work in film and television, with an increasingly obvious steer towards consumers who are only familiar with current, popular incarnations (to return us to Alonso's address to readers new and old from Chapter 1). More than basic cross-promotion, this is about stabilizing a way of doing things: if Iron Man loses popularity, or gets too expensive, a War Machine or Star-Lord will come along to replace him. A new team of Avengers is prepped and ready to go, with the narrative of *Age of Ultron* making this the case as if purely by the exigencies of story, as the schism of *Civil War* approaches. Meanwhile there is a whole alternate team-franchise in the form of the Guardians, as genuine efforts towards diversity in the schedules show an alert response to risk, as addressed in Chapter 6. Genre 'fractals' show the potential of extending the territory further, while respecting that individual artists and teams of artists no doubt genuinely feel that characters in Marvel's 'sandbox' offer dramatic opportunities that are universal in scope. The handling of *Daredevil* and its vigilante-over-superhero slant, as well as *Jessica Jones* (based on a much more recent addition to the MU canon, and pitched as the post-superhero life of a powered person: shades, in a different register, of *The Incredibles*), show other patterns asserting their presence: the more this happens, the more the superhero 'genre' enlarges – or becomes transparent.

Chapter 2 established that the early 2000s business resurgence of Marvel Comics, which generated enough confidence to lead a move into film production, was based on a return to core principles of organizational identity. These principles were set decades ago with a massive investment in the specifics of a rolling but diverse character universe. Marvel once again balanced faith in creators (within limits) with creative commercial approaches to engaging a new generation of customers (which meant adaptation to certain entertainment norms), all the while striving to make this play as respectful care for its repository of characters; as Johnson phrases it, in the context of MS, a virtually parental responsibility is the keynote struck, 'framed as a necessity for commercial and critical success rather than as meddling by an outside executive office' (2012: 17). In staging this return to its own history so well, MS has brought about a situation where – at this vaunted level of popular cinema – it succeeded in the race to 'own' the key category of 'shared universe'.

Expounding their *22 Immutable Laws of Branding*, Ries and Ries state that 'the most efficient, most productive, most useful aspect of branding is creating a new category; in other words, narrowing the focus' (2000: 66). As this 'new category' was the shared universe, which is no longer new, and has attracted competitors attempting to emulate its success, the organization must create fresh brands, and 'own' other newly forged categories, rather than simply adding products to the same brands. Along this same line of thinking, we put forward the proposal from Hooley et al. that organizations need to 'overcome inertia, narrow-mindedness and risk aversion' (2012: 333); that in order to 'stay relevant and to succeed, companies need bold innovative strategies' (333). Standing still was what led DC Comics to surrender market share dominance to Marvel in the early 1970s (Wright 2003: 224). Hooley et al. emphasize that the competitive advantage obtained from such innovation will be most effective when it emanates from within the embedded culture of an organization (331), allowing for an integrated approach to strategic marketing which ensures that goals are identified and aimed for across the piece. Along these lines, a snapshot of Marvel's comic operations can be seen as both an echo of the recent practice at MS, and a form of blueprint for possible directions.

Marvel rebooted its mainstream body of comic continuity following its 'Secret Wars' event across Spring and Summer 2015 (a complex rerun of the same essential idea as the 1984 version: the heroes are taken out of their everyday space and time, and forced into battle, with the continuity of the universe/multiverse at stake). Assessing the new line-up of creative talent which would take over the restarted titles in the autumn, Jesse Schedeen (2015) opines that Marvel is calculatedly pulling back from reliance on star writers such as Kelly Sue DeConnick (*Captain Marvel*), Jonathan Hickman (*New Avengers, Secret Wars*) and Rick Remender (*All-New Captain America*). A current trend falls in line with MS's strategy – as highlighted in Chapter 6 – of finding lesser known creative stars of the future and hastening their promotion. In the new crop, this would include names like writers G. Willow Wilson (*Ms. Marvel, A-Force*) and Marguerite Bennett (*Angela: Asgard's Assassin, Years of Future Past*). Not only can this approach make possible a Marvel claim that it has uncovered or made such stars, but such creators are also possibly more likely to tolerate rules placed within 'its' sandbox. This juncture brings another development with real relevance to the MCU, namely the shared talent now crossing comic book-scripting and MCU outlets: *Agent Carter* showrunners Tara Butters and Michelle Fazekas are replacing DeConnick on *Captain Marvel*, and the new solo title *Gamora* will be handled by *GOTG* scriptwriter Nicole Perlman, who is also now working on the film script of *Captain Marvel* (see Watercutter, 2015). The parallel appointments linking comic titles and MCU texts seem to show the strategy regarding what Feige has termed 'breadcrumbs' (see Philibrick, 2010), and the fashion in which followers are directed to pursue them, crystallizing into a distinct policy.

Kriston Capps (2014) reads Marvel's decision to 'kill' – for MU purposes – the popular Wolverine as a reflection of the rising exposure lent to one of Marvel's youngest, freshest characters, Kamala Khan (Ms Marvel). Alongside another recently created character in Miles Morales (Spider-Man), the young Muslim Khan joins more recognizable Avengers such as the Vision and Sam Wilson (as Captain America) in *All New, All Different Avengers*, headline title for the rebooted line. A timely appearance as a mentor figure made by Wolverine in *Ms. Marvel* (Vol.3, #7–8), shortly before his death, is interpreted by Capps as a torch-passing moment and symbolic move away from Wolverine's home franchise, the X-Men, the cinematic rights to which are not controlled by Marvel. The lore behind Ms Marvel's powers derives from the Inhumans, already primed for MCU exploration and soon to have their profile heightened considerably (see Chapter 5). Departmental interplay between Marvel's different universes and media was discussed in Chapter 6, where we looked upon the Guardians of the Galaxy team that was primed by Abnett, Lanning and Pelletier's run as a kind of market-testing on the page, years ahead of Gunn's film. The playing down of such as Wolverine and the FF attracts readings that see the wider Marvel, on behalf of MS, asserting an unwillingness to publicize other film studios' properties, hoping to weaken rivals; the substitutions into the rolling character and story landscape, though, also seem like overt signs of self-confidence in not just the characters but in the *treatment* of characters: a 'Marvel Way' of letting stories explode into life, which *GOTG* proved to the hilt. The system appoints the creatives needed to look through the right film culture prism at the material as already shaped by the comic creators: a textual environment – with familiar, nostalgic aspects, as we saw in Chapter 3 – seemed to spring up easily around *GOTG*.

We circle back here to the concerns of Chapter 2, and a brief reflection upon the 'essence' of Marvel. An argument could be made that many of the storylines used in MS texts up to now have drawn deeply and directly on the spirit of 1960s and 1970s Marvel, the phase of genesis and expansion; a – for the most part – fun phase that requires modest rewriting, rather a form of translation. Furthering this slightly crude argument, the repository of available stories appears bottomless by the standards of Hollywood adaptation, so why should it concern MS if standards drop in comics? This would fail to take into account something which the following have in common: Winter Soldier, the Chitauri invasion storyline (*The Avengers*), the Extremis formula (*Agents of S.H.I.E.L.D./Iron Man 3*), Civil War, Jessica Jones, a Guardians team led by Star-Lord, a female Captain Marvel, a younger Aunt May and more – all are elements hailing from post-2000 Marvel comics (many from the UU), and from key creators that are either still at Marvel in some form or only recently departed (Brian Bendis, Ed Brubaker, Warren Ellis, DeConninck, Abnett, Lanning and the associated artists on their runs, many of whom are directly responsible for the visual iconography of MS heroes).[6] The issue is not that supplies will run dry, as much as that the plots and thematics that have been interesting the writers and directors developing films share a common recency which expresses itself in terms of the world that the films and TV series' build, within appropriate generic limits. *Daredevil* may fudge issues of high-spec technology that might lock it into the present day (particularly in the unbelievably old school representation of its house journalist, Ben Urich, played by Vondie Curtis-Hall), but its Kingpin (Vincent D'Onofrio) is still a very recognizably post-financial crash (if not post-*Sopranos*) figure. The disoriented Hell's Kitchen in which Murdock/Daredevil practices is not just on its knees because the 'Battle of New York' occurred,[7] but because of high rents, absentee landlords, and untrammelled, socially punitive gentrification. Many of these innovations, and even the techniques for blurring their modernity into the classic roots of the characters' personalities, come straight from the UU textbook; arguably the last time a Marvel regime engaged in a thorough attempt to reinterpret what 'classic' versions of characters ought to mean.

Following Ries and Ries's analysis of maintaining competitive advantage, as highlighted above, MS has to keep staking out and ruling *new* 'categories'. The Captain Marvel and Black Panther intellectual properties are products, but have a territorial advantage which is tied up with the beginnings of a more diverse universe; it is only recently (and on television) that MS has allowed a female character to lead a text, for instance (although such as Black Widow/Natasha Romanoff and Maria Hill of S.H.I.E.L.D. (Cobie Smulders) have played significant roles). The introduction of Black Panther does not guarantee radicalism, but does suggest ways of exploring black characters with premises that are not dependent on white and American narratives, and with which more can potentially be done than with Sam Wilson (see Chapter 4).[8] If this period is correctly managed, and MS successfully integrates these characters as prominent, meaningful entries into its canon, it will be known as the first to the 'categories' of sustainable female and black, leading, mainstream superheroes for the cinema.[9]

Civil war … then what?

The thing I fear contains the thing I need.

(Thor, deleted scene in *Avengers: Age of Ultron*)

The know-how accumulated by Marvel in publishing may put its integrity as a division with control over its preferred methods – if not over sweeping creative direction – beyond any logic that might threaten its security. The possibility of a flow of new characters and stories that replenish the universe, while managing costs, is enhanced by the way that the comics market has reacted enthusiastically to the likes of Captain Marvel and Ms. Marvel. Captain Marvel fandom shows that to an extent, this is expanding to unfamiliar consumer areas (see Chapter 2); and the reception to the Inhumans in renewed-again *Agents of S.H.I.E.L.D.* gives Marvel a good gauge of what these characters may be capable. The film slate is well known (Marvel makes sure of that), release dates of new TV seasons are stacking up, and we have discussed what it means for all of these texts to 'gel' – or not to – within the chapters. What should be asked now is, what will happen if production and management structures go through bigger, more unpredictable and lasting change based on the speculations that were circulating by September 2015?

The September reports suggested that both Perlmutter and Feige, using different routes, have risen to positions closer to Disney command. 'Insiders say that with Feige breaking free of … the New York side of the company … the MCC's influence over the Marvel movies will be nominal at best' (Kit and Masters, 2015), with Feige apparently insisting that he should report only to Disney chief Alan Horn. Although this may bolster the idea of a 'Feige Era', with his authorial fingerprints over the strategy given form by Gunn, Whedon, the Russos and others, what would happen to the autonomy invested in structures of the division upon Feige's departure would surely be a matter which the Disney board would re-examine (and it would be unnatural for them not to reflect on the picture-making prowess of Walt Disney Studios at this point, although the way that Pixar was handled – its track record meaning something – balances this prospect).

Even while Feige is in place, if the move has gone down as reported, the result looks set to cut 'strings' from creative's accountability on the Perlmutter side, but to potentially lose a buffer from direct Disney control. Vital to how things will pan out is the future significance of the MCC. Along the lines just mentioned, if an assumption can be made that Marvel Comics will retain its established shape going forward (with no reason to assume Disney can bring in better expertise from within the corporate family), the committee has been portrayed (including by Johnson) as the collegial link between the wisdom requisite to prosper at this level of Hollywood, and the creative leadership – those working at the creative edge – in comics. There is an importance to that link which is very real, even if it is romanticized and given extra sparkle in the official narrative. The history of licensed movies and television – piecemeal, compromised, and sometimes slightly embarrassed to involve superheroes – testifies that something really is different about what Victoria Alonso has dubbed the 'Marvel Process'. If the MCC was dissolved, rearranged or rendered insignificant, could this flow and continuity be reconnected?

We are back in the territory of thinking about what counts 'as Marvel', whether this can be planned for and how it can be transmitted into new media vessels. Recent and important Film Studies work from Connor and Christensen maintains that both classical and (post-) modern forms of American studio expression should be read as, at least partly, allegorical: film narratives are stories about the business. 'The Hollywood studio ... does its business right there on the screen' (Christensen, 2012: 3). We have sensed support for this point in many of our MCU film texts, but have not wanted to labour that in their analyses; however, the broad strokes of the bigger narrative clearly present themselves for a reading in these terms. The narrative of brand mythology that Marvel activates around and through its own texts is partly a work of industrial reflexivity – and the case is highly similar with Pixar. With Pixar, individual narratives play out David versus Goliath, the tale of the boutique animator facing up to the Disneys of the entertainment world; a community of strong, happy, expressive individuals *with rights* is the ideal in so many Pixar narratives. Where Marvel is concerned, we can look to *Iron Man*, as we did in Chapter 3: the self-conscious starting-pistol shot of a super-narrative about the benefits and costs of innovation, risk, creativity and (business) control – was it a 'weapon you only have to fire once', a peaceful probe sent out into a 'bigger universe', or both? At some level, a notion of democracy is at issue (on one side of the camera, at least) – titans of innovation like Tony Stark (and Hank Pym of *Ant-Man*) also serve; theirs is not just to take. This is how we know they are not Obadiah Stane, or Darren Cross, the 'wrong' versions of capitalism in those texts. They are governed by their people – their audience – and power should be wrested away if they are not. But someone has to be empowered to take it away. *Iron Man*, of course, is no different from *The Incredibles* in that, however sophisticated it wants to cast its argument for why the strong should be liberated into their 'natural' position of protecting the weak, it can be understood very differently (see Mirrlees, 2013; Meinel, 2014).

Why Marvel Studios currently inhabits its own position of strength has hopefully been clarified by this book. In offering itself as a storyteller to be trusted – one that is soundly run and not going anywhere; one that understands its past, and the past of its form, and its own future, and the future of its forms – Marvel scripts its own fictive biography, its biggest ever epic. These ideas are reaffirmed every time a spectator sees its signature and quality hallmark, that cue of the flipping comic pages. Each time, Marvel becomes a studio again.

APPENDIX: TIMELINE

Date	Marvel Comics	Marvel Studios	Related activity
1960s	**1961**: *Fantastic Four* #1 – Marvel Universe is born **1962**: *Fantastic Four* #4 – Prince Namor, the 'Sub-Mariner', from the Timely era, returns **1964**: *Avengers* #4 – Captain America returns, in-continuity for the first time since the Timely era		**1967**: *Fantastic Four* and *Hulk* syndicated Cartoons **1968**: Martin Goodman sells Marvel to Perfect Film & Chemical Corporation (which became Cadence Corporation Industries in 1973)
1970s	**1970**: Jack Kirby leaves Marvel for DC (returns in 1976) **1973**: Death of Gwen Stacy in *Spider-Man* #121, widely seen as ending comics' 'Silver Age' **1978**: Mark Gruenwald joins Marvel after having contributed to the mapping of 'continuity' from the fanzine scene **1978**: Jim Shooter appointed Editor-in-Chief, returning publisher to a period of relative stability		**1977**: *The Amazing Spiderman* (CBS-TV) **1978**: *The Incredible Hulk* (CBS-TV) **1978**: *Dr Strange* (pilot only) (CBS-TV) **1978**: *Superman* (Richard Donner) Warner Bros.
1980s	**1980–1**: Marvel begins experimenting with direct market distribution. *Dazzler* #1 bypasses newsstand sales completely **1984**: *Secret Wars* marks the dawn of the age of comic book events		**1989**: *Batman* (Tim Burton) Warner Bros.

(continued)

Date	Marvel Comics	Marvel Studios	Related activity
1990s	**1990–1:** *Spider-Man* & *X-Men* issue new #1s and break comic sales records **1992:** Todd McFarlane and Jim Lee leave Marvel, forming Image comics **1996:** Marvel files for Chapter 11 bankruptcy **1998:** Toy Biz merges with Marvel to save the company, becoming Marvel Enterprises, Inc.	**1996:** Marvel Studios created. Headed by Avi Arad. Focusing on pre-production, increasing the presence of Marvel's characters on screen via licensing agreements **1998:** Kevin Feige onboard Fox's *X-Men* project as Associate Producer	**1992:** *X-Men* syndicated cartoon **1994:** *Fantastic Four* syndicated cartoon **1998:** *Blade* (Stephen Norrington) New Line Cinema
2000s	**2000:** *Ultimate Spider-Man* #1 marks the creation of the Ultimate Universe **2006–7:** *Civil War* is released. Series is widely considered to define the post-9/11 superhero landscape. In its aftermath, Captain America 'dies' **2009:** Marvel purchased by Disney	**2000:** Kevin Feige officially joins Marvel Studios as Arad's second-in-command **2004:** David Maisel joins as President and COO. Studio is steering towards independent production **2005:** MS secures Wall Street financing of $525 million to move into independent production **2006:** Arad leaves Marvel **2008:** *Iron Man* (Jon Favreau) and *The Incredible Hulk* (Louis Letterier) released; inaugural films of the Marvel Cinematic Universe (MCU)	**2000:** *X-Men* (Bryan Singer) Fox Studios **2002:** First serious business account of Marvel in Dan Raviv - *Comic Wars: Marvel's Battle for Survival* **2002:** *Spider-Man* (Sam Raimi) Sony Pictures **2003:** *Daredevil* (Mark Steven Johnson) Fox; *Hulk* (Ang Lee) Universal **2004:** *The Punisher* (Jonathan Hensleigh) Lionsgate **2005:** *Fantastic Four* (Tim Story) Fox **2007:** *Ghost Rider* (Mark Steven Johnson) Sony
2010–20	**2012:** 'Marvel Now' reboot reinvigorates the Marvel Universe **2015:** A new *Secret Wars* event 'destroys' the multiverse as it is known, to be followed by Marvel's 'All-New, All-Different' reboot	**2010:** Marvel Television created **2012:** Sixth MCU film *The Avengers* (Joss Whedon) brings current leading characters together **2013:** MCU enters network television via *Agents of S.H.I.E.L.D.* (*AoS*) [ABC-TV]	**2011:** Fox reboots X-Men franchise with *X-Men: First Class* (Matthew Vaughn) **2012:** First publication of Sean Howe - *Marvel Comics: The Untold Story* **2012:** Sony reboots Spider-Man franchise with *Amazing Spider-Man* (Marc Webb)

Date	Marvel Comics	Marvel Studios	Related activity
2010 – 20 continued		**2014:** Narrative events in *Captain America: The Winter Soldier* (Joe and Anthony Russo) impact directly upon the narrative of *AoS* mid-season **2014:** The tenth MCU film *Guardians of the Galaxy* (James Gunn) establishes a new franchise in the universe **2015:** *Daredevil* (Netflix) is first 'mature' instalment of the MCU and first venture into On-Demand television **2016–19:** The Marvel 'Phase III' film slate will encompass two *Avengers: Infinity War* films, *Spider-Man, Black Panther, Captain Marvel, Inhumans* which will follow *Doctor Strange* (Scott Derrickson, 2016) and *Captain America, Thor* and *Guardians of the Galaxy* sequels	**2012:** Marvel ceases to produce MCU videogame properties with SEGA **2014:** *Big Hero 6* (Don Hall and Chris Williams) Disney **2014:** Marvel ceases to produce videogame properties with Activision **2015:** Fox releases franchise reboot *Fantastic Four* (Josh Trank) to scathing reviews and poor box office

NOTES

Introduction

1. *Fantastic Four* Vol.1, #48–50.
2. *Avengers* Vol.1, #89–97 (collected in Thomas, Adams and Buscema, 2008).
3. The films that so far comprise this MCU are as follows: *Iron Man* (Jon Favreau, 2008), *The Incredible Hulk* (Louis Leterrier, 2008), *Iron Man 2* (Favreau, 2010), *Thor* (Kenneth Branagh, 2011), *Captain America: The First Avenger* (Joe Johnston, 2011), *The Avengers* (Joss Whedon, 2012), *Iron Man 3* (Shane Black, 2013), *Thor: The Dark World* (Alan Taylor, 2013), *Captain America: The Winter Soldier* (Anthony and Joe Russo, 2014). *Guardians of the Galaxy* (James Gunn, 2014), *Avengers: Age of Ultron* (Whedon, 2015), *Ant-Man* (Peyton Reed, 2015) and *Captain America: Civil War* (Anthony and Joe Russo, 2016).
4. Chapter 6 of Wright (2003: 154–79) provides a discussion of the turbulent period where senate scrutiny of comics led to the formation of the industry's own 'Comics Code'. As introduced by self-regulatory industry body the Comics Magazine Association of America (CMAA) in October, 1954, the code saw swathes of titles axed and prominent publishers going out of business. At the same time, the generic norms of those popular comics that aimed at a readership other than the very young were almost totally reset.
5. The issue sought to resolve why the then contemporary DC universe featured a different Flash from the one that appeared in 'Golden Age' comics. The need for this stemmed from the fact that 'only Superman, Batman and a handful of other characters were consistently published from the late thirties through to the present. Hence, DC introduced a new Flash, Barry Allen, instead of returning their original "Golden Age" Flash character, Jay Garrick' (Miller, 2011). Marvel had similarly to provide reasons for the same break between the 'Golden Age', and the 1960s re-visitations of characters like Captain America and the Sub-Mariner.
6. Disputation of authorship (as regards plotting/dialogue) attends many Ditko/Lee and Kirby/Lee works and characters. Such instances are frequently recounted throughout Sean Howe's comprehensive *Marvel Comics: The Untold Story* (2013). Clashes between Lee and Ditko regarding Spider-Man for instance (53), and many instances between Lee and Kirby, culminating in public court proceedings feature (278). Such issues shall not be specifically addressed here, but as a general note on authorship, we attribute equal credit to writers and artists on any comic book production. See also Howe (2013: 50–1) on the 'Marvel Method'.
7. During the days when comic books were almost exclusively sold at news-stands, a tradition evolved to label the issue with a date two months after actual publication ('cover date'). This practice continues today.
8. As in the case of Patsy Walker, a character from the company's 1940s early days who crossed genre several times (from humour/teen adventure/romance) to enter the MU as superheroine 'Hellcat'.

9. An example would be fantasy hero Conan the Barbarian, created in 1932 by pulp author Robert E. Howard, who interacted with the MU in a limited way when he received his own, long-running series. Other licensed characters like Rom the Spaceknight (based on a Parker Brothers toy) were, for a time, fully integrated, their adventures having repercussions in the wider MU, while the copyright-free Dracula has roamed its plains since 1972.

10. Over the years, Marvel Comics has tried 'Epic Comics' (adult-aimed fantasy) and 'MAX' ('R-rated' comics) lines, for instance. The MAX series *Alias* (2001–4), featuring the Jessica Jones character created by Brian Michael Bendis and Michael Gaydos, has spawned the adult-themed Netflix show *Jessica Jones* (2015–) for the MCU.

11. *Agents of S.H.I.E.L.D.* could be considered a 'spy show', although, as early as Season One (2013–14) generic boundaries were destabilized with hints that a key member of the team is powered. This development was further pursued in Season Two (2014–15) with the full-scale introduction of these powers, along with many other 'powered' individuals in the form of the Inhumans (see Chapter 8).

12. For more on this see Eder et al. (2010), Ryan (2013) and Buckland (1999).

13. Sean Howe (2013), in his *Untold Story*, lends a chronological view to the early expansion of Marvel's line under Stan Lee; see, for instance, 38–43, which details late 1961 to early 1963.

14. 'What exists and does not exist' – and how the division between the two is demarcated and policed – takes us into 'canon' discussions, which shall be touched upon within later chapters.

15. New consumers/spectators may have to acquire knowledge of these in order to become competent. Marvel deals with this by cross-promoting reprinted, reformatted comics alongside MS releases, such as *Marvel Platinum: The Definitive Guardians of the Galaxy* (Drake et al., 2014), released the same month as the James Gunn-directed *GOTG*. Character orientation is also provided by animated television shows and 'Infinite' digital comics, which are sometimes offered for free on the company's website.

16. There have, however, been efforts to calibrate the temporal flow of events in the comic to a historical scale; the company has referred to something known as 'Marvel Time', which is discussed by Troy D. Smith (cited in Tolworthy, 2014).

17. This is a fascinating aspect of the continuity debate that would require a lot of room to fully unpack. Gary M. Miller (2011) shows us that an institutional view is possible as he discusses certain continuity paradoxes: 'Never before in the history of culture has there been a group of characters like Marvel's and DC's who have continued to be published in new stories while their creators have died or moved on to other projects. They're corporate constructs and the corporations are now their custodians, which means they have to find ways to keep them in the public consciousness day in and out. That flies in the face of traditional continuity constructs like topical references about who's the President, or what the weather's like. … Marriage and children mark time, and for timeless characters, that's a no-no.' Marvel characters *do* get married and have children, but Miller's point stands since these decisions are frequently unpicked by later developments.

18. Marvel published the first series in late 1982, and there have been several waves and updated editions since.

19. In the 1980s, a series of writers including Mark Gruenwald and the British Alan Moore and Grant Morrison took this to dizzying levels. Moore's *Watchmen* (Moore and

Gibbons, 1987) – published by DC but not part of its mainstream 'universe' – is, on one level, a study of a 'Golden Age' set of characters (in fact, surrogates closely modelled on the Charlton company's heroes) transplanted into the environment of urban anxiety and apocalyptic prediction then current in 1980s genre cinema.

20. See Denson (2011) (*passim*).

21. In fact, it is a little more complicated than this, in that certain characters – Captain America, the original Human Torch and Prince Namor included – predated the 'Marvel' incarnation of the company once known as Timely Comics, and first appeared in the 1940s, only to be subject to a 'retcon' later. It was Lee's innovation to stitch once-popular characters like Kirby and Joe Simon's Captain America into the fresh round of post-1961 continuity. For more on the 'ages' conventionally ascribed to superhero comics, see Klock (2002: 3) or Denson (2011).

22. Use of the multiverse as a plot device is rife today, evidenced by 2015's major comics event 'Secret Wars', which revolves around the facade of the multiverse's near-desolation, complete with a rebooting of almost all of Marvel's comic titles and the proclaimed death of the Marvel (616) Universe and the Ultimate (1610) Universe (more on this universe later), as denoted on the final page of *Secret Wars* #1: 'The Marvel Universe – 1961–2015. The Ultimate Universe – 2000-2015'. (Jonathan Hickman (w), Esad Ribic (a), 'The End Times', *Secret Wars* Vol.1, #1. (July, 2015). Marvel Comics).

23. An argument has been made that 'MTU' – standing for 'Marvel Transmedia Universe' – may be a more appropriate term, particularly since the films were joined, in 2013, by TV show *Agents of S.H.I.E.L.D.* Yet, at the time of writing, 'MCU' had not been displaced by this term in fan and critical discourses, hence our preference for it. Citing convergence theorists Jonathan Gray and Will Brooker, William Proctor (2014) discusses the 'Marvel Transmedia Universe', and how it may fit into the Marvel Comics 'multiverse' in his extended review of *The Avengers*. Proctor notes that the dynamics of comic continuity inform MS's ambitions to develop its universe, taking it beyond the norms of cinematic practice.

24. See Wright (2003: 154–79); Genter (2007: 955–6).

25. The Sub-Mariner's public debut was in *Marvel Comics* Vol.1, #1, published by Timely in November 1939.

26. Up to 2015, this has not been generally true of the MCU; however, this looks ready to change with the introduction of *Doctor Strange* (due 2016) as part of the third 'phase' of MCU releases.

27. In the narration of the inaugural Spider-Man adventure (*Amazing Fantasy* #15, 1962).

28. We refer here to Black Bolt and his treacherous brother Maximus of 'the Inhumans', introduced in the mid-1960s pages of *Fantastic Four*, given their own title in 1975 and due for cinematic debut in 2019.

29. Characters such as Jim Hammond/The Human Torch (first introduced in Timely's *Marvel Comics* #1, 1939), Adam Warlock (first introduced [as 'Him'] in *Fantastic Four* Vol.1, #66, 1967), and Machine Man/X-51 (first introduced in *2001: A Space Odyssey* #8, 1977).

30. *Journey Into Mystery* Annual, Vol.1, #1 (1965).

31. See Howe (2013: 50–1) on the 'Marvel Method'. Demonstrating the later controversy around credit and payment for those involved in the 'Method', Lee's version of how it worked was recorded in a court proceeding involving Jack Kirby's family; this is reported by Seifert (2011).

32. His cameo appearance in *Fantastic Four* Vol.1, #4 (1962) gave the reason of amnesia for his absence of decades, thus stitching Namor back into the new continuity, while preserving what had gone before.

33. Editor's notes that broke into the diegetic panels were an early way of trying to help novice readers understand references to earlier stories or different planes of continuity (see Miller, 2011).

34. As an example, *Fantastic Four* Vol.1, #79 (1968) sees the narrator explain the narratively inessential appearance of a sports car thus: 'Okay, Jolly Jack [Kirby, the issue's artist] was just bustin' to draw a new Corvette – but now that he got it out of his system, onward!'

35. This tendency towards the 'meta' is another trait that has persisted within Marvel. As just two examples, we see the Marvel 'Bullpen' offices making an appearance in the action of *Invincible Iron Man* Vol.1 #123 (1979); in a more convoluted fashion, a 'retcon' saw writer Paul Jenkins inserted into the 'backstory' of his own superhero co-creation, 'The Sentry' (in the events of *New Avengers* Vol.1, #7–8 (2005)).

36. In *Amazing Fantasy* #15.

37. The controversy is outlined in Drucker (2012: 97–8).

38. See Schumer (1999).

39. This is Raymond Williams' term for a common set of values and perceptions, expressed in how cultural products document the experiences of an era. See Williams (1994).

40. To an extent, this did happen to DC, whose film imprint alienated a sector of fans with Superman's neck-snapping methods in *Man of Steel* (Zack Snyder, 2013). See Johnston (2013).

41. The soon to retire Goodman sold to Perfect Film and Chemical Corporation (later known as Cadence Industries). See Howe (2013: 91–3).

42. As reported by Howe, in 1990 Marvel sales were dominated by direct sales to comic stores to the tune of 73 per cent (2013: 324). Comics' general movement towards targeted, niche audiences is not out of keeping with developments in other media, although many of these settled in later; see Johnson (2013: 5).

43. See Flanagan (2004a: 20–2).

44. Included in this would be the post-*Secret Wars* move to regular 'events'. These interrupted (or, increasingly, incorporated) monthly titles and targeted seasonal sales (publishing more issues, for instance, in summer), forming a comic releasing strategy that mirrored the established Hollywood practice of a planned 'locomotive' hit trusted to pull the standard fare through the sales year (Gerbrandt, 2001). A related tendency towards 'sequels' (*Origin II*, Marvel, 2013), 'prequels' (the 'Before *Watchmen*' campaign launched by DC in 2012) and crossovers (superhero team-ups, sometimes inter-company ones, that mark the comic equivalent of the likes of *Alien Vs Predator* (Anderson, 2004)) can also be cited here.

45. The recruitment of auteurs to major studio franchises – *auteurs* being, by definition, those directors with a strong stylistic and/or thematic identity, the parameters of which may be significantly different from those attending the mainstream blockbuster – always presents a risk which may be expressed as the striking of a balance between allowing their talent to be expressed, while not rupturing the expectations of mass audiences and company stockholders both. More discussion of this theme can be found in Chapter 1 and additionally in Flanagan (2004a).

46. *Ultimate Spider-Man* was directly followed by *Ultimate Comics: Spider-Man*, which was subsequently replaced by *Miles Morales: Ultimate Spider-Man* and is currently *Spider-Man* Vol.2 (after the destruction of the UU in 2015's 'Secret Wars' event, as noted earlier). All iterations are written by Bendis.

47. In some ways, and without harming the 'mainstream' universe, this realized a dream of Jim Shooter, who wished to reset the tangled MU body of continuity in a way friendly to new readers. Certain figures within Marvel regarded the 'Shooter-verse' proposal with huge reservations, seeing it as a pointless cull of beloved characters (Howe, 2013: 255–9; 291).

48. Examples include the likeness that the UU's General Nick Fury bears to the international star Samuel L. Jackson (a fact commented upon diegetically by Fury himself in *The Ultimates* Vol.1 #4 (2002), years in advance of Jackson actually being cast in the role. The themes dealt with in *Civil War* are set to play out on-screen in 2016's *Captain America: Civil War*.

49. Johnson (2012: 13) clarifies that in 2008, the MCC included Kevin Feige (MS), Dan Buckley (COO Marvel Publishing), Alan Fine (Marketing Officer), Sid Ganis (Marvel Board Member and President of the Academy of Motion Picture Arts and Sciences), Craig Kyle (comics writer, and previous overseer of animated productions), Joe Quesada (Marvel Comics EIC), and as of 2009, Brian Michael Bendis (comics writer).

50. However, reports in September 2015 cited budgetary clashes over *Captain America: Civil War* as exposing tensions between Feige and the MCC, and portrayed Feige as straining to 'break free' of its influence (see Conclusion).

51. Post-Disney acquisition, success in this aim gets a little harder to ensure, it seems. The more successful the studio becomes, and the more projects are announced, the more commentary starts to express anxiety about the principle of trust in authors – based on affinity for material rather than previous track record – being able to be upheld. In many ways, this came to a head with the affair of director Edgar Wright and Marvel's *Ant-Man* project. See Lussier (2014).

52. The fact that comic sales to fervent fans and speculators did not stack up against a securely profitable company was indicated by the fact that Marvel went from selling a previously unheard-of eight million copies of *X-Men* Vol.2, #1 in 1991 (Wright, 2003: 279) to the verge of bankruptcy in 1996. The strength of the direct market meant that comic book retailing engendered a culture of consumption which forsook the balance of regular readership for the attainment of potentially valuable 'collections'. Early and rare editions became top sellers, and the industry's collusion in this behaviour ultimately proved catastrophic. The market became blocked with special edition, holographic, foil-stamped and 3D sleeves, all of which sought to capitalize on the perceived ability of comics to appreciate in value. Issue #1s proved the most alluring of all; therefore the tendency to reset long-running series for the short-term sales bump became an unwelcome addition to the major publishers' arsenal of gimmicks.

53. Warner Bros. ran a flawless campaign for the film, unleashing a strategy that paid off at various stations along a multinational ownership chain, redefining movie synergy in time for the new 1990s decade (see Eileen Meehan, 2000).

54. Marvel had directly benefited from its original involvement in the Hasbro toy line by agreeing to produce the accompanying tie-in comics.

55. The most famous case was that of the never-released *The Fantastic Four* (Oley Sassone, 1994), rushed through development under the auspices of Roger Corman's New

Horizons to help producer Berndt Eichinger retain his option on the characters (Ito, 2005: 108). The last entity to make any real money on a phantom production – if any were – was Marvel. Such contractual obligations and obstacles became so familiar in the comics world that the draconian FF stipulations were even deployed as a story arc within sitcom *Arrested Development* (2003–13), during which several characters endeavour to produce a low-quality 'Fantastic Four: An Action Musical' (see 'Smashed', S4E9) in order to prevent the franchise rights from lapsing. This is a telling example of a broader public witnessing the playing out of certain Marvel crises.

56. Johnson (2007: 72) provides some figures on these revenues.

57. Johnson's work arrived on the heels of the Fox release, *X-Men: The Last Stand* (Brett Ratner, 2006), a production which perhaps unlike any other, underlined the divergence in representations of the X-men characters from their origins, adducing discrepancies from the source material and subsequently experiencing a backlash of critical response (thereby illustrating the feedback factor postulated in a character wheel such as that presented by Wasko). Johnson's study provides not an emulatable critical approach as such, but a precedent for the necessity of such discussion.

58. *Blade* was, essentially, a vampire film, and came at an opportune time as Hollywood geared up for a renewed commitment to this sub-genre in the 2000s. We shall discuss in Chapter 3 how the MCU has been a playful arena with regards to genre.

59. All figures taken from Box Office Mojo (www.boxofficemojo.com), correct as of 30 September 2015.

60. Transmedia *storytelling* is a more specifically shared story across media, as opposed to a general transmedia approach, which could include disparate stories in different media. This is further explored in Chapter 8.

61. By way of example, it is noted that characters indigenous to the MCU – most famously, Agent Phil Coulson – receive exposure in Marvel-controlled but non-MCU texts like the animated *Ultimate Spider-Man*. In the live-action arena, complex deals mean that MS borrows characters that explicitly belong *simultaneously* to the stable of other franchises (notably Quicksilver, who, one year on from appearing in Fox Studios' *X-Men: Days of Future Past* (Bryan Singer, 2014), makes his MCU debut proper in MS's *Avengers: Age of Ultron* (played by different actors)).

62. The 'page turning' motif remains whether the text is 'official' MCU (such as *Captain America: The Winter Soldier*), or simply Marvel 'family' (such as Marc Webb's *The Amazing Spider-Man 2*, 2014). The omission of the word 'Studios' is the visible difference. In a further twist, the word 'Studios' does not appear on the fully MS-produced *Iron Man 3* yet Paramount (initial distributor of the series) has a brand presence, due to the terms of a deal whereby Disney/MS bought the distribution rights to Avengers/Iron Man franchise films back from Paramount. *Thor: The Dark World* (2013) thus became the first MS release to not be affiliated to a non-Disney distributor (see Stewart, 2013).

63. For broadcast on UK television, the title *Marvel's Agents of S.H.I.E.L.D.* has been used but the American version shall be preferred here.

64. Showing that, far from being a damage limitation exercise of salvaging hard-core viewership, such an event may be planned for, Joe Quesada – Chief Creative Officer of Marvel Entertainment, and one of the figures in the hierarchy most recognizable to comic book fans – comments: 'Really, you have to start with the loyalists. […] If the loyalists reject it, then we feel that everyone is going to reject it.' (cited in JabberTalky, 2014).

65. Leaving aside, that is, normative patterns of blockbuster film consumption such as repeat viewings that we can fully expect are part of the recipe of MCU films' theatrical success.

Chapter 1

1. The series in question are *S.H.I.E.L.D.* (Vol.3) by Waid (2014–) and *Operation S.I.N.* (Vol.1) by Immonen, Ellis and Boyd (2015).

2. The figure swelled to twenty-two with the 2015 announcement that Marvel would be presenting an untitled *Spider-Man* film in conjunction with rights owners Sony Pictures.

3. D'Esposito even directed the 'One-Shot' film *Agent Carter*, which became a calling card for the ABC co-produced series, in 2013, and Alonso describes the work of effects *co-ordination* across multiple pictures in different stages of production, emphasizing the idea of creative producing (see Thacker, 2011).

4. The MCC is a collection of creative and executive individuals, spread across separate Marvel divisions, who have collaboratively plotted the direction of the MCU (see Introduction for its composition and Conclusion for possible developments).

5. Much smaller producers, as well as independent exhibition interests, were also part of the logic of the Studio System because its practices drew them into its terms.

6. 'Fordism' refers to an economic system where mass production principles and a rigid division of labour were deployed to bring about economies of scale. Parts should be interchangeable and the end product predictable and standardized, just as were the automobiles produced in the factories of Henry Ford.

7. See Krämer (1998a) for a full unpacking of this term.

8. The other members of the 'Big Five' were Warner Bros., Paramount, Twentieth Century Fox and MGM. Sometimes referred to as the 'Little Three' were the more modest Columbia, Universal and United Artists.

9. As we shall see in Chapter 7, companies affiliated to Disney (the studio symbolically represented by a 'Magic Kingdom') tend to mystify the cutting-edge technologies of production with an appeal to those characters and to 'story'; this has long been a tactic in how Disney wishes to be viewed (see Wells, 2002: 40).

10. See Chapter 2, as well as Howe (2013: 91–3). Howe even refers to the head of Perfect Film and Chemical, Marvel's first owner other than Martin Goodman's company, as a 'minor-league version of the new moguls that were beginning to gobble businesses in the 1960s', specifically citing the notorious Charlie Bluhdorn. Bluhdorn's industrial conglomerate Gulf and Western bought out Paramount Pictures in 1966, and he was among the individuals whose attitudes in business set Hollywood's template for the 1970s and, arguably, much later.

11. See Taylor (2014) for a discussion of *The Avengers* as a 'fan oriented' production.

12. Connor uses *Raiders of the Lost Ark* (Steven Spielberg, 1981) as one of his case studies of studio allegories, but since the film shall be mentioned periodically throughout this book, we will not linger on it here (see Connor, 2015: 184–94).

13. Only the earliest of many such internal appearances by Lee, Kirby and the like can be found in Lee (w), Kirby (p), Dick Ayers (i). 'The Return of Doctor Doom!' *Fantastic Four* Vol.1, #10 (January, 1963). Marvel Comics.

14. It is important to note that Henry Jenkins – who would not endorse a pure political economy approach to studying large media entities – also centralizes the active role played by the reactions, preferences and actions of consumers in any convergence media process (see Jenkins, 2008: 9).

15. Some of these are discussed in Chapter 8.

16. Although increasingly marginalised in terms of financial contribution, the theatrical film may still be found at the centre of 'corporate identity' – exploited for a symbolic power other products do not possess, as argued by Connor (2012: 523).

17. Chapter 8 discusses the way a 'Feedback Loop' manifests itself in tie-in comics designed to elaborate on what production chief Feige has referred to as the 'breadcrumbs' dotted between MCU milestones. Slightly differently, the S.H.I.E.L.D. and Agent Carter comic stories mentioned earlier do not flesh out the MCU, but are rather incorporations into comic continuity of character incarnations made popular there.

18. Feige is directly implicated in an interesting example of brand legend-building associated with one of MS's most unexpected hits. In his commentary for *GOTG*, James Gunn describes the transitional edit from the young Peter Quill being beamed aboard a strange spacecraft, to the first shot of the Morag, the craft in which the adult Quill roams the galaxy in decades later, as 'too jarring' for test audiences. Gunn attests that the eventual solution came from Feige's suggestion: the placement of the page-flipping MS logo between the two moments.

19. 'Divorcement', sometimes known as the 'Paramount decree', was the culmination in 1948 of a series of contested legal decisions that ultimately saw the Supreme Court order the major studios to sell off their interests in exhibition (i.e., theatre chains). This, along with other practices that attached conditions to the booking of pictures by exhibitors, was seen as supporting a monopolistic business culture. See Casper (2007: 39–43).

20. Brannon Donoghue gives a very good account of some of the nuances involved in how major studios have sought to 'flexibly' globalize themselves, beyond merely tailoring their core English language products for specific national markets. See Brannon Donoghue (2014).

21. Kristin Thompson (2007: 268) gives an account of the international distribution deals behind event behemoth *The Lord of the Rings* trilogy (2001–3). In this franchise deal, marketing expenses were shared out among partners too. New Line was thus hugely protected from the film's possible failure; in the event, the series' success made a lot of small foreign distributors suddenly rich.

22. See Chapter 6 for a full set of financial figures on the 'Phase I' films which puts into context the slight disappointment of the second MCU film, *The Incredible Hulk*, which barely out-performed Universal's maligned attempt in 2003 helmed by Ang Lee. However, box office data alone does not justify the wisdom of carrying Hulk projects forward. The character is a significant marketing draw for Marvel (now, Disney) in key areas: 'Sales of the role play toys known as "Hulk Hands" (a pair of large costume gloves) [. . .] have been valued at US$100 million.' (Sudhindra, 2012); 'Marvel-related toys, such as Thor hammers and Hulk fists, are expected to generate a record $400 million in revenue this year for licensee Hasbro, according to Drew Crum, an analyst at Stifel Nicolaus & Co.' (Advertising Age, 2012).

23. Thompson herself (2006) has acknowledged that the power of Pixar's brand meaning to animation even overshadowed that of Disney at one point. *Toy Story* was directed by John Lasseter in 1995.

24. Although different films raise different complications here; see the Introduction.

25. Beginning in the 1980s – Indiana Jones and Tim Burton's *Batman* series were leaders – the once sacred studio logos started to be adapted and decorated according to the visual characteristics of the film's diegetic opening (covered in ice and snow for a wintry scene, say).

26. To be fair, other readings see more of a schism between the values of art/personal expression and commercial cinema, particularly in the 1980s; and ascribe a 'golden age' romanticism to products of the early 1970s New Hollywood who often in later career turned to sequels and franchises (Coppola, Brian De Palma, the once avant-garde inclined Lucas). See Chapter 7.

27. Usefully, Buckland provides a distinction between 'classical' and 'romantic' *auteurs* (2003: 84–5), indicating the multiplicity of the term. The classical variation does not bridle against studio economic and organizational parameters but works inside these, asserting thematic consistencies and perhaps improving stages of the conventional process by exploring their style. The romantic *auteur* is more along the model discussed in French criticism and advanced by Sarris: an artist whose free-thinking dominance on the material comes out in their intuitive touch on *mise-en-scène* and the whole textual environment, irrespective of whether they wrote the script.

28. An informed estimate provided by Thompson (2007: 33).

29. This included both those whose credit for creating alongside Lee was downplayed, and those whose story and art efforts maintained the expansion of the MU long after Lee downed his pen.

30. *Thor*, 2011 one-sheet poster – see The Blot (2011); *Guardians of the Galaxy*, 2014 one-sheet poster – see The Blot (2014).

31. Schatz summarises some of these kinds of views (1993: 32–4), but they are fairly easily found in writing (both from popular critics like Richard Schickel, cited by Schatz, and in academic commentary) on American cinema from the mid-1980s well into the 1990s.

32. To be fair, Schatz comments on the 'confounding' nature of the term 'New Hollywood' himself. On the two usages, see Smith (1998: 10–14).

33. The point is not lost on Stork (2014: 87–8) that MS's hiring policy may have been influenced by the recent critical success of DC's film division within Warner Bros., and the entrusting of the key Batman franchise to a fashionable but then relatively untested Christopher Nolan (*Batman Begins*, 2005).

34. As in the passing of the Avengers series to the less established directing pair (makers of *Captain America: The Winter Soldier*) after Whedon's relations with Marvel appeared to fray (Siegemund-Broka and Kit, 2015). We return to Marvel's definition of the 'sandbox' idea in Chapter 6.

35. Itself purchased by Disney in 1993.

36. The Academy Awards recognition accorded to *Lord of the Rings* in 2004 shows that no genre is beyond recuperation by this measure if it achieves the right mix of *auteur* filmmaker, quality production levels and financial success – not that winning acclaim has yet extended to superhero fictions, other than in technical and acting categories. Stratified into 'Best Animated Feature' category, Brad Bird's *The Incredibles* remains the exception. See Chapter 7.

37. See Chapter 7.

38. Instances could include the appointment of James Gunn (*Super*, 2010) or the Russo brothers (*Welcome to Collinwood*, 2002; TV's *Community*) to major MCU projects.

39. This is worth pointing out for when we describe the 'independence' of MS. In one sense, the vast majority of production for popular American cinema is 'independent', but a *term* like 'independent cinema' maps closely onto a set of economic, cultural and aesthetic delineations that need to be carefully understood, few of which would directly apply to Marvel films. See Newman (2011: 1–83).

40. Buckland (2003) notes that the greatest move towards tangibility taken by Dream Works (the 'vertically integrated' studio founded by Spielberg with David Geffen and Jeffrey Katzenberg) was to purchase a backlot. No doubt, this reflected a wish for the kind of respect demanded by an older Hollywood lineage. However, the deal foundered, leaving the company to rent space from the much older Universal (95).

41. 2014–15 saw stories that speculated on Marvel's publishing division taking instruction from a management presumably chiefly motivated by staying ahead of its 'strategic group' in blockbuster moviemaking (see Chapter 6), and cancelling the FF's comic title (a title which had enjoyed an uninterrupted run since 1961, many years of which were spent as the flagship comic of the whole company). The term 'sabotage' was used widely in reports, and the motive that most arrived at was that negating the extra publicity that comics could give to Fox properties the *Fantastic Four* and the *X-Men* was an opening salvo in an attempt to weaken the character brands, so that retaining their film rights seemed a less attractive proposition. See O'Connell (2015) and Weinman (2014).

42. The likelihood of a second MCU Hulk movie has attracted a lot of discussion in these terms. See Hughes (2015).

43. The ambiguity extends to a couple of characters in whom rights are 'shared', the most prominent of which – Quicksilver – was able to feature in one MCU film (*Avengers: Age of Ultron*) and, played by a different actor, in one from outside MS: Fox's *X-Men: Days of Future Past* (Bryan Singer, 2014).

44. An agreement to make and distribute at least one movie exploiting new computer-generated software and systems was signed by Pixar and Disney in 1991. Pixar went public in 1995, year of *Toy Story*'s release. Walt Disney Studios and Pixar set another agreement to jointly produce five movies over ten years from 1997, with Disney handling distribution and marketing. Before this agreement had run its course, Disney had purchased Pixar. For more, see Chapter 7.

45. Even Disney consumers – if the study by Wasko, Phillips and Meehan (2001: 45–53) is indicative – offer terms like 'capitalist', 'mass produced', 'manipulative', 'conservative', 'perpetuating false consciousness', 'totally white' and 'cultural standardization' when asked to list Disney 'values' (alongside many positive impressions). See also Budd (2005: 7–11).

46. In the few years prior to MS's development, Marvel had approved a pair of shows whose rights were connected to or inspired by film deals. One was *Blade the Series* for Spike TV (2006). The other, *Mutant X* (2001–4), a show about a team of powered mutants led by a paternal figure who seeks to locate and protect his kind, was an interesting case. Fox mounted a legal challenge to Marvel Entertainment and its co-producing companies in 2001 because of the similarities to *X-Men*.

47. The latter lasting until regulatory changes in the early 1970s (Hilmes, 1996: 467).

48. The way Walt Disney used media interviews to insist that creative control had been retained despite the shows being run by ABC, then a non-Disney company (Sammond, 2005: 319), was reminiscent of Marvel executives' claims when link-ups with ABC

and Netflix were initially announced. The claims focused on creative authenticity and embedding within Marvel Comics lore. See Draven (2013).

49. The implication of 'cord-cutting' is that a generation is abandoning broadcast television (like *Agents of S.H.I.E.L.D.*) for a variety of online ways of viewing.

50. This show played an important role in the careers of future Marvel directors Joe and Anthony Russo (*Captain America: The Winter Solider; Captain America: Civil War; Avengers: Infinity War* parts I and II).

51. North American monthly sales for the well-reviewed *Captain Marvel* series dipped below 20,000 units in February, 2015, a month where 50,000 sales were required to reach the Top 20 positions (ComicChron, 2015a). However, see Chapter 6 for an appreciation of the nuances of this character's value to Marvel/MCU.

52. Comixology (www.comixology.co.uk) is a third-party digital service that allows customers and subscribers to download comics from a variety of publishers, including DC and Marvel. The Marvel digital app can be downloaded from the main Marvel site and used to store individual titles purchased occasionally, differing from the 'Marvel Unlimited' subscription service where all of the current digital holdings of the company are available to customers as long as their subscription is active and paid for.

53. See FCC (2012).

54. These sorts of sentiments were expressed to the author by various interested friends with children below teen years. (Lisa Holden-Davision, Facebook message post to author, 11 April 2015; David Glynn, Facebook message post to author, 11 April 2015). The 'Back Issue' Facebook forum, a forum spun off Two Morrows' 'prozine' publication *Back Issue* and comprising over 4,000 international fans of 1970s and 1980s comics, hosted a discussion about the show started by Eric Fusco (13th April, 2015). The thread contained many references to how different its tone was from other corners of the MCU, and the consensus seemed to be that *Daredevil* was not viewing for all the family; this did not detract from the same conversants' appreciations of the quality of the show. Fans seemed to accept that MS/Netflix had intended the show for a specific audience that was different from MCU films, and there was an awareness about the role of Netflix in facilitating this. The forum can be found at https://www.facebook.com/groups/137494714050/?fref=ts.

55. This is exemplified by the Marvel Comics success story of 2015: the publishing triumph of the *Star Wars* relaunch. We won't go into the complicated history of publishing this property here, but Marvel held the license from 1977 to 1986; following suit with other accounts, Howe credits its huge sales as helping prop up a cash-strapped publisher at the time (2013: 196). With the film series dormant for most of the 1990s, the comic rights moved away. With the Disney-Marvel purchase of 2009 being followed by Disney's acquisition of Lucasfilm in 2012, an anticipated return of the title to Marvel's portfolio was set in motion. Top writers/artists were assigned to a main title plus (a first for Marvel), related solo series. Meanwhile, commentators quickly tracked fan resistance to a beloved film property coming under Disney control (Metrowebukmetro, 2012). With overt Disney markings absent, the Star Wars line returned in January 2015, with the highest US sale – just short of one million copies – of any comic issue in over five years (ComicChron, 2015b). Indeed, the sales dwarfed anything non-Star Wars that Marvel was selling. It took four more months for any Star Wars title to fall out of the top ten sales positions.

56. It could be argued that this period fostered changes that eventually polarised American cinema into a narrowly defined commercial mainstream on the one hand, and a more

radical and separate (certainly, than today) 'independent' alternative on the other, in the 1980s.

57. '"We're a new version of the old studio system" as Jeffrey Katzenberg said': this is Connor (2015: 13) supporting a view of Disney as a company with its own self-conscious relationship to history. Katzenberg ran its motion pictures division, 1984–94.

Chapter 2

1. Although not all of MS's releases have met with the same levels of financial success, with the possible exception of *The Incredible Hulk*, no individual film has fallen significantly below expectation. Language alluding to Marvel's consistent success with audiences and the critical community is frequently used not only by Marvel itself, but also in press coverage. For example, see Wheeler (2014a).

2. The title *Marvel Comics* was immediately altered to *Marvel Mystery Comics* with Vol.1, #2 (1939). It ran in this form until 1949, when it was replaced by *Marvel Tales* (1949–57).

3. Howe recounts many such instances. Clashes between Lee and Ditko regarding Spider-Man for instance (2013: 53), and many instances between Lee and Kirby, culminating in public court proceedings (2013: 278).

4. This also worked in the opposite direction, as the house styles of the 'Big Two' accommodated revisions inspired by individual star creators who swapped one for the other: Carmine Infantino, Neal Adams and Marv Wolfman were some of the noted talents to leave DC for Marvel in the 1970s and Kirby's exit for DC in 1969 was a defining moment (Howe, 2013: 106).

5. See Howe (2013: 28) for Goodman's willingness to trim staff if the business required it.

6. Stefanie Diekmann (2004) singles out Marvel as having made a significant contribution to popular culture, regarding its specially dedicated 9/11 titles *Heroes* (Vol.1, #1, 2001) and *A Moment of Silence*, (Vol.1, #1, 2002) as well as a 9/11 themed issue of *Amazing Spider-Man* (Vol.2, #36, 2001). She asserts that 'no competing publication received as much attention'.

7. See Francisco Veloso and John Bateman (2013) for a reading of Marvel's *Civil War* as commentary on the real life initiation of the Patriot Act, a reactionary policy regarding the erosion of civil liberties.

8. See Introduction for the development of the UU.

9. Such astute business acumen, it now appears, is supporting Perlmutter to an increasingly commanding position within the structures of Marvel's parent Disney, as Kim Masters (2014) reports: 'Perlmutter is one of the top individual holders of Disney stock'. She cites a 'studio insider' confessing that 'Disney owns Marvel, but Ike gets to control every budget and everything spent on marketing, down to the penny'.

10. Henry Jenkins remarks that 'more than twenty times the number of people went to see the Spiderman [sic] movies on their opening days than had read a Spiderman [sic] comic the previous year' (2006: 72–3).

11. All figures in this chapter are taken from Box Office Mojo (www.boxofficemojo.com) and rounded down to the nearest million dollars – correct as of 30 September 2015.

12. www.rottentomatoes.com.

13. In 2014, Marvel announced the nine feature films it would release between 2015 and 2019 (See Ford and Kit 2014).

14. Devin Leonard (2014a) cites Feige referring to a map of films that stretch out to 2028.

15. Johnson notes that upon the release of *Iron Man*, due to the different financing mechanisms involved with this independent production, as opposed to previous licensing agreements, 'Marvel Studios profited more than from its previous sixteen films combined' (2012: 26).

16. Perhaps the only qualification to this would be the distinction between exploring a character in television or feature film, which in critical terms is a much-weakened distinction anyway. For the question of American television's 'quality' lag when compared to theatrical film – and whether one exists – has received widespread comment in both scholarship and popular writing, against a background of industrial and delivery changes, the likes of which we looked at in Chapter 1 when discussing Netflix. See for instance, Pearson (2007) or, in the more populist vein, Heritage (2013). The order in which the influence travels is questioned in Joseph Oldham's account of the Marvel/ABC TV show, *Agents of S.H.I.E.L.D.* (Oldham, 2014).

17. Edward Norton was relieved from his role as the Hulk prior to *The Avengers*, due to him having not 'shown enough team spirit' (Child, 2010), which followed creative difficulties between him and the studio (Kirschling, 2008); Jon Favreau departed the Iron Man series after a troubled second instalment (Brodesser-Akner, 2010); Edgar Wright left *Ant-Man* during pre-production (Rosen, 2014); even Joss Whedon, who publicly supported Wright, was reported to have had issues with creative control during the production of *Avengers: Age of Ultron* (Gajewski, 2015).

18. See Mantlo (w), Keith Giffen (a). 'The Sword in the Star! Stave 2: Witchworld!'. *Marvel Preview* Vol.1 #7 (summer, 1976). Marvel Comics.

19. See Broderick (2014), Wheeler (2014b), Mazza (2014) and Johnston (2014) for such examples.

20. All episodes on Marvel.com (http://marvel.com/podcasts/12/women_of_marvel_podcast).

21. Danvers was previously established as the hero 'Ms. Marvel', although this happened some time after Danvers' initial appearance in *Marvel Super-Heroes* Vol.1, #13 (1968).

Chapter 3

1. Similar to the approach taken to Hollywood films and the companies that author them by Connor (2012, 2015) and Christensen (2012).

2. The music of AC/DC has become a signature of the film series, but using such hard rock to accompany scenes of high action is a virtual cliché in the broader genre. Its *diegetic* use here, supportive of Tony Stark's overconfident and superficially rebellious self-image, could be argued to have a dual function.

3. The approach to texture in the MCU is such that one media corporation has been featured as the 'in-house' diegetic media provider in the MCU. The level of detail is such that Leslie Bibb – the actor who in *Iron Man* portrays Tony Stark's inquisitor and later lover, Christine Everhart – is recalled into MCU service for the web episodes of its news programme 'Newsfront'. The 'show' covers aspects of *A:AOU* (the battle in Sokovia) and

the imminent release from prison of criminal Scott Lang, which acts as inciting incident of *Ant-Man*. The episodes are viewable at a 'WHiH World News' Youtube channel set up by Marvel Entertainment, and via a 'WHiH' Twitter account. The existence of WHiH mimics the function taken by 'in-house' newspapers in the Marvel comics universe like the *Daily Bugle* and *The Pulse* that have occasionally been used as a frame for the presentation of diegetic material. WHiH itself – taking the representational form of non-fiction news media – is a minor example of a genre 'fractal', with a role to play in the canon. Though Marvel's approach is particularly thorough, it is far from the first producer to associate such all-encompassing textuality with superheroes. See Owczarski (2015) on the blended textuality used in viral marketing strategies for Christopher Nolan's Batman films.

4. Included in this series would be at least three Spider-Man films, *Daredevil* (Mark Steven Johnson, 2003), *Superman Returns* (Bryan Singer, 2006) and others. The trope usually shows the character indulging and expressing their full powers in a positive way, having surpassed earlier identity struggles. Interestingly, few MCU texts use the trope; an exception would be the closing episode of Season One of MS/Netflix's *Daredevil*, where the familiar trope seals a particular treatment of the origin story, as denoted by the episode's unsubtle title: 'Daredevil' (S1E13).

5. At another level, Downey Jr's power needs to be contained, for 'it is the character – as opposed to the actor – who is the primary attraction for the present and future audiences of the superhero franchise' (Koh, 2014: 496). This touches on contracts and remuneration, as we discuss in Chapter 6.

6. See Schatz (1993); on the ambiguity in this phrase, see Murray Smith (1998: 10–14).

7. Stark's being a target for Middle Eastern politicized groups (although the 'Ten Rings' remains rather mysterious and ambivalent in the MCU, it is frequently dubbed a terrorist organization) foreshadows much later developments that touch on Stark's association with US hegemony. Particularly relevant is the sight of Iron Man's 'Iron Legion' peacekeeping sentries being greeted as an unpopular, imperialistic presence in the war-torn country of Sokovia (in *A:AOU*).

8. Stan Lee and Larry Leiber (w), Don Heck (p, i). 'Iron Man is Born!' *Tales of Suspense* Vol.1, #39 (March, 1963). Marvel Comics.

9. The traditional media actually has a rather good track record in MCU texts so far. Old-school journalistic integrity and passion for exposing social injustice stories are particularly foregrounded in the character of Ben Urich (Vondie Curtis-Hall) in *Daredevil*. The traditional fashion in which Urich's paper (the *New York Bulletin*, clearly a replacement for the more well-known *Daily Bugle* as that belongs to the Sony-controlled Spider-Man family of concepts) is represented in terms of influence contributes to a feel that the show is slightly at odds with aspects of the present day reflected in other MCU texts, although the paper is shown to be increasingly complicit with private financial interests in the city it serves. We have covered the omnipresent news station WHiH earlier.

10. See our discussion of S.H.I.E.L.D., in particular, Coulson and Fury, in Chapters 5 and 8.

11. In action-adventure, recent films like the Bourne series (commencing with *The Bourne Identity*, Doug Liman, 2002) or Antoine Fuqua's *Shooter* (2007) try to find ways of squaring traditional action forms of authority (super-competent spies and military men) with the critique of objectionable and deceitful state factions and their reduction of liberty. Combining conspiracy-thriller elements into the action film, they arguably create

a genre pathway for such as *Captain America: The Winter Soldier*. We return to this issue later in the chapter, and more fully in Chapter 4.

12. This is the case, if we can agree not to muddy the waters by discussing a putative 'blockbuster genre'. We offer some comments on how 'blockbuster' has a meaning that works in tandem with 'action' below, but stop well short of conferring genre status on the blockbuster, although the possibility has been discussed by others; see Hills (2003: 179–80).

13. See Chapter 7 for a discussion of this film's 'family-adventure' elements.

14. What is meant here is that, the Warner Bros. Superman and Batman adaptations aside, pre-2000, with no equivalent of the connected attitude to production that Fox, Sony and eventually – in an advanced form – MS would take, each new entry into the 'genre' was essentially, formally, an origin story. Superman's origin has been given cinematic expression at least twice in Hollywood's post-classical era; Batman's twice (with revisions); and the MCU sequence up until *Ant-Man* featured at least six narratives that were explicit origin stories (*GOTG* being an interesting exception with only the human Quill's presence in space briefly explicated, and the other characters' backgrounds condensed into brief dialogue amidst character-based moments – see Chapter 6). Including MCU television shows would boost the count, but, *Ant-Man* aside, the Phase II films are mainly continuations of established situations, providing some insulation from the requirement of an origin story. Here the advantages of a rolling continuity become obvious, and as discussed in Chapter 5, *The Avengers* recasts the previous MCU films as preamble for the main event, requiring only a few scenes to reintroduce those who have been off-screen for a while.

15. This is until *Avengers: Age of Ultron*, which contains an amusing visual detail. When the Vision is 'born' and meets the other heroes, his concept of dress (superhuman or otherwise) is completely blank; seeing Thor, he instantly manufactures a cape (or, is it a cloak?) for himself, in emulation – taking the Asgardian, perhaps, as a Lacanian 'ego ideal' figure (see Allen, 2014).

16. The early Captain America costume of comics is referenced in the United Service Organization (USO) show scenes of the film and therefore associated with theatricality and 'showbiz' over substance.

17. Flanagan (2004a: 27–30) discusses how Ang Lee was criticized for applying a pretentious and unsuitable aesthetic, redolent of art cinema 'taste', to the popular subject matter of his film *Hulk* (2003), suggesting a kind of inverted critical snobbery towards mishandlings of certain kinds of material.

18. Rivera's poster can be viewed at Headgeek666 (2014).

19. The work of J. J. Abrams – new creative force in charge of the cinematic fortunes of Disney's Star Wars universe, and thus a figure now officially presented as part of the Lucas-Spielberg tradition – is particularly instructive here. His *Super 8* (2011) was produced by Spielberg, and works in many of the nostalgic tropes of that cinema.

20. The term 'blissing-out' is associated with Andrew Britton (1986), but its essential idea also typifies Robin Wood's stance in work on the two directors (1986). Lewis summarizes Britton's critique: 'The prevailing effect of these films … is one of "conservative reassurance", a *feeling* that is consistent with the prevailing political climate of the times' (2007: 72).

21. *Alf* (NBC-TV, 1986–90) was a show that blended a sarcastic alien into the sitcom dynamics of American suburbia (essentially, reversing Quill's journey but reproducing

his fish-out-of-water predicament). The puppet star of the show also featured in a comic published by Star Comics, a Marvel imprint.

22. *Firefly* ran on Fox in 2002, was adapted/expanded into the Whedon-directed feature, *Serenity*, in 2005, and then enjoyed a further remediation in comic book form.

23. Chris Pratt was quoted, soon after the release, as being open to an appearance in *Agents of S.H.I.E.L.D.* as Quill. Speaking like a true ambassador for MS, he said: 'If it made sense for the brand and for the story, yeah, sure' (cited in Agar, 2014).

24. Pratt's textual history prior to Marvel is very different to that of Downey Jr, but the use of his previous roles, particularly in *Parks and Recreation* (NBC, 2009–15) to define Quill's good nature functions in a similar way to the invoking of the actor's past *mediated through* certain roles with Iron Man.

25. The name of the craft is a reference to the TV star Alyssa Milano, whose pop-cultural prominence as a juvenile sitcom actor at the approximate time of Quill's abduction, like all of Quill's referential exchanges, locks him into the period predating 1988.

26. The pop track most prominently placed in the pre-selling of *GOTG* (via a succession of trailers, for instance) was Blue Swede's 'Hooked on a Feeling'. Although a big hit on its release in 1974, for a wide cinema audience, the meaning of 'Hooked on a Feeling' is deeply tied to its exposure in one of the most acclaimed films of the 1990s, with its own high-selling and once omnipresent soundtrack: *Reservoir Dogs*. For those too young to be acquainted with that film, the song's longevity is still affected by the publicity afforded by Tarantino's patronage.

27. Marvel comic series' embed *noir*, espionage, Japanese *anime/manga* styles and more into their mix; applicable here are the various Captain America-related works of Ed Brubaker (see Chapter 4); Brian Bendis on *Daredevil* (2000–6) and *Alias* (2001–4); and the 2008–9 *Big Hero 6* (see Chapter 8). Of course in the case of embedding styles, the artists responsible for these runs (such as Steve Epting, Alex Maleev and Michael Gaydos) contributed hugely. Bryan Hitch of *Ultimates* fame, for instance, has become known as the artist who inscribes 'high concept' filmic storytelling onto the comic book page, whether dealing with the FF, Captain America or many others.

Chapter 4

1. As Fox readied new films, changes to Marvel's strategies on continuously publishing and/ or promoting FF and X-Men titles attracted conspiracy theories. For instance, Kriston Capps (2014) asserts that Wolverine's death in Marvel comics is part of a wider policy of shifting publishing focus from Fox's X-Men to the Inhumans, who shall join the MCU in their own 2019 film (and are discussed in Chapter 5). See O'Connell (2015) and Weinman (2014), and the discussion of Marvel's attitudes to negotiating rights in Chapter 1.

2. Wilson Koh discusses this, identifying in MS productions the 'superhero as postmodern star' with a greater 'primacy' for audiences than the actor playing the role. See Koh (2014: 485).

3. Scott Lang replaced Hank Pym (who had deserted the identity) in the 1970s. Lang has generally occupied the identity since.

4. Key 1980s/1990s Cap writer Mark Gruenwald comments on the effectiveness of this strategy in Zimmerman (1988: 5–23).

Notes

5. Jonathan Hickman's *Avengers* (Vol.5) run (also spilling over into his *New Avengers* title), #35–44 (November 2014 to June 2015).

6. Very little Captain America material was published in the 1950s; this shall be discussed later.

7. 'Harley-Davidson's $15,500 FLS Softail Slim motorcycle, the ride of choice for Captain America' (Advertising Age, 2012).

8. Interestingly, Wright (2003: 36) presents a quotation from co-creator Joe Simon that makes clear that the character's 1941 genesis was another effort of organization; to lend cohesion to the mobilization of comic efforts against the Nazis: 'The opponents to the war were all quite well organized. We [Simon and Jack Kirby] wanted our say too'.

9. See Chapter 5 for a further discussion of the unpowered perspective in relation to *Agents of S.H.I.E.L.D.*

10. Although as later developments show us, it is an agent of Thanos (Josh Brolin) who has empowered Thor's adopted brother with a sceptre infused with an 'infinity stone' (later important as the 'mind stone' in *Avengers: Age of Ultron*). The battle between heroes and villains for control of all six infinity stones ripples through *GOTG* and will culminate in the 'Infinity War' films (2018–19).

11. Kirby's son Neal discusses the 'profound effect' that his father's combat experiences had on stories including those involving Cap; in Overton (2015: 24).

12. Zola has a cameo in the final episode of *Agent Carter*, 'Valediction' (S1E8), showing the growth of HYDRA keeping pace with that of S.H.I.E.L.D.

13. Among the book's fictional reflections are the Jewish and Jewish-American roots of superhero saviours like Superman and, indeed, the Captain himself, many of whom were first published at the dawn of the Second World War.

14. Fleshed out, in the case of Howard Stark who was already introduced as an older version (John Slattery) in *Iron Man 2*.

15. These include the existence of Jim Hammond, synthetic human, original 'Human Torch' (briefly seen at the future technologies exposition attended by Steve Rogers and Barnes). At the same event, Howard Stark unveils a flying car prototype that will become familiar as a S.H.I.E.L.D. vehicle featured in many Cap adventures. Another barely glimpsed 'extra' that hints at storyline extensions to come is a blueprint hurriedly gathered up by a fleeing Zola, detailing the robotic body which generations of comic readers will recognize as vessel for the diabolical scientist's disembodied consciousness (in this form, Zola is central to the Rick Remender/John Romita Jr run on *Captain America* – Remender and Romita, Jr, 2013).

16. The compassion and comic timing of Tucci, honed in heartfelt 'indie' films like his co-directed *Big Night* (Campbell Scott/Stanley Tucci, 1996) and *The Daytrippers* (Greg Mottola, 1996), is one of several casting successes. Chris Evans, veteran of a former Marvel (non-MCU) franchise, *Fantastic Four*, swaps a character (Johnny Storm) who would never let duty present an obstacle to fun for one who is the personification of duty. Tommy Lee Jones goes one better, swapping universes from DC villainy in *Batman Forever* (Joel Schumacher, 1995). Jones is unlikely to be remembered as the definitive cinematic Harvey Dent, but makes up for it with a heroic turn here as Colonel Phillips.

17. More positive analogues and reflections also exist, as in Colonel James Rhodes/War Machine (Don Cheadle), who can be seen as Stark's counterpart. 'Rhodey' becomes the

more uncompromising-sounding 'Iron Patriot' only after the interference of dark forces falsely wearing the countenance of state authority (*Iron Man 3*).

18. Cap's involvement in the Second World War – curtailed, of course, by his disappearance into the Arctic ice – seems to end well in advance of August 1945 (fan estimates suggest a date of March 1945 for this event – see Anon., 2015b).

19. The first few panels that show Cap experiencing the new world, in *Avengers* #4, capture its strangeness to him with as much, if not more, pathos than does Johnston's film. See Stan Lee (w), Jack Kirby (p), George Roussos (i). 'Captain America joins … The Avengers!' *Avengers* Vol.1, #4 (March, 1964). Marvel Comics.

20. Ed Brubaker (w), Steve Epting (a). 'The Final Issue of Captain America'. *Captain America*. Vol.6, #19 (October, 2012). Marvel Comics.

21. However, Cap's long and convoluted comic history has seen him pressured into running for president, in a comic that arrived on stands in the run-up to the Reagan-Carter election. Cap withdraws on the grounds of being unable to limit himself to improving the reality of the country rather than fulfil its dream version. See Roger Stern (w), John Byrne (p) and Josef Rubenstein (i). 'Cap For President!'. *Captain America* Vol.1, #250. (October, 1980). Marvel Comics. Elsewhere, Captain America actually attains the position in the alternate continuity of the 'Ultimate Universe'.

22. Cap's relations with S.H.I.E.L.D. have always been uneasy. See the 'Secret Empire' story arc (Englehart, Friedrich and Buscema, 2005).

23. An operation which really occurred, of course, carried out by the Office of Strategic Services (forerunner of the CIA). The MCU version is revealed by the Arnim Zola-consciousness encountered by Cap and Romanoff in the secret base within Camp Lehigh.

24. Showing how *The Avengers* anticipates the ideas of trust that will really pay off in *CA:TWS*, during its events Rogers undertakes some off-mission detective work to force Fury's hand in abandoning a covert plan to weaponize the Tesseract.

25. Stark's English butler Edwin Jarvis (James D'Arcy) – discussed in Chapter 5 – is one more case of naturally honourable behaviour misunderstood and misrepresented by a distorted system (in this case, British military). The circumstances behind his own charge of treason are described in the episode 'Time and Tide' (S1E3). That this is then used by interrogating officers of the SSR to induce Jarvis to betray his employer Stark reinforces Carter's alienation among their ranks, with one or two exceptions.

26. Fury relates to Rogers an analogy he uses to explain decline. It is a tale of his humble grandfather's job running an elevator, and the steps he took to arm himself to protect his modest tips as society changed over the years. Fury, of course, is justifying the need for 'Project Insight'.

27. The diegetic Marvin Gaye reference (to the soul musician's soundtrack to Ivan Dixon's 1972 film) acknowledges the Blaxploitation cycle and the cultural tropes/situation that it reflected, giving rise to Sam Wilson, Blade and Luke Cage in comics (Nama, 2011: 37, 139). The early 1970s was a fertile if troubled period in Cap's comic history. A further link is to the wider era contemporaneously going on in 'New Hollywood' cinema. The casting of Robert Redford and certain genre tropes signal this.

28. The main difference in approach of the films regarding the fallout from *The Avengers* is telling, considering the ideological differentiation between the two heroes that is required as build-up to *Captain America: Civil War*. Stark suffers a form of post-traumatic stress disorder, addressed in his film as *individual* anxiety over events and contributing to

his frame of mind and stance on security (leading to Ultron). Cap's film, however, characteristically addresses the wider ramifications for *society* of the exposure of the Avengers.

29. Robert Stack played Ness in the ABC-TV show *The Untouchables*, running from 1959 to 1963. 'New Hollywood'-associated figure Brian De Palma directed Kevin Costner as Ness in the successful Paramount film of the same title in 1987.

30. The first occasion follows the important 1970s 'Secret Empire' arc, with disgust at the Nixonian politics of the day leading Rogers into the new identity of 'Nomad, the Man without a Country'. The next time that Rogers forsakes the identity, a fearful government installs one of many unimpressive specimens to attempt to preserve the symbolic role (this time John Walker, 'The Super-Patriot'), with predictable results. The Red Skull, himself using the physical likeness of Rogers at this time, is involved. In reaction to this, Rogers resumes service as 'US Agent' in a late 1980s run, regaining his iconic costume – for a while – in a key issue scripted by Gruenwald. See Gruenwald (w), Kieron Dwyer (p), Al Milgrom (i). 'Seeing Red'. *Captain America* Vol.1, #350 (February, 1989). Marvel Comics. See Walton (2009) on Nomad, and for rounded coverage of many of Captain America's alternate versions, identities and periods of retirement.

31. Issue #25 of *Captain America* Vol.5 became an enormous sales success (ICV2, 2007). The eventual reveal in 2009's *Captain America Reborn* storyline (Brubaker, Hitch and Guice, 2010) showed that, essentially, the Red Skull had banished Steve Rogers' consciousness into a temporal limbo while manoeuvring, once again, to take over Rogers' body.

32. Explicitly seen in *Captain America* Vol.1, #350 (February, 1989).

33. See for instance Unknown (w), Mort Lawrence (p), John Romita (p, i). 'Back from the Dead!' *Young Men* Vol.1, #25 (December, 1953). Timely Comics.

34. A version of the mind-manipulating villain who brainwashes Burnside into this service, Doctor Faustus (Johann Fennhoff), appeared in the MCU via *Agent Carter*, played by Ralph Brown; see the final four episodes of Season One. Faustus' name was also given to a mind-control technique featured in several episodes of *Agents of S.H.I.E.L.D.*, suggesting the character's influence within HYDRA. For the Grand Director, see Roger McKenzie (w), Michael Fleisher (w), Sal Buscema (p) and Don Perlin (i). 'Death Dive!' *Captain America* Vol.1, #236 (August, 1979). Marvel Comics.

35. *What If*... is a series instituted in 1977 but irregularly published. It allows the exploration of counter-narrative scenarios outside of regular continuity (a sort of limited forerunner of the Ultimate Universe principle). See Tony Bedard (w), Carmine Di Giandomenico (p), John Stanisci (i). 'What If ... Captain America Fought in the Civil War?' *What If? Featuring Captain America* Vol.1, #1 (February, 2006). Marvel Comics.

36. For some, the revision to Falcon's initial origin tale seemed to chip away at the idea of black self-determination that other Marvel characters and creators had been working towards. In it, Wilson's background as a socially conscious Harlem activist was revealed to be a fabrication of the Red Skull, with his 'true' background (itself, later, re-revised) being that of a streetwise low-level gangster (AKA 'Snap' Wilson) in need of redemption. The manipulative Skull remakes Wilson into the type of upstanding black man that would appeal as a potential partner for the liberal Captain America (Nama, 2011: 77) – with Sam thus representing a perceived vulnerability within Cap rather than a hero in himself. Even here, though, writer Englehart found ambiguity: the source of the character's bitter worldliness derives from his shock upon broadening his horizons from Harlem, only to discover the restricted lives blacks led in other parts of the country.

See Englehart (w), John Warner (w), Frank Robbins (p), Giacoia (i). 'Mind Cage'. *Captain America* Vol.1, #186 (June, 1975) Marvel Comics. This episode would not be the only time that the Skull would attempt to orchestrate racial clashes in Harlem to gain advantage in the war against Captain America (see Donovan, 2014: 77).

37. As seen in *Agent Carter*, S1E7 ('Snafu').

38. See Ed Brubaker (w), Alan Davis (p) and Mark Farmer (i). 'Powerless, Part 5'. *Captain America* Vol.6 #10. (June, 2012). Marvel Comics.

39. Ed Brubaker (w), Alan Davis (p) and Mark Farmer (i). 'Powerless, Part 5'. *Captain America* Vol.6 #10. (June, 2012) Marvel Comics.

40. Most of these events are inventions of Brubaker and technically 'retcons', since they unpicked the idea that Bucky was genuinely dead for decades. These events are covered in *Captain America* (Vol.5, 2005–9). Rogers and Bucky come face to face for the first time since 1945 in #8 (a scene which is reproduced quite faithfully in the Russos' film). The 'Winter Soldier's creation by Soviet intelligence is recounted in #11.

41. The Brubaker run shows that beneath the cover of the symbolic role, Bucky actually undertook covert killings that facilitated cleaner missions for the more scrutinized Cap, foreshadowing his later use by the Russians. See Ed Brubaker (w), Michael Lark (p, i), Steve Epting (p, i). 'Out of Time Part 5'. *Captain America* Vol.5 #5. (May, 2005). Marvel Comics.

42. Steve Rogers' 'death' in the celebrated postscript to *Civil War* instigates a chain of events whereby an extremely reluctant Bucky is persuaded to adopt the Captain America identity. Gimmicky though this may have been, three years were spent in carefully getting the arc to this point, and Bucky retained the mantle for a long run of issues (joining the Avengers for a time). The events surrounding the death and the need to seek justice for it bring Bucky and a very wary Sam Wilson together as a fighting partnership. See Ed Brubaker (w), Steve Epting (a). 'The Death of the Dream, Part One'. *Captain America*, Vol.5, #25 (April, 2007). Marvel Comics.

43. A recent offering was a period miniseries presenting some 1960s adventures in the form of *Winter Soldier: The Bitter March* (Vol.1, #1–5; April to September, 2014).

Chapter 5

1. Stan Lee (w) and Steve Ditko (a). 'Spider-Man Versus the Chameleon!'. *Amazing Spider-Man* Vol.1, #1 (March, 1963). Marvel Comics.

2. *MTU* initially rotated the FF's Human Torch with Spider-Man as lead character to be paired with a different guest star monthly; the webslinger soon became the mainstay. The Torch's team-mate Ben Grimm/the Thing had more success, leading the popular *Marvel Two-In-One* title for one hundred issues, 1974–83.

3. Daredevil once refused an offer to join the Avengers (Steve Englehart (w), Don Heck (p) and Mike Esposito (i) 'With Two Beside Them!'. *The Avengers* Vol.1, #111 (May, 1973). Marvel Comics). The moment seems like a manifestation of Daredevil's great self-under-standing as much as anything else; fitting it is, in MCU terms, that the character receives the most compartmentalised text (the period ones, aside) to date in his Netflix series.

4. First appearance in *Strange Tales* (Jim Starlin (w, a). 'The Judgement!'. *Strange Tales* Vol.1, #180 (June, 1975). Marvel Comics), then continuing in Warlock's revived solo title (1975–6).

5. When it comes to relations with the public, the heroes actually do well to not be explicitly accused as 'traitors' (*Avengers* Vol.1, #92, 1971), or have citizens seek to sell out their secret location in fear of a villain (*Fantastic Four* Vol.1, #20, 1963).

6. The editorial conversation with the reader that went on around boxes in certain panels of comics was intrinsic to Lee's style (Sweeney, 2013: 140). The even more continuity conscious Roy Thomas maintained this style when taking over in the early 1970s. A note in *Avengers* Vol.1, #110 (April 1973) from Thomas reprimands the reader for not reading Captain America's solo mag, where the explanation for his suddenly renewed super-strength can be found; the following month's (May, 1973) issue's commentary reminds the reader that picking up the previous issue of *Daredevil* will facilitate 'added dimensions' to the Avengers story. The continuous Marvel universe was subject to this method of wraparound plugging for decades. See Steve Englehart (w), Don Heck (p) and Mike Esposito (i) 'With Two Beside Them!'. *The Avengers* Vol.1, #111. (May, 1973). Marvel Comics.

7. An example would be Roger Stern (w), George Tuska (p) and Don Perlin (i) ''Tis the Season …'. *Giant Superhero Holiday Grab-Bag – Marvel Treasury Edition* Vol.1, #13 (1976). Marvel Comics.

8. An arc known as 'Planet Hulk' (*The Incredible Hulk* Vol.2, #92–105, 2006–7) by writer Greg Pak and artists including Carlo Pagulayan is a recent example of this strategy. To cope with the difficulty of lining Hulk up on a 'side' of Captain America/Iron Man's opposing social and moral clash over the 'Superhuman Reg. Act', then going on in the pages of *Civil War*, the clever Hulk writing/editing team simply opted him out and sent him to an entirely separate 'event' storyline. The moment was replayed at the end of *Avengers: Age of Ultron*. This time, although the macro-narrative is actually heading in a Civil War-like direction, the Hulk is arguably escaping from the difficulties of a likely romance with Black Widow, and his exile is voluntary, unlike in *Planet Hulk*.

9. German firm Constantin Film acquired the movie rights to the FF in the 1980s, leading to the never-intended-for-release Roger Corman version of 1994 and the two big-budget films made (with Constantin as distributor) by Twentieth Century Fox, with director Tim Story, in 2005 and 2007. Fox has retained the rights throughout the first decade of the MCU, despite the centrality of the FF to Marvel comic lore, and launched Josh Trank's *The Fantastic Four* – technically, the family's third live-action iteration – to generally poisonous reviews and weak box office three weeks after the release of *Ant-Man* in summer 2015.

10. Stan Lee (w), Jack Kirby (p) and Dick Ayers (i). 'The Fantastic Four Battle the Mad Thinker and his Awesome Android'. *Fantastic Four* Vol.1, #15 (June, 1963). Marvel Comics.

11. These appearances led to the Marvel careers of Lee/Kirby creations the Black Panther – joining the MCU in 2018 – and the Inhumans – already glimpsed on *Agents of S.H.I.E.L.D.* (as we shall see), and heading to big screens in 2019.

12. Lumpkin's co-creator, Stan Lee, got to play Willie Lumpkin in the non-MS *Fantastic Four* (Tim Story, 2005).

13. Stan Lee (w) and Steve Ditko (a). 'Spider-Man!'. *Amazing Fantasy* Vol.1, #15 (August, 1962). Marvel Comics.

14. Examples would include General 'Thunderbolt' Ross (played by William Hurt in MS productions *The Incredible Hulk* and *Captain America: Civil War*), who acquired Hulk powers as the 'Red Hulk' in 2008; Spider-Man's high school nemesis (but adult number one fan), Corporal 'Flash' Thompson, who became the heroic Venom (aka Agent Venom)

by bonding with Spider-Man's rejected alien costume (and recently joined the Guardians of the Galaxy in the MU) in a popular 2011–13 series; and even Gwen Stacy, murdered sweetheart of Spider-Man. A popular character but deceased in mainstream continuity for decades, the Gwen of a parallel universe became the recipient of spider powers rather than Peter Parker (*Spider-Gwen* Vol.1, 2015–). Aaron Taylor (2014) makes the interesting case that the usage of Gwen Stacy in Columbia's 2012 Spider-Man reboot *The Amazing Spider-Man*, and its 2014 sequel, actually improves upon the character, particularly from a standpoint of agency; long associated with being 'the Girl who Died' in Marvel's comics, a mere representation of the guilt part of Peter Parker's psychological make-up, Gwen's rebirth in the new continuity of Webb's films allows for the character to become 'an embodied and vital presence' involved in the solutions to Spider-Man's crime-fighting problems and thus (although Taylor cannot make this point), perhaps, presaging the 'Spider-Gwen' revamp (another instance of a potential 'feedback loop' from film to comics).

15. The 'fit' of writer to title was important, and difficult to predict. Steve Englehart was loved by fans on the Avengers, but criticized on the FF for breaking up formula and attempting to reflect growth in the characters by leaving Reed and Sue 'offscreen' to enjoy a family life with their son (Tolworthy, 2015).

16. Dan Abnett (w), Andy Lanning (w), Paul Pelletier (p), Rick Magyar (i). 'Somebody's Got to Do It'. *Guardians of the Galaxy* Vol.2, #1 (July, 2008). Marvel Comics.

17. The event that leads to the formation of the 2008 Guardians is tied up with an already in-play line of continuity following 'Annihilation Conquest' (2007–8); that is, the dispersed state of intergalactic 'police force' the Nova corps, leaving a vacuum of order in the galaxy. Gunn's film establishes the Nova corps but no more than this.

18. The only live action super-team, FF and X-Men aside, to truly emanate from America's Big Two publishers prior to the Avengers was a weak version of DC's 'Justice League' in a 1997 television pilot. A team of inept vigilantes made it to screens in the action-comedy *Mystery Men* (Kinka Usher, 1999), which had a more satirical intent.

19. Although later MCU developments confirm the Second World War-era missions of the Howling Commandos, sometime comrades of Captain America as well as Peggy (Agent) Carter, and a loose assemblage of spies and scientific mavericks forming the early version of S.H.I.E.L.D., the Avengers will represent its first team of (what become referred to as) 'enhanced' individuals; it seems certain that the Inhumans – discussed later in the present chapter – pre-dated them but were unknown to the public.

20. The chaos theme extends to the creation of the team by Lee and Kirby. This is often explained as the result of hastening product – any product – to already-booked printing time when a *Daredevil* title failed to be ready as planned. The members of the Avengers needed no individual origin stories, so it was thought quicker to work up their first adventure (Brevoort, cited in Darowski J. J., 2014: 1).

21. The packed sequel presents origins for Ultron and the Vision, as well as reporting those of Quicksilver (Aaron Taylor-Johnson) and the Scarlet Witch (Elizabeth Olsen), and giving major onscreen clues to that of future solo film villain, Ulysses Klaue (Andy Serkis).

22. Whedon's credits as creator, writer or writer-director include television's *Firefly* (Fox Network, 2002–3), *Buffy the Vampire Slayer* (various stations, 1997–2003), and for the cinema, *Toy Story*, *Serenity* (2005), *Alien: Resurrection* (directed by Jean-Pierre Jeunet, 1998).

23. Of the initial team in *Avengers* Vol.1, #1, Lee and Kirby created the Hulk; Hank 'Ant-Man' Pym and Janet 'The Wasp' Van Dyne created by Lee, Kirby and Larry Lieber; Thor (and

antagonist) Loki were also created by the pair with Lieber (based on existing archetypes of course); Don Heck and Lieber assisted in creating Iron Man.

24. IMDb reports that the film's working title was the apt 'Group Hug' (Anon., 2015c).

25. The team in attendance with Captain America at the end of the film consists of Falcon, Widow, the Vision, the Scarlet Witch and War Machine (Don Cheadle).

26. Calculated in fan estimates of in-universe time; see Anon (2015d).

27. Banner is also involved, making them co-creators (a nice condensation of tensions throughout Marvel history); Stark is the dominant partner, however, moving for the A.I. tech discovered in Loki's sceptre to be incorporated into their Ultron design.

28. Also on this issue, see Chapter 6 for a discussion of how MS's latest hit team, the Guardians of the Galaxy, hovers over the line between 'risk' – what cannot be prepared for – and 'planning' – what can be – both as a studio product and a diegetic feature of their screen adventure.

29. See Steve Englehart (w), Sal Buscema (p), Frank Bolle (i). 'A Dark and Stormy Knight'. *The Defenders* Vol.1, #11 (December, 1973). Marvel Comics.

30. *Amazing Fantasy* Vol.1, #15 (1962); Korvac and the Avengers' battle ran for ten issues and can be found in a collected edition (Shooter, Michelinie et al., 2012). Matthew Pustz argues that the hallmarks of this run – the Avengers' powerlessness and limited perspective combined with the fact that they misunderstood Korvac's chances of improving the world – carry a particularly strong sense of 1970s American 'malaise'. See Pustz (2012: 144–6).

31. Coulson is killed by Loki but, unbeknownst to the Avengers, later resurrected by technology from the alien medical project known as T.A.H.I.T.I. This is gradually revealed throughout the first season.

32. Peggy obtains this – aka 'the Diviner' – in S2E1, 'Shadows', and also appears in S2E8 'The Things We Bury'.

33. Howard Stark was involved, as we know, in 'Project Rebirth' – the creation of Captain America. In 'Shadows', Carter says that Howard Stark will be looking over the obelisk tech; that Carter and Stark's futures are entwined in the building-up of an intel service that becomes S.H.I.E.L.D., eventually reaching its top levels, is affirmed in the opening scene of *Ant-Man* where, in the late 1980s, they are shown discussing Pym's shrinking technology with Hank Pym.

34. The post-credits tease of *Ant-Man* shows the 'civil war' direction in which the MCU is heading by making mention of 'accords' binding Stark/Iron Man's activities after the Sokovia incident depicted in *A:AOU*.

35. That S.H.I.E.L.D. widely serves this function for the MCU is underlined by the presence of its logo – rendered in grainy form, as if witnessed in newsreel or archival form – upon the holding menu page while the (UK) *CA:TWS* blu-ray disc loads up. This leaks out of the diegesis and gives the user the impression that what they are watching is released data, playing in to the Widow's releasing of S.H.I.E.L.D./HYDRA intel files at the end of the movie itself.

36. The team consists of combat, scientific, technological and communications departments. There is a dedicated engineering staff (Mack, played by Henry Simmons), medical/biochemistry experts (Jemma Simmons, played by Elizabeth Henstridge), technology experts (Leo Fitz – Iain de Caestecker) and so on. Coulson's right hand is Agent May, who also provides transport (piloting the 'Bus', an airborne command station) and leads

the trained warrior side of the team. In this she is aided by (initially) Grant Ward, and later by Bobbi Morse aka 'Mockingbird' (Adrianne Palicki), former mercenary and SAS veteran Lance Hunter (Nick Blood), with others.

37. Oldham (2014) refers to this as 'telling the same huge-scale events [as seen in MCU features] from the perspective of the "little people"'.

38. The only top-billing star from the MCU to appear in an episode of *AoS* to date has been Samuel L. Jackson as Fury (in episodes '0-8-4'/S1E2 and 'Beginning of the End'/S1E22).

39. S.H.I.E.L.D. is treated with suspicion and envy by the regular military (represented in the show in the figure of Talbot). Although the WSC seems to carry out a similar function over 'peacekeeping force' S.H.I.E.L.D., it is shown that the United Nations does exist in this fictional universe ('A Fractured House'/S2E6).

40. S1E7 – 'The Hub' and S1E12 – 'Seeds'.

41. The show and the MCU films here pick up a theme voiced, very explicitly, by the Scarlet Witch in a 1970s *Avengers* story. Personally subject to the same anti-mutant bigotry that the X-Men have faced, the Witch notes that the public has a tendency to reify heroes: 'They treat us as *things*! Some *love* us as "*heroes*" – others *hate* us as "*non-humans*" – but none of them sees us [as] *real beings,* with *real feelings!*' (emphasis in original). See Steve Englehart (w), Bob Brown (p), Don Heck (i). 'Night of the Collector'. *The Avengers* Vol.1, #119. (January, 1974). Marvel Comics.

42. From Fury making his ally Stark vulnerable by using S.H.I.E.L.D. funds to buy up a controlling interest in his company with the intention of driving it back into weapon production (seen in *Iron Man* Vol.1, #129, 1979); to the readiness of high-ranking officer Victoria Hand – represented in the first season of *AoS* as played by Saffron Burrows – to serve supervillain Norman Osborn when he rises to command a version of S.H.I.E.L.D. (an event which unfolds in the 'Dark Reign' storyline running through many titles, 2009–10). 'Dark Reign' is an arc very clearly readable as a response to the ethical dimension of the 'War on Terror'.

43. Presumably as this story progresses, just as in various X-Men issues over the years, there will be philosophical and practical conflict within Inhuman society about the need to maintain this stance; significant shades here of the mutant community that is off-limits for MCU representation. Previous episodes indicate that the voice of change will be Skye/Daisy and her generation, e.g. the character 'Sparkplug' (Luke Mitchell).

44. S2E16 – 'Afterlife'.

45. Starting in Jack Kirby (w and p), Chic Stone (i). 'The Inhumans!' *Amazing Adventures* Vol.2, #1. (August, 1970). Marvel Comics.

46. One way of putting this would be to say that, characters who 'lose' their humanity – the Hulk, the Thing – are capable of feeling the same anguish as mutants like the X-Men or Prince Namor, or the much manipulated Inhumans; but transformed characters are not able to access the fierce pride and belonging that the latter characters sometimes exhibit.

Chapter 6

1. The AF films that preceded *GOTG*'s release are as follows: *Iron Man, The Incredible Hulk, Iron Man 2, Thor, Captain America: The First Avenger, The Avengers, Iron Man 3, Thor: The Dark World* and *Captain America: The Winter Soldier*. The films released after *GOTG*, but still pertinent to this discussion, are *Avengers: Age of Ultron* and *Ant-Man*.

Notes

2. The film's trailer includes a sequence from the film in which Quill (Chris Pratt), apparently mid-tomb raid, is asked at gunpoint: 'Who are you?' With a dramatic pause and the score's steady build towards a triumphant announcement, he asserts: 'Star-Lord'. At which point the dramatic tension is pierced for comedic value as the confused alien, Korath (Djimon Hounsou) – echoing what is the presumed response from a majority of the audience – exclaims: 'Who!?'

3. When compared to its predecessor *The Avengers*, *A:AOU* underperformed in every box office criterion, according to figures extracted from Box Office Mojo (www. boxofficemojo.com), correct as of 30 September 2015. Critical response follows a similar pattern, with critic aggregate Rotten Tomatoes (www.rottentomatoes.com) showing it to have a 74 per cent rating, versus *The Avengers'* 92 per cent. Yet, MS would no doubt counter such observations by pointing to a near $1.5 billion worldwide box office total, placing it easily in the top ten such grosses of all time.

4. This is consistent with Marvel choosing to accentuate certain elements in crafting its identity (and holding on to certain identity aspects associated with creative independence when seen in the context of Disney), as discussed in Chapter 2.

5. Based on figures retrieved from Box Office Mojo, August 2014 was the first August to breach $1 billion at the box office, a feat regularly achieved for June and July. The seasonal shift is reflected at the summer's start, with May – once too early to be included in summer revenue bonanzas – now regularly achieving such sales (the month has become an MS cornerstone, with all *Iron Man* and *Avengers* films, as well as *Thor*, enjoying May debuts in the US).

6. All figures taken from Box Office Mojo, correct as of 30 September 2015.

7. That first appearance was in *Marvel Super-Heroes* Vol.1, #18 (1969). They appeared in several titles over the next two decades, but didn't receive their own self-titled series until 1990.

8. The only notable exception to this is the film's inclusion of the character Yondu (Michael Rooker), who is loosely based on a character of the same name, and with a similar appearance, from the first Guardians line-up.

9. 'Annihilation: Conquest' is an event series that ran throughout 2007 and 2008, crossing over many of Marvel's more cosmically aligned titles, in which characters such as Quasar, Adam Warlock, Nova, Star-Lord and others fought to stop the techno-organic race known as The Phalanx, led by Ultron, from assimilating the universe to their ranks.

10. Dan Abnett (w), Andy Lanning (w), Paul Pelletier (p), Rick Magyar (i). *Guardians of the Galaxy*, Vol.2, #2 (August, 2008). Marvel Comics.

11. Dan Abnett (w), Andy Lanning (w), Paul Pelletier (p), Rick Magyar (i). *Guardians of the Galaxy*, Vol.2, #4 (October, 2008). Marvel Comics.

12. In box office terms, *The Avengers* set intimidating standards: at the time of writing, it sat in the all-time top five films for a host of criteria, including Domestic Box Office, International Box Office and Opening Weekend (Box Office Mojo).

13. The 'Marvel Now' umbrella covered a rebooting of Marvel's comic book line during 2013, intended to give the appearance of new beginnings in order to entice new readers, or to entice current readers to try new titles.

14. The MCC is a collection of creative and executive individuals, spread across separate Marvel divisions, who have collaboratively plotted the direction of the MCU (see Introduction for its composition and Conclusion for possible developments).

15. Infinite Comics are released by Marvel as digital comics that introduce limited animation techniques in the way the panels are presented, but are created in a way that can be replicated in printed form. All four issues of *Guardians of the Galaxy: Infinite Comics*, which focused in turn on Drax, Rocket Raccoon, Gamora and Groot, were released in 2014 and written by Brian Michael Bendis, with illustration by Mike Avon Oeming, Ming Doyle, Michael Del Mundo and Yves Bigerel respectively.

16. On an organizational level, Marvel Television is its own wing, separate from MS, although both contribute to the MCU (see Introduction, Chapter 1 and Chapter 8). There are hints that this structure is set to change (see Conclusion).

17. Complementors are organizations that are not formally linked, but whose functions contribute to one another's fortunes.

18. Chiefly DC, but also Image Comics (*Wanted*, Timur Bekmambetov, 2008), Dark Horse (*Hellboy*, Guillerrmo del Toro, 2004) and others.

19. Scott Mendelson (2015) discusses the box office performances of titles as diverse as *Fast & Furious 7* (James Wan), *Jurassic World* (Colin Trevorrow), *Star Wars: The Force Awakens* (J. J. Abrams) and *A:AOU*, all released in 2015. It is evident in this discussion that these films all have to consider roughly the same customer groups, and as such operate within the same strategic group. Similarly, Gant (2015) presents the top ten grossing films at the British box office (United Kingdom and Ireland), in which both *Ant-Man* and *A:AOU* figure. With the possible exception of Universal's *Pitch Perfect 2* (Elizabeth Banks, 2015), itself the second instalment of a franchise, every entry was either an MCU film, a Pixar or Pixar-style animated family film, or summer 'event' movie from the other big studios (Universal, Warner Bros., Paramount).

20. The risk posed by Rocket's inclusion has been noted by director James Gunn: 'When I came on board, the first draft of the script had him as Bugs Bunny in the middle of the Avengers, and I wasn't into it. I don't think of him as a toy. If Rocket didn't work, the movie wouldn't work. That meant fine-tuning how this character could be *real*.' (Gunn cited in Collins, 2014; emphasis in original).

21. Disney Infinity is available for numerous games console platforms. Figures of Disney characters are placed upon a digital platform connected to the console, which then reads digital information from the figure and loads the character into the game. This combines the narrative layers of a game, giving depth and context to the characters therein, with the popular act of toy collection – both features that are historically used to raise awareness of, and engagement with, entertainment IP.

22. A year after Pratt's breakout role as Star-Lord, he starred in *Jurassic World*, the film that toppled *The Avengers* as highest-grossing opening weekend of all time, as well as overtaking it in domestic and worldwide gross (see Box Office Mojo). MS's ownership of such a development can be seen in the jovial nature of Feige's public congratulations, via Twitter, to *Jurassic World*'s producers (again, perhaps, pointing up the inside Hollywood notion of 'strategic group'). The tweet also singles out Pratt, including a bespoke illustration of him riding a T. Rex that is holding Thor's hammer Mjolnir – which, as was made abundantly clear in the diegesis of *A:AOU*, is reserved only for the 'worthy' – whilst the Avengers are left scratching their heads (see McMillan 2015).

23. It is such organizational logic that also informs the process of corporate mergers and acquisitions. Marvel aims to promote or create new products to suit a slightly different need, whilst maintaining the same brand image. On a larger scale, Marvel was seen as a strategic fit for Disney to acquire; its mostly family-friendly entertainment

products fit with Disney's brand image, but can reach segments of the market in which Disney has little traction (see Chapter 1). One such vector in the market, according to Joanna Robinson (2015) is male children. She opines this in her coverage of the scandal surrounding Disney's minimization of the character Black Widow in *A:AOU* merchandising: 'Having already cornered the market on toys for girls with their irresistible princess line, they [Disney] were setting their sights on the lucrative world of male-oriented merchandise'.

24. 'Trade narratives' is a term used by Derek Johnson (2012), encompassing 'the self-reflexive trade stories that Marvel executives have deployed to legitimate their incursion into Hollywood production communities' (4). They are investigated further in Chapter 2.

25. We have already established the importance of *Raiders of the Lost Ark* to the aesthetic and business underpinnings of MS (in Chapters 1 and 3, respectively).

26. The use of 'teams' within the MCU is covered in more detail in Chapter 5.

27. The very direct scenes in both Avengers films where Stark and Rogers clash over methods are the most evident signs of this, but the treatment of each character in their most recent solo film is instructive also: Rogers as transcending the state-sanctioned, preset identity of Captain America to embrace the bigger but messily defined agenda of freedom in *CA:TWS*; the bruised and paranoid Stark as withdrawing, in a sense, and becoming more remote from his creation of Iron Man to the extent that suits fly around without him in *Iron Man 3*.

28. Unclear hints are given about latent abilities that may be related to the riddle of his father's identity.

29. All values taken from Box Office Mojo and rounded down to the nearest million dollars – correct as of 10 October 2015.

30. The stage for this was set by *Man of Steel* (Zack Snyder, 2013). Warner Bros. will release the first major crossover film deploying characters from DC's 'Justice League' team in the form of *Batman Vs Superman: Dawn of Justice*, with other League members due to have films released in the next decade (a very limited crossover of DC characters occurred in *Supergirl* (Jeannot Szwarc, 1984), but Supergirl is not a known member of the League, and the non-appearance of Christopher Reeve's Superman devalued the connection). Fox's X-Men series will be addressed in the main body of this text.

31. Such a trajectory is not atypical for Hollywood popular franchises, particularly where early successes establish public knowledge of characters. The Michael Bay-directed Transformers films, for example, follow a similar trajectory, with 2007's *Transformers* ($709 million), 2009's *Revenge of the Fallen* ($836 million), 2011's *Dark of the Moon* ($1.123 billion) and 2014's *Age of Extinction* ($1.104 billion). The addition of international grosses later in the series, as character properties mainly known in the US become established, has also factored in several cases.

32. The first wave of the X-Men franchise includes *X-Men* (Bryan Singer, 2000), *X-Men 2* (Singer, 2003) and *X:Men: The Last Stand* (Brett Ratner, 2006), which were later followed by *X-Men: First Class* (Matthew Vaughn, 2011) and *X-Men: Days of Future Past* (Singer, 2013). The first wave of Spider-Man films include *Spider-Man* (Sam Raimi, 2002), *Spider-Man 2* (Raimi, 2004) and *Spider-Man 3* (Raimi, 2007), followed by the more recent *The Amazing Spider-Man* (Marc Webb, 2012) and *The Amazing Spider-Man 2* (Webb, 2014).

33. It seems as though Fox intentionally eased off with this release, dropping the production budget from *The Last Stand's* $210 million to $160 million (Box Office Mojo),

concentrating instead on a rise in quality (as shown by its increased Rotten Tomatoes rating of 87 per cent, up from *The Last Stand*'s 58 per cent). The studio was therefore able to measure success on its own terms and allow the franchise to grow back into itself, demonstrating another way to manage risk and exposure to loss of vitality in a franchise.

34. Leonard (2014a) cites Kevin Feige referring to a map of films that stretch out to 2028.

35. Sean Howe (2013) explains of *Howard: A New Breed of Hero* [UK title]: 'Despite its $37 million budget – plus an additional $8 million spent on promotion – it bombed miserably, and received a critical drubbing that embarrassed everyone involved' (293). Interestingly for our next chapter which looks at a company which George Lucas had a hand in (Pixar), Willard Huyck's film represents the closest that executive producer Lucas has been to a direct Marvel production (with his interests quite separate from those of Marvel until they became related as parts of the Disney empire as of 2012).

Chapter 7

1. Across fifteen feature releases since 1995, Pixar entertainments had captured an average of $259 million in domestic takings per picture (when the average for the overall genre of computer animation – overwhelmingly stocked with 'family' titles – stood at $127 million (based on well over one hundred major releases from 1995 to 2015)). However, the top rating Pixar film *Toy Story 3* is bested by Dreamworks Animation's *Shrek 2* (Andrew Adamson, 2004) on the all-time domestic box office chart ($441 million for *Shrek 2*, $415 million for the Pixar film). All figures retrieved from Box Office Mojo (www.boxofficemojo.com), correct as of 30 September 2015.

2. For an example, see O'Hehir (1999) for a discussion of how 'norms' drawn from mechanically based photography – allied to perceptions of classical narrative, which is germane to the importance of 'story' to readings of Pixar – informed such criticism, see Cubitt (2000). A brief history of such views, pre-dating the emergence of digital cinema, is offered in Pierson (1999).

3. The initial deal between Pixar and Disney was that between an independent producer and distributor. An agreement to deliver at least one CG-based movie to distributor Disney was signed in 1991. Pixar went public in 1995, year of *Toy Story*. Walt Disney Studios and Pixar set another agreement to jointly produce five movies over ten years from 1997, with Disney handling distribution and marketing, but Disney had purchased Pixar, in 2006, before this elapsed.

4. www.rottentomatoes.com.

5. www.cinemascore.com.

6. Some measures would include the following: Box office grosses, which (at the US box office) total nearly $3.6 billion over twelve full releases; *The Avengers* is the fourth highest-grossing film at the worldwide box office. The modal average Cinemascore rating of MCU releases is 'A'. An MCU film has yet to dip below 65 per cent (i.e. be awarded a 'rotten' rating) on Rotten Tomatoes. (Box office statistics obtained from Box Office Mojo; correct as of 31 August 2015. Cinemascore and Rotten Tomatoes information is collated in the table at Anon. (2015e)).

7. *Luxo, Jr.* is a simple 1986 two-minute short. Its award-winning minimal narrative captures several Pixar themes for the future, including the endowment of inanimate technology with feeling; a forgiving family environment, and several motifs that become

recurrent signifiers of Pixar's deep connection to its own history later on, especially the logo/ident of the studio (a hopping lamp).

8. Lucas had sought the rights to Sci-Fi matinee adventurer 'Buck Rogers' (as well as the similar 'Flash Gordon') before making *Star Wars*. He included material from the Buster Crabbe-starring 1939 Rogers serial as a counterpoint to his dystopian sci-fi film *THX-1138* in 1971.

9. Invoking the feature *The Fox and the Hound* (Ted Berman, Richard Rich and Art Stevens, 1981) on which Lasseter worked, the narration connects the health of the final product to 'increasing budget cutbacks [which] had severely limited the multiplane dimensional look Walt Disney had achieved decades earlier' (see Iwerks, 2007). Multiplane photography was a hallmark of the 'realism' that Disney was credited as introducing to 2-D animation.

10. Genre fans might not always like it (Flanagan, 2009: 82), but the economic sense here is well-established and influential:

> With boomers taking their kids (or being dragged by them) to the movies, and with kids more likely than any other group to go to the theatre to see a film more than once, by 1991 PG and PG-13-rated films were twice as likely as R-rated ones to earn $60 million and three times more likely to earn $100 million at the box office.
>
> (Allen, 1999: 116)

Recent moves in the genre of which the MCU is a part (see Chapter 3), Action-Adventure, have tried to enhance their appeal through a return to 'basics' in terms of production methods (practical effects and graphic violence), but get stuck in a 'Catch-22' situation: if they prosper at the box office, pressure is invariably added to make subsequent films PG-13. This is what happened with Sylvester Stallone's Expendables trilogy (2010–14; *Expendables* 2 directed by Simon West, *Expendables* 3 directed by Patrick Hughes).

11. *Transformers* directed by Michael Bay (2007); *Frozen* directed by Chris Buck and Jennifer Lee (2013); *Jurassic World* directed by Colin Trevorrow (2015).

12. *Up*, directed by Pete Docter and Bob Peterson (2009); *Brave* directed by Mark Andrews, Brenda Chapman and Steve Purcell (2012).

13. In September 2015, commentary by Charles Gant on the UK box office bracketed together three traditions – that of the Spielbergian adventure, the computer-animated children's film (Pixar included), and the MS superhero film – in a brief summary of the busiest month of the summer:

> Admissions totals are in for July, and the number of tickets sold shows a big rise on July 2014. Thanks to July hits, including *Inside Out* and *Ant-Man* plus sustained runs by June releases *Jurassic World* and *Minions*, cinemas saw 20% more bums on seats than the same month a year ago. For the first seven months of the year overall, admissions are running an impressive 11% ahead of 2014.
>
> (Gant, 2015)

14. Shifts in how these markets behaved in relation to each other also need to take note of changes in the age-ratings methodology set for the industry by the Motion Picture Association of America (MPAA) in the late 1960s.

15. Both the period and the specific links between Disney and Lucas/Spielberg are discussed in Krämer (2006). The 'family-adventure' movie, Krämer's diagnosis of these changes manifesting in a form of filmmaking that became the most significant mainstream trend, is specifically explained in Krämer (1998b).

16. For a discussion of Spielberg's experiences with the MPAA over such matters, and his crucial role in the institution of the PG-13 rating, see Brode (2000) and Breznican (2004).

17. Examples include Jack Skellington of *The Nightmare Before Christmas* (Henry Selick 1993) and the manufacturing of Sid and his 'mutant toys' from *Toy Story*.

18. Co-founder Ed Catmull authored (with Amy Wallace) a 'management book' called *Creativity Inc.* which professed to offer business and management lessons based on his Pixar experiences. See Catmull and Wallace (2014).

19. Initiating, for instance, a Disney 'Story Trust' that worked on the conversion of Marvel Comics property *Big Hero 6* – see Roper (2014) and Collin (2015).

20. These nine animators, who are particularly associated with the studio's untouchable 1930s and '40s heyday, are frequently invoked as mentors of both Lasseter and Brad Bird, as well as fellow travellers like Tim Burton, all of whom studied under them at CalArts in the 1970s. CalArts is a private university set up by Disney to reproduce the animation principles that underpinned its 'classic' style. See Iwerks (2007).

21. See Amidi (2014) on Pixar's involvement in a story of wage-fixing among top animation outfits.

22. The MCC is a collection of creative and executive individuals, spread across separate Marvel divisions, who have collaboratively plotted the direction of the MCU (see Introduction for its composition, and Conclusion for possible developments around its current status in relation to the power structure around Feige, Perlmutter and Disney, which has recently become less clear).

23. Holliday cites the cases of *Cars 2* (John Lasseter and Brad Lewis, 2011) and *Brave*, from which original directors were either lost (Brenda Chapman of *Brave*) or found themselves in a directing collaboration (as in the case of Lewis).

24. Holliday extrapolates this to draw 'the implication … that when it comes to the desire for quality in the final dish, it matters little which gourmet chef is pulling the strings' (the culinary metaphor is drawn from Pixar's *Ratatouillle*, Brad Bird, 2007).

25. See Appendix: Timeline.

26. Although as we noted in Chapter 5, identity problems still arise for at least one member, Ben Grimm.

27. Representatives of Fox at a paid screening of Trank's version handed out surveys where fans could suggest directions for the franchise in future – a sign, apparently, that the choice had been made to cut and run after Trank's era. Although widely reported, as of this writing, the story was only based on some uncorroborated tweets. See Gonzalez (2015). No doubt some of the fans might have responded that the solution was to return FF rights to Marvel; that viewers had been petitioning Fox to this effect was also widely reported in August 2015.

28. *National Treasure* (Jon Turteltaub), *Troy* (Wolfgang Petersen) and, prototypically, Mel Gibson's *The Passion of the Christ* were all released in the same year as *The Incredibles*, 2004. More recent releases like *Hancock* (Peter Berg, 2008) used a superhero premise to explore the same tropes; even the rebooted James Bond series, from 2006, makes some allowances for these developments.

29. This is a tactic to make Bob seem more constricted, and is mentioned by Bird and producer John Walker on the R2 DVD commentary track.

30. Critics read the prologue as the 1950s, with the diegetic present transpiring twenty years later; yet Bob has a computer in his office (Meinel, 2014: 183).

31. The lack of subtlety strains credulity at times. In Iwerks (2007), narration that says 'it was the computer that would take us to new frontiers' is followed by interpolated footage from Kennedy's famous 1961 'Special Message to Congress on Urgent National Needs' speech, a talk that specifically refers to the impact that Sputnik and other space 'adventures' had on the world.

32. We will attend to their arguments more directly in the Conclusion.

33. Walt Disney, of course, literally 'signed' the trade dress of his company.

34. There is no 'pure' family film market, essentially; these days, any PG-13-rated event film inevitably becomes a 'family-adventure' title as long as the subject matter does not entirely mitigate against this. *GOTG*'s marketable members, and Oedipal sequel promise (the search for Quill's father; Gamora's tussle with Thanos), demonstrate this. On certain Spielbergian elements, see Chapter 3.

35. Gathering a smaller audience but over a longer period of time suggests a healthy audience appetite for this new character. To put this into perspective, if *Avengers: Age of Ultron* had achieved a similar multiple to *Ant-Man*, its final cumulative domestic box office would have been $592 million rather than the $458 million it did achieve. For comparison, the popular (and relatively unanticipated, which tends to correct opening weekend 'front-loading') *GOTG* had a multiple of 3.5; the high-grossing *Iron Man 3* achieved 2.35. Allowance must be made for the fact that sequels tend to attract 'front-loading' more than do original films. Even Pixar is not immune to this as a study of *Toy Story* trilogy releases demonstrates (All figures Box Office Mojo, correct as of 31 August 2015).

36. In fact *Big Hero 6* enjoyed only two miniseries (in 1998 and 2008). One of the aspects of so-called Disneyfication/Disneyization that is traditionally seen as negative is the annulling of cultural specificity to synchronize source material with the norms and expectations of Western audiences, seen as far back as its earliest fairy tale adaptations like *Pinocchio* (Ben Sharpsteen and Hamilton Luske, 1940). See Budd (2005: 7–11). In an example of forcing hybridity, *Big Hero 6* relocates the Japanese super-team of comics to the futuristic 'San Fransokyo', mixing the Bay Area technology associations of San Francisco – home to Lucas' company, Steve Jobs' Apple and a ten-mile ride from Pixar's Emeryville, Alameda County home headquarters – with the style (and muted cultural) elements of the original's Tokyo setting.

37. A late cameo 'appearance' by Stan Lee is the sole nod to including *Big Hero 6* in a Marvel environment.

Chapter 8

1. Certain scholars do use the term (see Hadas, 2014).

2. *Agent Carter* would also be useful in this investigation. A fuller account of how that show fits into MCU continuity can be found in Chapter 4, as a narrative development spinning out of the multi-movie saga of Captain America, but dealing well with the absence of that character.

3. These include titles/series like *Captain America: First Vengeance* Vol. 1, #1–4 (2011), and *Avengers Prelude: Fury's Big Week* Vol. 1, #1–4 (2012).

4. Recounted in Conway and Thomas (2006). The script was ordered by Orion pictures, a strong 'mini-major' outfit in the 1980s.

5. Figures obtained from Box Office Mojo (www.boxofficemojo.com), correct as of 10 October 2015.

6. Where Evans uses the term 'storyworld', we prefer the emphasis on 'story *universe*', though the two ostensibly mean the same thing.

7. Natasha Romanoff/Black Widow has been depicted several times in MCU films from different directors, remaining mostly consistent, but with minor character variations. One way these are denoted is the different hair style under each director. Scarlett Johansson wears long curls in Favreau's *Iron Man 2*, has shorter hair in Whedon's *The Avengers*, long straight hair in the Russos' *Captain America: The Winter Soldier* (*CA:TWS*), then back to the same short hair, when once again under Whedon's direction in *Avengers: Age of Ultron*. This system is akin to the way character iterations have been abandoned and returned to under different writers and artists in comics for decades.

8. Being depicted as a shady and mistrustful organization throughout (arguably essentially so, considering its charter for espionage, S.H.I.E.L.D. is used to drive the narrative in several One-Shots, and obviously *AoS*. Conversely, it is contextualized as an external, guiding force subordinate to the agency of the heroes in their own films (or even opposing that agency, as in *CA:TWS*, where it takes a bigger role). See Chapter 5.

9. The diegetic 'news network' WHiH, discussed in Chapter 3, is an example of a vehicle mostly consumable via the web (particularly Youtube), the content of which targets pre-consumption of theatrical releases such as *Ant-Man*.

10. The concept of 'remediation' elucidated by Bolter and Grusin – that is, the incorporation of old forms into new settings, the repurposing of material from an established medium rather than the introduction of a new one – could be helpful here. See Bolter and Grusin (2000).

11. Some of these would more accurately be described as mid-credits scenes, but the significance remains consistent.

12. The mistrust of authority frequently invoked throughout the MCU is no better exemplified than *AoS*'s bureaucratic attempts to compartmentalize information from both its characters and from the audience itself, embracing deliberate denial of information as part of its plot.

13. The Kree feature prominently in *GOTG*, a text that was released after the first season of *AoS*.

14. The MCC is a collection of creative and executive individuals, spread across separate Marvel divisions, who have collaboratively plotted the direction of the MCU (see Introduction for its composition and Conclusion for possible developments).

15. Christopher Yost and Craig Kyle (w), Scott Eaton (p), Andrew Hennessy (i) Vol. 1, #1–2 (August/September, 2013). Marvel Comics.

16. Web-based review aggregator Metacritic (www.metacritic.com) scores the game at 47/100 or lower across all platforms.

17. The only subsequent MCU-based videogame was the mobile device-only *Iron Man 3* (Gameloft, 2013).

18. The first entry to this series, 1996's *X-Men Vs Street Fighter* itself appeared informed by Fox's animated series, with character depictions following their likenesses in that show.

Conclusion

1. Christensen develops a very rich reading of the role of Jiminy Cricket (voiced by Cliff Edwards), noting that the character was an addition to Collodi's loosely adapted tale that indicated the moral direction Walt Disney wanted to go in (2012: 336–8). Nicholas Sammond, meanwhile, reads Walt – embodying the benevolent cultural-educational role of his company – as slotting into both the kindly old father role of Gepetto in the movie, and the conscience role taken by Jiminy. Thus, parents of 1940 were presented with a film studio executive/manager-figure as a model of the oversight needed to make a child 'a real American' (2005: 78). These, perhaps, are the conservative meanings taken from *Pinocchio* that a team led by Joss Whedon – familiar for a fascination and sympathy with his villains – might have been playing on with the inclusion of the reference.

2. Having seen *Beauty and the Beast* (Gary Trousdale and Kirk Wise, 1991), generally received as a return to form for Disney, beaten at the Japanese box office by Studio Ghibli's *Kurenai No Buta* (*Porco Rosso*) (Miyazaki Hayao) in 1992, Disney entered into a deal to present the Japanese studio's films, as distributor, in the West. The deal with sales company Tokuma Shoten Publishing Co. covered 'nine Studio Ghibli titles worldwide, including Miyazaki's next film *Mononokehime* (*Princess Mononoke*) (Schilling, 1997: 40). Miramax, for its owner Disney, oversaw an English language dub of the film that cast American star voices for the US market.

3. Among the current roster of shows in the (very traditionally named) 'Marvel Universe' block are *Hulk and the Agents of S.M.A.S.H.* (2013–), and a version of *GOTG* (2015–) that is highly synced-up, in presentation, story and even soundtrack terms, with the MCU film.

4. Jenkins was replaced as director of the film that became *Thor: The Dark World* by Alan Taylor.

5. In a wider and historical sense, it is difficult to be categorical about the health of the American comics business because many of the reference points cited shift according to who is reporting, and what agenda they may follow. The recent challenge of digital platforms (and other media, including film, reproducing similar content) to print comics is often interpreted pessimistically by established readers, yet a *Star Wars* comic sold a few thousand copies below one million for Marvel in January 2015, and an issue of TV adaptation *Orphan Black* – a far less pervasive franchise than *Star Wars* – sold half that huge number the following month for IDW comics (see ComiChron, 2015a and 2015c). This is a simple measure, no doubt; and a reliance on historical, non-comics franchises like *Star Wars* would not be a recipe for growing a long-term readership. It does, however, indicate – once again – the power of convergence and the shared universe principle.

6. Most well-known among these would be the MCU rendition of Nick Fury (by Bryan Hitch).

7. As the central battle with Loki and the Chitauri in *The Avengers* has become known in MCU lore.

8. The relation of African people to imperialism is certainly at issue in the origin of the character (Nama, 2011: 42–4), but this could potentially allow a critique of imperialism rather than the collusion with it observed by some in certain corners of the MCU (see Mirrlees, 2013: 9–11).

9. The fact that these characters enter during the same phase of expansion speaks of a concerted ambition. Add to this, the new Avengers line-up teased at the end of *Avengers: Age of Ultron* shows Falcon, War Machine/James Rhodes, Scarlet Witch/Wanda Maximoff and The Vision; that is, a woman, two black men and a definitively raceless character, who come in for the outgoing white men: Stark, Clint 'Hawkeye' Barton, Bruce Banner and Thor. Of course, such considerations will not be entirely divorced from industrial realities like the contracts of actors (see Chapter 6). The point is that the shared universe allows them to appear part of organic narrative ebb and flow.

BIBLIOGRAPHY

Adalian, Josef. (2015), 'How *Parks and Recreation* Managed to Survive for 7 Seasons'.
 Vulture. Accessed 1st August 2015. http://www.vulture.com/2015/02/parks-and-
 recreation-ratings.html.

Advertising Age. (2012), 'Avengers Bulking Up $6 Billion Marvel Licensing Machine'.
 Accessed 10th June 2015. http://adage.com/article/media/avengers-bulking-6-billion-
 marvel-licensing-machine/234572/.

Agar, Charles. (2014), 'Chris Pratt Won't "Rule Out" Appearance on "Agents of S.H.I.E.L.D."'
 Screen Rant. Accessed 17th September 2015. http://screenrant.com/agents-shield-chris-
 pratt-star-lord-guest-starring/.

Akass, Kim and Janet McCabe, eds. (2007), *Quality TV: Contemporary American Television
 and Beyond*. London and New York: I. B. Tauris.

Albert, Stuart and David A. Whetten. (2004), 'Organizational Identity'. In *Organizational
 Identity: A Reader*, edited by Mary Jo Hatch and Majken Schultz, 89–118. Oxford: Oxford
 University Press.

Allen, Richard. (2014), 'Identification, Theory of', In *The Routledge Encyclopedia of Film
 Theory*, edited by Edward Branigan and Warren Buckland, 237–41. London and
 New York: Routledge.

Allen, Robert C. (1999), 'Home Alone Together: Hollywood and the "Family Film."' In
 Identifying Hollywood's Audiences, edited by Melvyn Stokes and Richard Maltby, 109–31.
 London: BFI.

Alonso, Axel. (2015a), 'Untitled Foreword'. In *All-New All-Different Marvel Previews #1*
 Vol. 1, # 1. New York: Marvel Comics.

Alonso, Axel. (2015b), 'Jeph Loeb on *Daredevil's* debut, Netflix Advantage'. *Axel-in-Charge*
 blog. Accessed 15th April 2015. http://www.comicbookresources.com/article/axel-in-
 charge-jeph-loeb-on-daredevils-debut-netflix-advantage.

Amidi, Amid. (2014), 'New Evidence Emerges of Wage-Fixing by DreamWorks, Pixar and
 Blue Sky'. *Cartoon Brew*. Accessed 4th September 2015. http://www.cartoonbrew.com/
 artist-rights/new-evidence-emerges-of-wage-fixing-by-dreamworks-pixar-and-blue-
 sky-106529.html.

Anders, Charlie Jane. (2009), 'Are Superhero Stories Even a Genre?' i09. Accessed 4th
 October 2015. http://io9.com/5166889/are-superhero-stories-even-a-genre.

Andreeva, Nellie. (2012), 'CAA Signs Marvel Television'. *Deadline*. Accessed 24th September
 2015. http://deadline.com/2012/04/caa-signs-marvel-television-255502/.

Anon. (2004a), 'David Maisel Joins Marvel Studios as President & COO of Marvel Studios
 to Oversee New Initiative'. *Marvel.com*. 24th September 2015. http://marvel.com/news/
 movies/98/david_maisel_joins_marvel_studios_as_president_coo_of_marvel_studios_to_
 oversee_new_initiative.

Anon. (2004b), 'Profile: *The Incredibles*. Absolutely Super Yet Incredibly Human'. *The Sunday
 Times*. 21st November: 17.

Anon. (2009a), 'Marvel Decade: Kevin Feige'. *Marvel.com*. Accessed 24th September 2015.
 http://marvel.com/news/movies/10812/marvel_decade_kevin_feige.

Anon. (2009b), 'Marvel Studios' David Maisel to Step Down After Disney Deal'. *Los Angeles Times*. 24th September 2015. http://latimesblogs.latimes.com/ entertainmentnewsbuzz/2009/12/marvel-studios-david-maisel-to-step-down-afer-disney- deal-walks-away-with-huge-payday.html.

Anon. (2009c), 'Disney Completes Marvel Acquisition'. *Marvel.com*. Accessed 21st June 2015. http://marvel.com/news/comics/10809/disney_completes_marvel_acquisition.

Anon. (2015a), 'Captain America's Motorcyle: Alternate Realities Motorbikes'. *Marvel Wikia*. Last modified 29th July. Accessed 2nd March 2015. http://marvel.wikia.com/wiki/ Captain_America%27s_Motorcycle.

Anon. (2015b), 'The 1940s'. *Marvel Cinematic Universe Wikia*. Last modified 4th April. Accessed 5th April 2015. http://marvelcinematicuniverse.wikia.com/wiki/1940s#cite_ note-CAFV-0.

Anon. (2015c), '*The Avengers*: Release Info'. Internet Movie Database. Accessed 11th July 2015. http://www.imdb.com/title/tt0848228/releaseinfo?ref_=tt_dt_dt#akas.

Anon. (2015d), '2015' *Marvel Cinematic Universe Wikia*. Last modified 13th September. Accessed 15th September 2015. http://marvelcinematicuniverse.wikia.com/wiki/2015.

Anon. (2015e), 'List of Films Based on Marvel Comics'. *Wikipiedia*. Last modified 30th August 2015. Accessed 31st August 2015. https://en.m.wikipedia.org/wiki/List_of_films_ based_on_Marvel_Comics.

Ayodeji, Julius. (2013), 'Marvelization: The Rise of Complex Narratology on the Hollywood Screen'. *Avanca*. Accessed 11th April 2014. https://www.academia.edu/6461677/ Marvelization_The_Rise_of_Complex_Narratology_on_The_Hollywood_Screen.

Barbour, Chad. (2015), 'When Captain America was an Indian: Heroic Masculinity, National Identity and Appropriation'. *The Journal of Popular Culture*, vol. 48, no. 2: 269–84.

Barnes, Brooks. (2008), 'Disney and Pixar: the Power of the Prenup'. *New York Times*. Accessed 29th September 2015. http://www.nytimes.com/2008/06/01/business/ media/01pixar.html?pagewanted=all&_r=0.

Bather, Neil. (2004), 'Big Rocks, Big Bangs, Big Bucks: The Spectacle of Evil in the Popular Cinema of Jerry Bruckheimer'. *New Review of Film and Television Studies*, vol. 2, no. 1: 37–60.

Beckett, Jennifer and Thomas Apperley. (2014), 'Media X Building Branded Worlds: Marvel's Cross-Media Strategy'. *Inquire – Journal of Comparative Literature*, vol. 3, no. 2. Accessed 25th September 2015. http://inquire.streetmag.org/articles/123.

Bendis, Brian Michael and Steve McNiven. (2013), *Guardians of the Galaxy Volume One: Cosmic Avengers*. New York: Marvel Publishing.

Blot, The (2011), '*Thor* International Poster'. *The Blot Says*. Last modified 20th May. Accessed 15th May 2015. http://www.theblotsays.com/2014/05/guardians-of-galaxy-final- one-sheet.html.

Blot, The (2014), '*Guardians of the Galaxy* Final Poster'. *The Blot Says*. Last modified 22nd March. Accessed 15th May 2015. http://www.theblotsays.com/2011/03/thor-international- one-sheet-movie.html.

Bolter, Jay D. and Richard Grusin. (2000), *Remediation: Understanding New Media*. Cambridge, MA and London: MIT Press.

Bordwell, David. (2002), 'Intensified Continuity: Visual Style in Contemporary American Film'. *Film Quarterly*, vol. 55, no. 3: 16–28.

Bordwell, David, Staiger, Janet and Thompson, Kristin. (1991), *The Classical Hollywood Cinema: Film Style and Mode of Production to 1960*. London and New York: Routledge.

Brannon Donoghue, Courtney. (2014), 'Sony and Local-Language Productions: Conglomerate Hollywood's Strategy of Flexible Globalization for the Global Film Market'. *Cinema Journal*, vol. 53, no. 4: 3–27.

Bibliography

Brereton, Pat. (2012), *Smart Cinema, DVD Add-Ons and New Audience Pleasures.* Basingstoke: Palgrave.

Brevet, Brad. (2012), 'Meet Dr. Bruce Banner in New "Avengers" Clip'. *Rope of Silicon.* Accessed 3rd July 2015. http://www.ropeofsilicon.com/avengers-clip-bruce-banner-hulk/.

Breznican, Anthony. (2004), 'PG-13 Remade Hollywood's Rating System'. *Seattle Post-Intelligencer.* Last modified August 23rd. Accessed 30th August 2015. http://www.seattlepi.com/ae/movies/article/PG-13-remade-Hollywood-ratings-system-1152332.php.

Britton, Andrew. (1986), 'Blissing Out: The Politics of Reaganite Entertainment'. *Movie,* vol. 30/31: 1–42.

Brode, Douglas. (2000), 'Visionary Children and Child-Like Heroes: Steven Spielberg's "Primal Sympathy." In *A Necessary Fantasy? The Heroic Figure in Children's Popular Culture,* edited by Dudley Jones and Tony Watkins, 327–41. New York: Garland Publishing.

Broderick, Ryan. (2014), 'Marvel Held A Private Screening For The Brain Damaged Co-Creator Of Rocket Raccoon'. *Buzz Feed.* Accessed 17th September 2015. http://www.buzzfeed.com/ryanhatesthis/aint-no-thing-like-me-except-me#.qtxOl2ozX.

Brodesser-Akner, Claude. (2010), 'Jon Favreau Will Not Direct Iron Man 3'. *Vulture.* Accessed 14th September 2015. http://www.vulture.com/2010/12/jon_favreau_iron_man_3.html.

Brookey, Robert Alan, and Robert Westerfelhaus. (2006), 'The Digital Auteur: Branding Identity on the *Monsters, Inc* DVD'. *Western Journal of Communication,* vol. 69, no. 2: 109–28.

Brubaker, Ed and Steve Epting. (2011), *The Marvels Project: Birth of the Super Heroes.* New York: Marvel Comics.

Brubaker, Ed, Bryan Hitch and Butch Guice. (2010), *Captain America: Reborn.* New York: Marvel Comics.

Brubaker, Ed, Marc Andreyko and Chris Samnee. (2011), *Captain America and Bucky: The Life Story of Bucky Barnes.* New York: Marvel Comics.

Brzeski, Patrick. (2012), 'Disney's Marvel to co-Produce IM3 in China'. *The Hollywood Reporter.* Accessed 1st April 2015. http://www.hollywoodreporter.com/news/disney-marvel-iron-man-3-china-co-production-dmg-312323.

Buckland, Warren. (1998), 'A Close Encounter with *Raiders of the Lost Ark*: Notes on Narrative Aspects of the New Hollywood Blockbuster'. In *Contemporary Hollywood Cinema,* edited by Steve Neale and Murray Smith, 166–77. London: Routledge.

Buckland, Warren. (1999), 'Between Science Fact and Science Fiction: Spielberg's Digital Dinosaurs, Possible Worlds, and the New Aesthetic Realism'. *Screen,* vol. 40, no. 2: 177–92.

Buckland, Warren. (2003), 'The Role of the Auteur in the Age of the Blockbuster: Steven Spielberg and Dreamworks'. In *Movie Blockbusters,* edited by Julian Stringer, 84–98. London: Routledge.

Budd, Mike. (2005), 'Introduction: Private Disney, Public Disney'. In *Rethinking Disney: Private Control, Public Dimensions,* edited by Mike Budd and Max H. Kirsch. 1–33. Middletown, CT: Wesleyan Press.

Busch, Anita. (2014), 'Avi Arad Slams *Business Week*'s Marvel Story: "I Have Given Up On Journalistic Integrity."' *Deadline.* Accessed 24th September 2015. http://deadline.com/2014/05/avi-arad-slams-businessweek-marvel-story-email-724106/.

Busiek, Kurt and Alex Ross. (2004), *Marvels.* New York: Marvel Comics.

Calbreath-Frasieur, Aaron. (2014), '*Iron Man*: Building the Marvel Cinematic Universe'. *Scope: An Online Journal of Film and Television Studies,* vol. 26: 25–31.

Caldwell, John. (2008), *Production Culture: Industrial Reflexivity and Critical Practice in Film and Television.* Durham: Duke University Press.

Capps, Kriston. (2014), 'Escape Claws: Why Wolverine Had to Die for the Sake of Marvel Comics'. *The Atlantic*. Accessed 18th March 2015. http://www.theatlantic.com/entertainment/archive/2014/11/escape-claws-why-wolverine-had-to-die-for-the-sake-of-marvel-comics/382291/?single_page=true.

Casey, Dan. (2015), 'Interview: Executive Producer Jeph Loeb on *Daredevil, Jessica Jones & the Defenders*'. *Nerdist*. Accessed 23rd September 2015. http://nerdist.com/interview-executive-producer-jeph-loeb-on-daredevil-jessica-jones-the-defenders/.

Casper, Drew. (2007), *Postwar Hollywood: 1946-62*. Oxford: Blackwell.

Cassidy, Mark. (2015), 'Is Marvel Developing a THUNDERBOLTS TV Series for Netflix?' *Comicbookmovie.com*. Accessed 7th August 2015. http://www.comicbookmovie.com/fansites/markcassidycbm/news/?a=123330.

Catmull, Ed and Amy Wallace. (2014), *Creativity Inc.: Overcoming the Unseen Forces That Stand in the Way of True Inspiration*. New York: Random House.

Caulfield, Keith. (2014), '*Guardians of the Galaxy* Soundtrack Hits No.1 on the Billboard 200'. *Billboard.com*. Accessed 15th September 2015. http://www.billboard.com/articles/columns/chart-beat/6214496/guardians-of-the-galaxy-soundtrack-no-1-billboard-200.

Chabon, Michael. (2000), *The Amazing Adventures of Kavalier and Clay*. London: Fourth Estate.

Child, Ben. (2010), 'Edward Norton Dropped from Hulk Role'. *The Guardian*. Accessed 14th September 2015. http://www.theguardian.com/film/2010/jul/14/ed-norton-hulk-avengers.

Child, Ben. (2014), 'Benedict Cumberbatch is Just What Was Ordered for Doctor Strange'. *The Guardian*. Aceessed 11th March 2015. http://www.theguardian.com/film/filmblog/2014/oct/28/benedict-cumberbatch-doctor-strange-marvel.

Christensen, Jerome. (2012), *America's Corporate Art: The Studio Authorship of Hollywood Motion Pictures*. Stanford: Stanford University Press.

Cohen, David S. (2015), 'Marvel's Victoria Alonso Keeps Budgets of Superhero Franchises From Soaring'. *Variety*. Accessed 24th September 2015. http://variety.com/2014/film/news/marvels-victoria-alonso-keeps-superhero-budgets-in-line-1201266177/.

Collin, Robbie. (2015), 'John Lasseter: Hollywood Had Become Too Cynical'. *Telegraph*. Accessed 30th August 2015. http://www.telegraph.co.uk/film/big-hero-6/disney-john-lasseter-interview/.

Collins, Jim. (1993), 'Genericity in the Nineties: Eclectic Irony and the New Sincerity'. In *Film Theory Goes to the Movies*, edited by Jim Collins, Hilary Radner and Ava Preacher Collins, 242–63. London and New York: Routledge.

Collins, Sean T. (2014), 'The Rise of "Guardians of the Galaxy's" Rocket Raccoon.' *Rolling Stone*. Accessed 18th March 2015. http://www.rollingstone.com/movies/news/the-rise-of-guardians-of-the-galaxys-rocket-raccoon-20140729.

Colombe, Audrey. (2002), 'White Hollywood's New Black Bogeyman'. *Jump Cut* 45. Accessed 24th August 2015. http://www.ejumpcut.org/archive/jc45.2002/colombe/.

ComicChron. (2015a), 'February 2015 Comic Book Sales Figures'. *Comicchron.com*. Accessed 12th September 2015. http://www.comichron.com/monthlycomicssales/2015/2015-02.html.

ComicChron. (2015b), 'Comic Book Sales by Year'. *Comicchron.com*. Accessed 12th September 2015. http://www.comichron.com/yearlycomicssales.html.

ComicChron. (2015c), 'January 2015 Comic Book Sales Figures'. *Comicchron.com*. Accessed 28th September 2015. http://www.comichron.com/monthlycomicssales/2015/2015-01.html.

Connor, J. D. (2012), 'The Biggest Independent Pictures Ever Made: Industrial Reflexivity Today'. In *The Wiley-Blackwell History of American Film*, edited by Cynthia Lucia, Roy Grundmann and Art Simon. First Edition, 517–41. Oxford: Blackwell Publishing Ltd.

Bibliography

Connor, J. D. (2015), *The Studios After the Studios: Neoclassical Hollywood (1970-2010)*. Stanford: Stanford University Press.

Conway, Gerry and Roy Thomas. (2006), 'The Kon-Tiki Statue Blowing its Nose Was Our Favourite Scene!' Transcribed by B. K. Morris. *Alter Ego*, vol. 3, no. 58: 16–29.

Cook, David A. (1998), 'Auteur Cinema and the "Film Generation" in 1970s Hollywood'. In *The New American Cinema*, edited by Jon Lewis, 11–37. Durham: Duke University Press.

Crofts, Stephen. (1998), 'Authorship and Hollywood'. In *The Oxford Guide to Film Studies*, edited by John Hill and Pamela Church Gibson, 84–98. Oxford: Oxford University Press.

Cubitt, Sean. (2000), 'The Distinctiveness of Digital Criticism'. *Screen*, vol. 41, no. 1: 86–92.

Cubitt, Sean. (2015), 'The Contradictions of *Guardians of the Galaxy*'. *Deletion*, vol. 10. Accessed 9th September 2015. http://www.deletionscifi.org/episodes/episode-10-episodes/the-contradictions-of-guardians-of-the-galaxy/.

D'Allesandro, Anthony. (2015), 'Box Office Shocker: *Jurassic World* to hit $400m by Sunday; *Inside Out* 2nd Best Pixar Bow'. *Deadline*. Accessed 20th June 2015. http://deadline.com/2015/06/jurassic-world-inside-out-weekend-box-office-dope-1201448898/.

Darowski, John. (2014), 'The Earth's Mightiest Heroes and America's Post-Cold War Identity Crisis'. In *The Ages of the Avengers: Essays on the Earth's Mightiest Heroes in Changing Times*, edited by Joseph J. Darowski, 92–102. New York: McFarland Books.

Darowski, Joseph J. (2014), 'Preface'. In *The Ages of the Avengers: Essays on the Earth's Mightiest Heroes in Changing Times*, edited by Joseph J. Darowski. 1–4. New York: McFarland Books.

DeMott, Rick. (2009), 'Marvel Studios Promotes Louis D'Esposito to Co-President'. Animation World Network. 24th September 2015. http://www.awn.com/news/marvel-studios-promotes-louis-desposito-co-president.

Denson, Shane. (2011), 'Marvel Comics' Frankenstein: A Case Study in the Media of Serial Figures'. *Amerikastudien*, vol. 56, no. 4: 531–54.

Diekmann, Stefanie. (2004), 'Hero and Superhero'. *The Guardian*. Accessed 19th July 2015. http://www.theguardian.com/culture/2004/apr/24/guesteditors3.

Dittmer, Jason. (2005), 'Captain America's Empire: Reflections on Identity, Popular Culture, and Post-9/11 Geopolitics'. *Annals of the Association of American Geographers*, vol. 95, no. 3: 626–43.

Dittmer, Jason. (2007), 'The Tyranny of the Serial: Popular Geopolitics, the Nation and Comic Book Discourse'. *Antipode*, vol. 39, no. 2: 247–68.

Donovan, John. (2014), 'Cold War in comics: Clobberin' Commies and Promoting Nationalism in American Comics'. In *Ages of Heroes, Eras of Men: Superheroes and the American Experience*, edited by Julian Chambliss, 55–91. Newcastle: Cambridge Scholars Publishing.

Drake, Arnold, Gene Colan, Chris Claremont, John Byrne, Bill Mantlo, Mike Mignola, Jim Valentino, Keith Giffen, Timothy Green, Dan Abnett, Andy Lanning and Paul Pelletier. (2014), *Marvel Platinum: The Definitive Guardians of the Galaxy*. New York: Marvel Comics.

Draven. (2013), 'Rush Sheath Talks with Marvel Head of Television Jeph Loeb About All Things "Marvel's Agents of SHIELD" and the Future of Marvel Television!' *Aintitcool.com*. Accessed 15th April 2015. http://www.aintitcool.com/node/64954.

Drucker, Aaron. (2012), 'Spider-Man: MENACE!!! Stan Lee, Censorship and the 100-Issue Revolution'. In *Web-spinning Heroics: Critical Essays on the History and Meaning of Spider-Man*, edited by Robert Moses Peaslee and Robert G. Weiner, 90–100. New York: McFarland Press.

Duncan, Randy and Matthew J. Smith. (2009), *The Power of Comics: History, Form and Culture*. New York and London: Continuum.

Dyer, Mitch. (2014), 'Avengers Game Will Come When Marvel Finds the Right Developer'. *IGN*. Accessed 30th September 2015. http://uk.ign.com/articles/2014/05/01/avengers-game-will-come-when-marvel-finds-the-right-developer.

Ebiri, Bilge. (2014), 'Can *Guardians of the Galaxy* Break the Box Office Curse of Summer 2014?' *Business Week*. Accessed 16th March 2015. http://www.businessweek.com/articles/2014-08-04/guardians-of-the-galaxy-earned-94-million-this-weekend-dot-now-what.

Edelson, Richard. (2013), 'The Architecture of *The Incredibles*'. *Architizer*. Accessed 15th September. http://architizer.com/blog/the-architecture-of-the-incredibles/.

Eder, Jens, Fotis Jannidis and Ralf Schneider. (2010), 'Introduction'. in *Characters in Fictional Worlds: Understanding Imaginary Beings in Literature, Film and Other Media*, edited by Jens Eder, Fotis Jannidis and Ralf Schneidr, 3–66. Berlin: Walter de Gruyter & Co.

Edidin, Rachel. (2014), 'The Minor-League Superhero Who Changed the Face of Fandom'. *Wired*. Accessed 17th February 2015. http://www.wired.com/2014/04/captain-marvel-carol-corps/.

Eller, Claudia. (2003), 'Pixar's Flirtations Could Mean Trouble for Disney'. *LA Times*. Accessed 21st June 2015. http://articles.latimes.com/2003/feb/05/business/fi-pixar5.

Elsaesser, Thomas. (1998), 'Specularity and Engulfment: Francis Ford Coppola and *Bram Stoker's Dracula*'. In *Contemporary Hollywood Cinema*, edited by Steve Neale and Murray Smith, 191–208. London and New York: Routledge.

Englehart, Steve. (2015), 'Captain America III – 153-186'. *Steveenglehart.com*. Accessed 16th April 2015. http://www.steveenglehart.com/comics/Captain%20America%20177-186.html.

Englehart, Steve, Gary Friedrich and Sal Buscema. (2005), *Captain America and the Falcon: Secret Empire*. New York: Marvel Comics.

Erdemandi, Berkay M. (2013), 'Marvel Comics's Civil War: An Allegory of September 11 in an American Civil War Framework'. *Traces: UNC Chapel Hill Journal of History*, vol. 2: 213–23.

Erlichman, Jon. (2014), 'Iger: Marvel Brand Helps Disney Stay On Top'. *Street Smart* (online video). Accessed 15th September 2015. http://www.bloomberg.com/news/videos/b/28529bc3-f135-456e-87d0-217500882dc5.

Evans, Alex. (2010), 'Superman *Is* the Faultline: Fissures in the Monomythic Man of Steel'. In *Reframing 9/11: Film, Popular Culture and the 'War on Terror'*, edited by Jeff Birkenstein, Anna Froula and Karen Randell, 117–26. New York: Continuum.

Evans, Elizabeth. (2011), *Transmedia Television: Audiences, New Media and Daily Life*. Oxon: Routledge.

Fawaz, Ramzi. (2011), '"Where No X-Man Has Gone Before!" Mutant Superheroes and the Cultural Politics of Popular Fantasy'. *American Literature*, vol. 83, no. 2: 385–8.

FCC. (2012), 'V-Chip: Viewing Television Responsibly. The TV Parental Guidelines'. Last modified 16th May 2012. Accessed 29th August 2015. http://transition.fcc.gov/vchip/#guidelines.

Fellman, Paul. (2010), 'Iron Man: America's Cold War Champion and Charm against the Communist Menace'. *Voces Novae – Chapman University Historical Review*, vol. 1, no. 2: 11–12.

Fernandez, Jay A. (2008), 'Ongoing Storyline: Marvel-Par Alliance'. *The Hollywood Reporter*. Accessed 16th May 2015. http://www.hollywoodreporter.com/news/ongoing-story-line160-marvel-par-120073.

Ferrigno, Lou. (2003), *My Incredible Life as the Incredible Hulk*. Santa Monica: Lou Ferrigno Enterprises, Inc.

Bibliography

Fillipponi, Pietro. (2010), 'Exclusive Interview with THOR Video Game Producer Matt Powers'. *Comicbookmovie.com*. Accessed 30th September 2015. http://www. comicbookmovie.com/fansites/Poniverse/news/?a=20365.

Flanagan, Martin. (2004a), '"The Hulk," An Ang Lee Film: Notes on the Blockbuster Auteur'. *New Review of Film and Television Studies*, vol. 2, no. 1: 19–36.

Flanagan, Martin. (2004b), '"Get Ready for Rush Hour": The Chronotope in Action'. In *Action and Adventure Cinema*, edited by Yvonne Tasker, 103–18. London and New York: Routledge.

Flanagan, Martin. (2007), 'Teen Trajectories in *Spider-Man* and *Ghost World*'. In *Film and Comic Books*, edited by Ian Gordon, Mark Jancovich and Matthew P. McAllister, 137–59. Jackson: University Press of Mississippi.

Flanagan, Martin. (2009), *Bakhtin and the Movies: New Ways of Understanding Hollywood Film*. Basingstoke: Palgrave.

Ford, Rebecca and Borys Kit. (2014), 'Marvel Reveals Complete Phase 3 Plans, Dates "Black Panther," "Inhumans," "Avengers: Infinity War."' *The Hollywood Reporter*. Accessed 19th June 2015. http://www.hollywoodreporter.com/heat-vision/marvel-reveals-complete-phase-3-744455.

Frizell, Sam. (2015), 'Millennials Are Abandoning Their TV Sets Faster Than Ever'. *Time.com*. Accessed 5th July 2015. http://time.com/3713134/millennials-tv-cord-cutting-cable/.

Gajewski, Ryan. (2015), 'Joss Whedon on Fighting With Marvel Over *Avengers: Age of Ultron*: "It Got Really, Really Unpleasant."' *The Hollywood Reporter*. Accessed 14th September 2015. http://www.hollywoodreporter.com/heat-vision/joss-whedon-avengers-age-ultron-793502.

Gant, Charles. (2015), '*Paper Towns* Builds a Flimsy Number 1 Position at the UK Box Office'. *The Guardian*. Accessed 29th September 2015. http://www.theguardian.com/film/2015/aug/25/paper-towns-builds-a-flimsy-number-1-position-at-the-uk-box-office.

Gaudiosi, John. (2012), 'Marvel Exec Discusses "Avengers," "Amazing Spider-Man" Video Games'. *The Hollywood Reporter*. Accessed 30th September 2015. http://www. hollywoodreporter.com/heat-vision/marvel-games-avengers-amazing-spider-man-gdc-tq-jefferson-296842.

Gensler, Howard. (2015), '"Ant-Man" makes Amy Schumer Cry "Uncle."' *Philly.com*. Accessed 26th August 2015. http://articles.philly.com/2015-07-21/entertainment/64643742_1_ant-man-andrea-constand-cos-bill-cosby.

Genter, Robert. (2007), '"With Great Power Comes Great Responsibility": Cold War Culture and the Birth of Marvel Comics'. *Journal of Popular Culture*, vol. 40, no. 6: 953–78.

George, Richard. (2009), 'Brian Bendis: A Decade at Marvel'. *IGN*. Accessed 12th May 2015. http://uk.ign.com/articles/2009/10/23/brian-bendis-a-decade-at-marvel.

Geraghty, Lincoln. (2006), '"Realities … blending as one!": Film Texts and Intertexts in the *Star Trek/X-Men* Crossover Comics'. *Extrapolation*, vol. 48, no. 1: 108–19.

Gerbrandt, Larry (2001). Interview with Anon. *Frontline*. PBS. September. Accessed 20th May 2014. http://www.pbs.org/wgbh/pages/frontline/shows/hollywood/interviews/gerbrandt.html.

Giardina, Carolyn. (2014), 'Marvel Exec Talks "Avengers 2" and Why the Studio "Wants to Make Movies in L.A."' *Hollywood Reporter*. 24th September 2015. http://www. hollywoodreporter.com/behind-screen/marvel-exec-talks-avengers-2-741686.

Gioia, Dennis. A., Majken Schultz and Kevin G. Corley. (2004), 'Organizational Identity; Image, and Adaptive Instability Identity'. In *Organizational Identity: A Reader*, edited by Mary Jo Hatch and Majken Schultz, 349–76. Oxford: Oxford Universiity Press.

Goldsmith, Jeff. (2014), '*Guardians of the Galaxy* Q&A'. *The Q&A With Jeff Goldsmith* (podcast audio, 18th December) Accessed 14th September 2015. http://hwcdn.libsyn.

com/p/3/1/4/3146c4daace88f5b/GuardiansoftheGalaxyQandA.mp3?c_id=8075686&expir
ation=1426694006&hwt=5feaa60f4b5984cfa1af1513efbbdc02.

Goldstein, Patrick. (2008), 'Pixar Defies Gravity'. *LA Times*. Accessed 29th August 2015.
http://latimesblogs.latimes.com/the_big_picture/2008/06/pixar-defies-gr.html.

Gonzales, Adonis. (2015). 'Is Fox Actually Asking THIS At A *Fantastic Four* Screening?!'.
Moviepilot.com. Last modified 10th August 2015. Accessed 4th September 2015.
http://www.moviepilot.com/posts/2015/08/09/is-fox-actually-asking-this-at-a-fantastic-
four-screening-3455567?It_source=external,manual.

Grainge, Paul. (2008), *Brand Hollywood: Selling Entertainment in a Global Media Age*.
London: Routledge.

Graser, Marc. (2014a), 'How Marvel Guards Its Properties But Isn't Afraid to Take Chances
With Its "Galaxy."' *Variety*. Accessed 19th June 2015. http://variety.com/2014/film/news/
marvel-studios-guardians-of-the-galaxy-risk-1201266165/.

Graser, Marc. (2014b), '"Guardians of the Galaxy" to Break Records for "Disney Infinity."'
Variety. Accessed 18th March 2015. http://variety.com/2014/digital/games/guardians-of-
the-galaxy-breaks-records-for-disney-infinity-exclusive-1201302907/.

Graser, Marc. (2014c), 'Robert Downey Jr. To Join "Captain America 3."' *Variety*. Accessed
18th March 2015. http://variety.com/2014/film/news/robert-downey-jr-to-join-captain-
america-3-exclusive-1201312229/.

Graser, Marc. (2014d), 'Marvel Holding Off on Black Widow Movie, Focuses on "Captain
Marvel" Instead'. *Variety*. Accessed 26th August 2015. http://variety.com/2014/film/news/
scarlett-johansson-marvel-holding-off-on-black-widow-movie-focuses-on-captain-
marvel-instead-1201341771/7.

Gray, Jonathan. (2010), *Show Sold Seperately: Promos, Spoilers and other Media Paratexts*.
New York: New York University Press.

Gross, Larry. (1995), 'Big and Loud'. *Sight and Sound*, vol. 5, no. 8: 7–10.

Gunn, James. (2014), 'Audio Commentary'. *Guardians of the Galaxy*, 3-D edition. Blu-ray.
Walt Disney Studios Home Entertainment (UK and Ireland).

Hadas, Leora. (2014), 'Authorship and Authenticity in the Transmedia Brand: The Case
of Marvel's *Agents of S.H.I.E.L.D*'. *Networking Knowledge*, vol. 7, no. 1: 7–17. http://ojs.
meccsa.org.uk/index.php/netknow/article/view/332.

Hatch, Mary Jo and Majken Schultz. (2004), 'Introduction'. In *Organizational Identity:
A Reader*, edited by Mary Jo Hatch and Majken Schultz. 1–15. Oxford: Oxford
University Press.

Hawkes, Rebecca. (2015), '*Avengers Age of Ultron*: 7 Burning Questions'. *The Telegraph*.
Accessed 1st August 2015. http://www.telegraph.co.uk/film/avengers-age-of-ultron/
ending-spoilers-death-questions/.

Headgeek666. (2014), 'Untitled'. *Instagram post*. Accessed October 14th 2015. https://
instagram.com/p/l15llaM0jn/.

Hebdige, Dick. (2005), 'Dis-gnosis: Disney and the Re-Tooling of Knowledge, Art, Culture,
Life, Etcetera'. In *Rethinking Disney: Private Control, Public Dimensions*, edited by Mike
Budd and Max H. Kirsch, 37–52. Middletown, CT: Wesleyan University Press.

Heritage, Stuart. (2013), 'Ten Reasons Why Today's TV is Better Than Movies'. *The
Guardian*. Accessed 8th September 2015. http://www.theguardian.com/tv-and-radio/
tvandradioblog/2013/oct/23/10-reasons-tv-better-movies.

Hills, Matt. (2003), 'Star Wars in Fandom, Film Theory and the Museum'. In *Movie
Blockbusters*, edited by Julian Stringer, 178–89. London and New York: Routledge.

Hilmes, Michelle. (1996), 'Television and the Film Industry'. In *The Oxford History of World
Cinema*, edited by Geoffrey Nowell-Smith, 466–75. Oxford: Oxford University Press.

Hinkins, Jillian. (2007), ' "Biting the Hand That Feeds" ': Consumerism, Ideology and Recent Animated Film for Children'. *Papers: Explorations into Children's Literature*, vol. 17, no. 1: 43–50.

Holliday, Christopher. (2014), 'Inside Out: Collaborative Creativity and the Pixar Braintrust'. *In Media Res*. Accessed 28th August 2015. http://mediacommons.futureofthebook.org/imr/2014/04/21/inside-out-collaborative-creativity-and-pixar-braintrust.

Hooley, Graham, Nigel F. Piercy and Brigitte Nicoulaud. (2012), *Marketing Strategy and Competitive Positioning*. 5th ed. Essex: Pearson Education.

Hoskins, Colin, Stuart McFadyen and Adam Finn. (1997), *Global Television and Film*. Oxford: Oxford University Press.

Howe, Sean. (2013), *Marvel Comics: The Untold Story*. Paperback ed. New York: Harper Perennial.

Hughes, Mark. (2015), 'Details of Marvel's "Hulk" Film Rights – Fans Can Relax'. *Forbes*. Accessed 23rd June 2015. http://www.forbes.com/sites/markhughes/2015/06/19/details-of-marvels-hulk-film-rights-fans-can-relax-about-sequel/.

ICv2. (2007), 'Top 300 Comics Actual – March 2007'. (April 15). Accessed 18th April 2015. http://icv2.com/articles/comics/view/10404/top-300-comics-actual-march-2007.

IFPI. (2015), *IFPI Digital Music Report 2015*. Accessed 15th September 2015. http://www.ifpi.org/downloads/Digital-Music-Report-2015.pdf.

Ito, Robert. (2005), ' "Fantastic faux! It's clobberin" time! The unholy birth and mysterious death of the *Fantastic Four* movie Marvel Studios doesn't want you to see'. *Los Angeles Magazine*. March 106–11; 218–19.

Itzkoff, Dave. (2011), 'Modern Marvel'. *New York Times*. Accessed 22nd February 2015. http://www.nytimes.com/2011/03/27/movies/marvel-faces-a-mighty-foe-publishing-world-uncertainties.html?pagewanted=1&_r=1.

Itzkoff, Dave. (2014), ' "Guardians of the Galaxy" Character Creators Fight for Cash and Credit'. *New York Times*. Accessed 19th February 2015. http://www.nytimes.com/2014/08/07/movies/comic-character-creators-fight-for-cash-and-credit.html?_r=0.

Iwerks, Leslie. (2007), 'The Pixar Story'. Pixar Talking Pictures. *Wall-E* DVD. Walt Disney Studios Home Entertainment (UK and Ireland).

JabberTalky. (2014), 'Marvel has movies planned all the way to 2028!' *Movie Pilot*. Accessed 8th June 2015. http://moviepilot.com/posts/2014/04/04/marvel-has-movies-planned-all-the-way-to-2028-1317081?lt_source=external,manual,manual#!Wdwp2.

Jameson, Frederick. (1992), 'Postmodernism and Consumer Society'. In *Modernism/Postmodernism*, edited by Peter Brooker, 163–79. New York: Longman.

Jancovich, Mark. (2002), 'Genre and the Audience: Genre Classifications and Cultural Distinctions in the Mediation of *The Silence of the Lambs*'. In *Horror: The Film Reader*, edited by Mark Jancovich, 151–62. London and New York: Routledge.

Jenkins, Henry. (1995), 'Historical Poetics'. In *Approaches to Popular Film*, edited by Joanne Hollows and Mark Jancovich, 99–122. Manchester: Manchester University Press.

Jenkins, Henry. (2003), 'Transmedia Storytelling: Moving Characters from Books to Films to Video Games Can Make Them Stronger and More Compelling'. *MIT Technology Review*. Accessed 30th September 2015. http://www.technologyreview.com/news/401760/transmedia-storytelling/page/1/.

Jenkins, Henry. (2006), 'Captain America Sheds His Mighty Tears: Comics and September 11'. In *Terror, Culture, Politics: Rethinking 9/11*, edited by Daniel J. Sherman and Terry Nardin, 69–102. Bloomington: Indiana University Press.

Jenkins, Henry. (2008), *Convergence Culture: Where Old and New Media Collide*. Updated Ed. New York and London: New York University Press.

Jenkins, Henry. (2011), 'Transmedia 202: Further Reflections'. *Confessions of an Aca-Fan.* Accessed 30th September 2015. http://henryjenkins.org/2011/08/defining_transmedia_ further_re.html - Transmedia 202.

Johnson, Derek. (2007), 'Will the real Wolverine please stand up? Marvel's Mutation from Monthlies to Movies'. In *Film and Comic Books*, edited by Ian Gordon, Mark Jancovich and Matthew P. McAllister, 64–85. Jackson: University Press of Mississippi.

Johnson, Derek. (2012), 'Cinematic Destiny: Marvel Studios and the Trade Stories of Industrial Convergence'. *Cinema Journal*, vol. 52, no. 1: 1–24.

Johnson, Derek. (2013), *Media Franchising: Creative License and Collaboration in the Culture Industries.* New York and London: New York University Press.

Johnston, Rich. (2013), 'Controversy Over The Climactic Battle Of Man Of Steel (SPOILERS)'. *Bleeding Cool.* Accessed 12th April 2015. http://www.bleedingcool.com/2013/06/14/ controversy-over-the-climatic-battle-of-man-of-steel-spoilers/.

Johnston, Rich. (2014). 'Bill Mantlo, Co-Creator Of Rocket Raccoon, Gets A Private Viewing Of *Guardians Of The Galaxy*, Courtesy Of Marvel'. *Bleeding Cool.* Accessed 17th September 2015. http://www.bleedingcool.com/2014/08/03/bill-mantlo-co-creator-of- rocket-raccoon-gets-a-private-viewing-of-guardians-of-the-galaxy-courtesy-of-marvel/.

Jones, Gerard. (2002), *Killing Monsters: Why Children Need Fantasy, Super Heroes and Make- Believe Violence.* New York: Basic Books.

Keane, Stephen. (2007), *Cine-Tech: Film, Convergence and New Media.* Basingstoke: Palgrave Macmillan.

Kendrick, Ben. (2013), 'Is *Agents of S.H.I.E.L.D.* Getting Better as Ratings Fall?' *Screen Rant.* Accessed 14th April 2015. http://screenrant.com/agents-of-shield-improving-bad-ratings-abc/.

Kilday, Gregg. (2015), 'Paul Rudd and Marvel's Kevin Feige Reveal "Ant-Man's" Saga, from Director Shuffle to Screenplay Surgery to Studio's "Phase Three" Plans'. *The Hollywood Reporter.* Accessed 27th August 2015. http://www.hollywoodreporter.com/features/ant- man-saga-paul-rudd-804566.

Kimble, Lyndsay. (2015), 'A Superhero Never Rests: Robert Downey Jr. Posts Funny *Iron Man* – themed Labor Day Message'. Accessed 12th October 2015. www.people.com/article/ robert-downey-jr-iron-man-labor-day-tweet.

Kirschling, Gregory. (2008), 'New "Hulk": Behind-the-Scenes Drama'. *Entertainment Weekly.* Accessed 25th September 2015. http://www.ew.com/article/2008/04/17/new-hulk-behind- scenes-drama.

Kit, Borys and Kim Masters. (2015), 'Marvel's Civil War: Why Kevin Feige Demanded Emancipation From CEO Ike Perlmutter'. *The Hollywood Reporter.* Accessed 6th September 2015. http://www.hollywoodreporter.com/heat-vision/marvels-civil-war-why- kevin-820147.

Klock, Geoff. (2002), *How to Read Superhero Comics, and Why.* London and New York: Continuum.

Koh, Wilson. (2014), '"I am Iron Man": the Marvel Cinematic Universe and Celeactor Labour'. *Celebrity Studies*, vol. 5, no. 4: 484–500.

Krämer, Peter. (1998a), 'Post-classical Hollywood'. In *The Oxford Guide to Film Studies*, edited by John Hill and Pamela Church Gibson, 289–309. Oxford: Oxford University Press.

Krämer, Peter. (1998b), 'Would you take your child to see this film? The Cultural and Social Work of the Family-Adventure Movie'. In *Contemporary Hollywood Cinema*, edited by Steve Neale and Murray Smith, 294–311. London: Routledge.

Krämer, Peter. (2006), '"The Best Disney Film Disney Never Made." Children's Films and the Family Audience in American Cinema since the 1960s'. In *Genre and Contemporary Hollywood*, edited by Steve Neale, 185–200. London: BFI.

Bibliography

Kroll, Justin. (2014), '"Batman V Superman: Dawn of Justice" Moves to March 2016'. *Variety*. Accessed 29th July 2015. http://variety.com/2014/film/news/batman-v-superman-dawn-of-justice-moves-to-march-2016-1201277114/.

Lang, Brent. (2015), '"Ant-Man" Shows Power and Limits of Marvel Brand'. *Variety*. Accessed 21st August 2015. http://variety.com/2015/film/news/ant-man-box-office-marvel-1201543684/.

Lang, Jeffrey S. and Patrick Trimble. (1988), 'Whatever Happened to the Man of Tomorrow? An Examination of the American Monomyth and the Comic Book Superhero'. *Journal of Popular Culture*, vol. 22, no. 3 (Winter): 157–73.

Langford, Barry. (2005), *Film Genre: Hollywood and Beyond*. Edinburgh: Edinburgh University Press.

Lawrence, John S. (2009), 'Foreword'. In *Captain America and the Struggle of the Superhero: Critical Essays*, edited by Robert G. Weiner. 1–8. New York: McFarland Books.

Lazar, David. (2003), 'Introduction'. In *Michael Powell: Interviews*, edited by David Lazar. vii–xxi. Jackson: University Press of Mississippi.

Lee, Mark. (2011), 'The First Non-Avenger: *Captain America* and His Non-Struggles Against the Holocaust and Racism'. *Overthinkingit.com*. Accessed 5th April 2015. http://www.overthinkingit.com/2011/07/26/captain-america-holocaust-racism/.

Lee, Peter W. (2014), 'Stung by Stigmatization: Yellowjacket and Wasp Dis/Reassembled in the Age of Reagan'. In *The Ages of the Avengers: Essays on the Earth's Mightiest Heroes in Changing Times*, edited by Joseph J. Darowski, 65–78. New York: McFarland Books.

Lee, Stan. (2007), 'Synopses: *The Fantastic Four*, July '61 Schedule'. In *Marvel Masterworks: The Fantastic Four 1963*, edited by Stan Lee and Jack Kirby, 350–1. Tunbridge Wells: Panini Books.

Leonard, Devin. (2007), 'Calling All Superheroes'. *Fortune*. Accessed 24th September 2015. http://archive.fortune.com/magazines/fortune/fortune_archive/2007/05/28/100034246/index.htm.

Leonard, Devin. (2013), 'How Disney Bought Lucasfilm – and Its Plans for *Star Wars*'. *Business Week*. Accessed 11th April 2014. http://www.businessweek.com/articles/2013-03-07/how-disney-bought-lucasfilm-and-its-plans-for-star-wars.

Leonard, Devin. (2014a), 'The Pow! Bang! Bam! Plan to Save Marvel, Starring B-List Heroes'. *Bloomberg*. Accessed 20th July 2015. http://www.bloomberg.com/bw/articles/2014-04-03/kevin-feige-marvels-superhero-at-running-movie-franchises.

Leonard, Devin. (2014b), 'Marvel's *Guardians of the Galaxy* Test: Making Star-Lord Into an Actual Movie Star'. *Bloomberg*. Accessed 12th August 2015. http://www.bloomberg.com/bw/articles/2014-07-31/marvels-guardians-of-the-galaxy-test-making-star-lord-a-real-star.

Lethem, Jonathan. (2003), 'Izations'. *Randomhouse.com*. Accessed 19th February 2014. http://www.randomhouse.com/features/jonathanlethem/essay3.html.

Lewis, A. David. (2012), 'The Militarism of American Superheroes After 9/11'. In *Comic Books and American Cultural History*, edited by Matthew Pustz, 223–36. New York: Continuum.

Lewis, Jon. (2007), 'The Perfect Money Machine(s): George Lucas, Steven Spielberg and Auteurism in the New Hollywood'. In *Looking Past the Screen: Case Studies in American Film History and Method*, edited by Jon Lewis and Eric Smoodin, 61–86. Durham: Duke University Press.

Lewis, Jon. (2008), *American Film: A History*. New York: Norton.

Livesey, Ben. (2014), '*Captain America* Superpowers Extend to Third Week in Cinemas'. *Bloomberg*. Accessed 16th September 2015. http://www.bloomberg.com/news/2014-04-20/-captain-america-superpowers-extend-to-third-week-in-cinemas.html.

Lotz, Amanda D. (2014), *The Television Will Be Revolutionised*. 2nd Ed. New York: New York University Press.

Lussier, Germain. (2012), 'Exclusive: Katherine Sarafian, Producer of Pixar's "Brave," Talks Director Controversy, Pixar's Reaction to the Chilly "Cars 2" Reception And More.' *Slashfilm*. Accessed 31st August 2015. http://www.slashfilm.com/film-interview-katherine-sarafian-producer-pixars-brave-talks-controversy-marketing-cars-2-reactions/.

Lussier, Germain. (2014), 'Rumor: Edgar Wright Left Marvel's "Ant-Man" Over Major Script Rewrite'. *Slashfilm*. Accessed 6th July 2014. http://www.slashfilm.com/reason-edgar-wright-ant-man.

Lynch, Richard. (2006), *Corporate Strategy*. 4th Ed. Essex: Pearson Education.

Maltby, Richard. (1996), *Hollywood Cinema*. Oxford: Blackwell.

Masters, Kim. (2014). 'How Marvel Became the Envy (and Scourge) of Hollywood'. *The Hollywood Reporter*. Accessed 20th July 2015. http://www.hollywoodreporter.com/news/how-marvel-became-envy-scourge-720363.

Masters, Kim and Matthew Belloni. (2015), 'Marvel Shake-Up: Film Chief Kevin Feige Breaks Free of CEO Ike Perlmutter (Exclusive)'. *The Hollywood Reporter*. Accessed 30th September 2015. http://www.hollywoodreporter.com/news/marvel-shake-up-film-chief-819205.

Mazza, Ed. (2014), 'Bill Mantlo, Rocket Raccoon Co-Creator, Gets Private Guardians' Screening In Care Facility'. *Huffington Post*. Accessed 17th September 2015. http://www.huffingtonpost.com/2014/08/05/bill-mantlo-rocket-raccoon-screening_n_5649844.html.

McAllister, Matthew P., Ian Gordon and Mark Jancovich. (2006), 'Block Buster Meets Superhero Comic, or Art House Meets Graphic Novel?: The Contradictory Relationship between Film and Comic Art'. *Journal of Popular Film and Television*, vol. 34, no. 3: 108–15.

McClelland-Nugent, Ruth. (2010), 'Wonder Woman Against the Nazis: Gendering Villainy in DC Comics'. In *Monsters in the Mirror: Representations of Nazism in Post-war Popular Culture*, edited by Sara Buttsworth and Maartje Abbenhuis, 131–54. Santa Barbara, CA: ABC-CLIO.

McClintock, Pamela. (2014), 'Box Office Preview: "Guardians of the Galaxy" Tracking for $65M-Plus Debut'. *The Hollywood Reporter*. Accessed 17th March 2015. http://www.hollywoodreporter.com/news/box-office-preview-guardians-galaxy-722053.

McClintock, Pamela. (2015), 'Summer Box-Office Flops: "Tomorrowland," "Fantastic Four" Top List'. *The Hollywood Reporter*. Accessed 4th September 2015. http://www.hollywoodreporter.com/news/summer-box-office-flops-tomorrowland-820498.

McClintock, Pamela and Kim Masters. (2014), 'Executive Roundtable: 6 Studio Heads on China Plans, Superhero Overload, WB Layoffs, "Fast & Furious" Future'. *The Hollywood Reporter*. Accessed 18th September 2015. http://www.hollywoodreporter.com/news/executive-roundtable-6-studio-heads-748102.

McCulloch, Richard. (2014), 'Whistle While you Work: Branding, Critical Reception and Pixar's Production Culture'. In *Storytelling in the Media Convergence Age*, edited by Roberta Pearson and Anthony N. Smith, 174–89. Basingstoke: Palgrave.

McMillan, Graeme. (2014), 'Marvel's Negotiations with "Rocket Raccoon" Co-Creator Disclosed'. *The Hollywood Reporter*. Accessed 19th February 2015. http://www.hollywoodreporter.com/heat-vision/marvels-negotiations-rocket-raccoon-creator-723966.

McMillan, Graeme. (2015), 'Marvel Congratulates "Jurassic World" on Defeating "The Avengers."' *The Hollywood Reporter*. Accessed 29th July 2015. http://www.hollywoodreporter.com/heat-vision/marvel-congratulates-jurassic-world-defeating-802811.

Bibliography

McNeill, Darrel. (1984), 'Animation News: *GI Joe II, Transformers* Mini Series to Air This Fall'. *The Comics Buyers Guide*. 1st June: 22.

Meehan, Eileen R. (2000), '"Holy Commodity Fetish, Batman!": The Economics of a Commercial Intertext'. In *The Film Studies Reader*, edited by Joanne Hollows, Peter Hutchings and Mark Jancovich, 23–32. London: Arnold.

Meinel, Dietmar. (2014), '"And when everyone is super … no one will be": The Limits of American Exceptionalism in *The Incredibles*'. *European Journal of American Culture*, vol. 33, no. 3: 181–94.

Mendelson, Scott. (2014), 'Is Marvel the new Pixar?'. *Forbes*. Accessed 28th August 2015. http://www.forbes.com/sites/scottmendelson/2014/04/08/is-marvel-the-new-pixar/.

Mendelson, Scott. (2015), 'Box Office: "Furious 7" Close To Passing "Avengers" To Become 3rd Biggest Grossing Movie Ever'. *Forbes*. Last modified 24th June 2015. Accessed 12th August 2015. http://www.forbes.com/sites/scottmendelson/2015/06/24/box-office-furious-7-tops-avengers-is-3rd-biggest-grosser-ever/.

Metrowebukmetro. (2012), 'Star Wars fans beg Disney not to ruin franchise after £2.5bn Sale'. *Metro*. Accessed 21th June 2015. http://metro.co.uk/2012/10/31/star-wars-fans-beg-disney-not-to-ruin-franchise-after-lucasfilm-2-5bn-sale-610905/.

Millar, Mark and Steve McNiven. (2007), *Civil War*. New York: Marvel Publishing.

Miller, Daniel. (2015), 'How Robert Iger's "fearless" deal-making transformed Disney'. *LA Times*. Accessed 7th June 2015. http://www.latimes.com/entertainment/envelope/cotown/la-et-ct-disney-iger-20150607-story.html#page=2.

Miller, Gary M. (2011), 'DCnU-Inspired: Continuity – Please Use in Moderation (1)'. *Delusional Honesty*. Accessed 21st February 2014. http://www.delusionalhonesty.com/2011/07/continuity-please-use-in-moderation-1.html.

Mirrlees, Tanner. (2013), 'The Economics, Geopolitics and Ideology of an Imperial Film Commodity'. *CineAction*, vol. 92: 4–11.

Miskell, Peter. (2014), 'Hollywood Films and Foreign Markets in the Studio Era: A Fresh Look at the Evidence – Discussion Paper #IBH-2014-08'. University of Reading. Accessed 17th June 2015. http://www.henley.ac.uk/files/pdf/research/papers-publications/IBH-2014-08_Miskell.pdf.

Moore, Alan and David Gibbons. (1987), *Watchmen*. London: Titan Books.

Morris, Nigel. (2007), *The Cinema of Steven Spielberg: Empire of Light*. New York: Columbia University Press.

Moss, Charles. (2014), 'Captain America: McCarthyite'. *The Atlantic*. Accessed 23rd August 2015. http://www.theatlantic.com/entertainment/archive/2014/04/captain-america-mccarthyite/360183/.

Naficy, Hamid. (2001), *An Accented Cinema*. Princeton: Princeton University Press.

Nama, Adilifu. (2011), *Super Black: American Pop Culture and Black Superheroes*. Austin: University of Texas Press.

Newman, Kim. (2005), 'Review of *The Incredibles*'. *Sight and Sound*, vol. 15, no. 1: 55–6.

Newman, Kim. (2014), 'Film of the Week: *Guardians of the Galaxy*'. *Sight and Sound*. Last modified 25th April 2015. Accessed 12th August 2015. http://www.bfi.org.uk/news-opinion/sight-sound-magazine/reviews-recommendations/film-week-guardians-galaxy?utm_content=buffer1a24d&utm_medium=social&utm_source=facebook.com&utm_campaign=buffer.

Newman, Michael Z. (2011), *Indie: An American Film Culture*. New York: Columbia University Press.

O'Connell, Sean. (2015), 'Marvel Still Sabotaging *X-Men* and the *Fantastic Four*'. *Cinemablend*. Accessed 14th September 2015. http://www.cinemablend.com/new/Marvel-Still-Sabotaging-X-Men-Fantastic-Four-71801.html.

Office Videos. (2015), *The Collective Project: Robert Downey Jr. Delivers a Real Bionic Arm*. Youtube. Accessed 12th October 2015. https://www.youtube.com/watch?v=oEx5lmbCKtY.

O'Hehir, Andrew. (1999), 'Review of *Star Wars Episode I: The Phantom Menace*'. *Sight and Sound*, vol. 9, no. 7: 34–5.

Oldham, Joseph. (2014), '*Agents of SHIELD*: Agency, Institutions and Transmedia Serialisation'. *CST Online*. Accessed 5th August 2015. http://cstonline.tv/transmedia-serialisation-in-marvels-agents-of-shield.

Overton, Brian. (2015), 'Jack Kirby's *The Avengers*'. In *Avengers Magazine* no. 1, edited by John Rhett Thomas, 20–7. New York: Marvel Comics.

Owczarski, Kim. (2015) '"Why So Serious?" Warner Bros.' Use of the Joker in Marketing *The Dark Night*'. In *The Joker: A Serious Study*, edited by Robert Moses Peaslee and Robert G. Weiner, 146–64. Jackson: University Press of Mississippi.

Pearson, Roberta. (2007), '*Lost* in Transition: From Post-Network to Post-Television'. In *Quality TV: Contemporary American Television and Beyond*, edited by Kim Akass and Janet McCabe, 239–56. London and New York: I. B. Tauris.

Philibrick, Jami. (2010), 'EXCLUSIVE: Kevin Feige Talks *Iron Man 2*, *The Avengers* and More'. *Movieweb*. Accessed 28th September 2015. http://movieweb.com/exclusive-kevin-fiege-talks-iron-man-2-the-avengers-and-more/.

Pierson, Michelle. (1999), 'CGI Effects in Hollywood Science Fiction 1989-95: the Wonder Years'. *Screen*, vol. 40, no. 2: 158–76.

Porter, Michael. E. (2008), *On Competition: Updated and Expanded Edition*. Boston: Harvard Business Review Press.

Proctor, William. (2014), 'Avengers Assembled: The Marvel Transmedia Universe'. *Scope: An Online Journal of Film and Television Studies*, vol. 26: 8–16.

Pustz, Matthew. (2012), '"Paralysis and Stagnation and Drift": America's Malaise as Demonstrated in Comic Books of the 1970s'. In *Comic Books and American Cultural History*, edited by Matthew Pustz, 136–51. New York: Continuum.

Radford, Ivan. (2014), 'Captain America and Marvel's Great Political Shift'. *Little White Lies*. Accessed 18th September 2015. http://www.littlewhitelies.co.uk/features/articles/captain-america-and-marvels-great-political-shift-26251.

Rasmussen, Juli. (2009), 'Disney Acquires Marvel: Research Paper'. Florida: Full Sail University. Accessed 2nd August 2015. http://www.juli-rasmussen.com/work/negotiation/rasmussen_juli_research_paper.pdf.

Raviv, Dan. (2004), *Comic Wars: Marvel's Battle for Survival*. Sea Cliff: Heroes Books.

Rehak, Bob. (2008), 'Untitled'. *Blog post*. Accessed 13th July 2008. http://weblogs.swarthmore.edu/burke/?p=602.

Remender, Rick and John Romita Jr. (2013), *Captain America: Castaway in Dimension Z, Volume One*. New York: Marvel Comics.

Richardson, Anslem. (2012), 'Full Shadow & Act Report From Marvel Studios' "The Avengers" Press Junket'. *Shadow and Act*. Accessed 7th September 2015. http://blogs.indiewire.com/shadowandact/full-shadow-and-act-report-from-marvel-studios-the-avengers-press-junket.

Ries, Al and Laura Ries. (2000), *The 22 Immutable Laws of Branding*. London: Harper Collins.

Riesman, Abraham. (2015), 'The Secret History of Ultimate Marvel'. *Vulture*. Accessed 22nd June 2015. http://www.vulture.com/2015/05/secret-history-of-ultimate-marvel.html.

Robbins, Michaela and Fritz G. Polite. (2014), 'The Most Powerful Mouse in the World: The Globalization of the Disney Brand'. *Global Journal of Management and Business Research: F – Real Estate Event and Tourism Management*, vol. 14, no.1: 10–20.

Robinson, Joanna. (2015), 'Why is Scarlett Johansson Missing from the *Avengers* Merchandise?' *Vanity Fair*. Accessed 31st July 2015. http://www.vanityfair.com/hollywood/2015/04/black-widow-avengers-sexist.

Romney, Jonathan. (2006), 'Loud Candy'. *Sight and Sound*, vol. 16, no. 8: 44–7.

Roper, Caitlin. (2014), '*Big Hero 6* Proves It: Pixar's Gurus Have Brought the Magic Back to Disney Animation'. *Wired*. Accessed 28th August 2015. http://www.wired.com/2014/10/big-hero-6/.

Rosen, Christopher. (2014), 'Edgar Wright Leaves Marvel's "Ant-Man"'. *Huffington Post*. Accessed 14th September 2015. http://www.huffingtonpost.com/2014/05/23/edgar-wright-leaves-ant-man_n_5381567.html.

Ryan, Bill. (1992), *Making Capital from Culture: The Corporate Form of Capitalist Cultural Production*. Berlin: Walter de Gruyter.

Ryan, Marie-Laure. (2013), 'Possible Worlds'. *The Living Handbook of Narratology*. Accessed 1st July 2014. http://www.lhn.uni-hamburg.de/article/possible-worlds.

Sacks, Jason. (2014), 'Earth's Mightiest (Dysfunctional) Family: The Evolution of *The Avengers* Under Jim Shooter'. In *The Ages of the Avengers: Essays on the Earth's Mightiest Heroes in Changing Times*, edited by Joseph J. Darowski, 31–44. New York: McFarland Books.

Sammond, Nicholas. (2005), *Babes in Tomorrowland*. Durham and London: Duke University Press.

Sanderson, Peter. (1992), '*Spider-Man*: The First Thirty Years'. In *Amazing Spider-Man*, vol. 1, no. 365 edited by David Michelinie, Mark Bagley, Randy Emberlin, Stan Lee, Aaron Lopresti, Tom De Falco, John Romita Sr., Tod Smith, Andrew Pepoy and Peter Sanderson, 70–3. New York: Marvel Comics.

Sangiacomo, Michael. (2014), '"Captain America: The Winter Soldier" Starts Shooting in Cleveland'. *Cleveland.com*. Accessed 24th August 2015. http://www.cleveland.com/comic-books/index.ssf/2013/05/captain_america_operation_deep_1.html.

Sarris, Andrew. (1968), *The American Cinema: Directors and Directions 1929-1968*. New York: Dutton.

Schatz, Thomas. (1993), 'The New Hollywood'. In *Film Theory Goes to the Movies*, edited by Jim Collins, Hilary Radner and Ava Preacher Collins. 8–36. London and New York: Routledge.

Schatz, Thomas. (1998), *The Genius of the System: Hollywood Film-making in the Studio Era*. London: Faber.

Schedeen, Jesse. (2015), 'Is this relaunch really all-new all different?'. *IGN*. Accessed 15th September 2015. http://uk.ign.com/articles/2015/07/24/between-the-panels-the-marvel-comics-relaunch-already-has-a-big-problem.

Schilling, Mark. (1997), 'Miyazaki Hayao and Studio Ghibli, The Animation Hit Factory'. *Japan Quarterly*, vol. 44, no. 1: 30–40.

Schumer, Arlen. (1999), 'Neal Adams: The Marvel Years' [interview with Neal Adams]. *Comic Book Artist* 3. Two Morrows Publications. Accessed 29th September 2015. http://twomorrows.com/comicbookartist/articles/03adams.html.

Scott, Cord A. (2011), 'Comics and Conflict: War and Patriotically Themed Comics in American Cultural History from World War II Through the Iraq War'. PhD Diss., Chicago: Loyola University.

Scott, Cord A. (2012), 'Anti-Heroes: Spider-Man and the Punisher'. In *Web-spinning Heroics: Critical Essays on the History and Meaning of Spider-Man*, edited by Robert G. Weiner and Rob Peaslee, 120–7. New York: McFarland Press.

Seifert, Mark. (2011), 'The Stan Lee Deposition On The Origins Of The Marvel Universe For Kirby Family Vs Marvel Lawsuit'. *Bleeding Cool*. Accessed 22nd April 2014. http://www.

bleedingcool.com/2011/03/09/the-stan-lee-deposition-on-the-origins-of-the-marvel-universe-for-kirby-family-vs-marvel-lawsuit/.

Shooter, Jim, David Michelinie, Bill Mantlo, George Pérez, John Byrne, Sal Buscema and David Wenzel. (2012), *The Avengers: The Korvac Saga*. Tunbridge Wells: Panini Publishing.

Siegemund-Broka, Austin and Boris Kit. (2015), 'Russo Brothers to direct *Avengers: Infinity War* Parts 1 and 2'. *The Hollywood Reporter*. Accessed 16th May 2015. http://www.hollywoodreporter.com/heat-vision/russo-brothers-direct-avengers-infinity-783685.

Skipper, Ben. (2014), 'Marvel's Phase Four'. *International Business Times*. Accessed 23rd June 2015. http://www.ibtimes.co.uk/marvels-phase-four-what-happens-after-avengers-infinity-war-1472456.

Smith, Murray. (1998), 'Theses on the Philosophy of Hollywood History'. In *Contemporary Hollywood Cinema*, edited by Steve Neale and Murray Smith. 3–20. London and New York: Routledge.

Steirer, Gregory. (2011), 'The State of Comics Scholarship: Comics Studies and Disciplinarity'. *International Journal of Comics Art*, vol. 13, no. 2: 263–85.

Stevens, Tim. (2014), 'The *Guardians of the Galaxy* Join the All-Ages Marvel Universe'. *Marvel.com*. Last modified 13th November. Accessed 19th March 2015. http://marvel.com/news/comics/23665/the_guardians_of_the_galaxy_join_the_all-ages_marvel_universe.

Stewart, Andrew. (2013), 'Paramount's Super Pay-Off for *Iron Man 3*'. *Variety*. Accessed 23rd June 2014. http://variety.com/2013/film/news/iron-man-3-paramount-disney-1200479325/.

Stork, Matthias. (2014), 'Assembling *The Avengers*: Reframing the Superhero Movie through Marvel's Cinematic Universe'. In *Superhero Synergies*, edited by James N. Gilmore and Matthias Stork, 77–95. Lanham, MD: Rowman and Littlefield.

Strom, Marc. (2014), 'Nicole Perlman Writes the Galaxy'. *Marvel.com*. Last modified 19th August. Accessed 29th July 2015. http://marvel.com/news/movies/23099/nicole_perlman_writes_the_galaxy.

Subers, Ray. (2014), 'Weekend Report: "Guardians of the Galaxy" Obliterates August Record'. *Box Office Mojo*. Accessed 18th March 2015. http://www.boxofficemojo.com/news/?id=3885&p=.htm.

Sudhindra, Nicole J. S. (2012), 'Marvel's Superhero Licensing'. *WIPO*. Accessed 10th June 2015. http://www.wipo.int/wipo_magazine/en/2012/03/article_0005.html.

Sweeney, David. (2013), 'From Stories To Worlds – The Continuity Of Marvel Superheroes From Comics To Film'. *Intensities*, vol. 5: 133 – 50.

Tasker, Yvonne. (2004), 'Introduction: Action and Adventure Cinema'. In *Action and Adventure Cinema*, edited by Yvonne Tasker. 1–13. London and New York: Routledge.

Tasker, Yvonne. (2015), *The Hollywood Action Adventure Film*. Oxford: Wiley-Blackwell.

Taylor, Aaron. (2014), 'Avengers Dissemble! Transmedia Superhero Franchises and Cultic Management'. *Journal of Adaptation in Film & Performance*, vol. 7, no. 2: 181–94.

Thacker, Jim. (2011), 'Q&A: Victoria Alonso, Marvel's visual effects chief'. *CG Channel*. Last modified 18th September 2011. Accessed 27th September 2015. http://www.cgchannel.com/2011/09/qa-victoria-alonso-marvels-visual-effects-chief/.

Thielman, Sam. (2014), 'Finally, Some Actual Netflix Viewer Data – ComScore report breaks down viewership trends'. *Ad Week*. Accessed 5th July 2015. http://www.adweek.com/news/television/finally-some-actual-netflix-statistics-160753.

Thomas, John Rhett, ed. (2015), *Avengers Magazine*, no. 1. New York: Marvel Comics.

Thomas, John R. and Dugan Trodglen. (2015), 'The *Avengers*: Earth's Mightiest Interview'. In *Avengers Magazine* no. 1, edited by John Rhett Thomas, 38–50. New York: Marvel Comics.

Bibliography

Thomas, Roy and Peter Sanderson. (2007), *The Marvel Vault*. Philadelphia: Running Press.

Thomas, Roy, Adams, Neal and Buscema, John. (2008), *Avengers: The Kree-Skrull War*. New York: Marvel Comics.

Thompson, Kristin. (2006), 'By Annie standards'. *Observations on Film Art* blog. Accessed 7th June 2015. http://www.davidbordwell.net/blog/2006/12/10/by-annie-standards/.

Thompson, Kristin. (2007), *The Frodo Franchise: The Lord of the Rings and Modern Hollywood*. Berkeley: University of California Press.

Tilly, Chris. (2015), 'Why the Marvel Movie Guys are Annoyed with Joss Whedon'. *IGN*. Accessed 14th September 2015. http://uk.ign.com/articles/2015/04/27/why-the-marvel-movie-guys-are-annoyed-with-joss-whedon?utm_campaign=ign+main+twitter&utm_source=twitter&utm_medium=social.

Tolworthy, Chris. (2014), 'Marvel's Sliding Time Scale'. *Zaksite.com*. Accessed 20th June 2014. http://zak-site.com/Great-American-Novel/marvel_time.html.

Tolworthy, Chris. (2015), 'Behind the Scenes: Marvel Comics in 1989'. Accessed 15th September 2015. http://zak-site.com/Great-American-Novel/ff_end.html.

Tryon, Chuck. (2009), *Reinventing Cinema: Movies in the Age of Media Convergence*. New Brunswick: Rutgers University Press.

Tryon, Chuck. (2013), *On-Demand Culture: Digital Delivery and the Future of Movies*. New Brunswick: Rutgers University Press.

Tsui, Clarence. (2013), '"Iron Man 3" China-Only Scenes Draw Mixed Response'. *The Hollywood Reporter*. Accessed 29th September 2015. http://www.hollywoodreporter.com/news/iron-man-3-china-scenes-450184.

Turan, Kenneth. (2014), '"Guardians of the Galaxy's" heroes aren't what you'd expect'. *LA Times*. Accessed 12th August 2015. http://www.latimes.com/entertainment/movies/la-et-mn-guardians-galaxy-review-20140801-column.html.

Turner, Barry. (1995), 'The Rise of Organizational Symbolism'. In *The Theory and Philosophy of Organizations: Critical Issues and New Perspectives*, edited by John Hassard and Denis Pym, 83–96. Abingdon: Routledge.

Tyree, J. M. (2009), 'American Heroes'. *Film Quarterly*, vol. 62, no. 3: 28–34.

Veloso, Francisco and John Bateman. (2013), 'The Multimodal Construction of Acceptability: Marvel's Civil War Comic Books and the PATRIOT Act'. *Critical Discourse Studies*, vol. 10, no. 4: 427–43. Accessed 29th September 2015. http://dx.doi.org/10.1080/17405904.2013.813776.

Voger, Mark. (2006), *The Dark Age: Grim, Great & Gimmicky Post-Modern Comics*. Raleigh, NC: Two Morrows Publishing.

Walton, David. (2009), '"Captain America Must Die": The Many Afterlives of Steve Rogers'. In *Captain America and the Struggle of the Superhero: Critical Essays*, edited by Robert G. Weiner, 160–75. New York: McFarland Press.

Wasko, Janet. (1995), *Hollywood in the Information Age*. Austin: University of Texas Press.

Wasko, Janet. (2001), 'Introduction: Is it a Small World after all?' In *Dazzled by Disney? The Global Disney Audiences Project*, edited by Janet Wasko, Matt Phillips and Eileen R. Meehan. 3–30. London and New York: Continuum.

Wasko, Janet. (2005), *How Hollywood Works*. London and Thousand Oaks: Sage.

Wasko, Janet. (2007), *Understanding Disney: Manufacturing Fantasy*. Cambridge: Polity.

Wasko, Janet, Phillips, Matt and Meehan, Eileen R. eds. (2001), *Dazzled by Disney? The Global Disney Audiences Project*. London and New York: Continuum.

Watercutter, Angela. (2015), 'Writing "Captain Marvel" is Much Harder than Penning "Guardians."' *Wired*. Accessed 29th July 2015. http://www.wired.com/2015/07/nicole-perlman-captain-marvel/.

Webb, Janette. (2006), *Organisations, Identities, and the Self*. Basingstoke: Palgrave.

Weiner, Robert G., ed. (2009), *Captain America and the Struggle of the Superhero: Critical Essays*. New York: McFarland Press.

Weinman, Jaime. (2014), 'Marvel, Fox and the Fantastic Fracas'. *MacLeans*. Accessed 14th September 2015. http://www.macleans.ca/culture/movies/marvel-fox-and-the-fantastic-fracas/.

Weinman, Jaime. (2015), 'Comics: The Continuity Conundrum'. *MacLean's*. Accessed 22nd June 2015. http://www.macleans.ca/culture/arts/comics-the-continuity-conundrum/.

Wells, Paul. (2002), *Animation and America*. Edinburgh: Edinburgh University Press.

Whedon, Joss. (2002), 'Introduction'. In *Earth-X*, edited by Jim Krueger, Alex Reinhold, John-Paul Leon and Bill Reinhold. 3–4. New York: Marvel Comics.

Wheeler, Andrew. (2014a), 'Why Marvel Studios Succeeds (And How It Will Fail If It Doesn't Diversify)'. *Comics Alliance*. Accessed 21st August 2015. http://comicsalliance.com/marvel-studios-success-marvel-movies-diversity/.

Wheeler, Andrew. (2014b), 'Marvel Arranges Private "Guardians Of The Galaxy" Screening For Rocket Raccoon Co-Creator Bill Mantlo'. *Comcs Alliance*. Accessed 17th September 2015. http://comicsalliance.com/marvel-guardians-of-the-galaxy-screening-rocket-raccoon-bill-mantlo/.

Williams, Raymond. (1994), 'The Analysis of Culture'. In *An Introductory Guide to Cultural Theory and Popular Culture*, edited by John Storey, 56–65. London: Harvester.

Wood, Robin. (1986), *Hollywood from Vietnam to Reagan*. New York: Columbia University Press.

Worley, Rob M. (2004), 'Confirmed: Cassavetes Adds Emotion to *Iron Man*'. *Mania.com*. Accessed 10th May 2015. http://www.mania.com/confirmed-cassavetes-adds-emotion-to-iron-man_article_97183.html.

Wright, Bradford W. (2003), *Comic Book Nation*. Paperback Ed. Baltimore: Johns Hopkins University Press.

Wyatt, Justin. (1998), 'The Formation of the "Major-Independent": Miramax, New Line and the New Hollywood'. In *Contemporary Hollywood Cinema*, edited by Steve Neale and Murray Smith, 74–90. London: Routledge.

Yanes, Nicholas. (2009), 'Graphic Imagery: Jewish American Comic Book Creators' Depictions of Class, Race, Patriotism and the Birth of the Good Captain'. In *Captain America and the Struggle of the Superhero: Critical Essays*, edited by Robert G. Weiner, 53–65. New York: McFarland Press.

Yockey, Matt. (2005), 'This Island Manhattan: New York City and the Space Race in *The Fantastic Four*'. *Iowa Journal of Cultural Studies*, vol. 6: 58–79.

Zakarin, Jordan. (2012), 'James Gunn Confirms "Guardians of the Galaxy" Directorial Gig for Marvel'. *The Hollywood Reporter*. Accessed, July 29th 2015. http://www.hollywoodreporter.com/heat-vision/james-gunn-confirms-guardians-galaxy-marvel-371196.

Zimmerman, Dwight J. (1988), 'Mark Gruenwald'. *Comics Interview*, vol. 54: 5–23.

INDEX

Index

Index

Index